# TRADITION(S) II

# Studies in Continental Thought

John Sallis, *general editor*

# Tradition(s) II

## Hermeneutics, Ethics, and the Dispensation of the Good

STEPHEN H. WATSON

*Indiana University Press*

BLOOMINGTON AND INDIANAPOLIS

This book is a publication of

Indiana University Press
601 North Morton Street
Bloomington, IN 47404-3797 USA
http://www.indiana.edu/~iupress

*Telephone orders*   800-842-6796
*Fax orders*   812-855-7931
*Orders by e-mail*   iuporder@indiana.edu

The paper used in this publication meets
the minimum requirements of American
National Standard for Information
Sciences—Permanence of Paper for Printed
Library Materials, ANSI Z39.48-1984.

Manufactured in the United States of America

**Library of Congress Cataloging-in-Publication Data**

Watson, Stephen H., date
  Tradition(s) II : hermeneutics, ethics, and the dispensation of the good / Stephen H. Watson.
    p.   cm. — (Studies in Continental thought)
  Includes bibliographical references.
  ISBN 0-253-33900-6 (cl : alk. paper) — ISBN 0-253-21447-5 (pa : alk. paper)
    1. Tradition (Philosophy) 2. Philosophy, European—20th century. 3. Philosophy,
Modern—20th century.   I. Title: Tradition(s) 2.   II. Title: Traditions II.   III. Title.   IV.
Series.

B105.T7 W38 2001
148—dc21

                                                                    00-063424

1   2   3   4   5   06   05   04   03   02   01

# CONTENTS

Contents

# ACKNOWLEDGMENTS

Parts of chapter 1 appeared previously in *Research in Phenomenology 26*. An early version of chapter 3 appeared in *Man and World 21*. Papers reflecting various aspects of this work were presented at a number of conferences and colloquia. I especially acknowledge the following settings, whose papers directly resulted in parts of the book, and I am grateful both for the invitation and the comments of participants.

Parts of chapter 2 were presented as an invited address at the Canadian Society for Hermeneutics and Postmodern Thought (St. John's, Newfoundland) and at a conference on Rhetoric and Politics in the Work of Hans-Georg Gadamer (Heidelberg). Parts of the Introduction and chapter 4 were presented as an invited address on Post-Structuralism at the Twentieth World Congress of Philosophy (Boston).

Also, I thank a number of my students for their contribution not only in the preparation of the manuscript but in discussion of issues at stake within it: these include John Davenport, Robert Piercey, Matthew Halteman, and Michael Bowler.

In addition, I thank my colleagues at Notre Dame who have provided an exemplary context for my research, not only through their own work and in constant dialogue with my own, but in our common—and interdisciplinary—projects as teachers and scholars. Especially I thank Fred Dallmayr, Jerry Bruns, Ewa Ziarek, Krzysztof Ziarek, Karl Ameriks, Gary Gutting, Fred Crosson, Mark Roche. Grants from the Philosophy Department and the Institute for Scholarship in the Liberal Arts assisted in the publication of this work.

Finally, I thank John Sallis as well as Janet Rabinowitch and Dee Mortensen of Indiana University Press for their continuing interest in this project over the years.

# ABBREVIATIONS

### Thomas Aquinas
ST      *Summa theologiae* (Turin: Marietti, 1948)

### Aristotle
NE     *Nicomachean Ethics,* trans. Terrence Irwin (Indianapolis: Hackett, 1985).

### Jacques Derrida
Adieu  *Adieu à Emmanuel Levinas* (Paris: Galilée, 1997).

VM     "Violence and Metaphysics: An Essay on the Thought of Emmanuel Levinas in *Writing and Difference,*" trans. Alan Bass (Chicago: University of Chicago Press, 1978).

### Michel Foucault
AK     *Archaeology of Knowledge* [1969], trans. A. M. Sheridan Smith (New York: Pantheon, 1972).

### Hans-Georg Gadamer
EPH   *On Education, Poetry, and History: Applied Hermeneutics,* ed. Dieter Misgeld and Graeme Nicholson (Albany: SUNY Press, 1992).

HS     *Hermeneutics versus Science: Three German Views,* trans. and ed. John Connolly and Thomas Kneuter (Notre Dame, Ind.: University of Notre Dame Press, 1988).

PH     *Philosophical Hermeneutics,* trans. and ed. David E. Linge (Berkeley: University of California Press, 1976).

RAS   *Reason in the Age of Science,* trans. Frederick G. Lawrence (Cambridge, Mass.: MIT Press, 1981).

Reflections  "Reflections on My Philosophical Journey," in *The Philosophy of Hans-Georg Gadamer,* ed. Lewis Edwin Hahn (Chicago: Open Court, 1997).

TM     *Truth and Method* [1960], revised and trans. Joel Weinsheimer and Donald Marshall (New York: Crossroad, 1992).

### G. W. F. Hegel
Dif     *The Difference between Fichte's and Schelling's System of Philosophy* [1801] (Albany: SUNY Press, 1977).

HP     *Lectures on the History of Philosophy* [1833], trans. E. S. Haldane and Frances H. Simson, 3 vols. (New York: Humanities, 1953).

PR     *Philosophy of Right* [1821], T. M. Knox (Oxford: Clarendon Press, 1967).

Phen     *Phenomenology of Spirit,* trans. A. V. Miller (Oxford: Clarendon Press, 1977).

WdL     *The Science of Logic* [1812], A. V. Miller (New York: Humanities Press, 1969).

## Martin Heidegger

BP     *Basic Problems of Phenomenology* [1927], trans. Albert Hofstadter (Bloomington: Indiana University Press, 1982).

BT     *Being and Time* [1927], trans. John Macquarrie and Edward Robinson (New York: Harper and Row, 1962).

DL     "A Dialogue on Language" [1959], in *On the Way to Language,* trans. Peter D. Hertz (San Francisco: Harper Collins, 1971).

FS     *Frühe Schriften* (Frankfurt am Main: V. Klostermann, 1972).

HCT     *History of the Concept of Time,* trans. Theodore Kisiel (Bloomington: Indiana University Press, 1985).

LH     "Letter on Humanism" [1947], in *Basic Writings,* trans. Frank A. Capuzzi and J. Glenn Gray (New York: Harper and Row, 1977).

Par     *Parmenides,* trans. André Schuwer and Richard Rojcewicz (Bloomington: Indiana University Press, 1992).

## Thomas Hobbes

Lev     *Leviathan* [1651], ed. C. B. Macpherson (New York: Penguin Classics, 1985).

## Edmund Husserl

FTL     *Formal and Transcendental Logic* [1929], trans. Dorion Cairns (The Hague: Martinus Nijhoff, 1969).

K     *The Crisis of the European Sciences and Transcendental Phenomenology* [1943–37], trans. David Carr (Evanston: Northwestern University Press, 1970).

LI     *Logical Investigations* [1900], trans. J. N. Findlay, 2 vols. (London: Routledge and Kegan Paul, 1970).

## Immanuel Kant

(A . . . /B . . . )     *Critique of Pure Reason* [1788], trans. Norman Kemp Smith (New York: Macmillan, 1973). Following the standard practices, references to this work will list pages of the first [1781] and second [1787] editions, or "A" and "B" paginations.

CJ     *Critique of Judgment* [1790], trans. Werner S. Pluhar (Indianapolis: Hackett Publishing Company, 1987).

CPR     *Critique of Practical Reason* [1788], trans. Lewis White Beck (New York: Bobbs-Merrill, 1956).

Logic     *Logic* [1800], trans. Robert S. Harman and Wolfgang Schwartz (Indianapolis: Bobbs-Merrill, 1974).

**Jacques Lacan**

Ecrits   *Ecrits* [1966], trans. Alan Sheridan (New York: Norton, 1977).

**Emmanuel Levinas**

OBBE   *Otherwise than Being, or, Beyond Essence* [1978], trans. Alphonso Lingis (Dordrecht: Kluwer, 1991).

TI   *Totality and Infinity* [1961], trans. Alphonso Lingis (Pittsburgh: Duquesne University Press, 1969).

**Maurice Merleau-Ponty**

PoP   *Phenomenology of Perception* [1945], trans. Colin Smith (New Jersey: Humanities Press, 1981).

**Plotinus**

E   *The Enneads,* trans. Stephen MacKenna (New York: Larson Publications, 1992).

**Paul Ricoeur**

TN   *Time and Narrative* [1983], trans. Kathleen McLaughlin and David Pellauer, 3 vols. (Chicago: University of Chicago Press, 1984).

**Jean-Paul Sartre**

N   *Notebooks for an Ethics* [1983], trans. David Pellauer (Chicago: University of Chicago Press, 1992).

SG   *Saint Genet: Actor and Martyr* [1952], trans. Bernard Frechtman (New York: G. Braziller, 1963).

**Ludwig Wittgenstein**

OC   *On Certainty,* trans. G. E. M. Anscombe and G. H. von Wright (Oxford: Basil Blackwell, 1969).

PI   *Philosophical Investigations* [1953], trans. G. E. M. Anscombe (Oxford: Basil Blackwell, 1963).

TLP   *Tractatus logico-philosophicus* [1922] (London: Routledge and Kegan Paul, 1960).

WLE   "Wittgenstein's Lecture on Ethics," *Philosophical Review* 74 (January 1965).

# TRADITION(S) II

# Introduction

# 1. On the Inordinance of Our Time: The Effects of Detraditionalization and the Noncontemporaneity of the Present

> There must be a justice among incomparable ones. There must then be a comparison between incomparables and a synopsis, a togetherness and contemporaneousness; there must be thematization, thought, history and inscription. . . .
>
> —Levinas, *Otherwise than Being, or, Beyond Essence*

This book is the second of two works on the problem of tradition in Kantian and post-Kantian Continental philosophy.[1] The first book, *Tradition(s): Refiguring Community and Virtue in Classical German Thought,* articulated the experience of tradition intrinsic to the rational, albeit by a coherence that was internally (if not explicitly) differentiated and pluralistic—a coherence both interpretive and open-ended. The modern emergence of the concept of tradition thereby became linked to the critical practices of enlightenment, both augmenting and surpassing the latter's rational (or demonstrative) limitations, as thinkers attempted to invoke resources antecedent to the enlightenment and to articulate and refigure such resources within modern moral, political, and theoretical narratives of freedom, individuality, and rationality. Within these parameters the first book articulated a renewed account of hermeneutics, linked neither to a unique method (or countermethod), nor a set of proper names, but precisely the experience of historical rupture (the detraditionalization) out of which accounts of theory, self, and community would be refigured (or reconstituted) in the wake of modern reductions or constructions of these concepts. The result was complicated; to use Heidegger's terms for the rationality of the hermeneutic in general, it involved "a remarkable relatedness backward or forward" (BT:28)—a juxtaposition in which the link between the rational and the historical provides a resource for both intelligibility and critique.

This book begins the task of examining the effect of these transformations on the descent of twentieth-century philosophy in general and Continental philosophy in particular, tracing the latter's increasingly explicit encounter with the problem of traditionality and its effect on recent debates on topics as critical and widespread as the nature of subjectivity and personhood, the questions of law and legitimation, or interpretation and community. Unlike the earlier work on more classical German thought, where the transformation of the concept of tradition and its impact within Kant and post-Kantian sources remained more canonical, in this case the scope, of necessity, becomes less restricted, like the history that we have experienced in its wake, without being readily delimitable within the standard categories of philosophy as an institutional practice.

This effect is in the first instance disciplinary. On standard accounts the period denoted by the term 'modern philosophy' roughly still encompasses the same texts that Hegel's lectures on this topic did (Descartes to Kant and German Idealism). While it has been said that much of contemporary philosophy is a reaction to Hegel, it is surely true that contemporary philosophy became equally a monumental attempt to grapple with the advances of science (both formal and natural). Hegel, after all, had 'speculatively' (and somewhat fantastically) integrated the latter into the science of Absolute Spirit, a strategy which the reductive commitments of modern scientific naturalism had contested from its origins. Still, speculative purges like Hegel's seemed simply self-defeating; inquiries that descended from it could not be articulated within the demarcation principles of science, with the result that they inevitably instead seemed to become matters of merely historical interest. The concepts at stake in such 'speculation' seemed to express worldviews better grasped by the sociology of knowledge, the experience resolved by the analysis of its unconscious, or reduced to an epiphenomenon of a cognitive science that would do for the mental what Newton had done for the physical world. Hence emerged the epithets that accompany post-Hegelian 'Continental' thought: historicism, psychologism, nihilism, but equally the claim that all philosophy becomes a reaction to Hegel, a claim perhaps more conditioned than it had realized by the positivism to which it was initially opposed. Thinkers as diverse as Gadamer and Foucault concurred that, as a result, much of the philosophy of the time would be written by 'outsiders' such as Kierkegaard, or Nietzsche, or Schopenhauer (or for Foucault, even more radically, Sade and Goya). But in all accuracy, it would be no less necessary to include other 'outsiders' like Frege or Husserl or Wittgenstein, whose reactions to the crises in logic and mathematics had also articulated a domain that was "beyond the promise of dialectic," as Foucault put it, and equally unintelligible to Hegel.[2] And we will continue to insist on their presence here.

Doubtless, as has also been said, Hegel became the Aristotle of the post-Renaissance world—or as Jean-Luc Nancy has reaffirmed in a recent book, "the inaugural thinker of the contemporary world."[3] Still, if this is true, Hegel held the position in the first place by stirring up Platonist backlashes all around. This was true even perhaps in those most virulently anti-Platonist. It makes little difference, after all, if one argues for the historicist denial of truth or its defense, if truth is too timeless or 'separate' to be human, as Aristotle had realized. Such was the uneasy synthesis Hegel had bequeathed: a speculative logic that Gadamer declared even Heidegger had not fully comprehended (PH:231), coupled at the same time with a respect for law as objective as it was proclaimed to be real—both of which were supposed to be explicated through the schematism of history. Here, in any case, it was true: "[t]he general theme of the modern era, the *querelle des anciens et modernes,* is fought out monumentally in Hegel's philosophy."[4] Hence the antinomies that seemingly arose in Hegel's wake regarding what Gadamer himself called "the old stories [*alte Geschichte*]" of tradition—those denominated by Being, virtue (*aretē*), the beautiful (*kalon*) and that which lies beyond them, the Good (*agathon*) (RAS:77). Too often, in any case, claims to the timelessness of truth (or alternatively its dissolutions in Nietzschean inversions) simply omitted the history and the detraditionalization out of which the constructions of modernity arose: the quest for certainty and the search for foundations always attested to a lapse in their midst that was neither simply illusory nor apolitical. After all, the scientific and political failures of the past were real: the violence (of theory) so abhorred by much of twentieth-century thought was the result not of theory but of the withdrawal of principle or the authority that might sustain truth, the good from which even hermeneutic reason "must draw its nurture" (BT:194). And, the Stoicism that gave rise to the modern quest for certainty was time and again made by appeal to a virtue that might itself nurture peace, an argument constructed less out of the need to dominate than the 'hope' and the mutual promising of the social contract. The hope was that through science and oath such 'everyday' violence and dogmatism would be less 'wielded' or 'mastered', or even by a kind of voluntarism hubristically dominated, than internally constituted, 'regulated', and limited—making up thereby for what nature and tradition lacked.

Still, it was no less true that the method of such hope, indeed the hope of strict method itself, was that the rational might be reduced to one of its instances, that the internal 'regularities' of mathematics might not simply be the model of nature but the exemplar of reason itself. Here, ancient admonitions against expecting the same demands for explanation in all things sounded like defenses of folk psychology. Correlatively, when modern denials of the priority of methodological enquiry appealed instead to practice—and even 'praxis'—construing themselves to be against 'theory', often enough this too attested to the extent to which they were modern: the equation of theory and method was more indelibly 'modern' than it was 'metaphysical'. The distinction between theory and practice was not, after all, a distinction of opposition for the ancients: the appeal to practice, to pragmatism, as articulating an event over against the limits of theory, owed much more to its modern romantic ancestry than might have seemed plausible. For example, even Peirce's debts to Schelling here have much more to them than simply a commitment to realism or naturalism: both of the latter were encased in a rupture that had sought the solution to the illusions of metaphysics in reason's other, in its 'unconscious', as Schelling already termed it.[5]

The occlusion of the complexity of modern theoretics (an 'occlusion' as critical as the occlusion of the more ancient *Seinsfrage*) doubtless was widespread and overdetermined its polemics. Even justified demands for the 'deconstruction' of modern equations of reason with the *mathesis universalis* often remained parasitic upon the account of theory as construction and the substitution of techniques for the transcendence of *theoria*. And, often enough, many will charge, such deconstructive alternatives were shortsighted concerning the theoretical complications in their origins. While the pragmatics of theory construction seemed to derive from the experimentalism of modern science, the attempt to make explicit the working of nature precisely through exhibiting control over it, such (technical) ventures were taken less to simply dissolve theory than to shore up ancient foundations that had proven 'infirm'.

Here perhaps we can make sense of a second phenomenon. If Hegel indeed was the origin of our 'contemporaneity', he performed this function, as thinkers often enough concurred, only by acknowledging the dispersion of tradition in his midst and articulating a certain 'inquietude of the negative' which provided, as Gadamer put it, "the essence of the hermeneutic experience" (TM:346). Moreover, it might be argued that this 'negativity' had accompanied the modern from the outset. For both theoretical and moral reasons, this 'inquietude' reflected a detraditionalization to which modern thinkers like Bacon had already attested (TM:348). It was not accidental that this 'inquietude' was articulated by hermeneuts and poststructuralists, existentialists, and critical theorists alike. Hegel's 'contemporaneity' already attested to the fragmentation of 'modern time', *die neue Zeit*. Notwithstanding the modernist protocols that had enframed the science of the Absolute, if (by a certain naiveté) Hegel is to be read as the last speculative philosopher, his Absolute would only emerge in articulating the very fragmentation of modernity intrinsic to its experience, its 'phenomenology' reflecting explicitly the limit that lies 'beyond' it, divided between past and future, between, to anticipate Husserl's terms, retention and protention.

After Hegel, the 'subject' of philosophy would be fragmented between philosophies, histories, moralities, religions, arts, cultures, and politics. In one sense this fragmentation can be evidenced by the (formal) multiplicity that circulates 'encyclopedically' through Hegel's own texts, transforming the history he 'inscribes'. While Hegel sought in the *humaniora,* understood as the study of the ancients, a free plastic virtue (*freie plastische Tugend*), it became evident that this *syntagm* itself, combining if not the theories then at least the lexicons of modernity and ancient thought, attests to the differentiations—to use Benjamin's term, the 'translations'— such a practice would entail. While consistent with the problem of the *traditionis traditio,* and the idea that all thought may well (both by intuition and coherence) begin in remembrance (*Erinnerung*), Hegel's science of Absolute modernity attested to the very dispersion that is the noncontemporaneity of the modern, devoid of immanence, transcendental past, foundation, authority, or 'homeland'. And this provisionally indicates that the issue is not simply an epistemic or theoretical question, but equally a matter of the need for place (*polis*), a dwelling (*Boden*) and an ethics (*ēthos*)—the latter harking back to a theoretical 'translation' or refiguration already brought to light by Aristotle himself.[6] Still, paradoxically, if Hegel announced this 'noncontemporaneity' in linking 'Spirit' to history, he did so—despite the mechanism (and the logical machinery [*Räderwerk*]) of dialectic—by a certain dialectical 'delay'. The Absolute, which would reconcile the dispersion of 'contemporaneity' in demonstrating that the real is the rational, still found its own coherence through appeal to the mythemes of *theodicaea* (HP:457)—or as Gadamer states, by appeal to a certain "spiritualization" of Christianity (TM:346). Such theodicies, as becomes evident, may also still overdetermine thinking—and even phenomenology—in Hegel's wake. When in his 1935 Vienna lecture Husserl codified science as an ultimate "spiritual accomplishment" of unconditional universality he did so only by claiming that it clearly belongs to Europe (albeit linked to the United States and the English dominions) and not to "the Eskimos or Indians presented as curiosities at fairs, or the Gypsies who constantly wander about Europe" (K:272–73).

Granted his own 'cultural' history, that Hegel (or Husserl) had thus articulated this event might seem entirely 'natural'. It attests, in any case, to the overdetermined remainder of the sacred 'theodicies' (Christian or otherwise) in theoretical modernity, which may be both inextricable even if perhaps not simply (i.e., immanently [or universally]) endorsable.[7] Hegel himself found the 'figure' of Trinitarian speculation to be "diaphanous." He found it, for example, in 'oriental' religion (Hinduism), but he also found it in Plato.[8] Yet we are, it will be objected, beyond the time in which we would assert one 'religion' (theistic or otherwise) to be true at the expense of all others—as the very multiplicity of Hegel's text perhaps reveals.

For Gadamer, Hegel's position did not result in the 'hermetically sealed' totality of the mythical, which leaves "no room for the experience of the other and the alterity of history." In fact, Hegel's speculative experience had already (if not sufficiently) led him to acknowledge the contrary. Indeed notwithstanding his own emphasis on traditionality, Gadamer found in Hegel the continuing recognition that "the life of the mind consists in recognizing oneself in other being [*Anderssein*]" (TM:346). Kant's Copernican turn too involved the claim that concepts form a (limited) horizon of intelligibility. But it seemed obvious as well that Hegel's appeals to the 'horizons' of history, far from culminating in the Absolute of self-certainty (or epistemic con-temporaneity, the '*nunc stans*'), would not escape the 'dispersion' that gave rise to the modern. Indeed by a certain internal 'reversal', in 'recognizing' this multiplicity, such claims reemphasized precisely the problem of history that his 'science' sought to subsume: spirit's 'falling into time', the diaphanousness of its difference, and the problem of the unity in which reason might remain 'at home' with itself. While Kant had also written a history of pure reason as the concluding chapter of the *Critique of Pure Reason*, Hegel's 'conclusion' is exactly what now seems pre-cluded, its 'Copernican turn' fully decentered. Henceforth, in any case, the understanding of philosophy as the 'universal discourse of reason', and the history of philosophy itself would no longer be readily distinguishable. Hegel's account of the history of philosophy thus points to that moment in which reason would acknowledge, precisely in its recollection (*Erinnerung*) of the past, the 'division' (*Entzweiung*) which also adjoins reason to 'other'—but precisely as 'other'. The very 'tradition of reason', like the 'splitting' of time itself, apparently becomes 'multiple', divided between the present and the past, self and other, one culture and another. Unlike Kant's history, Hegel's begins with considerations on 'oriental' thought—albeit only by criticizing 'oriental' thought for an abstractness that it shared with Wolff and the scholastics (HP:I:119, 146). But here too, obviously, Hegel's limited vision testifies to his own historicity.

Surely Hegel's account of Spirit's "fall into time" was not an isolated phenomenon. The great natural histories and genealogies of the nineteenth century surely attest to the convergence of human knowing with knowledge of its own 'evolution' in what has been called the discovery of time. They do so however, by also attesting to the very dispersion of the present, a 'simultaneity', to use Bergson's term, whose diacritics had become anything but simply synchronic. And this term "simultaneity" (and its failure) itself was in a sense symptomatic—symptomatic, in any case, of Bergson's own crises with relativity theory.[9] As was the case with Heidegger, who too in 1925, as Pöggeler rightly reminds us, had sought to connect his account of time with the theory of relativity (hence not only with Dilthey or Bergson, but Einstein), here the specter of difference, the relative, and the 'decentering' of horizons will perhaps never be far away.[10] Heidegger himself was equally, however, inclined to view the interest in difference (e.g., concern, or at least curiosity regarding the multiple forms of ethnological or foreign difference) as a straying away from the care for what is near that accompanies human dwelling—and a symptom of our own 'uprootedness' (*Bodenlosigkeit*) (BT:43, 216–17).

Doubtless, as Levinas has said, in depending on its own totalizing practices, "the philosophical discourse of the West knows how to find again under the ruins or in the hieroglyphs, the interrupted discourses of every civilization and of the prehistory of civilizations that were set up as separated" (OBBE:169). But it is true too—as no one saw better than Levinas—that these 'hermeneutic' practices were equally in the end self-dissimilating, the contemporaneousness (the modernity) of such discourses implicitly disrupted. To open oneself to the other is inherently to call into question the univocal foundation of the past: "proximity is a disturbance of rememberable time," a simultaneity always differentiated (OBBE:89). At stake is an identity, a 'diachrony' that is precisely not "contemporary with itself" (OBBE:57). Hence it becomes clear that—and without denying the evidence or the problem of the symptom of our 'uprootedness'—the notion of the 'near' itself only emerges 'differentially', that is, as a 'universal' and uncircumscribable phenomenon—that is, one not to be circumscribed by any (ontic) 'place', language, nation, or 'people'. Claude Lefort saw this result to be characteristic of both "a society [which] is *historical par excellence*" and its democratic institutions, beyond the immanences of the traditional past. Indeed, "the present proves to be indefinable, covering many different social times which are staggered in relation to one another within simultaneity."[11] Here the 'near' and the 'strange' (and the interpretive care that attends them) are by no means antinomies but will emerge, as Merleau-Ponty already recognized before him, only 'laterally'—and democracy, Merleau-Ponty also claimed, was the institution of such difference, "the only known institution that guarantees a minimum of opposition and of truth."[12] The relations between identity and culture surely will not be 'nomadic', as some would claim, but nor will they be self-enclosed: rather, such identity itself will emerge only 'differentially' in the dialogues of the symbolic 'interworlds' that constitute both self and other, disarticulating its 'phenomenologies' from within.[13] As Levinas likewise saw, however, "paradoxically it is qua *alienus*—foreigner and other—that man is not alienated" (OBBE:59). At stake was surely a 'dwelling' or *ethos* which, without dissolving the near or assuming an indifferent cosmopolitanism, breaks up as "an impossibility to remain at home [*demeurer chez soi*]" (OBBE:184).

What is true of the complications of 'culture' is surely no less true of the complications attending the 'phenomenology' of nature. Here too Paul Ricoeur is right to insist on a discontinuity in the midst of such phenomenological 'experiences':

> Just as it seemed impossible to generate the time of nature on the basis of phenomenological time, so it . . . seems impossible to proceed in the opposite direction and to include phenomenological time in the time of nature, whether it is a question of quantum time, thermodynamic time, the time of galactic transformations, or that of the evolution of the species. (TN III:91)

Rightly seen however, this discontinuity, far from dissolving the 'phenomenological', is already at work in the dispersion between ordinary (and public) time and the singular 'experience' (if not the 'nature') that is Dasein. Here the immediacy of the present, the coexistence (or con-temporaneousness or community) of simultaneity and the after-effects of the past would be disrupted in the play of discontinuity itself, divided between the real and the imaginary, the 'given' and its concept, observation, theory, and metric.[14]

As a glance at Kant's table of categories reveals, the problem of such simultaneity (or coexistence) appeared already to be a transcendental one, linked by Kant to the categories of relations and the logic of substance—the latter ultimately understood through the principle and the problematic of "time-order" (and not simply its lapse) (A203/B248). Doubtless, moreover, the problems adherent to these categories (subsistence, causality—or freedom—and community) were both political and ethical in import—and had in fact been explicitly so linked since Leibniz's modern refiguration of the (now perspectival) Augustinian City of God.[15] In both cases, however, both in the case of truth and in the case of the Good, such a 'logic' now seemed to be internally disrupted in relativity, as thinkers from the post-Kantians to the modern phenomenologists continually worried. The problem seemed to be less one of instituting (or constructing) an order where there was one lacking than interpreting the 'order' that we share—if not in the 'lapse' of such 'monologics' then—in the differences (cultures, concepts, histories) through which their varying 'phenomenologies' would still be intelligible. And yet, the 'relativities' here are in one sense quite ordinary—those of history, life, and time itself. Indeed even Husserl himself acknowledged it in 1929, and did so increasingly in connecting truth to time and reason to history and

'everyday truth': "each and every truth . . . remains involved in *relativities* by
virtue of its essence" (FTL:278). And yet, as this admission already announces, any appeal to such 'origins' and the reliability of their evidence
would no longer be simple—and surely not timeless and ahistorical.

Despite his continuing appeal to the correlation of appearance and idea
of truth, if only as regulative idea and norm, the problem of tradition openly
erupted in Husserl's late manuscripts—strikingly enough precisely in those
texts that meditate on post-Copernican epistemic accounts—and which
problematically linked reason to Western and Greek origins. But as Derrida
realized, Hegel's concerns were not far away here either.[16] Whatever was left
of the ordinary (and of 'ordinary time') would be articulated through the
differences it announced, through the histories in which it was explicated
or narrated. The relations between reflection and its other(s)—the past, the
'other', the 'foreign', even its un-conscious—could no longer be opposi-
tional. It is almost as if, as Merleau-Ponty would indeed claim later, that in
order to fully confront this extension of reason before its 'beyond', the
phenomenology of consciousness in the end would require rapprochement
with a kind of psychoanalysis—every bit as much as would hermeneutics.[17]
"[F]undamentally," as Gadamer too would acknowledge, here "both
[hermeneutics and psychoanalysis] take part in the unconscious," where
questions become posed "to which there are no secure answers,"[18] where
neither time nor meaning are securable apart from one another, and where
the intelligibility of experience and concept become themselves interwoven
between histories, both 'archaic' or ancient and modern. Indeed, in a point
Gadamer once claimed to have learned "above all, from Jacques Lacan," he
stated that at stake in both psychoanalysis and hermeneutics is "completing
an interrupted process into a full history, a story that can be articulated in
language" (PH:41).

Even here, however, the result would be complicated. The 'perdurance'
of such interruption (i.e., the 'interrupted' status of narrative) has been attested to by postmodern and post-Heideggerian thinkers such as Nancy and
Lyotard, both thinkers understanding this interruption as an effect that
accompanies the end of myth and detraditionalization. The truth of the
matter doubtless lies between such views—not only between such 'post-
modernist' and 'neoclassical' accounts like Gadamer's but between such
'posttraditional' thinkers as Nancy and Lyotard themselves. Nancy had declared Lyotardian attempts to revive narrative in accord with Kantian precedent to be a revival of the "as if" that forgot the myth of totalizing narrative
(*mythos*), even as idea. For Nancy what is at stake is not narrative but being.[19] Lyotard himself however contested attempts to revive the 'myth' of

Being in any of its forms: "no one knows what 'language' Being understands, which it speaks, or to which it is referred."[20] It is perhaps in just
such rejoinders (*Auseinandersetzungen*) that the interpretive event itself becomes articulated, as doubtless the inter-rupted or fractured narrative of
the modern novel has long since attested.[21] The fact is that whatever remnants of 'being' there might be are also fragmented in the interpretations
that adjoin narrative and the experience of detraditionalization itself:
hence, as hermeneuts insisted, the interplay, the twofold synthesis of interpretive *Vor-struktur* and 'unconcealment'. But that was the point, the point
of the twofold synthesis; beyond the historical 'destructions' of dialectic,
something more would be needed. Indeed just such an extension beyond
dialectic had been at stake in Heidegger's articulemes for the hermeneutic
from the outset. In a fragment dating from 1924 Heidegger stated:

> Dialectic—historical destruction—understanding. . . . "Truth," uncoveredness, de-
> velopment of the uncoveredness, and dialectic. Dialectic in being negated does
> not lead to and call for *direct* grasping and having. A more radical possibility,
> new conceptuality: hermeneutics.[22]

## 2. The Koiné of the Hermeneutic

This much is true, however. If the term 'hermeneutics' is still retained for
such an 'interrupted' enquiry—as thinkers as diverse as Heidegger and Levinas did at points in their writings—it is not because hermeneutics provides
a method that might rival the explanations of natural science, nor because
it provides a science for the investigation of things mental or some presupposed spiritual entity, nor because it allows us to presuppose a deeper
meaning for the fragmentation of the human realm that might again unify
its referents. Rather, it is because this inquiry emerged precisely in acknowledging the problem of interpretation—a problem that neither conceptual explanation nor descriptive inventory can legitimately surmount.
In default of the monolithic authority of history or tradition (and since its
post-Kantian inception I have argued), at stake in this term 'interpretation'
was a task that neither attempts to escape that history nor the fragmentation
of its conceptuality—and consequently, as will become apparent, the task of
again reconfronting the history of philosophy.

It is doubtless true, as Arendt has shown, that the modern conception of
history in general arises in the event of a certain default of tradition in
which all things become dubitable—even perhaps, thereby, to use Nancy

terms, an *Ereignis,* beyond memory, of what escapes immanent represent-ability.[23] Lacking the assurance of either a science or a metaphysics for this event, however, the interpretations at stake must rely still on the link be-tween our experience and our history, acknowledging the necessity of both for any honest account of the rational. That is, the 'dissemination' of the present notwithstanding, and without denying the fragmentation and inde-terminacies of our concepts, it must still be insisted (as even a Lacan could still) that "interpretation is a signification that is not just any interpreta-tion."[24] But it is equally true that the ciphering of the history of our present (personal or cultural) likewise occurs only as a certain lapse in relation to the narratives of past.

Indeed notwithstanding the necessity of our reliance on experience in this *lapsus,* such 'old stories'—like that of the transcendence of Being or the Good—continually incurred upon the immanence of 'phenomenological' presence, robbing the latter of its obviousness, and motivating attempts to save the apodicticity of appearance 'otherwise'. If the experience articulated in these narratives in their modern guise remained best accessed through the science of phenomenology in their midst, even here, as Levinas recog-nized, we encounter a certain dissonance and interruption, "a plot (*in-trigue*) that is not reducible to phenomenology" (OBBE:46). Instead, against the latter's own stories of immanence within the subject, we would require an account (and correspondingly a hermeneutics) of what escaped egologi-cal reduction. As Proust put it, in the same year that Husserl published the first volume of the *Ideen* (1913)—again in explicitly opposing Bergsonian 'simultaneity'—what is required is a narrative of 'juxtapositions' or at least "a novel of the 'unconscious'," revealing what escaped "the reigning philoso-phy."[25] Here indeed, as Wittgenstein claimed of Freudian symbolism, we are confronted with events that "have something puzzling and in a special way interesting—so that we want an interpretation of them."[26] In appealing to the category of the interesting, Wittgenstein doubtless again attested to his proximity to Kierkegaard and the issue of discovery or recognition.[27] But the events articulated in such experiences, which equally call into ques-tion what Wittgenstein termed the (grammatical) obviousness of "seeing" (PI:212), do so in revealing that the links between tradition, narrative, and experience have become fully uncanny: the simple 'seeing' of the *lumen nat-urale* can no longer be univocally correlated with the reliability of a fixed in-herited framework (BT:221), or fixed inherited (or mythic) background (OC:§94f.). Instead our practices—and even the 'phenomenologies' of con-sciousness they once delineated—would not be free of the contingency, in-determinacy, and ambiguity that accompanied the problem of the historical everywhere. Indeed while Eugen Fink had aptly characterized the Stoic turn inward of the transcendental *epoché* as a dramatic caesura or disturbance within the natural attitude, here the "counter-play" of the world, of culture, of history, and the other would prove particularly disturbing to phenomenological harmony.[28]

Still, as Merleau-Ponty argued, while two consciousnesses might be mutually exclusive, two temporalities need not be (PoP:433). Yet neither, of course, are they thereby immanently con-temporaneous. Here the very 'plurality' of time is as much disjunction as identity. The time of eternity is always, for mortals in any case, an oneiric affair: the self is not a "motionless identity" but "opens itself to an Other" (PoP:423, 426). But, the problem, as he too saw it, is that, granted the ruptures of modernity, not only is such classical 'simultaneity' problematic but "nothing is left of the oneiric world of analogy"—and hence perhaps the old story of the *Seinsfrage,* through which the relations of same and other had been articulated (and interpreted).[29]

This perhaps further accounts for why those even closer to psychoanalysis, like Julia Kristeva, insisted that the critical role of interpretation cannot be simply limited either by experiment (or heuristic) or simple repetition of the past. Instead, again granted what she terms "the modern dislocated experience of temporality," the question of the 'imaginary' becomes even more crucial.[30] At stake in the question of interpretation is the necessity of the refiguration or 'transvaluation' of time itself, beyond the simple repetition of traditional identity. Hence it becomes clear (and without deciding a priori for or against 'the tradition') that, granted the requisites of the 'dislocated', pluralized, or decentered time of modernity, the rational demands, like the therapeutic process itself, not simply the transference of (received) interpretation but the 'transference' or appropriation of the (re)interpreting itself. Such reinterpretation thereby continually encounters in its midst, as did Freud's project itself, the problem (and the work in process or *Kulturarbeit*) of cultural '*symbiosis*'—that is, the problem of 'civilization'.[31] It is in just this sense that Gianni Vattimo has aptly said that hermeneutics—or in any case the problem of 'interpretation'—becomes "a sort of *Koiné* or common idiom of Western culture."[32] But from the outset, as Vattimo realized, too, the problem was a Heideggerian one. That is, it was a question, as Heidegger put it in his original retrievals of Aristotle, both of making explicit the interpretation which 'life' itself is and, in confronting the separation of the past, the problem of how such a 'con-temporalizing' occurs within historical life.[33] Indeed here especially the cyclopean vision of the modern encyclopedia soon revealed, to use the tragic terms Hölderlin introduced into transcendental philosophy, that we are all always internally divided, divided from the past as we are from our contemporaries—and thus endowed in both cases with "one eye too many." Hence, as Hölderlin rightly concluded, "what is familiar must be learned as well as what is foreign."[34]

Even so, it will be argued, the classical inheritance of hermeneutics has not simply been discarded. Indeed it was just here that this inheritance was claimed to be efficacious in domains such as aesthetics, or jurisprudence or moral casuistry. In all these domains the questions of interpretation remained unavoidable and hermeneuts acknowledged, in accord with classical accounts, both that there was an 'objective' nature of the thing to be decided and, to quote Cicero, often called the first casuist, that "the fundamental claim of social relationships (*humanitas*) is not identical in every circumstance."[35] Granted the contemporary dispersion of practices and cultures a thinker like Cicero did not face, the task seems ever more daunting. Indeed the ciphering of narratives (and the discernment or perception of the Good) here seemed to require at the same time both the ascertaining of our obligations and the renewal of the traditions themselves in the interplay of fact and idea, reason and nature.[36] The question was always whether the requisite interpretation now had sufficient rational resources on which to rely, once the unified horizon of tradition and ontic community had withdrawn, once the appearances, that is, had become, apparently, unreliable, indeed 'unphenomenological'. In fact this question had forged the demand for modern certainty as much as it forged the basis of the Pascalian charge against the excesses or 'overinterpretations' of seventeenth-century casuists, namely that, in the stress on interpretation, anything can be interpreted away—but not the *more geometrico*.[37] Apart from the demonstrative limits of the latter, reason lies lost in the (historical) interplay of same and other, its claims as illusory and unprincipled as the 'world' of the inverted image the moderns discovered at the heart of appearance, or Hegel at the heart of reason and phenomenology itself.

While again, all this may simply seem to depart from the critical tradition, we should tread carefully. Critically, Kant had already indicated the problem of the dispersion or 'polyhistory' which threatened unprincipled historical knowledge (*historisches Wissen*). Indeed pure polyhistory remains, Kant claims, "a cyclopean vision that lacks one eye, the eye of philosophy" insofar as it takes the latter to be dispensable (Logic:50). Yet, notwithstanding his own attempts to separate principle and history, he also indicated a certain disequilibrium in reason's midst. Equally as critically, the 'Copernican turn' (qua Copernican) itself clearly depended on historical precedent— and thereby, a certain parsing of "the ruins of the ancient systems" in its origins (A835/B863). Indeed in his lectures on *Logic* Kant openly acknowledged a certain historical ignorance (*Unwissen*) that threatens to reduce reason to 'polymathy': the rationalist alternative to polyhistory.

The problem, moreover, Kant asserted, is that the "historically ignorant are commonly the teachers of reason." The result of either pure unprincipled history or pure unhistorical cognition, that is, in either case when thought is "extended without definite limits may be called pansophy" (Logic:50). But such 'pansophy', for Kant, lacks all justification, being doubtless as transcendentally subreptive as any of our illusions of totality. Instead, both reason and history are necessary to what Kant already called the problem of the determination of one's horizon—recalling that Kant (perspectivally) identified our concepts with points of view.[38] While in this identification he may have followed Leibniz (and Lambert) in pairing optics and logic, the whole of the Kantian project hinged on denying the equivalence of representation and idea—and insisted on the transcendental 'distortions' that attended any such pure 'phenomenology'.

In this regard, as postmodernists like Deleuze readily argued, Kant had already articulated a 'fissure' within the Cartesian solidarities linking the I think and the Absolute, "even the subject can only represent its own spontaneity as that of another"—an origin that is always problematic.[39] Hence the problem becomes especially complicated: granted our reliance on the historical, determining what lies both within and beyond such horizons remains equally 'problematic'—and doubtless especially complicated for the problem of 'urbanity' and 'cosmopolitanism' Kant (and the critical tradition in his wake) still attempted to defend, a point to which we shall return. Suffice it to say, for reasons already evident, that such 'urbanity' would be less the common 'polarity' (or *polis*) of modern rationalism than the 'community' of differences it constantly eschewed. As Schlegel immediately realized after Kant, this form of urbanity would of necessity be more than a logical, analytic, or discursive matter, but would again require imagination and wit (*Witz*).[40] Indeed, he thought such urbanity to be precisely a question of "social wit"; the problem with its lack being that "there are fewer synthetic than analytic people."[41]

Rationally, in any case, rather than a schematic or internal conceptual analysis (and without denying the latter's necessities), the question of tradition, both uniting and dividing the ontic and the historical, entails a series of articulative encounters without which the facticity (and the cognitive 'horizon') of the present would be unintelligible. Here the internal play of temporal horizons both inaugurates and alters the rational, however: opening the limits of the lived-present both to its own past and in the encounter between (ontic) traditions, its own alterity—to what Hegel would soon call its own *Anderssein*. At the same time this alterity openly attests again to Hegel's modernity (i.e., our already-being-separate from the past). What Hegel's own 'phenomenology of spirit', structured by the figures *(Gestalten)*—and the refiguration—of the past, added to Schelling's account of the 'unconscious' was precisely the insistence on the question and the 'logic' of the historical. This logic in turn doubtless still overdetermines contemporary accounts of traditionality from Nietzsche to Heidegger, Gadamer to MacIntyre, Kuhn to Lyotard. That is, Hegel had already 'glimpsed' (albeit blinkingly) that the question of tradition would be inseparable from the problem of limits and alterity. The *Science of Logic* at the outset had explicitly linked the logic of finitude to a logic of limit and the finite's relation to its "outside" (WdL:122f.). The result however—*pace* Hegel (who clearly still had Kant in mind)—could neither simply vindicate the substantial or essential truths of the past ("Wesen ist gewesen") nor find guaranteed resolution in a future or more determinate or recuperative 'community' *(Gemeinschaft)* (WdL:389, 126).

Instead, the multiplicity of historical 'limits' through which we are united with the past and our 'contemporaries' both sustains and disrupts the rationality of traditionality—of being and time—from within. The fusion of historical horizons (both those of the past and the 'co-temporalizings' of the present) will be at best partial and underdetermined: the task always incomplete. The facticity of the present doubtless both makes possible the perdurance of the past as resource or 'example', to use Kant's term (its continuing 'reliability' to use Heidegger's term) but likewise institutes our opening onto another. And, this opening doubtless is equally divided between what confirms or informs our past but also onto what in confrontation has not been spoken within it (or even by a certain law of exclusion remains 'unspeakable' within it) or what remains still unsaid beyond it. Here instead we encounter the question of the incommensurable—again in Hegel's terms, the *Masslos* (WdL:371)—but equally, in what will not be reduced to a demonstrable criterion, the complicated remnants (the determinations and the overdeterminations) of the sacred, as has become evident. And, it will surely be relevant to the irreducibility of such 'excesses' or 'transcendences' that they remain linked with the problem of the practical and of ancient wisdom. This is true whether, for example, this link occurs by *phronēsis* and what extends beyond a science of the speculative, as in Aristotle's sense of the practical context in which "the particular is more true," or the Sophoclean question of the limits before which mortals must remain 'flexible' or 'plastic' or, Augustinian, *fide*—all of which, after all, withdraw from the structures of modern *mathesis universalis*. The history (and the problem) of the ethical will equally be tied to the irreducibility of this excess—as especially Levinas would see.

For now it doubtless suffices to acknowledge the lingering complications of the intertwining between the theoretical and the practical, divided between the constraints of the rational, the imaginary, and a present no longer simply homogeneous in its intelligibility. In this, the heterogeneity of the ethical, as Levinas saw (as many following Hegel did not) rejoined an ancient inheritance, in the problem (and the transcendence) of the Good—where the Good exceeds the conceptual requisites of the (demonstrably) true. Indeed Levinas himself went so far as to claim that "transcendence owes it to itself to interrupt its own demonstration" (OBBE:152). None of this necessarily 'interrupts' the reality of the Good, or what Murdoch aptly called the 'Sovereignty of Good'—nor the traditions out of which it 'speaks'.[42] What is clear however, at least provisionally, is that the problem of the Good will also be a problem of sovereignty, of what can be said, to use Wittgenstein's terms—and where the very 'unsayability', as he likewise saw, "points to something" (WLE:13).

Unlike others however, who appealed to such transcendence as trumping the truths of reason, both Wittgenstein and Levinas were in strict concurrence in calling this "place of the Good above every essence . . . the most profound teaching, the definitive teaching, not of theology, but philosophy" (Levinas, TI:103). While some declared Wittgenstein's proximity to Continental philosophy—to the tradition that emerges from Kant's third *Critique* and proceeds to Hegel, Schopenhauer, or Nietzsche (or Heidegger and Levinas)—to be a sign of his emotivism or irrationalism, we should tread carefully.[43] Doubtless it was more a sign of all these thinkers' 'modernity': the equivocity (strictly taken, the undecidability) attending the Good would need to be detached from traditional guarantees, whether by the truths of religion, culture, nature, or practice. The Good, accordingly, is already internally ruptured, in this sense already in fact detraditionalized: its 'narratives' always more interpretations than propositions. Still, such was the ancient lot of interpretation as Plato's *Ion* had revealed, always devoid of strict demonstration.[44] And this was the lot of hermeneutics in general as Heidegger had declared in linking the *Seinsfrage* to the question of the Good from the outset—and in explicitly recognizing its *figural* status (HCT:66). What will follow is that unlike classical accounts of natural law, where the narratives of authoritative transcendence provided first principles for ontic adjudication, 'postmodern' accounts of justice would begin in an acknowledgment of the excess (and the conflict) out of which such narratives much be ventured: hence 'justice' would now arise as a certain difference at the internal limits of law itself and the limitation of the sayable. And its hermeneutic, accordingly, as Manfred Frank

has seen, would always be in this respect 'heretical', devoid of the assurance of the *esse commun* that could still authoritatively bind together, say Aquinas and Leibniz.[45] The problem would be deciphering individuality in the latter's lapse—and especially, granted the lapse in community in which, as Heidegger put it in Hobbesian terms, "under the mask of 'for-one-another', an 'against-one-another' is in play," and in which conceptually others "are treated merely as numerals" (BT:291, 163). The problem in both Heidegger's and Levinas's lingering appeals to the Good was how to escape what politics had become, and whether, beyond its anonymous (or 'simultaneous') universality the modern state "can do without friendship and faces" (OBBE:160). It is in this way that "the contemporaneousness of the multiple is tied about the diachrony of two"—in the face-to-face (ibid.). Moreover, such diachrony is not without conceptual implications. Levinas claimed as well that the rationality of this event accordingly, beyond reflection on oneself, called for an account of philosophy as an intersubjective and dramatic event acknowledging "the critique exercised by another philosopher"—and hence philosophy as a dialogical interpretive history. Beyond the reminiscence of Platonic dialogue or the consensus of team workers in science, however, such rational diachrony would be empirically (and dramatically) realized "as the history of philosophy in which new interlocutors always enter who have to restate (*à redire*), but in which the former ones take up the floor to answer in the interpretations (*interprétations*) they arouse" (OBBE:20).

We shall return to the 'drama' between Heidegger and Levinas later, a relation further complicated in the question of tradition. Suffice it to say, however, that the problem of the 'dispensation' of the Good (the term is Heidegger's)—and doubtless 'ethics', Levinas will insist—will be uncannily ruptured, divided between the dispersions of modernity. Granted our breach with the past, such appeals to the Good will always seem internally threatened by egoism—or a narcissism that was again 'archaic', as Freud would argue in invoking an ancient mytheme. And yet there remained the problem of the Good's withdrawal, of what in its semantic irreducibility seemed still to 'speak' in such withdrawal, of the 'otherwise' that stands at the limit of the said still in need of interpretation—and witness. And if 'humanism', even the humanism of those who followed the trajectory of Heidegger's hope of "restoring meaning to this term," often seemed not up to the task (LH:224), both Levinas and Heidegger concurred that the Hegelian attempt to systematically unite subject and substance, the truths of the past and the truths of the present, would fail, missing the breach out of which the Good appeared.

### 3. Self-Understanding, the Inconvenience of History, and the Tasks of Reinterpretation

The relations between what Fichte had originally termed the task of 'self-understanding' and its own 'traditionality' would then always remain lacking in completeness. The task of such 'reflection', too, would inevitably be hermeneutic. As Manfred Frank concluded in his work on 'neostructuralism', it is precisely in confronting this "semantic undecidability" that hermeneutics discovered its "basic problem."[46] The internal plurality between one self and another, one culture and another, one tradition and another would always already require interpretation. If, as Hegel insisted in confronting the event, none of these 'indeterminacies' dissolved either law or analysis, "from here on," as Ricoeur put it, "by 'tradition' we will mean 'traditions'"—or since the 'virtue' of tradition is to indeterminately sustain both, as I have argued, 'tradition(s)' (TN:III:221). In encountering this indeterminate 'plurality' internally, however, we must still question whether the dialectical distinction between (formal) traditionality and (material or empirical narratives of) traditions is not abstract, and whether, consequently, the heuristic presumptions of Ricoeur's own (critical) third moment of the resolution of tradition grasps sufficiently the internal difference and plurality of 'traditionality' itself.[47] Even Ricoeur himself, in defending narrative's function in mediating between past and future, took seriously the problem of the end of narrating in the traditional sense, still hoping nonetheless that new narrative forms might already be being born (TN:II:28). At stake was the failure of 'monolithic' narration, the end of the grand narrative (Lyotard), and perhaps thereby the encounter with what cannot be narrated (Levinas). And the question is the extent to which Ricoeur had confronted it.

In this respect—and notwithstanding its considerable merits in presenting a Heideggerian rendering of narratival within-time-ness (TN:I:61)—Ricoeur's account perhaps still remained strictly too phenomenological: not only in his account's triadic dialectical resolution, Hegelian, but also in his argument for an ultimately or 'presumptively' determinate noematic correlate, Husserlian. As Ricoeur acknowledged, from the critical standpoint (e.g., Habermas's) "hermeneutics must . . . renounce its universal claim if it is to preserve a regional legitimacy."[48] But the question of traditionality (or 'sedimentation', to use Ricoeur's Husserlian term) had also seemingly rendered the logic of such phenomenologies problematic from within, as Heidegger's account of 'hermeneutic' ontological difference insisted.[49]

Hence the conclusion of *The Basic Problems of Phenomenology* (1927): "There is no such thing as *the one* phenomenology . . . " (BP:328). In one sense the issue is a matter of detaching the resources of phenomenology, the narratives that figure (and are refigured in) our experience from phenomenology's universalist or abstract commitments—if not to formalism, then the forms of strict science. If such a hermeneutics will inevitably be tied to a 'region', to its present, its *Vor-habe* and to the near, the latter as Heidegger continually insisted, can by no means be confused—either culturally or theoretically—with the 'primitive' (BT:76). Instead, the question of 'the near' became increasingly tied to the 'difference' through which it emerged. And this (critical) internal differentiation became increasingly as true of the 'theory' of traditionality as it was of the experience at stake, dividing its ontic 'concepts' or received views from within.[50]

The intelligibility of our contemporaneity thus emerges only in its 'diachrony'. At stake in the question of interpretation are the aftereffects (*Nachwirkungen*) of a traditionality that composes a history both conceptual and real. Doubtless, moreover, the 'separation' in such diachrony involves as much discontinuity as continuity. The very problem of interpretation emerges in historical remove from origins—and in this respect already entails the event of detraditionalization. Grasping the specificity of such a history requires, however, more than the logic of 'binary opposition' that underlies the concept of metaphysics, even the more complicated exclusions of 'metaphysics and its other'; it requires grasping the internal transformations that is its rational 'ciphering'.

Lyotard, having (like Ricoeur) appealed to Merleau-Ponty's expressivist account of language (*langagière*), most strongly contrasted the incommensurabilities between theory and narrative in our 'postmodern' age. While traditional (grand) narratives would be self-legitimating, the science of the modern age had been justified by appeals to progress, emancipation, and reason, all of which have been rendered delusory given historical reality. Still, as insufficiently as had Ricoeur's attempts to ground the 'free play' of interpretation through the logic of (noematic) reference, Lyotard's appeal to a paralogicism that exceeded all empirical determinations or totalization could not account for the rationality of scientific or theoretical change.[51] The denial of rational norms makes all legitimation, including its own, incoherent. And, the attempt to subsume interpretation and narrative within the logic of reference always presupposed such referents themselves to be uninterpreted. We will need an account of such narrativity that both acknowledges rational norms while, in the face of their failure, also allows for

us to narrate 'otherwise', a narrativity that never simply disappears from the
strongest sense of scientific objectivity—albeit one that does not simply invoke 'the other' against it.[52]

The risk in this regard is that the very notion of metaphysics as a systematic and exclusionary enterprise would prescribe an interpretation of 'the
other' that remains (putatively) 'metaphysical'—in just this sense, that such
'binary opposition' itself always assumes within the schematics of metaphysics the idea of a strictly delimited concept. As I have argued previously, such
a schematization presumes that such concepts ('subject', 'power', 'value', 'representation', 'certainty', etc.) were concepts with unified and determinate extension, defined (and definable) always and everywhere "as such."[53] But here
too the logic remains 'Hegelian', and the attempt to deny Hegel's encyclope-
dic vision by cataloguing its exclusions ironically risks again becoming his
'inverted world'. In such attempts, as Foucault put it, "Hegel, insidiously perhaps, is [still] close to us" (AK:235).

Rather, I have insisted on the interpretation and transformations in our
conceptual diachrony, suggesting that even our most 'contemporary' debates be articulated through the 'rejoinders' at issue in such diachrony. This
is not to privilege the past, it is instead to demythologize the present, to
mark its detraditionalization, and hence allow for its critical disavowal or
confirmation (BT:438). But as thinkers as diverse as Heidegger and Levinas
concur, this also entails that the history of philosophy be a more critical discipline than is typically thought. Far from being (at best) a heuristic reser-
voir—or (at worst) a museum of falsified beliefs—such a history and the
diachronous experience at stake within it comprise the weaving of our intelligibility.

It may well seem that, in recurring to such terms as Merleau-Ponty's or
Heidegger's emphasis on historicity, we must deny those like Levinas's
claims (on standard readings, in any case) to the unmediated demands of
the ethical. In one sense, this is true. Everything is 'mediated', Levinas's articulemes included, as will be seen. If we are never simply locked up in our
concepts, neither are we simply 'outside' them. Instead of such claims to immediacy, the 'absolute' is a question of their remainder, of when mediation
comes to an end, as Hegel saw (WdL:530f.). But rather than such an ending
regaining immediacy in fulfillment now, it is a question of grasping the fragmentation of such 'historicity' or perhaps, more relevant, grasping when
such historicity breaks down—and doubtless more to the point, practically,
when we shall intervene. Such claims to 'immediacy' cannot be a return to
the primitive, to use Heidegger's term (BT:76)—not even to the 'primitive'
terms of premodern theories, to an unmediated nature, nor to a God with-

out history, not even a divine command. In default of such markers, rationally we confront, as Lefort has emphasized, the problem of the empty place of the sacred, and the problem of its reinterpretation.[54] In this, as Levinas concurred, not only does ethics begin in ambiguity and equivocation, but encounters, even in attempting to 'unsay' it, the "inevitability of thematization and the said"—and as such, history (OBBE:94, 152).

Clearly then the very intelligibility of projects like Levinas's requires (and presupposes) the sort of history of philosophy he proposes. And lacking such an account we return to the primitive immediacies for which he is often accused. The point, in any case, is that if we are still to hope for a justice which cannot "do without friendship and faces" we will need to provide a path (and an account) beyond the agonistics of metaphysics—at the risk of rejoining the *Kampfplatz* and the "exhaustion" and "indifferentism" that Kant had already seen as its result (A:vii, x). Moreover, Levinas provisionally indicates the articulemes which delineate the conceptual 'space' of such a history, beyond the empty place of detraditionalized modernity. Against what he called "the veritable tradition (*tradition vénérable*) to which Hegel refers" in which "the ego is an equality with itself," Levinas himself referred continuously to the "good Cartesian tradition." In the latter, despite the demonstrative reductions of modernity, "the clear and distinct ideas still receive light from Plato's intelligible sun"—and doubtless, again, the encounter with the Good (OBBE:115, 133). But even were we to join him here, this too entails a complicated history concerning our past, the theoretical requisites of the present, and the interpretations of their remainder in our midst, a task which the present work explores. Indeed, beyond the totalizing hermeneutics of (modern) rationalism—and without sacrificing either the latter's critical 'distance' or its outrage with 'indifferentism'—we will need to articulate another account of interpretation that arises in its 'midst' and in connection with the ancient question of the Good. Indeed, as has become evident (both conceptually and etymologically), the problem of interpretation—the problem of this midst or between (*iter*), of what is near (*proti*) and its value (*pretium*)—is one to which the question of Good has always been linked archaically. What is incumbent is to grasp the specificity of its contemporary effect.

In a series of analyses this book will focus on critical problems that issue from this interpretive inheritance in contemporary thought, explicitly proceeding by 'reciprocal rejoinders' or, to use a Proustian term, a series of 'juxtapositions'. Juxtaposed, that is, through the concept of tradition, and departing from the hermeneutics of Heidegger and Gadamer, this work will articulate the problem (and the historical complications) of meaning and narrative, the question of law and personhood, and finally the interpretive status of the Good itself that results. The point, however, is not to present an objective history, whether it be a continuous, progressive, or interpretive genealogy or narrative (factual or propositional), but to acknowledge the logic of juxtaposition through which the 'objectivity' (the objectivity of an *Aspekt*) that accompanies such a history and its experience emerges. Doubtless from the perspective of a certain 'optics' such interpretations might seem arbitrary. Against standard (or 'metaphysical') accounts of objectivity, it might be objected, we could (legitimately) narrate the history of the 'outsiders' such accounts excluded—but only at the cost of the internal coherence that such a systematic concept of history presupposes. Or, alternately, we could articulate the internal development of hermeneutics as a science—albeit one its adherents admit to be inevitably, qua 'hermeneutic', incomplete. Finally, we might simply describe the ethical relations (or transcendentals) that always exceed such theories—but always perhaps at a certain loss of intelligibility, and by presupposing once more that their descriptions, phenomenological or 'otherwise', are incontestably (and univocally) 'evident'. Doubtless all these moments are at stake in the relation between analysis and synthesis, the ontic and the historical. Instead, here the account begins by acknowledging the logic of juxtaposition, Heidegger's "remarkable relatedness backward or forward" in order to articulate, as I have further articulated elsewhere, the remnants of a certain reciprocal rejoinder (*Erwiderung*), the traditionality—and doubtless whatever remains of its legitimacy—in our midst. Moreover, this word '*Erwiderung*' itself, as *Being and Time* attests, has both critical and legal implications—precisely as a 'rejoinder' that attests both to our 'belonging-to' the past as well as the necessity of our 'remove' or distance (and hence the need for adjudication and 'reinterpretation') regarding it.[55]

The point is a critical one. At the height of poststructuralism, in a 1971 text whose title indicates the fragmentation he had in mind (*Sade/Fourier/Loyola*), Roland Barthes proclaimed that, granted the omnipresence of the failure of tradition, "the only possible rejoinder (*riposte*) is neither confrontation, nor destruction, but only theft; fragment the old text of culture, science, literature, and change its features according to formulae of disguise, as one disguises stolen goods."[56] The account presupposed (again) not only a certain logic of traditional 'failure' but equally an account of tradition as (mythically) monolithic. But if tradition is not monolithic—neither systematically dogmatic (and false) nor a system of propositional truths—if, that is, it is 'always already' heterogeneous and diachronous, then it is also already fragmented. Indeed if so, the fragmentation that Barthes proposes is just the 'fragmentation' (and refiguration) that accompanies interpretation itself.[57] Interpretation is always already, to use another of Barthes's terms, 'cubist', already divided between destruction and retrieval, analysis and synthesis.[58] For all its anti-intentionalist fecundity, nothing was perhaps more mythic than the structuralist ahistorical (and instrumentalist) view of theory as bricolage, one which doubtless here still informs Barthes's 'writerly' performative of the 'theft' involved.[59] But it is crucial—and most poststructuralists neglected it— that even in maintaining the "violence" of the 'rejoinder' (an articuleme Heidegger too had invoked, for better or worse) this event remains linked to the question of legitimation. Indeed the conceptual and etymological history of 'rejoinder' itself (both in English and in German, as Heidegger's text attests) still maintains the legal (and genealogical) metaphorics of the critical tribunal—if it has abandoned its scientific paradigm. What Gadamer calls the "example" of legal hermeneutics, in short, is conceptually at stake (and at issue) in its own history, and internally reaffirms here the historical links between interpretation and the question of the Good.

As Benjamin rightly saw, this recognizes, on the other hand, that judgment is as much interpretation and translation as it is subsumption, where translation thus ultimately and 'ironically' "serves the purpose of expressing the central reciprocal relationship between languages"—texts, theories, experiences, and the 'transmissions' at stake.[60] But even this account of reciprocal relation becomes intelligible once more, less 'in itself' than against the backdrop of the history of the rational—in its scientific, legal, literary, and philosophical forms—through which the reciprocal relation becomes apparent. Accordingly, as has been pointed out, this means that such accounts share something in common with "rational reconstruction," through which hermeneutics, without succumbing to 'poetics', would articulate its "regional legitimacy."[61] The issue, nonetheless, may not be so simply expoundable—or reduced. Instead, on closer look, what is more clearly revealed is that the *topos* of the rational, to use Wittgenstein's terms, its 'multiplicity', may not be so readily 'circumscribed' (PI:§23:70). The notion of rational reconstruction, following a lineage that also dates back to Kant, still perhaps belongs too much to the logic of explanation (*Erklärung*).[62] This notion eludes, as hermeneuts always protested, alternatives to the rational hegemony of modern scientific theory, namely the (interpretive) 'explications' on which they continually relied. Still, it would be right to point out that the status of such explications themselves, in turn, in trading on more ancient accounts of dialectic, rhetoric, and experience (*empereia*), only become evident in being 'demarcated' from such positive reductions of the rational to theory construction, strict demonstrability, and deductive

decidability. Hence emerges, again, the complex 'genealogy' (and the rationality) of 'deconstruction'. The latter originated in the rational purities of
Husserl's (phenomenological) logicism, fully cognizant, however, of the
problems of institution, enunciation, historicity and tradition, the question
of truth and undecidability Husserl's account raises—and thereby the irreducible otherness that divides the self-identity of the transcendental 'living
presence'. It would not be accidental that Husserl and Joyce—and thereby
the problem of "historicity or traditionality"—were conjoined in Derrida's
itinerary from the outset.[63] But the equivocations in this 'conjunction'
doubtless could be accounted for only through the contested history out of
which they emerge. It may well be true, as Frank saw, that the 'tradition' of
hermeneutics only discovers its "basic problem" in such recent (largely
poststructuralist) accounts revealing the "semantic undecidability" of the
present; but these accounts themselves depend no less for their own intelligibility on this past—or in the series of reciprocal rejoinders their 'histories'
set off in the dynamics of coherence and critique. It is just in this tension,
again, that the question of tradition continually emerges and thus, the *topos*
of contemporaneity the present book engages, delineating the too often neglected status of its legitimacy.

## 4. Summary

This work, thus, traces the emergence of the question of interpretation in
contemporary thought, articulates the ethical concern that continually accompanies and supplements its theoretics, and finally reengages the detraditionalization out of which modern "humanistic" practices emerged—again
in hopes, to use Heidegger's term, that we might be able to restore (*zurück-
geben*) meaning to this term (LH:224). The opening chapter turns to the
remainder of tradition in recent Continental thought, as it became reconcep-
tualized in Gadamer and Heidegger. Here, inter alia, the effects of critical
modernity on the issues of hermeneutics and interpretation become most
pronounced. While standard accounts have sufficiently traced these thinkers simply to post-Kantian and phenomenological sources, we will more directly confront both the modern sources behind their accounts and
postmodern challenges in their wake, in which the concept of tradition itself
becomes fragmented between critique and appropriation, affirmation and
exclusion. This background provides the motivation for the emergence of
Heidegger's *Seinsfrage* itself: Heidegger does not simply undertake ontology

as first science, but rather turns to the problem of its lapse. After all, at issue is how to think the dispersion that results, divided between interpretation, affirmation, and deconstruction. While a number of accounts (from Heidegger's emphasis on care and human dwelling to Levinas's account of the ethical 'face-to-face') hinted that 'ethics' has sustained the critical explications of transcendental and phenomenological accounts, we will directly confront the issue by taking our cue (and protocol) from the concept (or the remainder) of 'friendship' in its midst. As a result—both as philosopheme and act— the interpretive event (*Ereignis*) becomes divided between the ontic and the ontological, virtue and the Good, self and other, singularity and community.

Still, if this analysis is correct, we will need to say more about the history at stake in the present. In chapter 2, I extend these resources through juxtaposition with the interpretive practices from which they emerge, again with an eye toward the question of legitimation. Here we take our clue directly from Kant's (modern) account of the *humaniora* as combining civility (*Urbanität*) and communicability in order to reexamine the problem of legitimation and the transition that underwrites the emergence of interpretive modernity (Logic:51). In particular, here the paradoxical status of the expressivist resources underlying the problem of interpretation become traced in detail, especially as this interfaces with the emergence of the modern concept of law. The latter indicated an event no longer graspable in terms of the mere wielding of force, but requires instead its internal 'regulation'—if only as promise. Still, if law is no longer reducible to the mere wielding of force (as is often claimed of Roman law, for example) its status nonetheless became especially problematic in relation to the modern demand for legitimation and the hope that the certainties of scientific method might intercede in the uncertainties of justice. Here we will further encounter the lingering remnants of medieval practices of interpretation and their modern transformations in the explication of the everyday. Coupled with the emergence of legal autonomy, the originary narratives of the everyday—too often simply confused with the 'levelings' of the secular—provided originary resources for articulating the 'lifeworld' anew. Indeed, it could be argued that the 'concept' of the lifeworld itself wears its synthesis of the ancient and the modern on its sleeve, divided between the ancients' *bios theoreticos* and the modern's conceptual (and Copernican) horizons.

Neither our legal nor our ethical practices are uninterpreted; we must always reengage the problem of meaning and narrative at stake within them. To do so, however, initially requires that we distinguish the latter from classical accounts in the philosophy of language. The approach thereby becomes seemingly nonstandard; yet, while hermeneutic, ethical or political issues often became excluded from standard discussions in what became philosophy of language, from the beginning of modern philosophy the investigation of meaning had been connected with issues of political significance. Hence Heidegger's own attempts to articulate the failures of modernity, continually and explicitly criticized what had come to be termed philosophy of language (BT:209), calling in the first instance for a retrieval of "the first systematic hermeneutic of everydayness of Being with one another," namely Aristotle's *Rhetorics* (BT:178). Still, even though Aristotle had seen the connection between rhetoric and political life, this would not be ultimately sufficient, granted what Heidegger had encountered in the leveling and dispersal of modern *Alltäglichkeit* and "our entanglement in words" (the term is Hobbes's); here neither the conventions nor claims of common usage are free of "jargon" (Hobbes's term again) and the need to interpret.[64] As Leo Strauss would similarly see in his famous study of Spinoza, the very idea that meaning could be both written and read with clarity and distinctness—deriving from each author's presumption of his philosophy as "the clear and distinct and, therefore, the true account of the whole," so that "questions of hermeneutics cannot be the central question"—presumed a politics both free from force and free from history.[65] It presumed, moreover, that such a history was not only inherently scrutable but immediately transparent, that an author or agent already knows and says exactly what she or he thinks, and that reading is unproblematic—that "reading between the lines" is not consequently essential to the rational.[66]

The relation between writing and power, or the question of 'persecution', would have little sense on such assumptions. But this 'clarity' seems to be rightly disputed. As will be seen, even in debates in the philosophy of language built around notions of clarity and necessity, such as those between Husserl and Frege, we need to say more, delimiting the problem of the unsaid not simply as ineffable mystery, but what in light of the requisites of normativity must appear as that which is unpermitted. From the beginning, and almost unbeknownst to himself, even Husserl, it might be argued, had struggled against the very paradigms that were contested in the 'crisis' of reason he outlined. The problem of reason's own narratives, the relation between norm and power, reflection and the 'unconscious', would increasingly become complicated. Such considerations would not only impact issues of a 'logical' character, but more extended aspects of the rational, as diverse as the modern narratives of the novel and the problem of the unconscious. Moreover, as Gadamer realized, even Strauss's great insights concerning the question of persecution and the art of writing did not grasp the problem of self-understanding, presupposing inter alia that the author has a "high degree of consciousness" of the 'ironies' of his or her accommodation (TM:295n): Strauss perhaps never fully grasped the complications between power and such an 'unconscious', where tradition itself has become fully "uncanny."

Next, the analysis turns to the interpretation of personhood in connection with a number of contemporary debates, in which the remainder of this concept had been divided—for example, between the concept of person as legal agent or representative, as tragic role, and as the site of relational or irreducible existential encounter. In chapters 3 and 4, I begin with debates surrounding the radicalized notion of person as first articulated by Levinas and then examine their current status, especially problematic with respect to modern accounts of theory, and trace their difference from premodern accounts. This strategy is invoked neither in order to escape nor to render homogeneous the present—nor to use Benjamin's terms, to dissolve the presence of the now (*Jetztzeit*)—but to confront the dispersion of our intelligibility. Again, it may well be true, as Frank has argued, that neither critical theorists nor existentialists and poststructuralists have succeeded in accounting for the 'eccentric' dignity of individual 'persons', but it is also true that these articulemes are themselves not without history, both conceptual and real.[67]

Here too the complex figures of *theodicea* may still have their impact: the question of personhood is again inextricably linked to the history of (Western) theology, a conceptual tradition (*Begriffstradition*) and semantic field Gadamer has again reinvoked, claiming that it remains still "extremely instructive."[68] Doubtless it is in just this sense, as Frank has pointed out, that Habermas himself insisted that, to be adequate, any position will require the binding force (*religare*) for the community that theology once had.[69] Moreover, beyond mere legalistic formulations, Frank argued, we will need a concept of individuality that safeguards the uniqueness granted traditionally to personhood. But as becomes evident, such 'individuality' remains as semantically indeterminate as the play of the signifier that Frank had linked to the problematic of contemporary hermeneutics in general. That is, such individuality will always require the figure and the reinterpretation or refiguration of narrative. Indeed, as Frank himself realized, in one sense the concept of individuality, the *terminus ad quem* of conceptuality, belies the logic of personhood, which is intrinsically relational. We will need to unravel all this and it will require, again, a ciphering of the historical narratives.

The point, moreover, is not that such historical accounts would provide the solution to modern theoretical conflicts—any more than modern theoretics, for example, provides a simple successor to antecedent paradigms of rationality, or than postmodern attempts to escape the exclusions of both paradigms resolve our questions. Instead, initially, in any case, we will need to avoid the logic of such resolutions (*Aufhebungen*). We will need to include (and parse) the narratives (ancient and modern) that articulate both the institution of such personhood (or rights) and the personhood (and experience) that escapes or remains 'eccentric' to (and remains potentially excluded from) such norms—and must ultimately justify them.

The theoretical articulemes by which we grapple with both the concept and the experience of personhood are, thus, neither readily affirmable nor readily discardable. The result, again, will be more a weaving of forms (again, 'translations' in the Benjaminian sense) that has nascently accompanied humanist practices from the outset, opening the problem of a 'differentiated' sense of community in its wake. Here also we encounter a 'being-with', a *Mit-sein* as Jean-Luc Nancy reminds us, that is as intractable as the 'claims' of being itself: differentiated between the ontic and the ontological, 'being' always emerges only through such a 'with'.[70] The latter remains, however, unintelligible apart from the history that delineates its excess, personhood, violence, norms, and alterity—the problem of what *Being and Time* still construed as Dasein's 'depersonalization' (*Entpersonalisierung*). If again, to use Nancy's terms, "we are in a sort of 'simultaneous tension' between the Enlightenment and Romanticism," or between the ancients and the moderns, this is because the time of this tension is itself already heterogeneous, detraditionalized, and fragmented.[71] In fact, it might be that the only community we 'share' in common, as Kristeva has argued vis-à-vis Proust, is the 'dislocated' or fragmented ('staggered', to use Lefort's term) form of simultaneity itself—a simultaneity fragmented between institutions, 'worlds', cultures, practices.[72] And yet whatever meaning this 'remainder' is to impart becomes intelligible, I will claim, precisely in the histories, dialogues (and theoretical articulemes) 'fragmented' in its midst—and with regard to the question of personhood, the contested historicity of 'the between', the '*convenientia*', as Heidegger signals in invoking an 'ancient' term, in which, among other things, the ethical relation itself might emerge (BT:170). Indeed Kristeva would later rediscover in the relationality of *convenientia*—precisely across the ontological differences articulated in the problem of the Good—a rupture beyond the exclusive limits of a relationality of the Same.[73] Moreover, this rupture continually supplants the (Western) 'tales of love' in their various permutations, refigurations both within and beyond narcissism and egoism, divided problematically between being from itself (*ens a se*) and being from another (*ens ab alio*).[74] It is just this problematic of the 'between' that Heidegger had articulated at the heart of the hermeneutic circle (BP:82).

Such appeals to the past—here to Aquinas's *convenientia,* but elsewhere in Heidegger, at least, to Augustine or Seneca for care, or Plato or Aristotle for the encounter with Being or the Good—were complicated, for reasons now evident. They were invoked both to critically lament the effects of tradition and to negotiate its remainder. Even before Aquinas, this *conveniens* had indicated for the Stoics a belonging or coming-together, a 'fittingness', 'justness', or *decorum* that escaped the manifest (or mathematical) 'objectivity' of proportion or *symmetria*—and acknowledged the context-specific character of the rationality that results.[75] The question is, what relevance would such 'reappropriations' hold for a (now literally 'in-convenient') community in which "mistrust," mutual "inconsiderateness," and "insensitiv(ity) to every difference of level and genuineness" circulate like the radio signals or trolley cars and newspapers exemplifying the masked anonymity Heidegger 'revealed' in the institutions of the public realm (BT:163–5)? If Heidegger had sought staunchly to separate his account "from any moralizing critique of everyday Dasein, and from the aspirations of a 'philosophy of culture'" (BT:211), the 'leveling' implications of the everyday for human authenticity remained inextricable: "neither highly developed and differentiated culture" nor low, neither foreign nor that culture most 'authentically' our own—all terms he uses—would in the end be unaffected. Hence, as Heidegger declared, "loaded down with a past that is unrecognizable . . . it seeks the modern [*Moderne*]" (BT:444)—a term invoked just once in *Being and Time.*

Finally, in chapter 5 these considerations will lead to a reencounter with the remainder of the practice of the humanities themselves, the character of the experience they 'venture', and the problem of the measure (or perhaps even 'demeasuring') that has accompanied their link to the problematic of tradition in Continental philosophy since Kant's critical system. Thereby, however, appeals to the ancients become further complicated in the (modern) question of norms. If the humanities are to be efficacious in confronting the fragmented remainder of a tradition that now "uproots the historicity of Dasein" (BT:43), simple recollection of the truths of the past cannot suffice. Instead, to use Arendt's terms, equally necessary is the acknowledgment that, however much the transmission (*traditio*) of the past may be connected to authority (*auctoritas*), it is also always an extension (*augere*)—and critique—by default.[76] Hence again the problem of legitimation. In order, finally, to confront the problem of legitimation and the task of interpretation (or the remnants of humanist practices) in contemporary thought I articulate anew a certain *Auseinandersetzung* between Heidegger and Wittgenstein on the problem of the Good—one that betrays again both the presence of the past and its modern dispersion. Whatever point there may remain in formulating the idea of a 'critical traditionality' relies on our being able to think these two moments of authority, normativity, and extension together. As the modern conception of rational norm and positive law demonstrates, the opposition between the 'internal' articulations of 'law' and 'Being' cannot be abstract. No more than claims about the rational 'purity' of law, neither the simple 'overcoming' of law nor the 'demeasuring' of the human will suffice to confront the discontinuous effects of detraditionalization: convention and interpretation, norm and judgment, testimony and statute will need to be thought together. The hermeneutics that is required will again be more complicated—or perhaps better said, the rationality (and the civility) required will be hermeneutic.

It is in just such 'uprooting' that the origin of a 'contemporary' hermeneutics emerges, as Gadamer acknowledged: "[T]here would be no hermeneutical task if there were no mutual understanding that had been disturbed and that those involved in conversation must search for and find again together" (PH:25). Now, in any case, what characterizes the 'universality' of the hermeneutic phenomenon is that the problem of the 'interpretation of texts' is "really only a special case of what is to be met in all human orientation to the world as the *atopon* (the strange)" (PH:25). It is just this dispersion of the present and the past, of the 'near' and the 'foreign', moreover, that both characterizes the 'incoherence' of our 'contemporaneity' and, as hermeneutic problem, makes evident the critical character of its rationality. Kant had already seen that the *sensus communis* would now require less a method than an extended manner of thinking (*modus*) devoid of the immanence of enduring examples (CJ:231–2). Hence for Kant it combined the (indeterminate) 'excess' of sympathy and the (iterable) possibility of communication. Now, however, as Kristeva insisted, it may well be that 'cosmopolitanism' would be inseparable from the differences that lie both within us as well as beyond us—an 'identity' fully uncanny.[77] But thereby the 'universality' of such cosmopolitanism too will be inextricably hermeneutic, the lapse in the exemplary authority of the past and demonstrable certainty (*methodus*) at stake inevitably 'estranging'—indeed 'puzzling', to use Wittgenstein's term for that which calls forth interpretation.

The recognition of this 'strangeness', however, attests to the critical status of hermeneutics in its 'remarkable relatedness backward or forward'—beyond the immanent authorities of nature, social practice, and the exemplary wisdom of the wise man or woman. As Pierre Hadot rightly pointed out this is not entirely new; most of the ancients did not deem it possible to live as a sage (*sophos*). But Hadot also saw that even should we be inclined to adopt their "spiritual exercises" we inevitably do so "at the same time separating them from the philosophic or mythic discourse which came along with them."[78] The same is true of all retrievals, "ransackings" (to use Harrington's term) of ancient prudence. Lingering appeals to *phronēsis* itself could not be viewed, after all, as replacing the modern conception of law as the internalization of principle; rather *phronēsis* would supplement law, thereby articulating resources that would allow us to confront the 'incommensurability' of contemporary debates anew. While hermeneuts sought to acknowledge the remainder of Aristotelian 'equity' by articulating justice as decency and practical philosophy, they did so under a simultaneous tension. Contrary to Aristotle, for whom nature, the *polis,* and the morally wise remained unproblematic, and where, consequently, the *problem* of the Good did not prevent him from both supplying definitions and 'exemplifications' of virtue, we are confronted by the shortfalls and suspicions of all invocations of 'transcendence'.

While Aristotle, after all, could claim that the opposition between the universal and the particular requires the interpretation of justice (or decency), he also claimed that this deficiency was external to law itself: "the law is no less correct" (NE:1134b). We are perhaps not only less sure about the latter, but equally convinced that the opposition itself is abstract. It is not a question of being 'beyond' all law or dismissing law but recognizing that internal to such reflection is the question of law's legitimation (i.e., "which law?"). Thus, the ambiguities of even Gadamer's more classical articulemes become apparent. Notwithstanding his own defense of tradition and the truth of 'prejudgment'—an account like Heidegger's in which we might "discover tradition [and] preserve it" (BT:41)—he had likewise affirmed what Heidegger had seen as the eventuality in which, through a kind of lapse in origins, "tradition thus becomes master" (BT:43). In this light, as Gadamer concurred, "we are always dominated by conventions" and "the very idea of a definitive interpretation seems to be intrinsically contradictory," with the consequence that "social life consists of a constant process of transformation" (RAS:82, 105, 135).

Still, the language of domination and transcendence may also forget the violence of its own past and, in particular, the transformation at stake in the detraditionalization of the law—risking the nostalgia for a 'good' without the contingencies of ontic connection. Here too the issues of the near and the 'far', tradition and its 'others', doubtless become complicated—and complicate the issue of justice in its midst. As Levinas saw, "justice remains justice only in a society when there is no distinction between those close and those far off, but in which there also remains the impossibility of passing by the closest" (OBBE:159). This is doubtless the 'hermeneutic' point: the historicity of understanding is always such that "we understand in a *different way, if we understand at all*" (TM:297; Gadamer's emphasis). To think that such understanding is devoid of norms (and not simply the 'norms' of the past), however, is to forget the very problem of meaning itself: even the meaning of being is always already 'plural'. As Nancy has also seen, if it is true that Dasein is always indissociably singular, it is also true that I *enunciate* 'I' only insofar as I am part of a 'we'—and here the point reencounters Husserlian and Fregean claims about the iterability (and normativity) of meaning (and judgment). This recognition has not only significative (and logical) consequences, but obviously both political and epistemic consequences as well. For Heidegger, "Dasein is *authentically itself*" only in "primordial individualization. . . ." That is "*(a)s something that keeps silent,* authentic Being-one's-self is just the sort of thing that does not keep on saying 'I'" (BT:369–70; Heidegger's emphasis). Yet it still remains the case that Dasein's "understanding of Being already implies the understanding of Others" (BT:161)—and in both respects it must equally "be Interpreted in terms of the phenomenon of care" (BT:157).

Doubtless, as has been seen, this emphasis on care emerged, as Heidegger pointed out, from Seneca and Augustine (BT:243). But it also had been found in Aristotle. Indeed if *Being and Time* still calls the *Rhetoric* "the first systematic hermeneutic of the everydayness of Being with one another," as earlier lectures on the *Rhetoric* reveal, all deliberate speech reveals most originally in our taking counsel with one another (*sumbouleuesthai*)—a concept very close, as Gadamer would again stress, to the issues of understanding, consideration, and forgiveness in Aristotle (TM:322; see NE:1442a ff.).[79] The question, again, is whether such ancient roots can be depended on in the 'inauthentic' heterogeneity of modern social conditions. In light of the lapse in traditional origins that accompanies modernity everywhere, such claims must still face the question of norms. Granted, the theoretical fertility of the Dasein analytic (critically and justifiably) depends on the recognition of Dasein's "most radical individuation" (and disclosure) of Being's *transcendens* (BT:62) over against the failures of the past or the public realm. Moreover, like the concept of care in which Heidegger had grounded knowledge in asserting that "knowing is a mode of Being of Dasein" (BT:88), this link between Dasein and *transcendens* articulates less the 'subjectivist' reduction of Being to an object than the remnant of a certain 'Stoic' epistemics that accompanies all of modern philosophy of subjectivity, granted the failure of the ancient authorities. Such subjectivity is truly less the center of the rational universe than its 'decentered' effect, less its own foundation than the effect of the loss of foundation, or 'abandonment'—and, consequently not only a 'divided being' in its origin, to use the traditional gloss on finitude, but a being divided between practices, cultures, passions, theories, and traditions.[80] Hence lingering appeals to transcendence can not be unrelated to principle, their 'opening' not without ontic facticity, their synthesis always 'analytically' articulated, and so on. Even were we to assert that the relations of such *Mitsein* are always plural and lacking 'determinate syntax' (Nancy), we will need to say more.

The problem involves avoiding an antinomy in accounts of meaning itself: to claim, for example, either that meaning is reducible to such immanences as those of Dasein's pre-ontological relation to itself (or even the 'immanence' of the intersubjective 'face-to-face') or that, granted the failure of tradition, such meaning is itself exhausted.[81] We are left wondering, as a result, how tradition had ever been meaningful, since its true 'meaning' was always 'elsewhere', or, alternately, how it had ever become challenged or transformed, granted its 'completeness'. Here too we must avoid the 'metaphysics' of meaning if we are grasp this history in its specificity. Even were one to concur with the claim that this history has often enough been that of the attempt to 'impose a figure'—as Nancy and Lacoue-Labarthe have claimed[82]—any account of its 'reinvention' will of necessity be a matter of figuration, or more precisely refiguration, indeed of figuring 'otherwise'.

Derrida himself has claimed that "deconstruction is inventive or it is nothing at all."[83] Moreover, he finds in Levinas's 'visage' or 'visages', an indication of such a reinvention out of Hebraic memory and the possibility (and impossibility, as has become evident), in the traditions articulated (and conflicted) in this 'reinvention' itself (Adieu:205). But in addition to the testament (the performative) of a saying that articulates the exclusions of law before the other, any such 'deconstruction' will also have to articulate the transformation of theory, law, virtue, and interpretation contested (and required) in its midst. Indeed that is just the point. We still must provide an account of a 'syntax', to use Nancy's term, that is open, acknowledging the complicated link between such a 'law', its history, and (the semantics of) interpretation. Here the plurality of interpretation in which 'Being' is said, the *pollakos legomenon*, would emerge from a history articulated between identity and difference, norm and construal, 'universality' and singularity: to use even Husserl's terms, the simultaneity of transcendental 'correlation' and the multiplicity of monads. 'Judgment' consequently would be no more simply entirely singular (or regulative) than it is determinate (or constitutive).

The result is a 'plurality' that is both regulative and constitutive at once—without dissolving the difference at stake between the two. The very semantic undecidability (to again use Frank's term) that accompanies our

interpretive phenomenologies would doubtless provide the articulation of
such a plural space. At the same time, however, the condition under which
this 'space' may rationally flourish becomes outlined. That is, the 'phenomenologies' that emerge from such a plurality would remain always internally
disrupted (as their 'ontological' critics charged), their narratives always
figurative (or 'interrupted')—and yet sustained by the *ēthos* (or care) from
which they emerge. Here after all, as will become evident, is where Levinas
still meets Heidegger, articulating anew the remainder of friendship as both
relation and event, an event no more simply 'ethical' than it is either ontological or epistemic. The point is capturing the 'belonging together' that attends all such determinations. Instead everything depends perhaps on
articulating this 'existential ontological event' as both singular and plural,
'ethical' and 'normative', in order to grasp the extent to which the regulation
of power entails both 'respect' for law and the 'care' that sustains it. Belying
both the "anonymous universality of the state," as Levinas termed it, which
would always view 'peace' as a calculated necessity and the idea of an absolute singular that would escape the necessity of the conventional, such an
account would center instead on the interpretation (and the civility) that attends the 'between' and the historicity that both democratic proceduralism
as well as appeals to natural 'law' always attempted to turn conventional.

Far from our simply being 'dominated by conventions', the result will be
more complex, involving a combination of principle and transcendence
whose first impetus for the problem of interpretation had been provided in
the schemata of classical German thought, as I have discussed in *Tradi-
tion(s)*. If, as Heidegger related, he had originally discovered the 'hermeneutics' of the *Seinsfrage* in a certain reciprocal rejoinder with the transcendental analogies of medieval speculation, it was likewise true that he
thought, as early as 1916—and doubtless very close to Benjamin—that this
hermeneutic could be made intelligible only in being linked to Hegel's account of the historical.[84]

Consistently, later, Heidegger argued against the *Sprachanalyse* of his
time (as would Derrida of his own) that truth cannot simply be reduced to
convention. The reduction of meaning to use or to practice, or even to iterable objectivity—and hence to the 'tradition' of truth—overlooks the exclusionary force of convention. If everything depends on recognizing 'the
sublime in the pedestrian', to use Kierkegaard's often-cited phrase, the danger is, as both Heidegger and Wittgenstein saw, that the sublime would become simply reduced to the pedestrian—hence, as becomes apparent,
emerges the problem of the Good. Such accounts miss, to use Heidegger's
term, the failure of a tradition 'hardened up'—or, to use Wittgenstein's

term, 'petrified' and the necessity of accounting for a truth that arises, to use Merleau-Ponty's term, by "coherent deformation."[85] Still, as such a deformation testifies, if 'truth' is somehow more than a predicate (and without reducing truth to conventions) it is also evident that truth will not be intelligible apart from the *Vor-habe* of such conventions, the problem of normativity, our "entanglement in rules" and the question of what Wittgenstein called, in articulating meaning and use, "the civil status [*bürgerliche Stellung*] of a contradiction" (PI:§325). This is the other part of what has been called Kant's mixed message to those in his wake: a 'regularity' (or at worse, mere averageness) out of which, even Heidegger acknowledged all intelligibility originated and (authentic or not) returns (BT:213). In this respect, if "the remarkable relatedness backward or forward" began in asserting that for all this, above all, the grammar is lacking (BT:63), the internal tension at stake is, recognizably both on ancient and modern grounds, the paradox of the Good itself. Doubtless revealed thereby was the problem of what lies beyond the determinately intelligible, beyond the hope of reduction to a primordial ground. But equally the paradox of the Good required, as both Wittgenstein and Heidegger perhaps agreed in attempting to liberate grammar from logic (BT:208f.), that we see in the question of this silence that exceeds simple determination an event (*Ereignis*) and an interpretation which "[w]e translate [*Wir übertragen*] . . . at one time into a proposition, at another into a demonstration, and at another into action" (PI:§459).

Still we must be careful to distinguish this event from the Spinozist thought that continually accompanied Wittgenstein's account and those influenced by it—as diverse, after all, as Quine and Deleuze. The 'expressions' or 'translations' in question are not modes of a single substance simply open to 'analysis' but—as 'translations'—remain always problematically interrelated. And, here again we are confronted with the ancient problem of being and the analogy of judgment. As Lyotard put it, in a strange pastiche of the ancient and the modern whose logic often enough escaped his accounts of the 'postmodern'—and aptly enough in responding to Rorty—"rationality is reasonable only if it admits that reason is multiple, as Aristotle said that being is spoken multiply."[86] But this is to say that the tasks (theoretical or practical) of the rational are multiply 'hermeneutic', a matter neither without norm nor interpretation (and reinterpretation) in the same moment that such tasks are neither without history nor the necessity of judgment.

# 1. Interpretation, Dialogue, and Friendship

## On the Remainder of Community

However the phenomena are no less falsified when they are banished to the sanctuary of the irrational. When irrationalism, as the counterplay of rationalism, talks about the things to which rationalism is blind, it does so only with a squint.

—Heidegger, *Being and Time*

"These fragments I have shored against my ruins."

—T. S. Eliot, "The Wasteland"

Our historical consciousness is always filled with a variety of voices (*Stimmen*) in which the echo of the past is heard. Only in the multifariousness of such voices (*der Vielfachheit solcher Stimmen*) does it exist; this constitutes the nature of the tradition in which we want to share and have a part.

—Gadamer, *Truth and Method*

It follows that the place of the 'inter-said' (*inter-dit*), which is the 'intra-said' (*intra-dit*) of a between-two-subjects, is the very place in which the transparency of the classical subject is divided and passes through the effects of 'fading' that specify the Freudian subject by its occultation by an ever purer signifier: that these effects lead us to the frontiers at which slips of the tongue and witticisms, in their collusion, become confused, even where elision is so much the more allusive in tracking down presence to its lair, that one is surprised that the *Dasein* hunt hasn't done better out of it.

—Lacan, *Ecrits*

Neither the same nor the other, the "friend" perhaps names only this difference itself.

—Jean-Luc Nancy, *The Birth to Presence*

# 1. The Fragmentation of Tradition

The concept of tradition has a long and overdetermined history in the descent of Western thought, articulated first in classical thought from Socrates to Lucretius as a sacred past with which philosophy must rupture in order to gain access to its truth—an account framed, that is, in the 'ancient

quarrel' between *logos* and *mythos* itself. The medievals' refiguration of philosophy perhaps only apparently broke with these constraints, albeit by attempting, beginning with Irenaeus and Tertullian, to revalorize the notion
of *traditio,* of the *parodisis,* by rational warrant. The result was a formalized
notion of the *ordo traditio* itself, safeguarding what must be remembered as
true and handed down from generation to generation: preserving it, that is,
from false interpretations or heresy.

It would be naive, however, to think that either the concept of tradition
or the sacred past it articulates simply disappear from philosophical modernism—any more than, as Claude Lefort has decisively shown, the religious simply disappears from modern conceptions of the political.[1] Notwithstanding modernist outcries against what Hobbes, for example, already
criticized as "vain" or "fabulous tradition" and "uncertain history," both the
sacred and tradition became obscurely refigured not only in such obvious
tropes as Newton's account of space as the divine *sensorium,* but porten-
tously in other more surprising places, for example, in Hobbes's own admo-
nition that, lest we fall into muddled linguistic nonsense, we must remember what the original meanings named—as if all, and only, those meanings
lexically completed the rational and linguistic universe.[2] Nor of course
would it simply overdetermine philosophy's narratives of the rational. As
Michel Serres has aptly noted, the figure of the divine *sensorium* would be as
appropriate for the classical novel as it would be for Newton's physics. "The
classical novel has the same history as the physics of this age"—both, that
is, determinist and determined, a system with a hierarchy, a closed narrative, homogeneous, open to evaluation on all points, regulated as much locally as it is globally.[3] Indeed, Kant's transcendental aesthetic would epistemically reinstitute this unity, now as a field of experiential determination—one which reduced not only the domain of the sacred, but both the
"experienced" and the true, under the constraints of the certainty by which
it equally figured re-presentation. Moreover, as is now all too fully evident,
the narratives of the political would be similarly invested. The transcendence and indeterminacy of the sacred would now be simply invested in
such (figured) concepts as the 'nation' and its 'people'. Nor, finally, should
we neglect the complexity of the cross-fertilization here. We should not in
this regard forget the mythic investments of the inductive method itself as
a political figure in the tropes of philosophical modernism, as writers from
Burke to Popper attested. The problem of traditions is doubtless inseparable
from such forgetfulness before the past. Science itself, as Popper, for example realized, was not only inseparable from both myth and tradition, but
was in fact part of a critical tradition to be traced from Socrates himself (and

onward to Derrida), and similarly was inseparable from attempts to grapple with (and to circumscribe) the sacred. Pointedly, even Bakhtin's attempts to elevate the revolutionary potential of the novel's articulation of the everyday had been similarly invested: while the epic would be linked by him to tradition, the novel, seemingly beyond all traditional forms, became linked explicitly to prediction—albeit only by means of a "quite specific problematicalness: characteristic for it is an eternal re-thinking and re-evaluating."[4]

In simply raising such matters, we consequently invoke the problem of historical distance and a certain re-move from origins which accompanies the descent of the concept of tradition and the splitting of the rational in the wake of such ruins. And Kant was perhaps the first to theoretically recognize it, in his Transcendental Dialectic. There, in summarizing what he termed the status of "the ruins of the ancient systems," Kant, every bit as much as Piranisi's etchings of ancient Roman ruins, had already focused on the mysterious past—and the inextricable speculations—of the ancients, long before those like Nietzsche or Benjamin had become appalled by their exclusions.[5] The problem of traditions, it might be said, to adopt the Freudian idiom, is just reckoning with the event of this *fort-da* that underlies traditionality itself. As Arendt saw, it was peculiar to the nineteenth century— and especially to Marx, Nietzsche, and Kierkegaard—to explicitly confront the "essentially negative experiences of foreboding, apprehension, and ominous silence" before tradition.[6] At stake was doubtless an interplay of the strange and the familiar, the *Heimlich* and the *Unheimlich*—even perhaps the repressed and the revealed—that had descended from the departures of Romanticism.[7] Schlegel had been the first to link such a *Wechsel* to the problem of historical criticism in his *Lyceum* fragments.[8] In the end, however, it was perhaps indicative of an event more generalized in effect, emerging from an interplay which underlies the economics of repetition and iterability, the real and the imaginary, the ontic and the ontological, justice and its articulation, the true and the certain.

It is, of course, just here that Heidegger's prolonged interrogation on Western thought too takes hold. Heidegger insisted that reason and tradition could no longer be thought without taking into account the ruins of the ancient systems, and, moreover, without reinterrogating—and retracing, to invoke again the terms of Freudian economics—its most fundamental investigation, the investigation of Being as such. The result is, to use Heidegger's terms, a repetition poised now between 'retrieval' and 'destruction'. In fact, to some extent this is again the legacy of German Idealism, which, more than any school before it, had seen itself as both provoked and overwhelmed by the need to integrate both the ancients and the moderns, knowledge and faith, desire and reason, history and system. But perhaps even more than any other thinker, Heidegger meditated on the intransigence of its 'ruins'. Indeed, at stake was a tracing of human existence within these ruins—*Existenz als Ruinanz,* as he put it in articulating the phenomenological 'ruins' of Aristotle in 1925. What is required here is less a systematic exposition of Heidegger's thought, than perhaps more considerations on the legacy and status of the thought in question. The latter will be linked in this regard to both the modern question of legitimation and, more to the point here, the complex link between hermeneutics and community. Hence the incursion of Gadamer, as will be seen, where this link becomes explicit. Moreover, as will become evident too, the status of Heidegger's (and Gadamer's) account and the 'hermeneutics' it bequeaths become perhaps evident only in articulating a certain *Auseinandersetzung* with its detractors.

We begin in fact with fragments, as both Heidegger and Gadamer attested in acknowledging the problem of distance and historical remove that inevitably accompanies the effect of detraditionalization. Indeed such a fragmentation was essentially connected to philosophical modernism's quest for certainty, inextricably interrupting its link with the past. As Gadamer put it, beyond the humanist rupture between traditions and beyond the historicist's collapse of traditions—in fact since both—"the continuity of the Western philosophical tradition has been effective only in a fragmentary way (*gebrochener Weise*)" (TM:xxiv). Indeed, it might be claimed that this fragmentation was already inherent to philosophy's origins, or so Heidegger claimed in the opening paragraph of *Being and Time.* Even Plato and Aristotle's investigations, in relation to which, he says, we have now grown deaf, are said to have originally emerged from the phenomena only in a provisional and fragmentary way (BT:2). It is just in this sense that we consequently would need to ask again the most fundamental question, the question of Being, to seek the status of its remainder anew. There was a sense from the outset that the project would not escape this fragmentation, that indeed the problem of fragmentation was at issue—that even our accounts of Being itself involve the dispersion of such (theoretical and experiential) fragments. There is a sense, moreover, in which such ruptures and historical distance were synonymous with even the origins of philosophy itself. Historically, perhaps, the problem of this distance already explicitly occurs with the transformation of the quattrocento, inevitably extending the tropological space of the rational and overtly encountering, for the first time, the conflict between narratives. Indeed retrospectively it might be seen as announcing the fracturing of transcendental authorities which would underlie theoretical modernism's quest for certainty of all sorts—

philosophical, ethical, and political. Hobbes in this regard, and those in his wake, had only thought to deduce their way out; *Scientia* might then still provide *Sapience,* and experience *Prudentia* (Lev:I.5); but in ways unrecognizable to his predecessors, both would be refigured, born out of a conflict between narratives in which all seemingly transcendental authorities had failed, a conflict between narratives—rational and otherwise ("they that trusting only to the authority of books, follow the blind blindly" [Lev:I.5]). It was doubtless indicative of a conflict much more archaic that had been at stake in all humanism and the study of 'letters'. And its legacy was apparent in the fragmented plurality modernism everywhere contested.

Indeed, Boccaccio's attempt in the *Genealogia deorum* to justify the study of the Latin gods, in this regard would only truncate a problem already nascent in Dante (and even Aquinas, before him), the hermeneutic problem of the interface and translation between narratives—in this case specifically, the problem of the synthesis of Christian and pre-Christian narratives.[9] Broadly construed however, it is equally the problem of the synthesis of the ancient and the modern, the past and the present. Moreover it is a problem that reiterates itself (not only in Philo's synthesis of Athens and Jerusalem but) in the emergence of the concept of the *ordo traditio* itself. On the one hand, the latter had been invoked by Irenaeus to delimit the truth of what had been authoritatively handed down, while, on the other hand, such pronouncements were held to be the expression of—and were justified by— what had been openly and everywhere believed.[10] Already complications become apparent in the relations between analysis and synthesis, determination and event, universal and singular, interpretation and horizon. Tradition itself, like analogy in general—likewise, as its defenders declare, 'everywhere analogous'—is similarly 'traditional'. The concept of tradition itself, that is, adheres to the history of concepts, to 'traditionality' as such. If, it should be insisted as a result, that at stake in the rational is precisely the art of such synthesis (i.e., what Nietzsche called the art of interpretation), the exposition of such genesis (and genealogies) emerges always and only as part of the problem which accompanies questions of the *traditionis traditio.* More originally, however, as Heidegger realized, the problem opens with the beginnings of philosophy itself. In considering the question of the propriety and impropriety of writing and how we may best please the gods, Socrates states in the *Phaedrus,* "I can tell you the tradition that has come down from our forefathers, but they alone know the truth of it."[11]

This is not to say, obviously, that no account of rational legitimacy is possible under such construals, nor even that Heidegger or Gadamer failed to provide one, even though the problem of legitimation, as is often charged, may remain too implicit in their accounts. If we are to avoid the dogmatisms they both sought to overcome we will need to confront the question of legitimation anew. To begin to do so however, we will need to wrestle with the paradoxes they present to theoretical modernism: in Heidegger's case the status of an interrogation concerning the remnants of the question (and the science) of Being; in Gadamer's case, a brief—on its basis—against all monologics. In the first place, Heidegger declared, such a science (like all sciences) would be a totality established through an interconnection of true propositions (*das Ganze eines Begründungzusammenhanges wahre Satz*) [BT:32]. And yet such a (formal) totality, Heidegger reminds us, still lacks a certain completeness (*Vollständigkeit*), lacks, that is, an account of the origins, the history, and the procedures which clarify and legitimate such propositions. As such it does not reach the meaning of science, provoking a question concerning its *Sinn*. In one sense it was simply the acknowledgment that the basic concepts of scientific enquiry determine beforehand the subject matter. Science, that is, remains 'theory' laden. Thus the need arises to account for its 'production', a matter different in principle from the kind of 'logic' that "limps along after investigating the status of some science as it chances to find it in order to discover its 'method'" (BT:30). And here too there will be a certain debt to Nietzsche: 'science' is always more than a 'method'. Hermeneutics—like standard accounts of theory in general—always previously had presupposed there was an exacting account of such an enquiry. Hence the significance of interpretation for the most 'fundamental' questions of traditionality. But, of course, if we are to say positively what is at stake, we will need to say more.

Of necessity, at stake will be a rupture with classical transcendentalism. Such an enquiry could not follow Kant's transcendental 'retroduction', nor could it simply seek the conditions of the "sciences objectively so called" under the assumption that this founding had already been accomplished. The 'positive' outcome of Kant's first *Critique*, for Heidegger, was instead always an ontological one. In a gloss perhaps already indicating his affinity—perhaps even debt to Fichte and Schelling—Heidegger declared that the first *Critique* concerns "what belongs to any Nature whatsoever, not in a 'theory' of knowledge," (BT:31) and not at all a regionally circumscribed nature (i.e., mechanics). Indeed, as Heidegger claims in taking a privileged example, "what is philosophically primary is neither a theory of the concept-formation of historiology nor the theory of historiological knowledge, nor yet the theory of history as the Object of historiology" (BT:31). Rather this investigation of Being and tradition requires a step beyond the closure of theory, a "productive logic," as he calls it, which would initially clarify the entities that form the protocols for theory. Not without irony—and surely not without connection to the history of irony that accompanies all such hermeneutics—he claims that "such research must run ahead of the positive sciences, and it *can*" (BT:30; Heidegger's emphasis). Moreover, it is just in this regard, as has been seen, that the enquiry would become foundational:

> Laying the foundations, as we described it, is rather a productive logic—in the sense that it leaps ahead [*vorspringt*], as it were, into some area of Being, discloses it for the first time in the constitution of its Being, and, after thus arriving at the structures within, makes these available to the positive sciences as transparent assignments for its enquiry. (BT:30–31)

Encased in the very language of foundations it would ultimately belie, however, Heidegger's claim here is that this primordial step beyond theory, this laying out of Being itself explicitly clarified, this explication, that is, which would articulate the remnants of tradition and Being, is precisely interpretation. In fact, it is in this sense, Heidegger claims, that instead of the circumscribed inventories of historiology, "what is primary is rather Interpretation." It carries, however, all the paradoxes of Heidegger's *Being and Time* with it. First he states explicitly that this "genealogy of the different possible ways of Being" cannot be understood to be deductively constructed. Rather this leaping ahead would be interpretive through and through and complicated thereby within the text of *Sein und Zeit*. If Heidegger is clear in insisting, "and you can do it [*und Sie können es*]," its status will be unclear, linked time and again to an encounter toward an event not only yet unknown but both uncanny and strange in a twofold difference—ontic and ontological—which divides even *homo interpretans* from within.

## 2. The Refiguration of the Past and 'the Between' of Care: Interpretation and the Leveling of the Everyday

It is in this way that Heidegger himself explicates the ruins of what still cannot be thought within science. To accomplish this task he returns, curiously and uncannily perhaps, in the first place, to premodern narratives, to Aristotle and the problem of Being as *pros hen* and to Augustine (and the Stoics), to *cura* and the problem of finite transcendence (BT:492n). This retrieval occurs precisely in order to rearticulate what lies behind these fragments, yet to be brought to light. It is just in this sense, however, that, for example, if Werner Marx was right in claiming of Heidegger's investigation as search

for a new "other meaning of Being, as departing tradition," this investigation still remains figured through the articulemes of the tradition itself.[12]
'Tradition' just denotes our inevitable reliance on the past for significance
(*Bedeutsamkeit*)—our facticity—as well as the encounter that is the provocation of the problem of its meaning (*Sinn*), an event not functionally determinable by it. If interpretation is tradition bound, it likewise inevitably
affirms our distance from it. Hence, then, the problem of the new emerges,
and the inevitable question of its excess, its *Vorausspringen,* one whose ambiguous status results precisely from our separation from tradition—even
in our attempts to appropriate it.

Readers of the above text, moreover, will perhaps immediately hear the
connection with that other form of *Vorausspringen,* problematic in standard
interpretations of the ethical, that is all too briefly alluded to in Heidegger's
discussion of *Mitsein*. There Heidegger refers to an authenticity in which
Dasein "does not so much leap in for the Other [*für ihm einspringen*] as *leap
ahead* of him [*ihm vorausspringt*] in his existential potentiality-for Being,
not in order to take away his 'care' but rather to give it back to him . . . for
the first time" (BT:158; Heidegger's emphasis). If both instances consequently will be matters of interpretation, of Dasein's resolute being-ahead-
of-itself, and ultimately its self-projection as care, it may well be true, too,
that both in fact mutually enlighten one another. If, after all, this extension
beyond theory is the 'foundation' of theory, and if thereby fundamental ontology belies all fundaments and all ontologies, it is, too, an extension dependent on an encounter that belies all theory, uproots all categories in the
presence of an event foreign to both. It involves thereby a matter neither
simply ethical nor simply theoretical, but rather the origin of both 'ethics'
and 'theory'. Of course, preontologically we are not strangers to ourselves
(BT:36). From the beginning, however, the question of interpretation could
not simply be removed from this encounter with the strange nor could 'ethics' be removed from the encounter with the stranger, both opening precisely for Heidegger in the problem of ontological difference that spurs
philosophic enquiry in general.

Indeed, it could be argued—and as this text demonstrates—interpretation
too is just this uncanny event, a reciprocal rejoinder between past and future, between received views and the possibilities they portend. At stake remains a complex itinerary, indeed an economics or *Wechsel* extending from
Fichte to Nietzsche and beyond, one which likewise articulates a certain
post-Kantian indeterminacy within Heidegger's own text—again, to use
Merleau-Ponty's term, a "coherent deformation." The *Daseinanalytik,* on the
one hand, that is, would articulate the meaning of Being and, on the other

hand, explicate meaning itself as temporally affected, an event complicated between historical projection and encounter, projected between the ontic and the ontological, and between past and future. And if Dasein is, as care, this Between (*Zwischen*) [BT:427], and even if it is clear that the 'who' of Dasein cannot be articulated without the primacy of the first person, the *Je-meinigkeit*, it is true too that to be denotable in this respect would always be a complex gesture, answerable to no definite description but an 'experience' divided between self and 'community'. As both historical and ontological Dasein's 'between' is doubly—and ambiguously—ontic and ontological, the *Zwischen* of Being and entities, self and other. Moreover, the 'interpretations' at stake—primordial, inextricable, ventured both beyond and in default of all categories, are likewise then neither simply theoretical nor practical—neither ethical nor singular, neither passive nor active, but precisely their intertwining, the care in which Dasein's Being is already beyond itself, again precisely as this 'between', this 'entity'—but equally this 'we' [BT:238].

The status of the latter is often articulated in accord with the archive of traditionalism, as a matter of 'generations'— without the character of 'generations' itself perhaps being ever sufficiently articulated (BT:436). And *Being and Time* would only reinstitute this archive, still invoking Irenaeus's ancient predicates of *traditio* as the handing down (*Überlieferung*) of a treasure (*Erb*), and its heritage (*Erbschaft*), declaring that "everything good is a heritage" (BT:435), albeit now by truncating the history of its decline within our generation—but also without perhaps ever sufficiently articulating its status. And if *Being and Time* likewise 'neglects' the matter, if in fact this primordial community as being beyond itself remained too often instead articulated in terms of its leveling and failure—indeed generating the death throes of a particular tragic gesture—that is perhaps not accidental. If Heidegger began by retrieving certain premodern narratives, here he will perhaps remain closer to moderns like Hobbes, from whom he sought to distance himself, than to Aristotle or Augustine.

What perhaps Heidegger ever failed to sufficiently provide was less an account exposing the failures of modern civil society—nor considerations concerning the *Augenblick* of its authentic alternative—than an account of how the everyday might be salvaged within such dispersions and *Ruinanz*. The final word instead remained too clear and almost intransigent—as was perhaps the debt to Nietzsche within it: the whole project of fundamental ontology as a negative critique would remain directed upon the ossified perversions of the today (*das "Heute"*)—even (and perhaps especially) when he hoped that in the moment of vision "existence can even gain mastery over the 'everyday'" (BT:422). Moreover, the critique of such ossifications is general in extent: including not only the play of imagination or its failure that underlies Gadamer's own account of *Spiel* and *Spielraum,* but equally such distant kin as Wittgenstein's language games: *Sprachspiel.* Doubtless all these figures obliquely share—and participate in—modern accounts of transcendental imagination, invention, and perhaps even the permutations of formal construction and the history of formalism. The question is, perhaps, how does this interface with the complications of the ancient science, of Being as such, and how might we still talk about either Dasein or its community without simply succumbing to the fate of irrationalism—or perhaps simply mourning their 'demise'. But in many ways, of course, this is just Heidegger's question: the question of the remainder, the meaning of Being, in the wake of the techniques of modernity. And its task, in this regard, becomes equally divided, then, between the legacies of Aristotle and those of Hobbes.

It suffices perhaps to recall that originally in the *Scotusbuch,* Heidegger had appealed to the benevolence of this *pros hen* and its medieval gloss as *transcendens* to overcome the leveling of modern society, albeit already aware of the onslaught which awaited. In fact the *Scotusbuch* closed, recognizing the need to confront Hobbes, if only under the *persona* of 'Hegel'.[13] *Being and Time*'s analysis had further seen the hegemony of the latter's complications, now perhaps more fully aware of the difficulties—logical and political—which attended the conflict between the ancients and the moderns, a conflict which is already evident perhaps in the very syntagm 'fundamental ontology'.

Thus, the ambiguity of the *Daseinanalytik*—like that of the ancient institutions of analogy itself—becomes equally complex. If the hermeneutic circle had relied on a multiplicity which need not be opposed to truth, if, that is, Being can still be said in many ways, and the interpretative circle consequently need not be vicious, the ambiguity of the 'everyday' seemed instead perhaps only to threaten in its lack of univocity, which always in turn seemed simply to imply, as had ambiguity in general for Husserl before him, a failure of foundations. Even this *Sinn,* in whose horizons the *Seinsfrage* became intelligible, however, seemed simply too univocal for the task at hand: the explication of *Sinn,* in its opposition to ambiguity, seemed always to itself presuppose—fundamentally—a resolution both epistemic and ontological. And perhaps Heidegger himself came to see it. The figures of the everyday, on the other hand, lack such univocal foundations. But for Heidegger the *Zweideutigkeit* seemed always—and only—to mask a certain leveling of transcendence. The problem with the everyday is that even its *Füreinander* masks an "against-one-another [*Gegeneinander*]" (BT:219). Diversity here endangers. Both endangered and isolated, the truth of modern subjectivity requires a virtue that, like that of Kierkegaard's Abraham, remains "purely personal," confronted with an "either/or!" that makes dialogue with the other impossible. And yet while such accounts, linked inherently to divine command, might aid the theologian, here they ultimately fall short. The problem then is how to break free from the distortions of *Mitsein,* how might authentic dialogue be possible: how, granted its historicity, might the figures of the everyday be liberated? And more specifically, the problem seems to be one of knowing how we could even start to generate 'principles' for such a 'liberation'.

The problem with such principled enquiry here, in any case, the problem with such 'methodological' requisites, is that they remain ultimately too underdetermined. Such is the lot with all interpretation, as with all theory, it will be objected. Hence emerges, however, the problem of 'method' as *Mitsein,* that is, as dialogue, a complication which has, as becomes evident, accompanied the descent of modern transcendentalism, in the lapse of 'singular' or 'monolithic' authority. And here, it might be thought, recourse to Gadamer may explicitly 'augment' Heidegger's lacunae. For whatever else is implied in the account of hermeneutics as dialogue, its interpretive question openly affirms not simply the problem of traditions, but equally the status of the received views and everyday practices, and hence the possibility of an event which is less—or at least not only—the distortion of *logos* than its emergence.

First however, it should be noted that, even in the later works, while Heidegger never simply denies the importance of dialogue, it is true too that he 'downplays' its significance before the *Sache* itself. As he puts it in *What Is Called Thinking?*

> Every interpretation is a dialogue with the work, and with the saying. However, every dialogue becomes halting and fruitless if it confines itself obdurately to nothing but what is directly said—rather than that the speakers in the dialogue involve each other in *that* realm and abode about which they are speaking, and lead each other to it. Such involvement is the soul of dialogue. It leads the speakers into the unspoken. The term "conversation" does, of course, express the fact that the speakers are turning to one another. Every conversation is a kind of dialogue. But true dialogue is never a conversation.[14]

We should of course beware of false contrasts here: clearly, here too it is the *Vorausspringen* and the excess of its 'hermeneutics' that Heidegger has in mind. Moreover, the "Dialogue on Language" would replace the hermeneutic circle with the event of dialogue (albeit now explicitly without foundation, without 'why')—and yet a dialogue which also terminates before the silence of the unsaid, a dialogue "with more silence than talk" (DL:52). What will be at stake in this regard are differences regarding the account of dialogue: to speak classically, differences regarding its *Elementlehre*, precisely, that is, differences regarding "the elements of a theory of hermeneutic experience" (TM:265). And as will become further evident, Heidegger and Gadamer's difference here may well indicate not only differences in the account of language, but in the end a difference in archives and the rational itself.

Gadamer's *Truth and Method* cannot be taken to be simply a denial of the rigors of method—any more than Heidegger's careful leaping ahead and clarifying could be. Instead it must be read as a book that, its author contends, polemically heightens the tension between truth and method (TM: 554), proceeding on the example of Heidegger's own "methodological program" vis-à-vis this underdeterminacy. In both cases, as has been seen, there are doubtless, or provisionally, certain concurrences with Nietzsche's claim—that "it is not the victory of science that distinguishes our nineteenth century, but the victory of scientific method over science."[15] Hobbes, again, in a sense had furnished its protocols; the *Leviathan* had distinguished philosophy from ratiocination in general (which even the "American savages" have quite naturally) precisely in terms of "Method" (i.e., deductive certainty). On the basis of the latter, moreover, he had claimed that its origins were not Greek but Indian, Persian, and Egyptian (Lev:IV.46). In this regard Hobbes not only repeats but reinvokes Thales' own debts regarding the origins of geometry and natural science.

What perhaps differentiates Gadamer and Heidegger at this point—even perhaps without their knowing it—is the status of 'tradition' itself. For Heidegger, tradition, a claim with which Nietzsche too could concur, was first and foremost, or at least proximally and for the most part, an impediment to truth: "tradition blocks our access to those primordial 'sources' from which the categories and concepts handed down to us have been in part quite genuinely drawn" (BT:43). And here Heidegger's account of the rational follows Husserlian (and Hobbesian) foundational protocols: a search for the origins is traced that would provide the original meanings and authentic (i.e., fulfilled) evidence for received truths, the opening of what lies 'beyond' in founding all interpretation. It is a question of tradition itself blocking what is transmitted: again, to speak Hobbesian, a certain forgetfulness regarding what the original names stood for. We may wonder whether Heidegger too, especially in his attention to the semantic origins of philosophemes (e.g., *Grundwörter* such as truth as '*aletheia*' or nature as '*physis*'), may still think the name primary—like other foundationalists of the early twentieth century, Russell or the early Wittgenstein.

Gadamer's interpretive considerations, on the other hand (as he put it), focused on the sentence, the question of the articulation, and hence the dialectic—and our distance from such primitives.[16] In not only consigning the word to poetics but the latter to *dialectic*, Gadamer explicitly follows a complex itinerary in the history of rhetoric that descends from the ancients to the humanists and beyond, dividing the legacy of interpretation between the poetics of the word and the rhetorics of assertibility, indicative once more of a synthesis between the ancients and the moderns—a venture of what lies beyond demonstration without succumbing to 'substantialism'. Hermeneutics so construed is less the return to origins than it is the critical venture of their possibility. Moreover, if as a result, no interpretation can be final, definitive, ultimate, or original, then it is less the return than the transfiguration (or re-figuration) of origins that is at stake, requiring the art of invention as much as the art of memory. Here no principled inventory can claim ultimate adequacy—we may have our principles, but we also have our detractors. But this requires that the very rationality of our claims depends on our acknowledging such competitors, actual or possible—again the recognition of the Hobbesian moment. Heidegger of course does not specify his relation to Hobbes explicitly, save the critical remarks that occur in the *Basic Problems of Phenomenology* (BP:183ff.). There Hobbes is criticized for having *equated* truth and judgment, on the basis of the convertibility of the transcendentals. The latter, as Heidegger realized, was by no means a matter of equivalence, however, but of analogy for the scholastics, who even themselves had not, he claimed, thought through its significance.[17] From this he argued, however, that the question of the *Sache* itself had not been broached, Hobbes having denied the interpretive *ekstasis* in which Being is disclosed—in the same way that he had denied that words such as "Entity, Intentionality, Quiddity" were meaningful at all (Lev:I.4).

Characteristically of all nominalism, Heidegger charged, Hobbes had surrendered his own approach in the hope of reestablishing a direct relation between names and things, investing once more in the myth of the given that nominalism had denied. If it is essential for memory to retain the significance of the first names, it is true too, as Hobbes put it in the *Logic*, that "the original names are 'arbitrary'" and (a matter Bakhtinian enough) "new names are daily made, and old ones laid aside."[18] It was a question of attending to the original link between the 'arbitrary' name and its particular thing, recognizing both that the naming of things is necessary for science (since unless the scientist "communicate his thoughts his science will pass with him") and that not all names signify something. In an example portentous enough, Hobbes points out that "this word *nothing* is a name, which yet cannot be the name of anything: for when, for example, we subtract 2 and 3 from 5, and so nothing remaining, we would call that subtraction to mind, this speech *nothing remains,* and in it the word *nothing* is not unuseful."[19] Heidegger himself, like Husserl before him, on the other hand, follows the same trajectory inversely, moving from the *Sache* (or the question of the *Sache*) to its sign, an attempt to acknowledge an excess which escapes circumscribed signification—and then, in the later works, ultimately to the poetic primacy of the signifier, for him the only resource identifiable after the *Gestell* of modern theory. To circumvent this antinomy, however, it will be necessary to further investigate the dialectics of the circle in which such distinctions arise.

### 3. On the Reckoning of Accounts: Between Invocation and Assertion

If it can be agreed with Heidegger that "Hobbes' view is of particular significance for the understanding of contemporary logic,"[20] Hobbes's legacy at the level of judgment also lingers in the very problem of assertability itself—the problem of alterity and lapse in epistemic authority that underwrites both the quest for certainty and the elevation of modern *mathesis* before skepticism. Henceforth, Hobbes had asserted, words would no longer be accepted as the "uncertain signs" of traditional prudence, derived from former authors, "the money of fools, that value them by the authority of an Aristotle, a Cicero, or a Thomas." Instead, reason is calculation and words, rather, are "wise mens counters." Consequently, what can be named "is whatsoever can enter into, or be considered in" the "accounting books of reason," as Hobbes put it (Lev:I.4). While those in Hobbes's wake may not at all be similarly committed to the equation of truth and assertion, for reasons Heidegger had already demonstrated, they will be left with the challenges that the problem of assertability logically entails (one's lingering in the problem of sufficient reason), the problem of the conflict of interpretations itself, the collapse of traditional authority, and the encounter with the other.

Notice that all this cannot be merely reduced to the problem of *ethical* respect for the 'other'—with which, after all, it likewise emerges in Hobbes's challenge. The problem of the 'other'—and the quest for certainty—is of a piece in the collapse of transcendental authorities, and both will need to be addressed in its wake: both, that is, the ethics *and* the epistemics of 'alterity', the plethora of words, passions, and 'manners' having become in both cases too 'various' to be univocally relied on (Lev:I.11). Despite Hobbes's reductionist views of both the Good and the rational, the question of certainty was politically charged in this regard, poised, as the *Leviathan* itself makes evident, not only against the abuses of theoretical speculation, but equally against the abuses of private conscience, the latter under the pretense of being "face to face with God almighty." Thus, the singular truths of inspiration became equally charged with a failure to remember the origin or with a "lucky finding of an Error held generally" (Lev:I.8) and one not at all a matter of in-spiration or the divine face-to-face. In all this, Hobbes is convinced that 'Spirit' is not an event but a metaphor or at most the mere blowing in of a Phantasme (Lev:III.34).

Clearly, Hobbes's views are of no less significance for the problem of metaphysics, a domain he already abhorred for its "jargon" (Lev:IV.46). But no matter what one thinks of Hobbes's 'demythologizings' or semantic reductions, his legacy, both theoretically and politically—the issue after all was civil war—remains in the problem of judgment itself. It is true: Gadamer will claim—doubtless *pace* Heidegger's 'antihumanism'—that the very tradition of the *sensus communis,* which now "we must laboriously make our way back into," involved a model for overcoming such agonistics, one which we will ultimately reaffirm. But first and foremost it will be necessary to acknowledge the lapse in transcendental authorities out of which such a retrieval emerges. If there ever were a language capable of originally naming things independent of the interpretation of ratiocination, a speech that would 'say' things as God named them—and perhaps Adam after him, Hobbes allows—this language "was again lost at the tower of Babel." As a result of this "dispersion" we face instead the "oblivion" of this prior language in "the diversity of tongues" (Lev:I.4). And, while Gadamer's humanist appeal to the *Koinonoemosune* of Marcus Aurelius (TM:24) opens once more the possibility of a community which would honor the faculty of opinion, both in oneself and the other, Marcus Aurelius did so only by appealing to a narrative of a common nature, a universal reason, and an inherited religion that has long seemed lost.[21] Such traditions for Hobbes were already nothing but "wives fables" (Lev:IV.46) now in need of justification. In this regard the modernist question of certainty, however, becomes as intractable as the *Seinsfrage* itself. Moreover, we can formulate both in tandem: to forget the problem of 'assertability' would be to think that the 'other' is not a problem; to think that truth were simply assertability would be to think 'Being' is not a 'problem'.

In this sense, were I simply to deny the claim of the other, I would have no grounds for 'asserting' my own, which is also not to say that I simply submit to the other's summons—at most that is when things turn ethical, perhaps even theological. It is rather to recognize that claims concerning tradition(s) will inevitably suffer from a certain disequilibrium, ventured within an agonistic which is the very condition of legitimacy and authentic dialogue. It is precisely in this sense that Gadamer's claim includes, allows for, and ventures "the elements of 'conflict'" that summon its participants "to come with one to 'judgment'" (TM:261n). To refuse this agonistic, consequently, would be no less dogmatic than to claim to have solved it, to have determinately conquered it. While expressivists or hermeneuts might insist on the good ambiguity that fosters humanistic translation and interpretation, Hobbes would be adamant in his commitments in this regard. Such, it should be added, is the plight of civil society, as everyone from Hobbes to Hegel and all their multiple descendents realized. To think that justice is the same as the democratic contract is to think that 'sovereignty' is not a problem. It may be necessary again to add, however, that this dispersion is perhaps as rationally necessary as it became historical fate. The demise of ultimate transcendental authorities is what modern society and modern science share in common—though neither should be simply construed thereby to be simply matters of 'decline'. It is rather to recognize that even the most disputational genres of philosophical enquiry modeled on deductive proof cannot be detached from "the inner connection between knowledge and dialectic" (TM:364). The question instead is what to do with the ensuing possibilities.

Provisionally, to say all this is just another way of saying that traditions will be matters of interpretation and, methodologically, inevitably problematic, a point on which a variety of thinkers in the ruins of idealism agree—not only Gadamer and Heidegger, for example, but Josiah Royce, in the wake of pragmatism, or Eliot, in the wake of early analytic philosophy. This is a complex matter, however. Initially, the point about traditions seems to be simply a matter of coherence, that intelligibility requires the iterability and continuity of meaning. Knowing that reason has semantic connections with its past, claiming therefore that even a certain transcendental semantics will be necessitated—knowing, that is, that the evaluation of truth claims requires that one meet certain standards of coherence (to speak simply, knowing that interpretation is part of a language game)—does not on its own convert the satisfaction of such criteria itself into truth. Even preservation or verification (*Bewahrung*) is an act of reason (TM:281). Coherence, mere iteration, consequently, does not deliver truth. Claims to truth remain inevitably claims to *Sachlichkeit*—if perhaps not simply to *Objektivität*, even for hermeneuts like Gadamer.

"Understanding is an event" (TM:309) will inevitably mean more than such a factical claim about its conditions, then, inaugurating a separation that distinguishes us from the authorities of the ancients: distinguishing in turn *phronēsis* from the authority of the *phronemos*—or its 'hero'. And correlatively, tying understanding to its event will never simply imply restricting it thereby. To say that understanding is an event is, however, to say that it is a community matter, an issue to which we will need to return. Provisionally, however, this sounds like Peirce or Dewey. And many of Gadamer's commentators have seen it to be such, as Heidegger's English readers anglicized him as a Schwabian version of Dewey. In one sense, of course, this is not false; Dewey's own proximity to Gadamer's hermeneutics is undeniable. As the former claimed in his *Ethics,*

> Adoption of the experimental method does not signify that there is no place for authority and precedent. On the contrary, precedent is . . . a valuable instrumentality. . . . But precedents are to be used, rather than to be implicitly followed; they are to be used as tools of analysis of present situations, suggesting points to be looked into and hypotheses to be tried.[22]

Still none of this attention to use authorizes the reduction of truth itself to use, to warranted assertability. This is, after all, both the significance and the vagueness of application—and why Hegel (fatefully) had rejected it at the outset of the *Rechtslehre*. Applications are dangerous: lacking determinate rules (i.e., formulae) for judgment (i.e., subsumption), we can apply concepts and articulate things wrongly, after all. Without simply turning substantialist, we will still need a more substantial account of truth, and we will need a more complex account of its justification. What must likewise be insisted, however, is that the commitment to the traditionality of truth cannot be limited to either (1) a commitment to the substantive truths of the past, or (2) a commitment to the mere semantic coherence (the historicity) of such truths, or even (3) a commitment to a specific (ontic) community of investigators on their way to a final truth, a Peircean (or Husserlian) infinite. Rather, the art of interpretation not only is lacking in foundations but lacking the assurance of ends—and its complex coupling of both is precisely what preserves its rational warrant. Interpretation is not only 'anarchical' but 'ateleological'.

To say this may doubtless seem paradoxical, granted the other commitment of hermeneutics—that reason *is* historically bound. Even so, the first
part, that we lack foundations, is straightforward. Only those bound by Platonist construals of timeless, unimpeachable propositions could read Gadamer simply as a historicist. This is true even though hermeneutics will play
hard for them, since he denies, after all, that any interpretation of tradition
will be ultimately definitive (TM:535).

Still, perhaps even more problematically for Gadamer's *Elementlehre* of
hermeneutic experience, he also denies the teleology of truth as much as its
archaeology. "We might regard as one-sided the principle that experience
should be evaluated only teleologically, by the degree to which it ends in
knowledge" (TM:349–50). This, perhaps, is more difficult. And it may well
be decisive for understanding the theoretical status of Gadamer's own
hermeneutics, coming in fact precisely in his section on the logic of prejudices (*Voraussetzungen*). For Gadamer, to deny the problem of truth, to simply endorse the teleology of knowledge, would again be to forget the
negative. History will not do everything—not even our being-in-it. Teleo-
logical claims (even the teleologies of analysis) cannot decide everything;
they presuppose, moreover, that there is something ultimate to decide. But
interpretation "cannot be understood teleologically in terms of the object
into which it is enquiring. Such an 'object-in-itself' clearly does not exist at
all"—which is not to say 'objectivity' *tout court* (TM:285) does not exist at
all. Hence, as Gadamer recognized, this is the importance of the critique of
skepticism by Bacon, who had detached experimentalism from such teleologies at the outset of philosophical modernism (TM:348f.)—or of Hegel's
appropriation of dialectic as skepticism in action at its end (TM:354). But,
as has been seen, if there are remnants of classical dialectic here, they will
be as much Aristotle's as Hegel's.

None of this initially seems to require the elevation of tradition as an essential part of experience. The invocation of the negative does, however, in
the wake of both Bacon and Hegel, pay homage to the critical moment too often thought to be missing from the hermeneut's account—indeed converging
upon Popper's falsificationism, as Gadamer's English editors are likewise
quick to footnote (TM:353n). But this is not simply Popperian either, after all,
since it is not certainty but truth that is at stake. And consequently it will not
suffice to limit our encounter with truth to falsification, precisely because it
will not suffice to limit truth to theoretical certainty (nor ultimately thereby
to deductive exemplars). If Hegelian *skepsis* will inevitably be linked to this
*Erfahrung,* interpretation will, after all, extend beyond it. Popper's falsifica-

tionism, on the other hand, really is Hegel's dialectic turned on its head: instead of the truth of negation, the negation of truth, as Feyerabend would ultimately see.

For Gadamer, on the other hand, the dialectic at stake in interpretation is 'deregulated' with respect to such commitments:

> The dialectic of experience has its proper fulfillment not in definitive knowledge but in the openness to experience that is made possible by experience itself. (TM:355)

This openness to experience doubtless has its 'positive' critical edge: taken phenomen-ologically, it retains the 'openness' to the requisites of verification (the 'iterability' of knowledge). Hence the lingering trace of Husserl's teleology of consciousness, and the problem of the coherence of *Erfahrung*. Forgetting this critical moment is the transcendental illusion to the tragic: commitments to 'unknowing', after all, presuppose at least the articulation of something about which we do not know—if not knowledge of it. The early Schelling's "There is nothing left but to fight and fall," still abandoned philosophy to what he criticized as "the horrors of ecstasy (*Schwärmerei*)."[23] And yet this much, it will be said, is true: if not in terms of the tragic, then at least in those of the fallible—to speak Kantian, the recognition of limits (TM:357)—this opening lingers on. The science of consciousness—phenomenology, that is, as its positivist and neo-Kantian detractors rightly recognized—never attains knowledge, if it remains always regulated by its *telos*. 'Tradition' in this sense emerges only within a certain splitting within the science of phenomenology, undercutting its Cartesian commitment from within. In Husserl himself, in fact, this was the case; the underdeterminacy of the multiple traditions in which "we are always involved" becomes thematic only in the move from static to genetic phenomenology and the acknowledgment that static analysis in itself is insufficient. The immediacy of consciousness depends on the past and the anticipation or 'protention' of the future for the very origins of its reflective coherence. The attempt, consequently, to complete the reduction to pure immanence inevitably fails. Gadamer's account of prejudice, on the other hand, begins in fact by purging experience from the idols of "exact scientific experience" (TM:347). The encounter with the Absolute, the revelation or disclosure of Being which phenomenology was to articulate from Fichte and Hegel—and, as has been indicated, on to Freud and Husserl—would undergo a certain withdrawal; understood within the finite sequences of consciousness, it now indicates, to speak Kantian, a purposiveness without ultimate purpose or finality.

Paradoxically then, it is precisely in this 'ateleological' purposiveness, precisely in this 'transmission' of the series, that all phenomenology broaches the problem of *traditio* (TM:290), of what is received and handed down (*parodisis*). Moreover, it is here that Gadamer's account resumes the most ancient accounts of traditionality, linking the structural and genetic features of experience in an appeal to the perdurance of time—one which at the same time would provide the means of its legitimation. Finally it is precisely here that Gadamer's reappraisal of the classical, "the basic category of effective history," emerges, "the binding power of the validity that is preserved (or verified) and handed down"—and yet as, again, an uncanny event beyond all simple coincidence of the present, always "unattainable and yet present" (TM:287, 577). While the result allows for "preservation amid the ruins of time" (TM:289), it does so precisely by calling into question the primacy of the discrete present. "[T]he discreteness of experience (*Erlebnis*)—however much it maintains its methodological significance as the intentional correlate of a constituted meaning value—is not an ultimate phenomenological datum" (TM:245).

Hence, however, the impact of Husserl's great (but as we have just seen, loaded) discovery emerges, that, *pace* Brentano and Meinong, the present is not simply a perception but the result of a production within the sequences of temporal retention and protention. It is only thereby that the discrete experience retains its critical value. The present, while not phenomenologically ultimate ("there is no such thing as 'the present'" [TM:534]), and while fallible, is nonetheless corrigible—related to the past in the same way that the past is corrigibly linked to the present and the anticipations of the future. The present thus is a ciphering or weaving (and 'testing') of hermeneutic forms (TM:306). Still, it must likewise be insisted that, at the same time, temporality undergoes a certain splitting with respect to *not only* its past or its future, but *equally other* presents, its transcendental 'polarity' inevitably decentered.[24] The genealogy of experience that links all 'static' analysis semantically and historically to its transcendental past, by the same epistemic 'insufficiency', likewise links the 'phenomenology' of reason (problematically) to its 'rivals', to alternative iterative series and traditions. If interpretation is always historically bound, it is "never absolutely bound to any one standpoint and hence can never have a closed horizon" (TM:304)—a point tantamount to saying that there can no more be traditions in themselves than there can be truths in themselves. Hence the complication and fecundity of its 'opening', the openness to experience and the emphasis on the dialogues of traditions. As Merleau-Ponty put it, "our relation with the true passes through the others. Either we go towards the true with them, or it is not towards the true that we are going."[25]

If Husserl had acknowledged the importance of temporality, never did he fully see (as Heidegger had) its *ekstasis,* a dependence which again, to use Gadamer's Nietzschean term, "reverses" the simple reductions of Cartesian consciousness (TM:257). It is in this regard that, while the inextricable dependence on time as a necessary unity opens thought to the transcendence of temporality itself and thus to the possibility of truth, this temporal bond likewise links it, not simply "to methodological sureness" (TM:362), but also to the transcendence of historicity—and hence the opening of its 'internal' horizons to 'external' horizonality, splitting the present and its founding interminably and irretrievably before its facticity. The reversal (*Umkehrung*) of Cartesian Platonism does not lead to empirical reduction but to a 'return' of transcendence: always an opening out beyond itself. But this *ekstasis* is not simply 'elevation', but equally 'exteriorization'. Experience, as Gadamer saw, will not only mean more than coherence, it will also involve an opening up within a certain alterity, its 'hegemony' always worked out only before and between determinate "rival projects (*rivalisierende Entwürfe*)" [TM:251]—and attesting doubtless thereby to its 'Hobbesian' inheritance. We should not forget that Hobbes (like Bacon) declared the end of knowledge to be power—and their conjunction would overdetermine both in the quest for certainty. We should notice provisionally, however, that having recognized the necessity of such theoretical competitors, when Gadamer initially parses Husserl's failures on intersubjectivity, he does so not in terms of an alter ego but instead in terms of an I and a thou (*Ich und Du*)—an event in which hermeneutics and the problem of tradition receives if not its foundation, then, to use Gadamer's term, its theoretical "analogue" (TM:361).

The logical point, however, in this matrix of exchanges is this: if we are limited to our own finite perspectives, our theoretical 'competitors' may be at least as open as we are to our mistakes—perhaps even to our own pain, as Wittgenstein (and perhaps Benjamin) realized. The iterability of tradition, in short, is not a concept with limited extension, but is openly divided—indeterminately 'pluralized', to speak Derridean, opening upon the other and transformation. Experience, that is, is itself interminably divided, an *Ur-teilung*, as Gadamer imparts, reinstating Hölderlin's account of judgment (TM:251). Nor will its *Erlebnis*—if synthetic and 'a priori' with respect to its content—be a simple 'lived unity'—either simple memory or simple

expectation. Interpretation, that is, will always inevitably involve a heterogeneous synthesis, opened within a divided origin, distanced from tradition
as much as it is bound by it; *logos* is always *dia-logos*, the opening of a certain transcendental indeterminacy, the problem of truth, and the question
of the other.

## 4. The Dis-Possession of Dialogue and the Symbolics of Law

We should be clear about the complexity of this dialogue. Dialogics, after
all, has been neither owned nor controlled by such accounts of hermeneutics. And if in the end we should be prepared to endorse Gadamer's account of dialogue, we will need likewise to measure it against its own
antecedents and competitors, of which there are at least two. Of these Gadamer himself, as has been seen, openly discusses one, but both in fact
have open antecedents in the philosophy of Kant and German Idealism,
and they result in the agonistics represented by relational accounts of dialogue that, as Theunissen has recognized, emerge in the thought of Cohen,
Rosenzweig, Buber, and Levinas—the tradition of *Ich und Du*.[26] The other
'tradition' worth recalling, though probably equally or genealogically a
product of neo-Kantianism, is most prominently at work, as Albrecht Wellmer has recognized, in the dialogics of recent critical theory and its attack
on the philosophy of the subject. Turning briefly to these views reveals the
extent to which both these accounts have open antecedents in Kant's critical systems. On the one hand, both accounts affirm the critical question itself; on the other hand, both affirm the Kantian account of philosophy as
achromatic, that is, dialogic, discursive, and not simply constructive.
Against both of these, however, Gadamer will see himself as attempting
(successfully or not) a via media in ultimately retrieving the classical tradition of Aristotelian friendship.

As Albrecht Wellmer points out in his *Ethics and Dialogue,* the linea-
ments of these polemics can already be seen to emerge from the protocols
of Kant's account of objectivity and, in particular, its articulation of theoretical rationality within the second *Kritik*.[27] The effect of this articulation ultimately results in the distinction between ethics and the moral
law, the latter itself originating from the distinction between procedural
and substantive (for Kant, empirical) accounts of truth. The universal-
izable condition of the categorical imperative, the formal demand for the
iterability of maxims, already opens up the outline of an account of pure
rational dialogue.

Those immediately in Kant's wake nonetheless saw the problem with Kant's formalism, its underdeterminacy or "specious philosophical legitimacy," and hence the return of interpretation which haunts it.[28] And hermeneuts will largely agree then that Wellmer is right in recognizing that the facts of reason will "as a rule . . . in fact be determined by my own, preexisting normative convictions."[29] But they will likewise agree with Wellmer that Habermas's attempt to reckon with the problems that ensue by means of analogy with empirical induction becomes (transcendentally) illusory, "a covert scientistic residue," lacking, in fact, the complexity recognized in the links between concept and intuition, theory and observation, schema and translation—in short, the questions of interpretation confronting the rational.[30] We will need again to acknowledge the complexity in play in the two orders in the account (the empirical and the transcendental, the ontic and the ontological), certainty and truth. While acknowledging the formal requisites of obligation, at the same time we will need to acknowledge what withdraws in this event, granted its theoretical complications. In the demise of transcendental authorities, what Axel Honneth terms 'post-traditional theory' will inevitably deal with the complications affecting modernist issues of formal equality, representation, and transfer: in short, the problem of recognition (*Anerkennung*).[31] Following the departure of transcendental authority, "the logical grammar of basic normative terminology almost inevitably assumes a universalistic significance."[32] And yet such formalistic requisites—even if limited to particular schemata—remain insufficient. As Carnap rightly realized about logical syntax, "in logic there is no morals."[33]

We can note here again Honneth's own recognition that, while Habermasian emphasis on communicative rationality represents a "needed corrective for Marxism," it likewise does so by an exchange which "reduces the rigor" of critical theory.[34] Indeed this reduction is one which can be spelled out precisely in what is lost in its transformation of Hegel's and Adorno's "basic notions of rationality" grounding the rational in experience.[35] Thus, in contrast with Habermas's critique of Hegel, focusing on the monological character of the concept of absolute spirit, Adorno upholds—as even Gadamer did in the ruins of classicism—the cynical truth of Hegel's system. Now this cynicism became directed at the view of the history of humankind's attainment of consciousness as the product of totalitarian reason in order to take into account the historical specificity of the particular, according to the tradition of leftist Hegelianism.[36] Whatever else might be gained in this substitution, it cannot occur *salve veritate*, and without reductionism—precisely as dialogics had recognized from the outset.

The point here is both the achievement in the 'criteriological' issues at stake in those such as Habermas's accounts and the problematic status of their application: both the rational (procedural) demand for 'iterability' and the lingering (substantial) delusion that it might be both necessary and sufficient. The problem is that it remains, to use terms Wellmer too endorses, both logicist and monological.[37] Wellmer's distance from this formalism can be gauged further, in fact, by his assenting to the Derridean claim that iterability involves alteration, that iterability inherently always implies underdeterminacy and the problem of remove—"what we call a single meaning can only be elucidated by recourse to a—real or potential—*plurality* of situations."[38] The history of legitimation becomes equally the history of alterations and transformations—and the history of the rational becomes a history of interpretation, dialogue the schematism of and the venture of the rational.

While classical hermeneuts like Gadamer have not specifically acknowledged this claim, it is the very condition of their own account of legitimation as application. And doubtless, Wellmer's ultimate attempt to deny the Habermasian separation of theoretical, practical, and aesthetical discourse amounts to a certain rapprochement with Gadamer on the issue of rhetoric. In that case, granted the split between procedural requisites and substantial truths, we will indeed have to affirm Kant's own recognition of our fallibility in practical matters. Lacking procedural guarantees of our cognitive competence, as Wellmer himself still quotes Kant, "it is advantageous (to morality) to 'work out our own salvation with *fear and trembling*'."[39] But it will demand equally a rapprochement with nonformalist accounts of dialogics.

As Theunissen (among others) rightly realized, the second theory of dialogical intersubjectivity as reciprocal recognition emerges in Fichte's account of the ethical.[40] While, on the one hand, Kant's commitment to the iterability of law led to an implicit formal dialogics, however, on this second account, it led to the problem of rational difference, alterity, and possible conflict. It would accordingly require, as Rosenzweig saw in relation to Cohen's neo-Kantianism, an overcoming of constitution for correlation, and the discovery of a (communal) factuality antecedent to constitutive factuality.[41] As Gadamer too put it, here the thou is not an object but a relation (TM:358). The dialectics of recognition (or epistemic constitution) extrinsically has no holds barred. It is potentially a Hobbesian fight to the death, which, Gadamer claimed, could be overcome only by confession and forgiveness (TM:343). If, as Honneth realized, Hegel was early on 'tempted' by Hölderlin's account of love, it was true too, as has been seen, that he never quite extricated himself from his reliance on the algorithmic of tragedy—to use Gadamer's term, the presupposition that the antinomies of knowledge might extrinsically be resolved.[42] The point is that what Hegel early on called 'the perception of recognition' will require not simply external procedure but internal transformation and (reflective) judgment: hence the way of "the between" now, to cite Buber.[43]

A certain impasse thus seemingly arises in the contexts of theory between the logical grammar of norms, the semantics of persons, and the question of practice. Moreover, this impasse may indeed be present in single texts. While, as Theunissen suggests, the archive of contemporary dialogics in the tradition of Rosenzweig, Buber, Marcel, and Levinas finds its antecedents in Fichte's *Science of Ethics,* Fichte's ethics itself contains the contradiction of both forms. Fichte remains committed both to the '*Du*' that limits conscience and the constitutive foundations of the '*Ich*', both the iterability of truth and its epistemic origins. The paradox is perhaps the paradox of all transcendentalism—as Husserl too himself would ultimately affirm.[44] If "reciprocal communication" is demanded, insofar as "the more extended this intercommunication is, the more does truth (objectively considered) gain, and I likewise," Fichte from the outset acknowledged that "from the standpoint of transcendental consciousness . . . it is quite possible that philosophizing individuals do not agree on a single point."[45] While the former may be a transcendental condition of truth claims, the latter is a possibility that theorists of the rationality of communication too often forget—the forgetfulness that Gadamer (after Hegel) had seen as the potential danger and transcendental illusions of univocal judgement. Husserl's attempts, even in the later works, to articulate the rational traditions underlying science in terms of a "community of empathy and of language" would thus fall short: Husserl was never sufficiently cognizant either of the dangers awaiting the idols of communicative purity nor of the plurality of narratives that underwrote the rational.[46] And it is just here that the motivation for the opening to the other in hermeneutics arose.

The paradox returns nonetheless. Dialogue without regard to criterion, dialogue without 'constitution' (indeed epistemic or political), in default of transcendental authority, verges upon non-sense. The appeal to the 'sign' before the sign, the face, or the ineffability of Being threatens equally to lose sight of the underdeterminacy and withdrawal of substantial truths, the problem of 'assertibility'. Here again, as Wellmer realizes, we lack transcendental authorities.

Now here too Gadamer's interface is in fact complex. *Truth and Method* recognizes that the immediacy of the I-thou relation will not suffice: "[t]he thou is not something about which one speaks but that to which one speaks" (TM:536). Knowing that discourse, silent or otherwise, takes place before the other, knowing that Dasein is always *Mitsein,* does not solve the problem of the complexity of their 'between', nor does it explain the possibility of the "reciprocal translations" of the other's position—nor finally does it simply entail the venture toward "recognizing the value of the alien" of hermeneutics (TM:387). In a telling gloss on Levinas, Gadamer has recently reaffirmed the problem: "The 'completely Other' of God, the otherness of the others, neighbors, that other of nature enclosed in itself—they all do not surrender to our 'savoir'" (EPH:210). But once more it will be necessary to unpack the ramifications of this encounter.

In a 1929 review of Löwith, Gadamer had already insisted that dialogue could not simply be viewed as communication, as the transference and agreement of propositions. Nor, however, will the question of rationality be solved by the summons of the thou; it will, as has been seen, instead be opened up by it. As Gadamer realized, in a phrase whose dialect sounds closer to Frankfurt than to Freiburg, such appeals still lack "the objective communicative nature of the state and society" (TM:536). In making this claim, *Truth and Method* concurred with Leo Strauss (but also Heidegger) that the I-thou cannot by itself found the bond of the *polis.*[47] In this regard "[t]he appeal to immediacy—whether of bodily nature, or the Thou making claims on us, or the impenetrable factualness of historical accident, or the reality of the relations of production—has always been self-refuting, in that it is not itself an immediate relation but a reflective activity" (TM:344). The appeal to the immediacy of such friendship, if necessary, being inextricably bound to prejudice, does not guarantee justice: there is after all friendship among thieves. More will need to be said. And this was exactly the force of Strauss's response to Kojève's hope that mutual recognition or friendship might solve the problem of underdeterminacy—the Hegelian problem of subjective certainty—by means of an objective spirit whose consensus might form the biconditional of truth.[48] But no more than truth just *is* certainty (nor the modern construction 'objectivity' for that matter) can its recognition be limited to any ontic or empirical community.

If such appeals are to be made, we will need an extended form of friendship—perhaps what Aristotle calls the friendship of the citizen (NE:1171a), or what Kant called the cosmopolitan extensions of common sense, a matter that concerns a "universal communicability" devoid of ultimately determinable concepts and which is still the opening of "a universal standpoint."[49] The problem that accompanies this 'opening', however, is both intractable and unavoidable for dialogue. As Theunissen realized, for all their fecundity, dialogical 'betweens'—like reflective judgments in general—neither simply replace nor solve issues of transcendental constitution and determination.[50] And yet, as has also been seen, the reflective stronghold of transcendental constitution remains (monologically) insufficient, technically (or logically) incapable of grasping the question of what escapes determinability in its 'strangeness': a question of acknowledging the presence of the stranger. Even epistemologically, however, it will be a question of articulating the adumbration of dialogue in its specificity and the reversal (*Umkehrung*) that "belongs to these forms of inner self-enlightenment and to the intersubjective representation of human experience" (TM:562). It is in this extension that Gadamer's hermeneutics emerges as dia-logics, not simply as the co-presence of I and thou, but equally as the possible venture of shared tradition and practices—in Aristotle's language, shared activities—thus filling out the complexity of the hermeneutic event.[51] Such an extension will be complex for reasons now evident. The rationality in question will require, as Gadamer puts it, that understanding likewise articulate anew the 'positive' relation between understanding and life. The latter, moreover, will involve precisely the dialogical event in which Dasein opens itself to the new, to transformation and to the other:

> Belonging together always means being able to listen to one another. When two people understand each other, this does not mean that one person "understands" the other. Similarly, "to hear and obey someone" [*auf jemanden hören*] does not mean simply that we do blindly what the other desires. We call such a person slavish (*hörig*). Openness to the other, then involves recognizing that I myself must accept some things that are against me, even though no one else forces me to do so. (TM:361)

To authentically hear the other is neither simply to come to common agreement, to re-iterability, or even to consensus. Moreover, the leap ahead (*Vorausspringen*) undertaken by all interpretation in the encounter of the 'entity', which "discloses it for the first time" remains—even if transcendentally (theoretically) necessary—still, taken by itself, a 'monological' event. In all this, as Levinas has said, the "depths semantics" of I and thou will be inseparable from the issues of 'heteronomy', transcendence, dis-association.[52] And yet neither, of course, can this dis-association simply imply slavishly acceding to the other's claim upon me. As modernists rightly realized in the end, even the account of virtue itself remains an interpretation and cannot go critically unlimited.[53] Here even 'Levinasian' claims concerning an obligation beyond the vagaries of theory may in the end still suffer, from not only Sartrean protocols but Hobbesian blinders—resulting from lingering (false) antinomies between 'theory' and 'ethics', desire and recognition, self and other, egoism and respect, power as violence and knowledge as calculation. Yet if as Gadamer put it (as Heidegger, explicitly in any case, did not), Dasein's *perfectio* depends on friendship—if, that is, "to participate with the other and to be a part of the other is the most and the best that we can strive for and accomplish" [EPH:235]—it remains true too that the question of Dasein's singularity remains unsurpassable. And Gadamer's hermeneutics doubtless sought to capture both: both, that is, the critical vagaries (and requisites) of theory and the unsurpassable character of Dasein's singularity.

In further confronting the problem of legitimation, aptly granted his own Aristotelian commitments, and moving from dialogical 'subjectivity' to 'objectivity', Gadamer has concentrated on the hermeneutic relevance of Aristotle and the natural law tradition. Specifically—and openly in relation to Leo Strauss—in this appropriation Gadamer distinguishes Aristotle and the 'natural-law tradition':[54] "Aristotle's position on the problem of *natural law* is highly subtle and certainly not to be equated with the later natural-law tradition" (TM:318; Gadamer's emphasis). Unlike the later tradition, Gadamer claims that the distinction he has in mind can be grasped neither simply by the distinctions between the demonstrable and the indemonstrable, nor simply the changeable and the unchangeable, the promulgated and the Absolute. Instead, he claims, in explicating *Nicomachean Ethics* (V.10), at stake is an interplay between nature and interpretation, experience and judgment, that is identical with hermeneutics itself:

> The true profundity of his insight has been missed. Certainly he accepts the idea of an absolutely unchangeable law, but he limits it explicitly to the gods and says that among men not only statutory but also natural law is changeable. For Aristotle, this changeability is wholly compatible with the fact that it is "natural" law. The sense of this assertion seems to me to be the following; some laws are entirely a matter of agreement (e.g., traffic regulations), but there are also things that do not admit of regulation by mere human convention because the "nature of the thing" constantly asserts itself. Thus it is quite legitimate to call such things "natural law." In that the nature of the thing still allows some room for play, natural law is still changeable. (TM:319)

This *Spiel* has of course been at stake from the outset of *Truth and Method*, the play between beings and Being, the self and the other, the interpreter and the text, I and thou, and so on. Here he articulates the relation of determinacy between law and things appealing specifically to Aristotle's own examples. While the right hand may be stronger than the left, the latter through training can become as strong as the right. Second, one and the same measure always proves smaller when we buy wine in it than when we sell it. Here, however, "Aristotle is not saying that people in the wine trade are constantly trying to trick their customers, but rather that this behavior corresponds to the area of free play permitted within the set limits of what is right." If the best state is everywhere one and the same, it is not the same state that is the 'same' but justice: and justice in this similarity is so in different ways than the case in which "fire burns everywhere in the same way whether in Greece or in Persia" (TM:319–20).

Now the point to all this, Gadamer claims, is that the *pros hen* which underlies 'natural law' also has an equivocal function. That is, far from it being restricted to the formulation of the unchangeable, its function is to refute the changeable. "For Aristotle the idea of natural law has only a critical function. No dogmatic use can be made of it—i.e., we cannot invest particular laws with the dignity and inviolability of natural law" (TM:320). On Gadamer's reading, that is, appeals to natural law do not univocally characterize or determine things *simpliciter;* instead things by their nature form the limit of the underdeterminacy of such interpretive appeals.

What is striking here, however, is the problem of critique itself. While negative critique is possible on this view, what is *precluded* is formal or simple prescription—except of course in accord with the model which underlies such appeals, namely, hermeneutic prescription in an 'analogical' fashion. And consequently, prescriptions will be equivocally dangerous when they conflict about justice. While interpretations legitimately bind together words and things, dogmatism here amounts to the claims that they do so independently of the *Spielraum* in which they arise. 'Dogmatism', that is, consists in univocal claims to determinacy beyond interpretation—and 'critique'. On this view, such critique is a matter of the articulation of things 'otherwise' than the already interpreted—in accordance with the things themselves. To speak phenomenologically, then, the positive experience of the 'cancellation' of interpretation provides an experience that acknowledges both the indeterminate plurality (the *pros hen*) in the ancient account of the unicity of truth while acknowledging the requisites of rational critique.

Gadamer's distance from classical claims concerning the objectivity of natural law is obvious, even 'classical' phenomenological claims. Adolf Reinach's 1913 work, *Über die apriorischen Grundlagen des bürgerlichen Rechts,* a work Husserl had described as a masterpiece in the field, had sought to show that there are a priori truths in this area "in exactly the same sense in which primitive arithmetical or logical axioms are a priori."[55] Thus such concepts as 'claim', 'liability', 'property', and 'transfer' are all held to have meanings that might be fixed a priori. Without simply denying the formal character of law—a matter to which we shall return—Gadamer refuses the paradigm of fixed *mathesis universalis* at this level, emphasizing the interpretive event which of necessity underlies such terms. Again, this is not to speak of the simple and equivocal or arbitrary character of interpretations, nor even simply to deny that such things are univocally fixed by the nature of things. Indeed Gadamer can still claim regarding this *pros hen* as he has again recently, now in a quite modern gloss which wears its 'Hobbesian' conscience on its sleeve.

> The "nature" of humans does not change. Abuse of power is the original prob-
> lem of human coexistence and the complete prevention of this abuse is possible
> only in utopia. (EPH:218)

Far from our claims regarding the human being dissolved thereby, such claims must be recognized to involve a complex (and threatened) weaving of univocity and equivocity, of identity and difference in interpretation. And yet at the same time this recognition likewise authorizes the possibility that "despite all the variety of moral ideas in the most different times and peoples, in this sphere there is still something like the nature of the thing" (TM:320). But while it precludes the possibility of a univocally unchangeable, positive, and unchallengable stipulation, it reaffirms the possibility of our warranted appeals to justice.

Here again, however, it may seem that we simply encounter the (metaphysical) echo of Marcus Aurelius's Stoic affirmation of the unity of reason, nature, and community—that unity through which "we are especially for one another."[56] Gadamer's respect for the dialectic of assertion seems once more both to honor the faculty of opinion and to reinstate Marcus's two rules regarding it: first, "to do only what the reason of your legislating faculty suggests," and second, "to change your opinion, whenever anyone at hand sets you right and unsettles you in an opinion."[57] Once more, however, we will need to mark the trace of the withdrawal in which its venture occurs—indeed the same withdrawal out of which all Stoicism emerged. It is not accidental that Heidegger would recur to Seneca for the account of care, or Gadamer to Marcus Aurelius for that of community and the remnants of natural law, raising their opponents' ire against Stoic unities that underlie dialogue—as 'against dialogue' as they were themselves "against method."[58] And yet, 'remnants' is the point: as Pierre Hadot has noted, it is "the uncertainty of care" that is the origin of Stoic virtue.[59] Seneca already writes of humans whose essence occurs in the withdrawal of nature, and Marcus Aurelius is plagued by the necessities which plague all Stoicism; divided between *chaos* and providence, his defense of community is already undertaken under the failure of traditionality itself: "Consider how many have already lived in mutual enmity, suspicion, hatred, and conflict, and now lie dead, reduced to ashes; and be quiet at last."[60] Nor would it be accidental that Walter Benjamin would join them precisely at this point, claiming too that, like the notion of tradition itself, the notion of allegory would require a further consciousness of human default that no simple or substantive commitment to nature could provide (or resolve).[61] Hence, again Benjamin claimed, the Greeks would know neither fragment nor allegory, nor melancholy—even in tragedy. Instead, divided between *chaos* and community, here is precisely where 'hermeneutics' would begin, in the distance between mortals and gods, in the frailty (but surely not the dissolution) of all theory, precisely in the default of the immanences of *theoria* itself. The affirmation of the other can occur, not simply by recourse to the foundations of nature, mutual self-consciousness, recognition, or community, but in the venture of their possibility—precisely as the encounter which occurs between *chaos* and community.

The failure Heidegger encountered in the anonymity of *das Man* is precisely to have lost the agency (*das Meiste*) or the opening in this event. Instead it dissolves the difference of community in a reification in which "everyone is the other and no one is himself [*Jeder ist der Andere und keiner er selbst*]" (BT:165). The point is that the 'we' of Dasein neither dissolves nor absolves its 'I' or its 'you'. To hear the other is to be 'summoned', but *not* to what can make demands because he or she is '*other*' (hence the Hobbesian inversion) but because of all that opens up in the call: ethically, so that we might heed the obligation to assist, but equally, epistemically, namely, the opening of a corrigibility concerning all that arises between us in our 'hold' upon Being. And it is just in this sense that we can begin to accommodate the later Heidegger's own gloss on dialogue, not as the silence before language, but the silence of language and Being itself. To think that it occurs without dialogue—and even conversation—would be to remain Hobbesian about both naming and friendship, and it would be to forget what Heidegger called "the promise which dedicates itself to the nature of saying" (DL:54).

## 5. The Remnants of Friendship

It is just here in fact that Gadamer's recourse to Aristotle's important meditation on friendship (*philia*) in practical wisdom (*phronēsis*) becomes critical, precisely, that is, "in the indeterminate position of the concept of
friendship between the doctrine of virtue and of the good" (TM:536).
'Friendship', thus construed, becomes the articuleme of the 'between' of Being and logos, mediated by institution, by language, the logic of question
and answer, and tradition—all in an attempt to circumvent the antinomies
between assertion and alterity, silence and projection: in short to open the
event of dialogue.[62] In this positivity, beyond the leveling of civil society, in
the process of conversation, the other would be reduced neither to the an-
tagonist, nor to the mutual investigator—not the reiterative extension of
my truth, my presuppositions, but rather, to use terms from Bacon's essay
on friendship, to "faithful council."[63] Here, as Kant realized—already aware
perhaps that the practices had been dispersed—friendship is not simply
identity of thought, but perhaps better a matter of difference.[64]

As becomes evident throughout, Gadamer wants to maintain that "a *polis*
is always grounded in an ethos—I remain an Aristotelian" (EPH:130; Gadamer's emphasis). Nonetheless, the attempt to acknowledge "the social realities
into which we grow through upbringing and education" equally acknowledges their implicitly dialogical standpoint—and implicitly the opening of
the horizons of human dwelling—implicitly (but always only implicitly)
the demand for an extended or cosmo-politan standpoint. Like truth, the
question of friendship equally involves the recognition of the between. And
experience in the opening of the between becomes the outline of the universal beyond classical immanence. It is just in this sense that the classical remains uncannily both "unattainable and present"—divided between self
and other, the ontic and the ontological (TM:289). Hermeneutics will again
be precisely the articulation of this 'between'.

The importance of friendship had already, albeit briefly, culminated
*Truth and Method's* discussion of the hermeneutic relevance of Aristotle—
not only in its obvious retrieval of understanding (*sunesis* [*das Verständnis*])
emphasizing the particular and application, but equally in the retrieval of
considerateness (*gnome*) and consideration or sympathetic understanding
(*syngnome*; *Einsicht und Nachsicht*).[65] Such 'sympathy' indeed remained
problematic for modern accounts of reflection and formed something of a
hemorrhage within transcendental phenomenology—as authors such as
Husserl, Stein, Scheler, Sartre, and Levinas testify. This rupture doubtless

itself attested to a Hobbesian inheritance, as classicists like Strauss insist. And, Gadamer too was not simply unaware of these epistemic protocols and the problem of the difference it entails even for sympathetic judgment.

In the first place, in accord with this difference, and invoking the Hobbesian terms (i.e., those of transfer and transposition) that now accompany this archive, Gadamer claims, "Someone's sympathetic understanding is praised, of course, when in order to judge he transposes himself fully into the concrete situation of the person who has to act" (TM:323).[66] But against Hobbes, for Gadamer in *Truth and Method* this means that, in accord with sympathetic judgment, "the person who is understanding does not know and judge as one who stands apart and unaffected, but rather he thinks along with the other from the perspective of a specific bond of belonging, as if he too were affected" (TM:323). Such being bound-together—if only by the logic of the subjunctive, the *als ob*—is for Gadamer a being bound-together in friendship. Moreover, it requires at the very least the goodwill, which Aristotle identifies at the origin of friendship (NE:1167a), and which Kant would refigure through the objective requisites of practical reason. It is worth recalling in this connection that if Kant was never sure whether the goodwill ever existed in its purity, he was sure that moral friendship did: "This (purely moral) friendship is no mere ideal, but (like the black swan) actually exists now and then in its perfection."[67]

Although Aristotle's protocol becomes the model for hermeneutics, as has equally become evident, we will need to keep in mind the complications that govern this 'retrieval'. Aristotle's account in the *Ethics,* in accord with the habituated wisdom of the *phronemos,* immediately warns us to respect the "inheritance of the years" and, consequently, the person who has experience in these matters (NE:1143b), while Gadamer claims that it is a characteristic of the experienced and of human flourishing to be open for more experience—and thereby a certain forgetfulness of the past, an opening *to* experience (TM:355), as he puts it in his gloss on Hegel. And this gloss is not accidental. Gadamer's account of such openness—as well as of friendship in general—remains in this regard formulated in thoroughly modern (indeed post-Kantian) terms, refusing to simply reject the dialogical relation between the I and the thou. That is, the problem of friendship will again be linked immediately by him to the problem of *recognition* and the dialectic of experience—consequently as much to Hegel as to Aristotle, a link poised to forge a passage between the ancients and the moderns. Although Aristotle had understood that friendship involved the awareness of reciprocal goodwill, he had not been concerned with the modernist issue of its recognition. Indeed, it might well be thought that Gadamer suggests, in accord with good hermeneutic claims regarding understanding the author better than she understands herself, we can claim of Aristotle "that he could not understand himself in the way that we understand him" (TM:536)—in just this sense, perhaps, that, beyond simple appeals to nature or universal reason, *we* understand the middle realm of friendship with respect to virtue, historical practice, and the Good as what "comes after" modernity.

The importance of this understanding of friendship becomes perhaps even more prominent in this regard in Gadamer's more recent writings—and from this vantage point forms something of a culmination to the writing of *Truth and Method* itself.[68] Now wisdom itself, as he puts it, must be seen "as shared perception, shared knowledge, shared life and shared being [*Mitsein*]," a certain *Mit-Struktur* that is given along with the opening of every world (*die mit aller Weltoffenheit mitgegeben ist*).[69] However, it must be equally insisted, as has become evident, that this transcendental dyad or *Mit-Struktur* is equally the removal of every world as simple substantialized identity, as indeterminately erupting in this 'between'. We will need then to think Gadamer's later pronouncements as of a piece—both those which emphasize the splitting of the 'One' and those which trace the 'reconciliation' of friendship.

It will be equally incumbent then to recognize that what complicates this retrieval is that it is irretrievably a modern venture, its retrieval, not simply a 'repetition'. Hermeneutics always involves a certain remove from origins, a certain decline in traditional determinacy: all that provokes the need, that is, for interpretation—and all that threatens hermeneutics from within. The 'sympathy' operative within hermeneutics operates, that is, always perilously under what Nietzsche called the belief in truth, or to invoke the convertibility of the transcendentals, the belief in the Good. Indeed, Gadamer's descriptions follow this strategy almost deliberately to the point of illusion—almost to the point where it is hard to see, granted its presumption of truth, if one could ever simply say that the *interpretans* is false except on its own terms. The 1984 paper "The Hermeneutics of Suspicion" admits as much in adjudicating between the hermeneutics of integrity and the hermeneutics of suspicion inaugurated by Nietzsche: "I see no way of reconciling the two."[70] And here it is worth noting that if Gadamer had invoked the beneficence of Plato's dyad, so, as Lacan notes, did Freud, precisely in acknowledging its negativity and illusion (Ecrits:12). Specifically, rather than a dialogue based on *Einfüllung*, Lacan returns again to the social ontology of Hegel's master and slave, now as a dialogue of pretense and *méconnaissance*. Beyond that, as has become evident, it is Hobbes's truth that is proclaimed by Hegel—and perhaps even a 'truth' be-

yond that, since the step at stake in the constitution of the Freudian subject, beyond egoism and self-interest or 'Hobbesian' liberty, is a confrontation of simple aggressivity. In this regard what Lacan insists on is an
event which has contested philosophy and its dialogues since its origins—
or at least, as he points out, since Thrasymachus's "stormy exit at the beginning of the *Republic.*" We may need, in this regard, to confront the uncomfortable rapprochement that awaits Gadamer's gloss on *Erfahrung* "as
openness to experience" by invoking Lacan's gloss on dialogue as "the experience constituted between two subjects": the psychoanalyst relies on a
"blind intentionality that has no other purpose than to free [the patient] from
an illness or an ignorance whose very limits he is unaware of" (Ecrits:12).
Doubtless such blindness affects the illusions of beneficence itself, even
the charity of interpretation. In this light it is not at all surprising to see the
hermeneut's *cura* and *caritas* again confronted by Lacan with Augustine's
*cupiditas,* with its primal "envenomed stare," precisely as a truth which
"foreshadowed psychoanalysis" (Ecrits:20). If true 'friendship' may be a
significant condition for the encounter with truth, we still lack its rational
demonstration: we will lack its criteria and we will lack its method—at
stake, as Kant realized, *pace* Hobbes's concern, is always more a 'manner'
than a 'method'.[71] The extension of application or recognition will equally
force us to grapple with the violence of the encounter.

While Gadamer is right—as was Aristotle—to connect the opening of
experience of the other with the formation of self—and right also, for reasons now more fully evident to connect the flourishing of humans with
such openness (TM:355)—it will preclude, as has been seen, a simple "return to self." The account, consequently, diverges from Aristotle's account
of self-knowledge, a denial both of self mastery and perfect application (or
perfect reconciliation)—without substituting the merely expedient for it
(TM:322). Here the problem of the self and the question of the Good will
truly remain hermeneutic: as Ricoeur realized, a moving back and forth between current practices and "far off ideals."[72] We will deliberate not only
about the means but the ends.

Unlike with Aristotle, for whom the virtue of friendship involved shared
activities whose criteria were (traditionally) determinate and, consequently,
a matter of 'like-mindedness', the hermeneutics of friendship will operate by
a certain deficiency—to speak Sartrean, a dialogue of "reciprocal inadequacies"—one which is exactly the need for invention and justification and
which will require the so called 'conflict of interpretation' precisely for the
latter's fecundity in the venture of the true. Indeed if the other, to invoke the
figure appealed to from Aristotle to Lacan, is the "mirror image of myself,"

it is true too, to invoke the figure on which Sartre depended, that "the trouble is I don't see my own face."[73] To borrow the Kantian (transcendental) figure at stake, the result will be a *Mit-Struktur* composed of "incongruent counterparts," one in which the idealist's 'congruence' will be out of the question; the idealist's I = I is precisely precluded. As George Herbert Mead, a figure to whom Habermas also appealed against classical subjectivism, likewise affirmed, "We talk to ourselves, but we do not see ourselves."[74] And yet here too it remains a complicated event. If consequently "the import of what we say is the same to ourselves as it is to others,"[75] it sets off a complex dialectic of socialization and rationalization dividing once more self and society (or the 'I' and the 'me' as both Sartre and Mead realized) repeating once more the splitting of the Hegelian self emphasized by Idealists to psychoanalysts in its wake. Even Lacan, however, still appealed in this regard to "a discrete fraternity" and "a task for which we are always too inadequate" (Ecrits:29).

The "logic of 'friendship'" would then appear to be irrevocably divided between identity and difference—perhaps even more archaically, once more between ancient metaphysical antinomies: Empedocles' attempt to articulate friendship by means of the affinities which underlie the Cosmos and Heraclitus's attempts to found friendship on difference. Aristotle himself, at the outset of the *Ethics,* sought to delineate the specificity—and the identity—of friendship between this metaphysical opposition founded on identity and difference. In accord with the 'middle realm' or the 'between' in which humans dwell, Aristotle founded the latter both on shared practice and the '*pros hen*' of virtue—knowing full well that the Good itself ultimately escaped such ontic instantiation.[76] Hobbes would not allow it to be so easy, dividing the issue again between the question of Being and the question of certainty, ultimately reducing the former to the latter and making it once more parasitic on the demonstrations of nature. The effect of such demands, in discarding the appearances, would shatter the ordinary narratives, discarding the heterogeneous practices that had made friendship itself possible. Hence emerges the voluntarism which underlies the contract—always threatened by the desire for power that accompanies the need for certainty and sovereign judgment. The sharing of wisdom, the dialogue of truth, would now be fragmentary—as much Schlegel as Socrates, as Gadamer too relented.[77]

This is not to say that Aristotle's appeal to shared activities must now simply be left behind. Indeed, it is just the indeterminate status, the fragility of friendship and virtue with respect to the Good, that has attracted Gadamer's retrieval of Aristotle from the outset—the division tacitly acknowledged thereby between the ontic and the ontological and the analogical fragments the account of friendship had ventured. It is just this, moreover, that classical readings of Aristotle like Strauss's, Gadamer claimed, had missed.[78] The appeal to the Good will be neither without interpretation nor without the need for dialogue—nor will the appeal to dialogue guarantee its resolution.

Even Buber, in his demurral from monologics ultimately acknowledged as much, and recognized too, at his best, this 'Aristotelian' moment in articulating the drift and whither of dialogue in his 1929 work *Dialogue*.

> Whither? Into nothing exalted, heroic or holy, into no Either and no Or, only into this tiny strictness and grace of every day [*nur in diese Strenge und Gnade des Alltags*], where I have to do with just the same "reality" and with whose duty and business I am taken up in such a way, glance to glance, look to look, word to word, that I experience it as reached to me and myself to it, it as spoken to me and myself to it. And now, in all the clanking of routine that I called my reality, there appears to me, homely and glorious, the effective reality, creaturely and given to me in trust and responsibility. We do not find meaning lying in things nor do we put it into things, but between us and things it can happen.[79]

But what ultimately is to be made of such a 'between'? First, the 'between' in question is not simply the between of looks and glances, or I's and thous, but likewise the between of words and things: the shared activities of the everyday, which, homely and pedestrian as it is, is likewise whatever indeterminately and uncannily remains of the 'glorious'. We can now perhaps further characterize this 'between' for what it is, articulated by means of the *factum* of the everyday. It is again, after all, precisely what *Truth and Method* understood as the (analogical) relation of understanding and life (TM:263f.). This 'it can happen'—echoing Heidegger's own 'and you can' of the hermeneutic circle—is doubtless complex. It involves not simply coherence but encounter and event—and not simply a face-to-face, but a belonging together based on shared venture and exchange of activities, practices, legitimation, inventions, interpretations. It is just in this respect, as we have seen, that Gadamer can claim that "[t]he true locus of hermeneutics is this in-between [*In diesem Zwischen ist der wahre Ort der Hermeneutik*]" (TM: 295). If Dasein as 'care' too exists as this 'between', it is as Heidegger recognized (disclosing its Augustinian transformation originally linked with *caritas*) as both concern (*Besorge*) for beings and solicitude (*Fürsorge*) for others, all of which depend, as has become evident, on interpretation and the fragmented remainder of hermeneutics.

We should likewise then note, though provisionally, the proximity of this 'between' to the later Heidegger's discussion of the event of the *polis*, where we find again the complex exchange between Being and beings, the polarities between the utopian and the polis, the ordinary and the extraordinary. But we do so provisionally, keeping in mind, as Castoriadis has likewise insisted, that we recall—as Heidegger did not—that the Athenians were responsible for not only the birth of tragedy but also the birth of democracy— that both were in fact narratives of the 'middle realm', that realm in which virtue became fragile, ventured, and at risk.[80] Nor finally should we forget that this birth likewise occurred, as Hecataeus, Herodotus, and Thucydides all attested, not without a certain skepticism of tradition—that in this regard, the figures of democracy, tragedy, and *historia* are that which the Athenians and the moderns share in common. It is then a question indeed of thinking the status of this between and the *Mit-Struktur* that is its remainder and the 'belonging together' that may foster 'hermeneutics' in its wake.

Another name for this 'between' is friendship. And, justice, Derrideans have similarly stated, is another name for deconstruction.[81] To paraphrase Aristotle, then, it might be replied that, if you *have* friendship you do not need deconstruction, but if you *have* deconstruction you still need friendship, hermeneutics (NE:1155a). The Derridean gloss on friendship must force the reply "perhaps"—'but not the friendship of identity, of presence, and *ousia*, but of difference. Against Aristotle, we still need Nietzsche: against the constancies of Aristotelean friendship, we must still acknowledge our enemies'. The point, as has become evident, is that we never simply possess either.[82] Accordingly we can trace the illusions of both as ultimate determinations of *co-mmunio*. If the 'belonging together' that underlies Aristotle's ancient definition of 'community' now seems suspiciously like 'shared property' in posttraditionary settings, and the Stoic bonds of law, nature, and community are irrevocably disrupted, then demands for submission to the thou seem no less so.

Heidegger's Hobbesian glosses, consequently, should not be forgotten: "Into primordial Being-with-one-another idle talk first slips itself in between (*zwischen das ursprüngliche Miteinandersein schiebt sich zunächst das Gerede*)" (BT:219). Moreover, it is precisely here that the problem of recognition becomes explicitly acknowledged in Heidegger's critique of classical phenomenologies of empathy: the "hermeneutic of empathy" emerges only "from the unsociability of the dominant modes of Being-with" (BT:162–63). Nor should we forget the effect of Derrida's critical descant in its wake: "Oh, my friend, there is no friend."[83] All 'friendship' remains a venture always at risk, trading upon the risks and the illusion (the paralogy) of analogical extension and reflective idea. Thus, as even Gadamer admitted, "no one wants to assert that the romantic image of friendship and a general love of one's neighbor are the supporting bases for either the ancient polis or the modern technocratic metropolis" (EPH:219). As Aristotle put it—already mindful of the Straussian reproach—"though we love both the truth and our friends, piety requires us to honor the truth first" (NE:1096a).

What Gadamer did claim was that these forms of friendship remain "important presuppositions for solving the modern world's problems"—precisely, as has been seen, in articulating the positive remnants (both epistemic and practical) in the passage between the ancients and the moderns, the positivity of interpretation—to use Lefort's term—in "the dissolution of the markers of certainty." The problem that "re-interpretation of the political" now inaugurates, as Lefort likewise realized, belongs to a social history in which people "experience a fundamental indeterminacy at the basis of power, law, and at every level of social life."[84] It is this indeterminacy, beyond either sacred or metaphysical immanence, that underwrites both the virtues of interpretation and democracy—that *ethos* that has been, as Aristotle already put it, deprived of a master (NE:1161a).

Tradition exists, to use Gadamer's terms, only in this between, and specifically, only in the multifariousness (*Vielfachheit*) of its voices (*Stimmen*) (TM:284). It is then, to use Bakhtin's term, a "polyphonic" event. Indeed Bakhtin had similarly stressed its dialogical status, in stressing once again the breakup of idealistic philosophy, the plurality, the infinity, and even the 'carnivalesque' character of interpretation—over against the ideology of philosophical modernism and "its cult of unified and exclusive reason."[85] We would again require a narrative of tradition beyond the genre of the epic and its virtues. But this 'beyond' would be ambiguous, its fragmentation as much descriptive as prescriptive, as much a promise as the absence of transcendence it indicates may be mourned.

## 6. Polylogue: Beyond 'the Paradise of Decoreous Idealism'

The dialogue in question will be equally complex then, as recent accounts on all sides have affirmed. As Blanchot has put it (once more in rejecting 'dialogism' in general), it will again need to be subtracted from "the paradise of decoreous idealism," confronted with the interruption of totality which all conversation entails—always irreducibly a *polylogue*, to use Kristeva's term.[86] Moreover, our accounts of dialogical exchange must acknowledge both the requisites of the rational and the ambiguities that accompany their entailments. As Charles Taylor has aptly noted, the relation at stake in this encounter will be problematic when subsumed beneath the modern gloss on equality. If, as Rousseau for example seems to have thought, xRy is compatible with a free society only when x = y, the margin to recognize difference is very small.[87] But, as obvious as it may seem, we should not in fact reject either dialogism or equality because of the complexity. Although Aristotle himself had acknowledged that "friendship is said to be equality" (NE:1157b), the 'equality' in question was anything but 'formal', but instead remained one internally and 'analogically' differentiated—an equality differentiated, that is, always with respect to the Good itself. The dangers are equally blatant then: such differences were precisely those that furnished the 'justifications' for Aristotle's most blatant inequalities: the 'friendship' of 'master' and 'slave' and 'man' and 'woman'—'friendship' always underwritten by the categories of the superior and the inferior. Better doubtless is the Stoics' demurral: "Be neither the master nor the slave of another."[88] But it is the post-Kantian dialectics of recognition that allow us to think beyond such failings and precisely, in this regard, what the 'modern' discourse on friendship adds to the ancient.

To think 'beyond' does not mean to think 'without': the problem of Being will not simply dissolve the problem of certainty, any more than the step beyond theory can dissolve all theoretical constraints. To goodwill we shall need to add the venture of reciprocity—precisely in order to avoid substituting one violence for another, as modernists always realized. Postmodern critiques of reciprocity, on the other hand, too often confuse equity (*epieikeia*) with simply matters of distributive justice, confusing (as did Hobbes) the venture of reciprocity with the calculations of contract, exchange, and debt. Both moves, after all—both the denial of the *Seinsfrage* and the denial of the transcendence of the Good—were at stake in Hobbes's reduction of the copula to mathematical equity and reason to its accounting ledger.[89] It is just in this sense, that, beyond the syntactics of such 'equality', we will indeed need to be open to the semantics of difference, a semantics to which Bakhtin's (Rabelaisian) interpretation of modernity was closer, in claiming that the novel requires the openness of the everyday, and which Gadamer, as has been seen, connected with the flourishing of being human (TM:355). The result, again, is not a "return to self" but to use Bakhtin's term, a reciprocal dialogue that is semantically "open and unresolvable": as much the ruin of the 'poetics' of immanence as of its canonical 'legalistics'.[90] To demand the difference of reciprocity is by no means to deny either the other or alterity. This was, after all, just Aristotle's demand, that *philoi* wish the good for the other's own sake (NE:1155b)—indeed that such persons are friends most of all, for they have this attitude because of the friend himself" (NE:1156b). Before this *pros hen*, consequently, all other forms of friendship would remain deficient and analogous (NE:1157a). And, surely it would re-occur even in Kant's critical refiguration of goodwill, which acknowledges the other as an end in itself, both retrieving the Stoic love of community while anticipating the problem and the task of recognition—a retrieval thus fragmented, as was the concept of humanity itself in Kant, between "the universal feeling of sympathy, and the ability to engage universally in inti-mate communication."[91]

We need, then, not only respect for the other but the acknowledgment of difference: hence the task of recognition. But not simply this either. For *pace* many contemporary accounts that emerge from this new archive of en-lightenment regarding difference, we will likewise still need even more than this. We need, after all, precisely in acknowledging the complex rela-tions that obtain between identity and difference, a *Mit-Struktur* that flour-ishes in preserving difference, a difference as dia-logical, a 'one', again, which is always indeterminately two (*ahoristos dyas*)—and thereby perhaps the venture of friendship itself.

Against the failures articulated in the *das Man* analysis then, in which we are all the other and nobody is himself, there remains the uncanny event in which as Gadamer puts it, "we are all others and we are all ourselves" (EPH:234), again the possibility in which, as Aristotle had ventured, the friend is 'another self'. To acquire a horizon surely means that one learns to look beyond the close at hand: we do so also however, "not in order to look away from it but to see it better" (TM:305). For all this we will need perhaps quite ordinary virtues, indeed the virtues Aristotle refers to as ordinary hon-ors—amiability, meekness, and veracity. 'Hermeneutic' virtues it might be said, those virtues which Aristotle initially articulates—in contrast with magnanimity—as pertaining to "associations with others, in living with them and sharing words and deeds with them . . ." (NE:1126b). Doubtless they were construed in confrontation with the "mistrust," mutual "inconsid-erationess," and "unsociability" that Heidegger had encountered in the pub-lic realm (BT:163–65). Surely the whole of *Truth and Method* should be read as their hermeneutic elaboration in an age threatened, as well, as Gadamer would later put it, with "the flattening technological destruction of all that has flourished" (RAS:58–59). Moreover, this elaboration animated Gada-mer's thought from the outset. Gadamer's 1931 ethics book, a book its author has described as written as an attempt to emancipate himself from the style of Heidegger, doubtless in this regard ended with precisely the same conclusion in turning from Plato to Aristotle—and perhaps equally a return to the ambiguities of the everyday, beyond the Heideggerian condemnations of civil society. Beyond fate and inconstancy, Gadamer declared, we may still "make visible this actual self-understanding of Dasein in its unchanging averageness."[92] But if in all this we have apparently moved beyond Heidegger, it is doubtless important to remember that it is Heidegger whose remembrance—that is, the recollection of the problem of Being and its analogics— that opened the questioning itself: the question of Being, of Dasein, the self, and the other and the possibility of their renewed belonging-together, one both made possible and risked in the *Vorausspringen* of interpretation.

If Gadamer viewed himself always as Heidegger's disciple and, on the basis of Aristotle, the "real vindicator of his philosophical purposes" (TM: 540), doubtless the charity of interpretation is operative here too—even in their difference. But perhaps in *Truth and Method's* conclusions, after we have followed this long itinerary, we can still 'hear' them both:

> Our first point is that the language in which something comes to speak is not a possession at the disposal of one or the other interlocutors. Every conversation presupposes a common language, or better, creates a common language. . . . This is not an external matter of simply adjusting our tools; nor is it even right to say that the partners adapt themselves to one another but, rather, in a successful conversation they both come under the influence of the truth of the object and are thus bound to one another in a new community. (TM:378–79)

The 'dialogue' in question and the friendship that sustains it remain then inevitably hermeneutic: the community it announces inevitably at risk, inevitably political. Aristotle had in one sense again said nothing else: "all community would be part of the political community" (NE:1160a)—and all friendship, thereby, as we have seen, inherently related to the friendship of the citizen. Even in Aristotle, however, the latter remained oblique. Devoid of traditional foundation, however, be it by nature, by essence, or by prior exemplification of the wise (or 'heroes'), surely such a 'friendship' would appear even more oblique—community having become founded less on the noble wielding of power than demands for the latter's constraint. And doubtless it was precisely this complication that would overdetermine interpretation and debate concerning not only community but both friendship and law in its wake.

# 2. The Respect for Law

*On Civility, Irony, and the Emergence*
*of Hermeneutic Modernity*

"All the partisans of different forms of government speak of a part of justice only."

—Aristotle, *The Politics*

It is a misunderstanding which has given rise alike to the demand—a morbid craving of German scholars chiefly—that a legal code should be something absolutely complete, incapable of any fresh determination in detail, and also to the argument that because a code is incapable of such completion, therefore we ought not to produce something 'incomplete', we ought not to produce a code at all.

—Hegel, *Philosophy of Right*

I am thinking especially of Heidegger's early fondness for referring to "the famous analogy"—"die *berühmte Analogie*. . . ." He welcomed the Aristotelian teaching of *analogia entis*—the analogy of being—from early on as a brother-in-arms against dreams of a final grounding. . . .

—Gadamer, "Reflections on My Philosophical Journey"

# 1. Regulation, Iterability, and the Antinomies of Power: On the Modern Conception of Law

Analyses of the political in recent Continental philosophy have often viewed it either as transcendentally 'constituted', the result of rational agents whose actions are rationally veridical *simpliciter,* or (almost as transcendentally) as an exclusive process in which the differentiations of power at stake are intrinsically, viciously, or tragically self-serving expressions of the will to power. The result, with its 'Spinozistic' remnants that have continually haunted Continental thought since Kant, is divided between analyses concerning the veracity of reason's constitutive reflections on its practices—the Spinozistic *idea ideae,* as Sartre liked to remind us—and analyses viewing the latter as a mode of expression of event(s) antecedent to it. Correlatively, the philosophy of law seems to become divided between antinomies concerning the analysis of decision procedures or the analysis of complex facts or events, social, natural, economic, libidinal, or otherwise. Granted these alternatives, that a Jacques Lacan would provide an analysis linking Kant and Sade at the end of this history seems in retrospect if not fitting, then all but inevitable.[1] Such accounts, it is often objected, remain insufficient before the history and the logical complexity that underlies the modern conception of law, the complicated venture from which it emerges in detraditionalization, and the question of interpretation that accompanies it. The modern conception of law—the point initially sounds Hegelian—is reducible neither to the mere wielding of power (and hence of the account of private law), as had been the case in the Roman paradigm that had preceded the modern transformation of law, nor to the singular judgment of political agency.[2] As a result, the form of justice would not be determined simply by a wielding of power, but by its internal limitation: the rule of justice would be internally divided between subjective agents.

Hence the modern conception of law, recent theoreticians such as Blandine Kriegel have again insisted (explicitly following Hegel), is based not on the wielding of power, nor even a democracy with limited application founded on the subservience of slavery (as in ancient democracies) but instead the internal regulating of power itself.[3] The point is crucial: Roman law did not think of power in terms of law but of fact—any more than much of contemporary theory thinks of "day-to-day governance" in terms of law, but rather by more 'modern' concerns regarding the need for revolution against the illusions of illegitimate power.[4] And yet, neither the internal disequilibriums tolerated in doctrines of "separation of powers" (or doctrines of checks and balance), nor the heterogeneous and 'external' 'exceptions' (and guarantees) of natural right are readily conceivable thereby. Indeed, natural right was similarly divided between those who would reduce it to the rights of subjective constitution (or again, private law) and those who would seek its origin more broadly in the ancient appeals to transcendence that stood behind it. Kriegel herself notes, in accord with standard accounts, not only St. Thomas but also St. Francis as precursors to the modern account of natural right in separating the realm of the political and the day to day from the hierarchies (and subservience) of divine patronage.[5]

While Kriegel, like the later Hegel, strongly argues against the romantic abandonment of law for *Naturphilosophie,* she nonetheless argues elsewhere for her own 'Spinozistic' version of natural right, acknowledging that a human being "can neither sever himself from life nor seize complete control of it."[6] Indeed, in this regard, she claims that "the fate of natural right depends upon our being able to return to natural law and further enlarge the clearing it has already carved out for itself in the texts of our tradition."[7]

The problem—as no one realized more than Strauss concerning such Spinozistic retrievals—is that the rationality of such a "return" would be complicated, to say the least.[8] Thinkers as diverse as postmodernists like

Gilles Deleuze, or ecologists like Arne Naess—both again, like many post-Kantians, following Spinoza—may all have "returned" to natural law accounts to heal what ails modernity, but the question is what to make of such "returns," and which return is now relevant. Doubtless, moreover, the very quest for objectivity itself is involved here in ways that recent philosophers of science have found similarly hard to come by. Whatever Spinoza's legacies regarding the *interpretatio naturae* are—and they are considerable—they remain figured *more geometrico:* a deductive 'immanence' which could surely be no more simply presupposed in politics or ethics than it could be in science itself.

The problem then is by no means simply a postmodern one. Surely we will need more histories than those to which we have grown accustomed: neither a return to the ancients nor simply recognition of the end of metaphysics will suffice. As early theoreticians of modern political theory realized, the problem is how to interpret such a law. It is especially, as Hobbes claimed, the natural law that is most in need of interpreters—and hence his hope that the new physics might help us. Even Kriegel acknowledges that if natural rights "originated in the thought of St. Francis . . . they point the way to a transcendence that has little to do with faith"—or in any case traditional scriptural exegesis.[9] In the midst of debates over political matters, Bacon, for example, appealed both to the laws of the land—legal precedent and "transcendent reason"—and to the "original grounds of nature and common reason." The whole problem perhaps was how to interpret the mix. Here Bacon's appeal to history as "another way of philosophy," one to which hermeneuts like Gadamer still appealed for precedent long after Hegel, would be complicated indeed.[10] To the extent that transcendence might still remain at stake, its interpretation could not simply derive from scriptural exegesis.

If, like other commentators, Kriegel still credits Aquinas's *Treatise on Law* with opening an independent realm, "trusting to 'reason and its capacity to know the temporal order by means of observation',"[11] in Aquinas this natural order still remained ultimately ordered by its theological *pros hen* and political legitimacy required monarchy as its *lex animata,* just as judgment itself requires a last judgment, a final grounding, *Letztbegründung.* But it is precisely here that, with the emergence of the modern account of law, such judgment became internally limited: its transcendence could no longer simply be fixed by reference beyond it, nor simply located by a singular judgment immanent within it. Internally divided between its agents, it became the problem of how such a 'transcendence' might be interpreted, and how, so construed, justice might interface with day-to-day law. Nature would not simply be elsewhere or transcendent: the hierarchy of authority would be dispersed within 'equity' itself. Freedom and law, if by no means simple equivalents, are still by no means simply opposed either. And, property would no longer be regarded as a matter of simple domination but of entitlement. Doubtless, as Kriegel notes, then, the classical remnants refigured in modern natural law "contained a cluster of ideas."[12] And yet nothing was more evident than that, as the critical practices of modernity and debates over the interpretation of such topics intensified, so equally did the *problem* of their interpretation—demanding equally a kind of hermeneutics no longer circumscribed by exegesis of tradition.

Still, as is evident from both its late modern defenders and its detractors, especially granted its defense of the 'prejudices' of tradition, it is precisely the critical status of the modernity of what we now call hermeneutics—here and elsewhere—that has similarly seemingly always been in doubt. And thus the question of its legitimacy has itself always seemingly been 'infinitely deferred'. Moreover, that it is the status of legitimacy that is at stake seems only to affirm the historical antinomies out of which 'hermeneutics' emerged, divided over the 'retrievals' that constitute the specificity of its 'classicism', the ensuing question of the limits or exclusivity of tradition—and hence the exclusions that underwrite the traditional. Nowhere perhaps is this more evident than with issues surrounding law and its interpretation. While its proponents pointed to legal hermeneutics as a rich example of their account's fecundity, critics could see in it only the continuation of a romanticism that had dissolved the rule of law, exchanging universal principle for traditionalism, abandoning law for something more original or primordial—and in the process dissolving the principle (and the legitimacy) of law itself. The opposition between tradition and law seems almost synonymous with the Hegelian recognition of the modern conception of law. Indeed, as Hegel put it, while animals have their law as instinct, it is humans alone who have law as custom, and the latter must be overcome by freedom (as much as instinct) and codified by "the principles of jurisprudence in their universality" (PR:135). But the hermeneutic point was surely that, rather than the dissolution of principle, it was the interpretation of law that was in question: the rationality of interpretations could be grasped only by recognizing the difference between the ontic and the historical, to invoke Count Yorck's famous distinction (BT:451). While the rationality at stake in law required both principle and transcendence, hermeneuts still seemed to be foiled by the charge of historicism and irrationalism. Even Gadamer himself has related hermeneutics to motives that remain enigmatic, unclarified, or 'unconscious', which through dialogue, facilitate "completing an interrupted process into a full history (a story that can be articulated in language)." And, in the same text he claims this is a fact that he "learned . . . above all, from Jacques Lacan" (PH:41). While doubtless the charity of interpretation may be operative here too, these links between hermeneutics and such seemingly 'nonpolitical' practices as psychoanalysis, rhetoric, or aesthetics only emphasize the problem of hermeneutic 'legitimacy' and the question of the law anew. The obvious issues remain still outstanding: will just any story do? Or, is it a matter of completing a history or tradition already undertaken, and if so, when is such a tradition legitimate, when repressive, and which 'stories' are relevant?

The question surrounding the modern interpretations of law, obviously, is a complicated one, uniting, for example, issues concerning not only political revolution, the status of the emerging 'revolutions' in scientific practice or philosophy of mathematics, but such seemingly disparate practices as those at stake in poetics, and, as has begun to appear evident, even the semantic excess or remainder of the medievals' theological speculations. Indeed that precisely such diverse questions interfaced in the problem of tradition from the outset of modernity is evident from the differences (but common practices) at stake in Bacon and Galileo, or Machiavelli, Hobbes, and Vico—issues doubtless with which we have still not dispensed. The bond between classicism and modernity not only complicates hermeneutics in particular but interpretation in general. What Kant had already called the "ruins of the ancient systems" remained a continuing and complicated problem—and surely not simply in philosophy: the attempt to return to the classical, even within the most modern upheavals of the avant-garde, would in fact be widespread, as Eliot and Pound, Mondrian or Klee, Schönberg or Berg, Wittgenstein and Heidegger would attest.

The politics of classicism in twentieth-century modernism is, of course, equally complicated and doubtless involved in the theoretics of (modern) hermeneutics. If the claim could be advanced (as it was) that phenomenology appealed to certain antemodern forms of theory—indeed if Gadamer, for example, called the classical, that "consciousness of something enduring," the fundamental category of effective history—classicism was equally constituted only through "the awareness of decline and distance" (TM:288). Here as well we will need to separate the inextricable question of tradition from reactionary traditionalism—and doubtless perhaps much of standard accounts of hermeneutics. Whatever remains of the classical will likewise provide a basis for interpretation only in separation from the past. Thinkers widespread would be struck by the problem of classicism even in the midst of the most Nietzschean meditations, whose unwieldy status

might be prefigured, for example, in Hölderlin's appeal to Empedocles. Indeed, both Heidegger and Gadamer at the origins of their theoretical speculations explicitly linked their accounts to what both referred to as an
"Aristotelian tradition." Even the claims of strict science made in their Husserlian background still sound Aristotelian, both in their refusal (albeit ambiguous, admittedly) of a univocal and mathematical method and their
appeal to the semantic priority of the theory of meaning as intentional reference to being as such. This was, after all, Husserl's reply to logicists and
formalists alike: that mathematics could not be ultimate, a claim that would
not be inconsistent with the charge that phenomenology appealed to resources that were antemodern.[13] Lingering appeals to the lifeworld only of
course further confirmed such reservation. Even in the midst of full-fledged
existential revolt, authors like Merleau-Ponty still appealed to Hegel's "heritage" as the origins of a "new classicism."[14] And yet surely it is unclear what
such invocations of the classical implicate. If the legitimation that emerges
from hermeneutic practices were 'phenomenological'—and in the end few
would deny it (surely neither Heidegger nor Gadamer, their transformations of the phenomenological research program notwithstanding)—such
legitimation would become inevitably complicated by returns to the ancients. Appeals to the things themselves and the admonishment that we
would let the texts speak were critical in this genre. But when all is said and
done, its detractors could claim, who didn't hold such things? Such appeals
to the given were regarded as naive as all ancient science. Here thinkers as
diverse as Freud, Einstein, Schlick, or Adorno were of a piece, long before
Habermas or Ferry, in consigning such claims to the museum.

On the other hand, such condemnations of phenomenological naiveté as
nostalgia must be contested historically. Notwithstanding its own internal
reductionism, the radicality of Husserl's scientific and reductionist construal of the *epoché* in the end had as much in common with Hobbes as it
did with Aristotle (or Brentano for that matter); even the term 'phenomenology' emerges at the end of the eighteenth century (in Lambert) along with
the term 'semiotic' or the doctrine of signs to which Husserl originally opposed his work.[15] More recent scholarship has sought, for example, behind
the work of Schleiermacher, to which thinkers like Gianni Vattimo or Manfred Frank for example have already returned it,[16] the origins of modern
hermeneutics in Humboldt's task of universal characteristic—one, it should
be added (as Kant did) that is as overdetermined as the word 'character' itself, divided between the semiotic and the moral sense. As such, 'hermeneutic phenomenology' would be similarly overdetermined. It was, that is,
divided between the ancients and the moderns, divided between ancient

speculations about 'life', whose ambiguities all declared should not simply be abandoned, and a certain modern nominalism linked to the problems of articulation and representation and thus Cartesianism (or more perhaps to the point, in the conjunctions of perspectivism and characteristic perhaps to Leibnizianism). And yet beyond Leibniz, in Kant's wake, and beginning with Humboldt, individuality had itself become problematic, no longer determinably explicable (i.e., subsumable under determinate rules) but a matter of 'reflective judgment' and interpretation—and explicitly thereby an attempt to combine Kant with Aristotle.[17]

## 2. Toward a Genealogy of Interpretation: Between Tradition and Oblivion

In one sense 'fundamental ontology', the discipline to which Heidegger appealed for the basis of hermeneutics in *Being and Time,* might seen to be a similarly 'oxymoronic' result. It was less a theory or art of interpretation than, as is claimed in his "Dialogue on Language between a Japanese and an Inquirer" (both his most hermeneutic and most dialogically 'multicultural' text), "the attempt first of all to define the nature of interpretation on hermeneutic grounds" (DL:11). But the "fundamental flaw" of this early work, Heidegger contended (not without Nietzschean overtones) was that he "had ventured forth too early" (DL:7)— without sufficiently making his way back into the problem of Being. While the problem of the Western tradition as 'leveling', as 'self-differentiated' from its Greek origins, surely acknowledges the internal plurality of this tradition—a plurality which I have argued is internal to traditionality as such—in the resume of the "Dialogue with a Japanese," Heidegger thought he was fitting phenomenology back into the place that is properly its own within Western philosophy (DL:9). In one sense, as he himself points out, the task was already outlined in his *Scotusbuch,* which united the theory of meaning and the doctrine of the categories, the problem of the meaning of being (DL:6). But the result—again as classical (and traditional) as it may sound—would indeed be paradoxical: as these terms themselves betray, the *Scotusbuch,* in its attempt to construe *grammatica speculativa* as "theory of meaning," was already modern—and indeed explicitly Husserlian. Yet, as Heidegger acknowledges, his familiarity with 'hermeneutics' emerges from his studies in theology, where he was particularly agitated about the "relation between the word of Holy Scripture and theological-speculative thinking" (DL:9–10). Here indeed there may be

a case of what Hegel thought to be *always* the case, that the figures of personal and cultural or historical development (*Bildung*) coincide—a matter
to which we shall return [Phen:50].

While the question of law emerges against the backdrop of the theological-
political problem, the account of hermeneutics as a "general theory of understanding," to use Schleiermacher's terms, emerges against the backdrop
of speculative-theological thought. This is not to say—any more than the
philosophy of law does—that hermeneutics reduces to theology. As Heidegger acknowledges, "without this theological background I should never
have come upon the path of thinking" (DL:10). But, apart from considerations that might be restrictedly theological in import—as becomes evident
for Heidegger—nothing perhaps would be more 'godless' than to think that
hermeneutics was strictly or intrinsically a theological matter. Until we have
grasped the theoretical significance of this background, we undoubtedly
will not grasp whatever hermeneutic modernity might be about. Otherwise
all talk of hermeneutic 'appropriation' will amount to historicist nostalgia,
a refusal to abandon the ancient's speculations, on the one hand, or, on the
other, the limitations of Cartesian representation, call it the subject, or experience, or—to use Humboldt's term—"individuality." And as Humboldt
realized as early as 1792, explicitly refiguring Aristotle through Kant, the
question of individuality was critical to the flourishing of the political.[18] Indeed this refiguration can be regarded as symptomatic. Before the charge of
irrationalism or the abandonment of law could be sustained, we would inter
alia need further to investigate the complex links between Humboldt's
'characteristic' of individuality, his dialogical account of language, and the
liberalism of his political theories. All lie in the background of post-Kantian
hermeneutics, every bit as much as the task of recognition and community,
what Schlegel would call the sympathetic virtue that "concerns itself with
promoting the freedom of others" and whose criterion is friendship.[19]

Humboldt's liberalism, like his account of the articulation or 'characteristic' of individuality must preclude the strict correlation of consciousness
and universality—or consciousness and self-consciousness. It disarms in
advance Hegel's *Phenomenology of Spirit*'s correlation of meaning, universality, and consciousness, and the resulting charge that the attempt to characterize the singular is self-refutational: an event in which literally "we cannot
say what we mean" (Phen:60). For Humboldt, on the contrary, the task of
articulating the specific *individuality* of another is basic to the rational and
to the political, where "the principle of the true art of social intercourse
consists in a ceaseless endeavor to grasp the innermost individuality of another," a care that promotes both individual and "manifold diversity."[20]

Doubtless it is just such a 'virtue' that was at stake in Scheler's famous account of sympathy and still at stake (and doubtless threatened) in Heidegger's account of authentic *Mitsein*, a care which, beyond the domination of *das Man*, frees the Other in his freedom for himself" in order that "the Other [might] become transparent to himself *in* his care and to become *free* for it" (BT:159; Heidegger's emphasis). Still, such accounts are complex and accessible perhaps only by grasping the transformations and the histories (conceptual and real) at their origins—a task we shall provisionally begin here. Moreover, these transformations are overdetermined, emerging out of the problem of detraditionalization at the origins of modernity, precisely in refiguring what historians of liberalism refer to as "the theological-political problem" in its origins.[21]

Manfred Frank has thus aptly called for "a genealogy of [such] individuality." Here he appeals to a certain "heretical tradition" extending from Gilbert of Portier and Richard of St. Victor to Schleiermacher's reading of Fichte and Hegel and contests both the speculations of the ancients (and the demonstrations of the modern). Such a genealogy again explicates a notion of an *Individualität* irreducible to a logical particular, an *individuum*—one reducible neither by the medievals' *esse commune* nor the infinite gradation of the modern infinitesimal calculus.[22] The result might appear to be equally 'unwieldy', defenseless against the claim that such appeals had either abandoned the objectivity of the eternal verities and the Good or the legitimation procedures which might vouchsafe rationality in the former's lapse. What is critical is demonstrating how such a notion of individuality acquires legitimacy, lest such 'good' heresy should succumb to historicism: but what is required in both respects is a certain genealogy of interpretation perhaps.

Here the extent to which such claims concerning legitimacy have generated if not succumbed to a series of antinomies between hermeneuts and their detractors again becomes evident: between those who charged hermeneutics with nostalgia, romanticism, and simple historicism. Simply denying either aspect of hermeneutics, either its antemodern speculative precedents or its (evidential) interpretive characterizations, will inevitably be fruitless. On the one hand, to interpret is to appeal to what exceeds demonstration, while, on the other hand, the charge that metaphysics is somehow simply a bygone art is notoriously ideological. It is after all what both positivists and deconstructionists share in common and why Levinasian ethical defenses against totalizing ontologisms doubtless felt the need to defend in turn a certain 'retreat' to metaphysics. Yet, until we have a broader account of the descent of hermeneutics, its appeal to the theoretical fertility of interpretation

will either seem fruitless or seem to be a nostalgic pastime—and the implications here are (as everywhere with the cluster of problems associated with
hermeneutics) both theoretical and practical. It is striking in this regard to
recognize that Gadamer, for example, has recently traced his early work in
the 1930s not only to Plato or Aristotle but also to "Moritz Schlick's convinc-
ing critique of the dogma of protocol sentences in 1934."[23] However we construe hermeneutic commitments to the past, we cannot construe their noncontemporaneity to be simply nostalgic or naive commitments to origins,
scientific or otherwise. Heidegger similarly railed against the "romanticism"
in phenomenology "which believes it can step directly into the open space,
that one can, so to speak, make oneself free of history by a leap."[24] Again
what is critical in hermeneutics, to use Hegel's terms, is the rational *transition* (*Übergehen*) between the ancients and the moderns, not simply the
quarrel or antinomy between them. What is in this regard crucial are the
refigurations at stake in modern origins of hermeneutics, refigurations
which exhibit both its ancient legacy and critical advance.

It is not of course that attempts at such a genealogy have not been made.
Such an account was given by Michel Foucault, for example, under the (again
Hegelian) guise of "the prose of the world." Here Foucault returned to modern hermeticism, rightly pointing to the complicity between hermeticism and
arguments by analogy, ultimately claiming the failure of the former in its inability to stop the process of infinite semiosis. Here anything and everything,
to use Michel Serres's formalist term, "interrefers" and as a result, the evidence in question became, as Foucault saw, "infinitely poverty stricken."[25]

In a rare reference to hermeneutics, Sartre before Foucault had similarly
railed against attempts at hermetic totalization (and ideology) for which,
like "the medieval clerk every apparent analogy is a sign of deep identity"
(SG:471). Against such a hermeneutics, the *Notebooks for an Ethic* suggested, we should wonder, "What is the structure of our society that provokes the appearance of this emphasis on hermeneutics?" (N:435). And yet
Sartre did not mean to deny the analogical extensions of thought (and in
particular the epistemic function of *l'imaginaire*); rather he recognized the
difference in which imagination erupts, the difference that both separates
and unites the imaginary and the real, which can be grasped only through
subjectivity itself. Foucault, on the other hand, had little recourse other
than to subsume such appeals to individuality beneath his reading of the
history of ideas as a series of *episteme,* leaving out the transitions or precisely those moments of rupture Sartre's *l'imaginaire* had been invoked to
explain. Foucault questioned whether the appeal to individuality did not

mask a conceptual failure underlying the failure of the substantialist claims of humanism to *humanitas universalis*. He attempted to see the systems of formation and transformation that unite individual and concept within successive episteme (AK:129–30). Such matrices, like the rules of language to which they are connected, are less constituted by any empirical subject than they are the very condition for being a subject. And here the fictions of the imagination, like the individual ecstases of an Artaud or Roussel, remain devoid of epistemic function, and become at most an epiphenomenon or excess at the limit of scientific change, an aesthetic or literary moment excessive to any systematic functional (and thus epistemic) bridge "between tradition and oblivion" (AK:130).[26] But to leave the transitions out is to leave out the passage of judgment to reduce invention to function and to substitute rule for evidence. Admittedly, however, not without a reductive inversion (call it the philosophy of subjectivity) can evidence and intention simply be identified with rule, objectivity, and determination. Beyond the systematic reductions of enunciative archive or constitutive acts of transcendental intention, we will need an account of the 'belonging-together' of principle and transcendence, of the relation between individuality and objectivity. Beyond iterative stabilizations of the enunciative event we will need to say more to account for the recognition, in Foucault's terms, that "reason is the difference of discourse, our history the difference of times, our selves the difference of masks. That difference, far from being the forgotten and recovered origin, is this dispersion that we are and make" (AK:131). What is missing, however, is the figuration (and judgment) of such difference, which would involve not the mere exegesis of a preexisting archive (or tradition) nor the naiveté of subjective or 'phenomeno-logical' constitution, but the event which unites both—and doubtless united both in the emergence of the problem of interpretation at the outset of modernity. To grasp this event would be precisely to demarcate the modernity of hermeneutics itself, the account of the specificity of this passage itself—or to trace the genealogy of individuality and literature (and of course the expressions that unite them) at the origin of modernity.

In a tale of metaphysical if not characteristic mysterious suspense, Umberto Eco similarly provided the genealogy of a certain extension that occurs between the *esse commune* of Thomas Aquinas and Dante, which occurs, as he puts it, in his attempt to still defend "the old and still valid 'hermeneutic circle'."[27] In fact the story is one he recites often in such defenses,[28] and itself indicates inter alia the close link between narrative, history, and demonstration. Moreover, like all such hermeneutic narratives, it occurs both against a certain renewal of hermeticism (the problem of over-determination, as Eco calls it) and in the full recognition that underdeter-minacy does not simply dissolve the evidence of appearance. This was after all precisely the claim of the hermeneutic circle: that, lacking a demonstra-tion, a circle of 'interdependencies' "need not be vicious," to use Heidegger's term. Without succumbing to what Eco also argues against—that is, the *over-interpretation* or the hermeticism still lingering in postmodern hermeticisms —I think it is fair (and perhaps critical) to say that the complicated syntax of this 'need not claim' on behalf of the hermeneutic circle attests to the ten-sion in its midst. Heidegger's fundamental ontology would not avail itself of the idealists' genre of transcendental argument, whose appeals always either presupposed a prior certainty (Kant), or by reductionism detached inten-tionality from the problem (and the principles) of objective enunciation (Husserl). And yet the hermeneutic circle did not dissolve the need to appeal to the evidence of appearance. As Eco puts it, still appealing to the phenomenological-Aristotelian remainder, "in everyday life, however, it is a fact that we generally know how to distinguish between relevant significant similarities, on the one hand, and fortuitous, illusory similarities on the other."[29] But this is not simply Aristotelian because it involves an event that occurs against the archive of traditional allegory, an event fully acknowl-edging its distance from tradition via modern detraditionalization: the tra-ditional unities on which Aristotle could seemingly precritically rely—nature, the *polis,* and the wisdom of the ancients—has become, if not falsified, or a mere 'wives' tale' (as Hobbes declared), yet still problematic. Whatever we make of the classical, and Gadamer acknowledges this even in retrieving it, the classical is accessible to us only at a certain distance: we might call it the distance of detraditionalization that inextricably an-nounces hermeneutic modernity. Narrative can no longer mean mere tradi-tional 'archival' exegesis, but will require the distinction that underlies judgment as *Ur-teil,* to cite Hölderlin's famous gloss. At the same time this 'distance' is not, to use Heidegger's term, simply a 'leveling', as in his ac-count of *Alltäglichkeit.* And this has too been missed. The everyday to which Eco (and modern hermeneuts) appeal does not simply lack transcen-dence but needs to be construed 'otherwise' than by its simple dissolution: we need, as Bacon put it at the beginning of the modern period, "another way of philosophizing." Bacon's claim is made with respect to the emer-gence of history as a paradigm of the rational, in particular its relevance to the moral. Strauss would lament it as the birth of historicism.[30] But the point is that the relevance of history emerges precisely out of the failures that underwrite this detraditionalization. Even the vaunted Cartesian problem of the prejudices begins similarly before the recognition of "warped knowledge"—and hence similarly differentiated from the past.

Hermeneuts—as much as their detractors—will still need to give us an account of the rationality of this interpretive differentiation between past and future. And Eco himself does so precisely in returning to the very transition that Foucault dissolves. Instead Eco reconsiders the emergence of hermeneutics at the dawn of modernity, returning to a point before the cosmic semiosis of the Renaissance *corpus hermeticum,* in which the mechanism of analogy had become unlimited, as Foucault claimed.[31] At the same time, he likewise passed beyond the limits of the allegorical rigidly circumscribed by the medieval archive of scriptural exegesis. As Bacon provides Gadamer's account with an alternative basis of modern hermeneutics (or Rabelais provides a paradigm for Bakhtin), Eco's account pivots on the importance of Dante.

In fact like Gadamer, Eco acknowledges the importance of all three domains: the originality of the modern is neither simply scientific, nor aesthetic, nor political. Still, Dante's transformation of scriptural exegesis articulates his poetry through a new investment in the allegorical, investing, that is, its polysemous message with an accomplishment almost theoretical in import.[32] Poetry itself is not simply an emotional or obscure link to the literal but would now provide a certain allegorical articulation of the real. The medievals before Dante had limited allegory to the practices of scriptural allegory. Nowhere was this more complicated, for example, than in the notion of the figured *transcendens* that would attach itself to 'personhood', whose complexities perhaps still elude us. The concept of personhood remained divided from its inception between sacred transcendence and its individual but finite refraction—as is evident in Boethius's attempt to define it by a syntagm almost as anagrammatic and as complicated as are all such reinterpretations: "rational individual substance."[33]

That this medieval archive is not irrelevant to hermeneutics had been recognized by Gadamer in his discussion of the Inner Word, where his explication of immanence and transcendence imparts "an idea that is not Greek, which does more justice to the being of language, and so prevented the forgetfulness of language in Western thought from being complete" (TM:418). Even before that, as we have seen, such considerations had been at stake in the origins of Heidegger's own account of hermeneutics in the *Scotusbuch.* There, in fact, Heidegger too had appealed to the intimate relation of the inner person to God as a domain that was lacking in the leveling of modernity— albeit by a metaphysics still firmly entrenched in the analogical. Later he himself would both contest and rely on this 'metaphysics' in the narratives of

the fourfold and the *analogia* of Being in *Ereignis*.[34] It would now be necessary, Heidegger had declared, following Count Yorck's distinction between
the ontic and the historical, to link such considerations to an examination of
historical possibility and articulation. In this light Heidegger's ensuing considerations on Aristotle or Plato, Hobbes or Leibniz, or Hölderlin, Kierkegaard, or Nietzsche would only further adumbrate a problem already lurking
from the outset—the problem of Being and its interpretation, a problem less
resolved or concluded than explored as a task of thinking, as he put it time
and again. Even if, as Gadamer too claimed, "the nature of historicity becomes conscious to the human mind only with Christian religion"—hence
again the overdetermined effects of conceptual theodicy—it remains true
that this historicity remained articulated by "deriving the present from a
mythical past or by seeing the present in relation to an ideal and eternal order" (TM:531). Hence, for example, Bacon's debt to and transformation of the
past: the problem of the present, the modus of modernity had not been
grasped. If (Augustinian) illumination provided then "the first hint of the
speculative interpretation of language" (TM:484), the problem of the ontic
could not be reduced to the *intus*—since intuition itself would be figural, interpretive. To use a term of the early Heidegger, all intuition would be
"hermeneutic intuition," opening beyond the fixed appearance of the ontic,
forcing us to recur to the history and the narrative in which the present itself
becomes problematically 'recited'.

## 3. Narrative, Trope, and History: 'Another Way of Philosophizing'

In transforming the speculative-theological limits of the medievals, Dante,
(as Eco argues) had begun such explorations beyond the ontic, albeit in el-
evating the vernacular: the truth (or the problem) of the poetic and the allegorical could not be restricted to theological speculation. In so claiming,
however, he likewise opened up two dimensions that remain problematical.
First, the problem of narrative itself: beyond the exegesis of canonical
forms, narration would here arise as the problem of interpretation. Second,
the political: the articulation of the relations between 'this world' and the
'beyond' will impact in turn the domain of the political.

Regarding the question of narrative, Boccaccio saw that it made possible
the opening of the space of ordinary experience through the modern emergence of the narrations of the novel. Late-twentieth-century avant-garde
novelist and theoretician Philippe Sollers, for example, would still claim in
this respect that Dante had opened up a temporal line on which we still rest,

an intersection between two planes, one horizontal (historical) and the other vertical. Indeed as a "symbol of antiquity's resumption and herald of modern times" this intersection will become, to use Sollers's poststructuralist term, already the Nietzschean "drama of individuation"—a certain opening of language whose constraints would be unlimited, the opening of a multiplicity that anticipates Baudelaire.[35] "Novellando," in any case, Boccaccio decreed, would suspend the space of theoretical agonistic in order to narrate, to "tell stories."[36]

Dante's move may well in fact have prepared the way again for a semiotic metaphysics emptied of transcendence, as Eco argues.[37] As he also recognizes, however, the "old and still valid hermeneutic circle" that he defends could not simply be a reinstatement of past constraints, but must acknowledge what Derrida (or Kant) calls the 'illusion' that is necessary for representation. Indeed that was the point of the circle. To use Derrida's terms: "this is where the story (history) will have taken place, if it takes place."[38] The background of hermeticism in one sense may well portend romanticism (a modern neo-Platonism) and a new kind of fundamentalism in which "every text speaks of the irrational and ambiguous discourse of Hermes."[39] It is true, as Derrida says of Sollers's *Nombres*, for example, that it critically "deconstructs the transcendental illusions of representation."[40] But such 'deconstructions' "need not," as Eco realizes in *The Limits of Interpretation*, dissolve all presentation—any more than transcendental illusions in general need simply be false. As Kant realized, such 'illusions' are less "mere figments of the brain" than narratives whose venture is lacking in ultimate demonstration and determinability: this is their 'undecidability'. The point is that no such narrative exhausts the matter at hand—any more, for that matter, than the modern period can simply be read as a new form of Pythagoreanism that elevates number itself: the "limitations" of the latter became fully evident in the nineteenth century every bit as much as the *ecstases* of symbolism. Here, as Derrida rightly saw, by a strange affinity that is by no means simply hermetic, if we are to grasp the complexity of the matter the researches of a Husserl and Frege, or Proust and James, or Joyce would be thought together. But as early as 1929 Beckett had read Joyce as part of a tradition extending from Dante, Bruno, and Vico.[41] Gadamer similarly had related hermeneutics, via Cusanus and the 'concept' of *explicatio* that accompanies the *exhibitio* of transcendental logics, to "the nominalist breakup of the classical logic of essence (in which) the problem of language enters a new stage" (TM:435). Here too *explicatio*, which is not simply the inner *verbum* of past theology, reveals the "positive significance that things can be articulated in various ways (though not in [just] any way at all) according to their similarities and differences" (TM:435). Indeed in a significant study on the language of angels according to the scholastics, Jean-Louis Chrétien concurs regarding Dante's elevation of the vernacular: humans alone were given language because it was necessary to them alone. According to the scholastic accounts, angels, on the other hand, more immanent to the Radiance of the Divine, communicated in full transparency—an account that would, Chrétien points out, still overdetermine, indeed provide the measure for later projects concerning universal language that would escape the 'entanglements' of natural language.[42] Modernity would be neither fully emptied of such transcendence through its appeals to l'imaginaire and the symbolic realm—indeed that was the problem of the 'separation' at stake—nor was transcendence a matter of self-contained algorithmic or 'perspicuous' immanence. Just here is the problem of modern narrative, literary or philosophical.

The question is how to understand such narratives and the risk that haunted them. If, as Dante asserted, all language originates as a "response" to a (divine) call, in the end what call is it?[43] The modern elevation of the vernacular immediately confronted—as is clear from Dante's text as much as Hobbes's[44]—the Babel and "confusion" of languages. Postmodernists like Lyotard would be even more direct: "no one knows what 'language' being understands, which it speaks, or to which it can be referred."[45] Moreover, the project of a universal language of perfect transparency and perspicuity that always accompanied the modern seemed, as Chrétien has suggested, an angelic "dream," indeed, to speak Nietzschean, a venture "all too human."[46] The question was what to make of this rupture out of which language responds and to which, to use Dante's terms, I owe so much—indeed, Dante asserted, even my being, since the vernacular has been responsible for what I am.[47]

These new 'allegories' would not take place simply by mere exegesis of the sacred past—'locally', as it were. The articulations in question were more complicated; like the novel itself such ventures were neither simply devoid of their sacred past nor simply its replacement. Despite the fact that, as Michel Serres quite rightly put it, a dominant tendency of modern thought was to exchange the 'elsewhere' of transcendence for the 'immanence' of the here—and the classical novel thereby becomes as determinate as the determinacy of classical physics—it is precisely the indeterminacy of such immanence that we must note.[48] Indeed the point has been made that the passage between Dante and Boccaccio is itself not only the opening of modern narrative but, in that very moment, the rupture between exegesis and interpretation and a modern philology that recognizes a rupture between the present and the past.[49] It is this same distance that Gadamer acknowledges to be that out of which classicism always emerges in discontinuity.[50] In this regard the novel would now narrate the ordinary, not a realm other than itself, and consequently not simply one true elsewhere—or simply false, as all 'fictional' discourse was regarded. The emergence of the modern novel, as thinkers like Bakhtin have insisted, would involve the introduction of new narratives, concerning individuality, experience, embodiment, and freedom. When modern philosophers saw notions like freedom to be irrational, consequently, it was as much because such an experience involved less a singular event or power—let alone a theory—than a transformation, and even a certain transformation within storytelling itself—one that doubtless awaited post-Kantian 'expressivists' to rightly retrieve.

Again, as Eco admits, this 'telling' of the new poetic could not simply be poesy. What Dante's transmutation of allegory into the poetic portends is the transfer of theoretical predicates into the telling of narrative; the ancient (Platonist) conflict between philosophy and poetry has neither been dissolved nor made *aufgehoben* but rewritten from within. Even the "polysemous" allegorical truth of theological speculation will have its locus neither in the past nor in the beyond but in the task of narrating the here and now. This doubtless accounts for the modern link between the ordinary and Aristotelianism: transcendent form would not be 'separable'. Nor, however, could the 'ordinary' simply be correlated with the description of the particular, substituting the myth of the given for *mythos* itself, a mythic reinvestment that accompanied all 'demythologizing' in its 'scientific' reduction and ensuing simple descriptions of the so-called 'real' content of myth. Instead the inventions of narrative, reducible neither to a simple inventory of the particular nor regulated by self-subsistent transcendent form, articulated the problematic (and hermeneutic) status of the ordinary, both ontic and historical, present and transcendent. Doubtless Dante pre-figures it here as well.

*The Divine Comedy* and the literary practices that would come after it would thus not only allegorize the 'secular', but likewise articulate its genre through predicates that Aquinas, for example, had restricted to philosophy and theology. Dante openly suggests that the manner of treatment (*modus tractandis*) employed in *The Divine Comedy* is "poetic, fictive, descriptive, digressive, and transumptive"—predicates reserved for traditional poetic discourse. But, as Eco also notes, Dante further claims that the treatment "also consists in definition, division, proof, refutation, and the giving of examples," and here the "poets continue the work of the scriptures but with the aperture of philosophy itself."[51]

The telling that results would thus be a showing: an *exhibitio*, not despite, but because of the polysemous character of the sign. Literally there is always more than one way to tell the story. In fact the story—like the ancient account of Being itself—is never told in any other way than in these "many ways." If, in its rupture with description, to interpret is always to 'allegorize', allegory, similarly detraditionalized, too had thereby undergone a change that was fundamental. Allegory had previously always depended on a fixed tradition. But now that tradition, devoid of ultimate foundation, was in ruins. As Sollers put it, this became the opening of a certain literary generalization, or *lisabilité,* whose economics would remain formally (if not pragmatically) unrestrained. The allegorical would no longer be subsumable beneath traditional exegesis: to use Hegelian terms, it would be instead internally "disrupted," dispersed in plurality, particularity.

As the historian of Christian tradition Jaroslav Pelikan has observed, it is not that this conflict had gone unrecognized. Long before the intense debate about the Reformation's question of interpretation of faith *solus scriptura* versus appeal to tradition had erupted, the question of differences internal to the tradition itself had already surfaced. As Pelikan notes, particularly after Peter Abelard's *Sic et non* (Yes or no) had been written, dealing with apparent contradiction in the tradition, the harmonization of biblical or other authoritative texts became one of the most important aspects of scholastic thought. While Abelard was convinced such internal contradictions were formally resolvable, others, like Bernard of Constance, argued that "failure to pay attention to historical differences . . . could lead a careless observer to the hasty conclusion that different canons were 'absurd or contrary,' when 'a consideration of the times, the places, or the persons' would show that the diversity was to be attributed to the special circumstances surrounding the case. . . . "[52] In fact the dialectical status of the past had been (explicitly) evident, beginning with the theological debates concerning the Gnostics, where Irenaeus and Tertullian formally framed the concept of tradition itself.[53] And as Pelikan has noted elsewhere it is no accident that Irenaeus and Marcus Aurelius are contemporaries.[54] Not only do both meditate on time and providence, but both write besieged, to use the Stoic term, by a necessity whose 'immanence' has withdrawn. Walter Benjamin likewise has noted that such 'withdrawal' is the origin of allegory.[55] In this light Gadamer's claim that allegory depends upon a fixed tradition is itself 'overdetermined'; the question of tradition, as Irenaeus exemplifies, is 'always already' allegorical.

What inter alia became obvious in the detraditionalization of modernity, then, was the problem of discontinuity that threatens such resolutions.[56]

The speculation that had incited Heidegger's fascination with the Word could not but be a matter of rupture and interpretation. It could not be simply a matter of making the implicit explicit, as with archival exegesis, nor even, to speak Wittgensteinian, a matter of making the meaning logically perspicuous. In addition, as has been seen, interpretation requires a judgment other than the mere subsumptive—its interpretive narratives are equally a kind of picturing or exhibiting. Here, as Heidegger saw, even though his account of 'the speaking of language' remains perhaps again dangerously close to exegesis, analysis would not be enough. Judgment would be complicated between analysis and synthesis—without dissolving the rigors of either. Even "incalculable justice requires us to calculate," as Derrida acknowledges.[57] And of course the dangers are not simply theoretic, but real, as Hobbes realized in his discussions of exegesis and tradition in general. Hence the radicality of his transformation—that power would not simply be wielded, as had been the assumption of traditional legal theory, but itself regulated.

At the origin of this *transformation* were both Hobbes and Machiavelli—and both were too often simply seen as villains in such narratives. The 'emptying' of *transcendens* is not simply its dissolution but the emergence of the problem of its lack or "empty place," as Lefort has put it, whose reading of Kantorowicz's study of medieval political theology had in a sense provided his protocols. Moreover, the space of the "ordinary" itself opens up the task of interpretation that occurs in this lapse—the question of the prose of the world, to use Bacon's terms, which Strauss decried as the origin of historicism. Kriegel follows Strauss here, at least this far, in being able to conceptualize the venture (and risks) of this 'prose' of the ordinary only as abstract (Roman) dominion formed "by violence and maintained by force."[58] For, as we have seen, the Hegelian state makes *aufgehoben* such 'prose', rather than (on the most charitable reading) opening within it—and thereby its absolute idealism would simply dissolve the difference and plurality (and the dangers) in its origin. For Kriegel instead, "the return" of the Hegelian monarchy remained benign, indeed "the opposite of a master."[59] It is true Hegel attempts both to assert that law is rooted in historical tradition and that "right must become law."[60] But this doubtless overlooks the heterogeneous relation between tradition, right, and law, one by no means simply rationally 'equitable or immanent'.[61] The Hegelian monarch as "the final subjectivity of decision" (PR:187), in which "the personality of the state is actual" (PR:182), not simply resymbolizes but reinstantiates the immanence and the danger of Averroistic totality that had accompanied philosophical modernism since

Dante: that there is an individual in which individual and totality coincide. In accord with the immanent development of science, as Hegel puts it, this "absolutely decisive moment of the whole is not individuality in general, but a single individual, the monarch" (PR:181).

But Dante is surely not to be held responsible for such dangers: what instead his text portends is the rupture in the hierarchies that bound the present to the past. And in his wake Boccaccio's narratives obviate a certain distance from the continuous past that no theory will surmount or overcome. It is just for this reason that the question of law will be less a matter of mere exegesis than interpretation: subject and object, to speak a latter theoretical language, will be divided, exegesis or analysis and interpretation will be moments of the rational. Tradition is not quite what Hobbes will claim, a matter of "wives' tales": Aristotle, Cicero, and St. Thomas are not simply "fooles money." And yet as this division announces, a certain rupture has inextricably taken place, a certain discontinuity is irrefutable—a certain detraditionalization and pluralization accompanies the descent of traditionality.

As previously noted, nowhere, especially granted the critical limits that underwrite medieval theological exegesis, is this rupture more obvious again than in the philological and hermeneutic practices that underlie Boccaccio's study on the genealogy of the gods, linking such narratives to an 'exemplary unveiling' more general in scope. This transformation is now fully evident. Here Boccaccio articulated and defended the study of the pagan gods, in a sense fully dehierarchizing our rational practices.[62] It is in "this prose of the world" that the problem of narrating the fragmentation of experience emerges: the problem of the novel, never simply devoid of link with *transcendens* of the sacred, the past, or nature and yet already perhaps beyond the hope of immanence with respect to such authorities. Thus construed the question of interpretation inevitably is accompanied by the question of how we belong to, and the nature of our co-mmunity both with the present and the past.

## 4. Contract, Transcendence, and Community: Modern Averroism and the Politics of the Everyday

But this returns us to a second consequence of Dante's generalization. As writers as diverse as Max Scheler and Etienne Gilson explicitly worried in their retrievals of medieval thought, Dante's elevation of the vernacular (as in a good deal of modern political theory) smacked not simply of a kind of voluntarism, but of Averroism, its appeal to the potencies of the vernacular dissolving the individual in the universal, in a kind of shared or communal 'agent intellect'.[63] Indeed the charge had been made in Dante's own lifetime by figures such as Guido Vernani. The refiguration of the sacred allegories led to making transcendence immanent to the community of humankind; hence the risk again of *humanitas universalis*. Doubtless the charge of Averroism against Dante is too strong, as Kantorowicz shows in the concluding chapter to his study on *The King's Two Bodies*.[64] And yet, as he acknowledges, "if ever there existed a secular 'mystical body', it existed in Dante's *humana civilitas*," whose perfection would be independent of the transcendent realm of the sacred, a realm of acts good in themselves (*de se bonus*) independent of divinely infused virtue.[65] Here we see again the problematic status of individuality that Manfred Frank has emphasized—albeit one at stake in the figured "relational identity" (to use a term of Irigaray's) that one finds already in Boethian personhood. Such a universal had remained indeterminate in the figured relations of medieval personhood: both dignity and community were never simply 'universal' except by reference 'beyond' themselves; hence Dante's 'transmutation' here becomes as 'equivocal' as all modern theories concerning the immanence of reason and nature.

While Dante did not say (as did his teacher, Remigio de Girolami, described by Kantorowicz as "curious thomistic proto-Hegelian") that an individual could not possibly reach perfection on his own, he did say that the totality of human knowledge, the totality of that by which man became Man, or briefly, the totality of *humanitas* could become actuated only by the collective effort of the corporate body of mankind.[66] Here, there is no doubt that "Dante conceived of the *genus humanum* as though it were a single person."[67] But it is this threat that would continually overdetermine the levelings of modern political theory, confusing autonomy and immanence, certainty and truth, agency and transcendence—when it is precisely the status of such immanence that became increasingly problematic. Even Kant himself appealed to the figure of a species of rational being developed from generation to generation, each of which provides the foundation for succeeding generations to erect a higher edifice in accordance with Nature's goal.[68] Moreover, this "justification of Nature—or better Providence" is posited in hopes that "the discord also natural to our race may not prepare for us a hell of evils however civilized we may now be"—and in hopes of articulating a universal history with the outcome of perpetual civic peace.[69] Yet its status remained 'figured', an idea and not fact. One can agree with Kantorowicz that the doctrine of the king's two bodies—like the conceptual elaboration of traditionality, it might be added—is "a landmark of Christian political theology," having inter alia a formative role for the problem of political, social, and individual incorporation in its wake.[70] Still, its allegories, from *corpus Christi, corpus ecclesiae mysticum,* and *corpus republicae* to the *corpus morale et politicum,* commonwealth, and finally the body politic could never again be substituted for the immanent icon of transcendence. To grasp its rational status, it is crucial perhaps to recall that the Tudor doctrine of the king's two bodies still belonged to the analogical principles of common law and not to theoretical first principles: it exemplified the interpretive status of law and the problematic status of its institutions.

Derrida, in his readings of Searle and Austin in *Limited Inc.,* notes that *"jeu de massacre,"* as Eco calls it, would reraise the problem of such incorporation and reemphasize the figural status of incorporation and institution. The question was whether appeal to the background of performative practice, convention, or context, could simply suffice for juridical legitimacy, always a problem of 'the police', as Derrida worried. As trumped-up as the rhetoric on both sides of this debate might have seemed, it surely involved a modern problem. Hegel had similarly worried about the extent to which the (Fichtean) appeal to reason's limits or constraints, which was lacking in intrinsic communal life, did not entail the need for extrinsic authority, the universalization of the police of external regularity (Dif:146–48). The point is the underdeterminacy of juridical concepts. Such concepts are neither demonstrably univocal nor unproblematic and they are never politically neutral, or totally devoid of the problem of force or power—nor are the performatives that they enact simply transparent.[71]

The attempt to univocally (and legitimately) *demonstrate* the force of law would inevitably fail, *pace* the modern attempts of Grotius, Pufendorf, Locke, and others. Principled demonstration will neither replace the transcendence of its medieval predecessor nor will natural law be made rationally immanent. Kriegel is correct, for example, in pointing out the subjectivism of the collapse of natural law into the individual as possessing, as Pufendorf put it, "the seeds of supreme sovereignty."[72] If even Kant would still appeal to such "seeds," he did so fully aware of their figurative status. The immanence appealed to in such guarantees would not suffice. Both nature and right will inevitably remain figured, less bound theoretical variables than what remains at play in judicious interpretation. Hence Hobbes's concern that we will especially need interpreters with regard to the natural law, but what he did not realize is that the 'nature' at issue will not simply be calculated. The physicists would not solve but complicate the problem of the *interpretatio naturae.*

It is precisely this complication that must be thought if the rationality that underlies the analogies in question is to be grasped, divided between principle and transcendence, transcendental reduction and its excess. Granted the modelization of theory, as Wilfred Sellars understood before Kuhn, science itself would not be devoid of analogy. Hence the process of analogy while "obscure and difficult" is as "essential to the philosophy of science as it has been to theology."[73] Nor should we deny what is decisive about the physicist's causal demonstration in putting an end to the hermetic drift of analogy—a point acknowledged by Foucault as much as it is by Eco. The difference in question, as postmodernists like Deleuze argued, may not be reducible to analogical identity but nor is identity simply the former's mere 'epiphenomenon'.

It may well be true, as Deleuze thought, that individuation cannot be conceived to be simply in Scotus's terms, "the ultimate actuality of form": all interpretation is underdetermined. We may even admit that there is, beyond the simple correlation of transcendental representation (or the forms of judgment) and the individual, something like what Deleuze argues for: a transcendental principle that is "plastic, anarchic, and nomadic, contemporary with the process of individuation."[74] Still this need not lead to infinite semantic or epistemic drift in the relations between difference and repetition. While the 'contingency' Deleuze cites may disrupt transcendental necessity, it does not dissolve it, turn its appearances epiphenomenal, nor simply erase its evidence. The point is that individuation cannot be seen simply in systematic propositional sequences; its process is both historical and conceptual, its rationality always 'underway', a matter that holds for legal theory as much as scientific theory.

It suffices to recall in this light that what distinguishes the demonstrations of legal theoretics from the analogics of common law—as writers from Bacon onward have taught—is an account of the 'mixture' of intuition and proof, transcendence and principle, probity and probability, that is at stake in common law juridical reasoning.[75] Hobbes, on the other hand, complained that the indeterminaries of the common law required monarchial supervention—but he had from the outset constructed the figure of the Leviathan, "that *Mortal God*, to which we owe under the Immortal God, our peace and defence" according to the concept of personhood—the "real Unitie of them all, in one and the same Person" (Lev:II:17; Hobbes's emphasis).[76] And the acts that resulted were as certain and as determinate, consequently, as the constructions of the geometers.[77]

Rightly understood, the appeal to the everyday poesy of history at stake in the tradition of 'the common' indeed required a "new way of philosophizing," where transcendence and principle were connected otherwise than by hierarchical immanence. If law requires judgment, it could not be resolved in the *lex animata* of monarchial kingship; juridical agency would equally need to be understood otherwise (as the very notion of personhood itself nascently acknowledged). It is in just this light that law is hermeneutical, as

Gadamer recognized in distinguishing Bacon as a precursor of his account of hermeneutic rationality.[78]

Still it is also important to recognize the limits of such interpretation: again interpretation is always more than mere exegesis—this is the effect of the separation that underwrites judgment. Hence arises, granted the epistemic shortfall that separates demonstrable certainty and interpretation, the question of defeasibility and suspicion which Derrida and others emphasized. If such interpretation, to use terms from the later Kant, becomes justified through the "schematism of analogy," the judgments that result are after all reflective (i.e., do not yield ultimate determinacy). Nor, as Gadamer realized, was the character of the narrative that accompanied the "old story of the Good" intended "to yield an ultimate determinacy" (HS:322). This indeterminacy would be further complicated in the modern narratives of freedom, power, and the institutions of law. But far from being dissolved it is precisely here perhaps that this indeterminacy finds its critical edge. As Heidegger saw, such "multiplicity of possible interpretation does not discredit the strictness of the thought content. . . . Rather multiplicity of meaning is the element in which all thought must move in order to be strict thought."[79]

The attempt to replace such indeterminacy with collective judgment, decision procedure, and consensus was surely a seductive one—and, as has been seen, accompanied modern humanism from the outset. Hobbes and his followers in retrospect missed the complexities of the humanist break. In the very origins of humanism, beyond its nominalist, Averroist, voluntarist, or even rationalist alternatives, its interpretive resources still reveal themselves. Foucault was not, after all, the first to pronounce humanism dead. Indeed Count Yorck's own distinction between the ontic and the historical had a similar corollary, cited by Heidegger in Being and Time: "The 'modern man'—that is to say, the post-Renaissance man—is ready for burial" (BT:452). But the point surely could not be the dissolution of homo interpretans nor the politics of the everyday that had arisen in modernity. This is not to dissolve the question of interpretation any more than it is to dissolve the question of certainty—a point too often missed by defenders of the Seinsfrage. It is after all, the question of certainty (or default of univocal tradition, as we saw with Abelard) which dissolves the immanences of Being and nature—and which raises the question of Being. With interpretation the problem of certainty and the problem of Being emerge concomitantly, even if by a certain "uneven development" historically—and neither are resolved in appeals to the community of investigators or political collective. Here Heidegger's Letter on Humanism was surely right in attempting to think the 'dispensation' [Schickung] of Being distinct from the idea of nationalism (or internationalism) thought of as "the subjectivity of man in totality" (LH:238, 221). The effect of politics had surely taken its toll—but clearly as has become evident, it had not dampened Heidegger's sense for history or acumen of philosophical analysis. If Heidegger's writings of the early thirties verge on committing just such a fallacy regarding ontic totalization, grasping what was at stake would require both a knowledge of the withdrawal of such immanence—its detraditionalization—and the requisites of critique in its wake. Only thereby, he claimed, is there hope of restoring a sense to humanism (LH:224). And surely this can be done only by acknowledging the withdrawal of Being that occurs in its midst, the necessity of interpretation, and the plurality in which this occurs.

While it is true that democratic contract theory often enough avoided the 'immanentization' of the political collectivity, this attempt to reduce the (transcendent) figure of Boethian personhood as individual rational substance and the complicated structure of the king's two bodies to the immanence of (transcendental) rational agency or technical or procedural rationality would not end. In one sense such theoretics had already been undermined in the desubstantialization of personhood undertaken in Kant's paralogisms. To again use a term of Irigaray's, already at stake in the medieval paradigm was precisely an identity that was figured, a "relational identity" without immanence.[80] And yet the modern transcendental tradition, following Descartes and evading the problem of Being (or the given) for the certainty of representation, also substituted a form of immanence for this transcendence (BT:126). Even Kant himself almost restored such immanence (if only as idea) and those in the transcendental tradition following him from Fichte onward would simply affirm it *in actu,* even if under the regulative guise of the bad infinite. Indeed Scheler himself wondered whether Heidegger's own account of Being-in-the-World had not falsely correlated Dasein and the world. What, after all, precluded there being many worlds?[81] But that was the hermeneutic point. Nothing precludes this: 'worldhood' is always indeterminately open and 'Dasein' is already *'Mitsein'.*

## 5. The Differentiation of Transcendence and the Politics of the 'Empty Place'

The result of such 'desubstantializations' is that the modern community, devoid of immanence, would be too little thought through, and hence its inherent link to otherness, to difference—which is not simply a link to the Other, either as person or as substance—remains unrecognized. Rather, this 'alterity' is what figures relations between persons, institutions, and texts, without dissolving the evidence and judgments at stake within them. This is "the multifariousness of voices" that not only is "the tradition to which we want to belong," as Gadamer puts it (TM:284), but to which (historically if not ontically) we always already belong. But it is just this "plurality of voices," now to directly invoke Hobbes's terms, that the modern *Leviathan* sought to level or "reduce" (Lev:II:17) in figuring political deliberation as the Averroistic act of one person—or one community, or one nation, although all of these 'unities' arise only differentially in the breach of tradition that modernity announces, the 'between' that only a hermeneutic can articulate. In the end that is why it is especially the natural law that requires interpreters. Beyond both nominalism and essentialism, classical liberalism and the romanticism of organic society (which Gadamer too construes as an uninterpreted and unjustified "relic of natural law" [TM: 274]), this multifariousness belies all attempts of strict theoretical reduction. Neither nature nor law can be simply the uninterpreted correlates of 'objectivity'. Indeed there is a sense in which, granted the multifariousness (or multiplicity) in question, objectivity itself will be indeterminately divided in their midst, the interplay of principle and transcendence.

Here, however, we might also wonder about the formal implications of what Gadamer terms "the prejudice of completeness (*Vollkommenheit*)" (TM:294). Gadamer defends such a 'prejudice' as part of an appeal to the integrity of the text and the possibility of its "preservation amid the ruins of time." Hence: "The prejudice of completeness, then, implies not only this formal element—that a text should completely express its meaning—but also that what it says should be the complete truth" (TM:294). And yet it is precisely the ruins of time that makes even the classical remainder, as we have seen, appear only in its difference and multifariousness. While it is true that we only attempt to 'understand' the text when "the attempt to accept what is true fails," there is another sense in which completeness fails: in the recognition that such completeness is unattainable—to use predicates again that now attach to the classical, that domain that is "unattainable and yet present" (TM:288). And this too surely has formal (and more than formal) implications—and Gadamer's continuing meditation on the dialogical status of the hermeneutic event continually acknowledges it. The provisional appeal of completeness here would yield to a meditation on plurality—a point at which Gadamer rejoins Levinas, for example, in similarly appealing to "the good beyond the true." The question is what to make of reason—and its politics—as a result.

Recently Gadamer has claimed that "the argument for the significance of temporal distance, as persuasive as it is in itself, is a poor presentation for discussing the significance of the otherness of the other and the fundamental role played by language as conversation." After all, as he put it, interpretive distance does not always have to be historical distance (Reflections:45). Surely this is true: such 'alterity', as I have argued, can be quite con-temporary and ready to hand. Yet it surely is critical to note that the problem of such alterity became problematically present to hand only within the specific temporal distance that became explicit in the detraditionalizations of modernity—the point at which, as Hobbes puts it, "manners" become too "various" to be relied on, giving rise to the problem of certainty and alterity, in the humanist ventures of modernity. Indeed, elsewhere Gadamer himself claimed that "when the historical tradition in its entirety up to the present moved into a position of . . . remoteness, the problem of hermeneutics entered intrinsically into the philosophic awareness of problems" (RAS:97). The simple affirmation of immanence had been precluded in the event of detraditionalization itself. Hence emerges, as we have seen, the modern importance of dialogue as the "indeterminate two (*ahoristos dyas*)." The simple affirmation of the other became no more readily a possibility than the simple affirmation of tradition—both, as he realized, and he still used Aristotle's terms, would be 'slavish'.

Doubtless it can be argued that the modern conception of autonomy depended on a dehierarchization of law readily available in the mathematization of mechanics as analyzable *partes et partes*.[82] Here precisely each part (materially) contributes efficaciously to the whole, which in turn depends on the interaction of parts. Such a paradigm may also make possible the 're-spect' for individual qua individual, as a particular irreducible to the identity of substance—and this in turn, paired with the question of certainty, perhaps lead to the question of the recognition of difference. Ironically, to this extent, postmodern affirmations of difference would forget their modern debts. Precisely the conceptual paradigms of the Enlightenment may have provided the schemata for the problem of difference. This is not to say of course that the Enlightenment's politics were actually construed as a politics of difference as opposed to equitable 'domination', even when it was the modern account of law that was at stake. The question of such recognition and the emancipation of difference doubtless is nonetheless both a principled and a modern affair. The ancients surely could identify 'others' but not 'respect' them—that would require both a universality and individuality that remained too much unthought within the ancient hierarchies. Contested in its origins between virtue and autonomy, this explains perhaps both why modern thought served to open the problem of difference and the foreign, and yet remained tortuously complicated by the history of its own exclusions. What is required is an account not simply capable of functionally or iterably articulating difference individually, but of *welcoming* its possibility. But if this is true the situation will be more complicated than Gadamer pictured. If the *humaniora* still present "the integrative function" of reason (RAS:167), they are not unaffected by the natural sciences they integrate, as the modern accounts of freedom and law doubtless attest.

I am inclined, however, to say the modern opening to difference in the *humaniora* (or to use Humbolt's term, diversity) still involves a classical account of both truth and community, albeit now surely a multifarious one—but one that also escapes the simple leveling of modernity precisely by acknowledging a virtue that informs democracy. It is the remainder of what the ancients understood as the problem of friendship, an event where truth, dialogue, and virtue occur only by a certain in-between. Here Gadamer again has reemphasized, and did from the outset, both the Aristotelian notion of friendship and associated notions of sympathetic understanding, or considerateness [*synesis*], and fellow feeling [*syngnome*] which all remain in the background of modern accounts of sympathy from Hume to Scheler and beyond (TM:322–23). To this, however, Kant had added the problem of rational communication—precisely in defining *humanitas* itself—and the post-Kantians, attempting to acknowledge the violence of political modernity, have added the otherness at stake in the question of recognition. Both doubtless would overdetermine the problem of interpretation—and overdetermine the *humaniora* themselves, as Kant had realized in adding communicability to sympathy, thereby acknowledging the (modern conception of the) principled rule of law.

The enigma of 'intersubjectivity', the problem of other minds, the question of the other, what Henry James[83] would still obliquely call "the question of manners," is a distinctly (or at least critically) modern one. Accordingly, Kant already acknowledges, both the requisites of objectivity and its limits are dependent in sympathy (or care) on an excess, an openness, an 'extension', and a transcendence that sustains it. The *humaniora* thus understood, are constituted, Kant claims, in furthering the "communicability and urbanity [*Urbanität*] in which humaneness [*Humanität*] consists" (Logic:470)—or as Kant put it elsewhere, the combination of "sympathy and the ability to engage universally in very intimate communication," in both respects a matter of "integrity and character" (CJ:231, 206). Even Levinas would not be far off in recognizing the remains of obligation in the little humanity that adorns the world, "if only with simple politeness or the pure polish of manner"—albeit always threatened by the threat (and seduction) of violence (OBBE:185). If, as has been said, Gadamer urbanizes Heidegger in drawing out the implications of his thought, the result is also perhaps a modern conception of law and civility that remains both open-ended and limited, divided between self and other, regulated and free, circumscribed in principle and yet always unfinished. The result is, to use Gadamer's term, precisely "hermeneutic virtue" (Reflections:96) itself, a matter both of interpretation and (*pace* the 'wielding' of force) communication, sympathy and care. The closest Hegel himself could come to it is in recommending "the illogicality of the Roman jurists and praetors that must be regarded as one of their chief virtues, for by dint of being illogical they evaded unjust and detestable laws" (PR:20). It is just such a 'virtue' that was to underlie the rationality of common law's mix of precedent and judgment, retrieval and renewal. And, it is surely not irrelevant that when Hegel reintroduces the immanence of monarchy into the question of modern law, it is precisely to make up for what he perceived, following Montesquieu, to be the English failure of the virtue needed to sustain democracy (PR:178, 183).

Instead, while declaring the deceptive protocols of Roman law illicit, exchanging it for the 'speculative' dialectics of the implicit and the explicit, Hegel could only find the interplay of the written and the unwritten, precedent and innovation in English common law monstrous (*ungeheuer*) (PR:135–36). And while he also claimed that the very concept of *Bildung* required such multiplicity—as well as a flexibility of mind—in order to overcome simplistic (externalist) views of *Naturrecht* (PR:129), he continued to argue for strict codification (and realization) as the condition for rational law, where the spirit's freedom would "stamp its seal" "maturing (*bildet*) itself inwardly" until it "attains objective reality in the finite" (PR:125). But, it could be argued, precisely here he had abandoned his own transformation of modern civility—or, as he also understood it, his own modern transformation of Cicero's notion of *decorum*, the appearance of justice (PR:121).[84] Here "the end of reason is neither the manners [*Sitteneinfalt*] of an unsophisticated state of nature, nor as particularity develops, the pleasure for pleasure's sake which education [*Bildung*] procures" (PR:125). Yet, such 'civility' would require perhaps precisely the complex interplay between subjective and objective, universal and particular, principle and transcendence which simple univocal codification could only reduce. Moreover, while Hegel could admit such a multiplicity of objects and situations required a flexibility or plasticity of mind for theoretical *Bildung*, practical *Bildung* required a discipline of objective activity and universally recognized attitudes—but in either case the result was precisely to overcome diversity for the sake of Absolute Objectivity.

## 6. Hermeneutics, Sovereignty, and the Machinations of Power: On the Unwieldiness of Civility

In a brief reference to the reception and transformation of Roman law in later Europe (referring to the quarrel over the exempt status of the caesar [*lege solutus*] under the Justinian code), Gadamer aptly claims that "under the changed circumstances of modernity it became an ongoing hermeneutical thorn" (RAS:96). Gadamer himself again saw in this issue the point that jurisprudence sustains the law, that "the just interpretation of the law is not simply a doctrine concerning a technical skill" (RAS:96). But it is equally decisive that in the same gesture he explicitly links hermeneutics to the principle of the modern conception of law:

> The ideal of law implies the idea of equality under the law. If the sovereign himself is not subject to the law but can decide upon its application, the foundation of all hermeneutics is destroyed. (RAS:96)

Doubtless it is just this interplay of transcendence and principle, jurisprudence and law that underlies both the civility—and the modernity—of hermeneutics.

When we invoke the notion of civility, in any case, we should also note the modern transformations it involves, which surely also lie in the background of hermeneutics as well. The conceptual past of *civility* is too quickly linked to the diacritics of the Greek *politiké*,[85] even perhaps as Heidegger had in claiming that the "wielding" (and later self-assertion) of Roman humanism has predetermined "every kind that has emerged from that time to the present" (LH:202). Heidegger thereby missed the reinterpretations that occur in the emergence of modernity itself, buried over in positivist (and antipositivist) revisionism. Both reeling from the Nietzschean alternatives, neither Carnap nor Heidegger were perhaps able to respond to the hermeneutic (and justificatory) complexities of modernity. It is true enough that whenever liberalism exchanges this humanist past for "pragmatic liberalism," whenever it turns simply 'scientific', it is "liberalism betrayed."[86] And when Gadamer, for example, acknowledges his own Aristotelianism, he is likewise quick to divorce it from the substantialism and hierarchicalism of communitarian politics. Rightly so, and in this he is consistent both with the detraditionalization that accompanied the modern notion of the everyday and the internal regulation of principle. In this respect hermeneutics remains fully in accord with the modern humanist treatises on civility itself, as readers like Bakhtin have noted. When, for example, Erasmus writes his own *de Civilitate* (1530) the concept of manners could no longer be a hierarchical notion. Civility is not restricted to the self-glorifying egoism (or heroic 'virtues') of nobles, as Strauss, for example, argues vis-à-vis Castiglione's *Book of the Courtier*—its 'other-directedness' one step removed from Hobbes's fear of violent death.[87] But neither is it simply the tacit introduction of Hobbesian constraint, any more than it is simply dependent on traditional mores.[88]

Leery of the differences at stake, in declaring manners too various to be relied on, Hobbes and those after him were led to divorce all politics from ethics; but it was just this move perhaps that the humanist notion of *civilité* contested, pointing to the possibility of a 'hermeneutic' that might not only *not* conflict with civil society but even sustain it. Instead Erasmus declared—adding that the point was of cardinal importance—"no one can choose his own parents or nationality, but each man can mould his own talents and character for himself."[89] Even if we acknowledge the naiveté of modern humanism's neglect of power, Erasmus writes in hopes of a virtue or nobility not based on the hierarchical *wielding* of power: "Let others paint lions, eagles, bulls, and leopards on their escutcheons; those who can display 'devices' of the intellect commensurate with the grasp of the liberal arts have a truer nobility."[90] This view no longer simply seeks to wield or to escape power. 'Civility' is not unlimited '*caritas*'; it is differentiated instead in the midst of the 'syntax' of power itself. The attempt to purge the pure internal (syntactic) regulations of law from the indeterminacies of virtue clearly would be fallacious. No law was, to use Montesquieu's analog, so 'machinelike' that it did not depend on virtue—or risk subversion without it.[91] This was, after all, precisely the remainder of what Aristotle called decency and its 'extension' before the shortfall in the written law.

Again, Hegel's attempt to substitute the purity of the speculative monarch for the indeterminacies of virtue would not suffice. From the beginning, Hegel had sought to ground law in the possibility of strict or external determination. The *Differenzschrift* thus criticizes the conflict between reason and nature in Fichte as a "realm of freedom where every truly free reciprocal relation of life, every relation that is infinite and unlimited for itself, that is to say, beautiful, is nullified" (Dif:144). The result, suspending

the opposition between freedom and nature, is the "true infinity of a beautiful community where laws are made superfluous by customs, the excesses
of an unsatisfied life by hollow joys, and the crimes of oppressed forces by
the possibilities of activities directed at great objects" (Dif:146). The claim
is that "through a genuinely free community of living connections the individual renounces his indeterminacy or (as Fichte calls it) his freedom. In a
living connection there is only freedom in the sense that it includes the possibility of suspending itself and entering into other connections" (Dif:145).
But such a 'suspension' surely entails the reduction that accompanied the
speculative from the beginning to the end of his career. While the later Hegel would renounce romanticism, he did not renounce its protocols. And
those who would follow him here in connecting socialization with such objectification surely would too.

By contrast, the constitution of law would indeed be internally regulated,
and thus not a mere wielding of force, but the 'autonomy' it makes possible
cannot be guaranteed without the life of virtue that might sustain it from
without. The 'body politic' literally would require another body than the automaton that had opened Hobbes's Leviathan. Law is not a machine; its interpretation is not a matter of mere analysis, and the problem of its meaning
cannot be exhausted in simple objective calculation and codification: law
would not escape the problem of its own indeterminacy, nor the problem of
interpretation. We should doubtless wonder in this regard about the complicated relations that link politics, philosophy of language, and analysis in the
wake of Hobbes. Hobbes's hope that the physicist's objectification of nature
would provide a model for morals only complicates such problems.

In the end the political requires that the heart must be more than a
spring—or a springboard to objective mind and social practice—and interpretation is more than analysis and procedural or methodological calculation. Hegel had at least seen this in criticizing Fichte's own version of the
machine state (although he continued to argue that custom and imagination might simply overcome the opposition between nature and culture)
and he later denied that dialectic could be a Rädenwerk.[92] Fichte also had
seen that the question of the lived body would be fundamental to natural
right, and that the figure of the 'body politic' involved the complexity of
principle and transcendence. Still Fichte also remained curiously entrenched in the need to dominate nature, to objectify the will, to reduce the
'accident' of singularity before the universality of reason's concept, through
which the art of statecraft would be, to use Hobbes's term, a matter of human industry, fully oblivious to its complications. And Hegel did not see his
own complicity in such reductions in identifying social practice simply

with immanence and objectified individuality—or, for that matter, the *telos* of practical labor to be abstracted from individuality, that is, to become "more and more mechanical, until finally man is able to step aside and instill machines in his place" (PR:129). But doubtless here too it is the history of these concepts themselves that articulates their intelligibility, and hence perhaps the increasing importance of Kant's own gloss on the ancients' *humaniora*.

As we have seen, Kant himself was not far from this intuition, providing both the principle of law's internal regulation and its extension, acknowledging both the modern sense of law as the internal limitation of power and a certain 'transcendence' (or 'sympathy') that remains necessarily in its midst—but in both cases still a question of character. And, as has been seen, Gadamer similarly pointed to the role of *synesis* and *syngnome* play as a political event in Aristotle. Such *synesis,* however, is not naive, nor simply the 'mechanism' of communitarianism, nor is its tolerance unlimited. The 'virtue' of hermeneutics and the decency to which it appeals remain always already critical, a differentiation that accompanies the distance (and reciprocal rejoinder) out of which all interpretation and all dialogue emerges. The 'tyranny of virtue' dissolved not only the internal regulation of law, but the transcendence of its past. As Montesquieu insisted, within the internal regulations of law, even appeals to virtue must be limited. Unlimited generosity no more suffices for justice than the algorithmics of pure universality. But in this recognition, *pace* Hegel's charge of Aristotle's formalism (PR:108; HP:2:206), we can perhaps still see the remainder of Aristotle's claim that virtue must avoid the extreme—or at least a modern construal of the doctrine of the mean, devoid of its Pythagorean past. Similarly, we will need to see the question of interpretation as internally regulated by the requisites of critique and judgment, and sustained by a transcendence that remains in its midst. Here the problem of Being and the problem of certainty are, again, of a piece.

Still, while the principles of civility depend on the 'internalization' of virtue, civility likewise required, as Erasmus's account already acknowledges, a certain externalization, that is, to the extent that such civility would involve a virtue not simply restricted by determinate community practice or social status. When theorists of civility like Oakeshott, again following Hegel in identifying *lex* as a self-contained system of law, attempt to grasp *cives* as "related solely in terms of their common recognition of the rules which constitute a practice of civility," they have missed this history and the transformations in its midst.[93] If 'civility' is unintelligible apart from the (modern) notion of law, the 'care for law' civility entails emerges only in reciprocal rejoinder with the failure of univocal traditions and the 'dialogue' that emerges in its lapse. Such an account cannot be provided by understanding practices to be simply rule governed; they must be hermeneutic as well. Civility must emerge instead not simply from the 'internal' differences that constitute community but also from differences between communities, between peoples, between moral codes, in reciprocal rejoinder with the past and with other practices, codes, and possibilities. Indeed Erasmus's text (no less than Montaigne, for example) instantiates such interpretation, appealing both to the ancients and to differences between cultures for its evidence—and its criticisms. Likewise having fully analyzed the internal legalistics of obligation, Kant's account remains fully in accord with these new practices of the *humaniora*. Indeed, as I have argued, in thus articulating the possibility of virtue Kant's *Metaphysics of Morals* becomes a paradigmatic hermeneutic text—or to use Gadamer's terms, still a book of "unshakable truth" (Reflections:56). The difference is that we must acknowledge the hermeneutic or narratival status of such a metaphysics if its accomplishment is indeed to be 'unshakable'. Seeing Kant in this light requires that we explicate a different account of the rationality of practices than as simply 'rule governed', or at least one more implicit than explicit in Kant's account, acknowledging its hermeneutic interplay of principle and transcendence, law and narrative.[94]

The result is paradoxical—both "Stoic" and "ironical." As Schlegel saw in such irony—an irony far removed from Castiglione's (or Hobbes's), which had simply subverted theory for practice at the door of modernity—a new or a higher "urbanity" devoid of determinate *polis* arises—and he adds, a republicanism both devoid of the monological rule of mon-archy in precisely the sense that both modern society and modern law are devoid both of substance and "of unity of person."[95] Here again, our own traditionality too would always be encountered in separation, in plurality, divided from the past and before the other, the unity between them always only ideal. Hence beyond the immanence of individual and universal the cosmopolitan idea reemerges, but for reasons now clear, always as internally differentiated. It is true: granted all that we rely on, granted our *Faktizität,* our *Vor-struktur,* the practices on which we rely, to say that our tradition is simply or wholly wrong always verges on incoherence.[96] But it is also true that both our affirmations and our negations remain finite—'ontic or determinate negations', to use Hegel's term. The result is that our traditions themselves remain underdetermined, unfinished, neither fully self-contained nor simply eternal. Paradoxically—or ironically, since it is the irony of hermeneutics that is at stake—it is the destiny of our 'tradition' (or the virtue of its hermeneutic remainder) to make such encounters with the 'other' both possible and necessary.[97] But, as has become evident, this is by no means the irony of Theophrastian duplicity (or dissimilation) but the 'good ambiguity' out of which the plurality of Being itself must always be encountered. Thus, beyond the mere exegesis of traditional authority, as Gadamer put it, "it is the *world itself* which is communicatively experienced and continuously entrusted (*traditur*)" (Reflections:29; Gadamer's emphasis).

The *Begriffstradition* invoked by hermeneuts (both formally and ontologically)—as they always argued—required and authorized another account of truth than one articulated through propositional equivalence, and another legitimacy than that supplied by strict demonstration. This account acknowledges that both judgment and legitimacy are divided, laterally and not hierarchically: to use Kant's terms, the result would be not constructive, but "achromatic" and "dialogic."[98] The medieval account of legitimacy, fully invested in a specific, hierarchical mytheme that assured the links between the finite and the infinite, could claim that judgment requires a judger and hence that the monarch's voice would be the juridical and, a monologic 'last judgment', the *lex animata*. The multifariousness of the modern hermeneutics (implicitly, in any case) recognizes something else: democratic authority, which, as we have seen, does not dissolve *transcendens* but acknowledges its figurative status, even while acknowledging both the requisites of principled rationality and *lex*.

Such a hermeneutic account of rationality and legitimacy is not devoid of tradition, even if always already detraditionalized: it is a mistake to think that, deprived of determinate *ethos*, a detraditionalized account of justice might do without '*ethos*' entirely. Habermas, for example, is fully aware of the cognitive indeterminacy that accompanies postconventional morality,[99] and hence the necessity of supplementation by principled law. But he thinks nonetheless that the latter might provide a deduction of all human rights, even those concerning human welfare in its social, technological, and ecological aspects[100]—as if such notions were not themselves theory dependent and requiring interpretation and the cipher of tradition. As Gadamer put it to Strauss, the effect of detraditionalization cannot, at the risk of loss of intelligibility, be as complete as proceduralists had claimed. For the very intelligibility of their procedures, after all, depends on our being able to remember "the one world . . .which in all decay has lost far less of its evidence and cohesion than it talks itself into."[101]

In the afterword to *Truth and Method*, Gadamer thus presents his case concerning the 'between' of hermeneutics and rhetoric: "It is the realm of practice and humanity in general, and its province is not where 'iron-clad

conclusions' must be accepted without discussion, nor where emancipatory
reflection is certain of its 'counterfactual agreements' but rather where controversial issues are decided by reasonable consideration" (TM:569). It is
just in this sense that the history that exceeds the ontic would not be merely
a "tissue of effects, *Geflechten Wechselwirkungen*," (TM:283) but the narrative *exhibitio* of tradition itself, the working out of tradition as an event divided in dialogue, history, and possibility. As Gadamer claimed of irony "the
result of this situation is that such deciphering interpretation remains 'uncertain'. Its 'truth' cannot be demonstrated 'objectively', except in terms of
that agreement about the subject matter . . ." (TM:538). Rather than falling
short of demonstration, irony augments the latter in acknowledging the
'plurality of voices' out of which consensus emerges.

We live, it has been said, in at most one world. This is true enough—
always in fact transcendentally true, it might be said. But our concepts, as
Kant explicitly realized, are divided between many worlds. This has been
part of our history at least since the Copernican Turn.[102] Our concepts are
irretrievably divided, figured: this too, it could be claimed, is part of what
Machiavelli as early as 1519 called the "experience of modernity" (*lunga es-
perienza della cose moderne*). The agonistics of theory, as Kant saw later,
would equally have its own battle over the remainder of speculative metaphysics, divided between the first principles of cosmotheology or ontotheol-
ogy, as Kant put it.

Postmodernists were doubtless much too prone to search beyond history—and beyond metaphysics—for an understanding of the present moment. The latter could not be accounted for either by an absent or a present
sublime 'now'; the givens to which such 'paganisms' still immanently appealed would not suffice.[103] Pierre Manent, for example, has claimed that to
rightly grasp the fertility in the modern conception of law—the fertility of
the division between nature and law—requires that we seek its key "in the
long neglected artisans of the eighteenth and seventeenth centuries, who at
least knew that the question is that of nature and law."[104] To overaccent
either side of this division "necessarily weakens the other." Similarly, rather
than simply seeing metaphysics at an end, Eco viewed the fertility of modern interpretation in the disruption at issue in Dante's inner transformation
of the canon of poetics. And Manfred Frank also found the origin of such
hermeneutics not simply in the canonical history that returns to Schleiermacher, but in the question of individuality that precedes him—that is, in a
'heretical' tradition that disrupts the strict determinacies of modern
thought. We would be mistaken were we not to see Gadamer's or even
Heidegger's hermeneutics to be of a piece here, less the attempt to surpass

history (or metaphysics or philosophy) than rethinking and refiguring the history in its midst—as much Scotus as Hölderlin, as much Cusanus as Dilthey. The problem, as Gadamer ultimately saw, is that there is simply no "language of metaphysics"—just because there is no metaphysics "in itself."[105] The question of the dispensation of the Good will not be dispensed with. Instead there is the problem of justice, the problem of adjudicating—with decency—the constraints of law, and thereby the endless task of interpreting the 'old story' of Good. The task of hermeneutics has become both much more critical and much more historical than its antagonists might have suspected.

In this light, in fact, we should return perhaps to the 'modern' conception of law from which we began. In a decisive addition to paragraph 216 of the *Philosophy of Right,* on right as law, Hegel brings a number of issues into focus:

> It is a misunderstanding which has given rise alike to the demand—a morbid craving of German scholars chiefly—that a legal code should be something absolutely complete, incapable of any fresh determination in detail, and also to the argument that because a code is incapable of such completion, therefore we ought not to produce something 'incomplete' [*Unvollkommenen*], i.e., we ought not to produce a code at all. (PR:139)

Decisively, the question of law, universality, and incompleteness are here brought together. Neither the completeness nor the determinacy of law precludes innovation, nor does their 'plasticity' preclude universality. Doubtless here lies the fertility of the Hegelian account of "determinately existent law [*das Dasein des Gesetzes*]." At the same time we must surely question whether this same morbid German tendency [*Krankheit*] concerning absolute completeness ultimately 'affected' even Hegel's own account of ultimate determinacy—if not in the return of the monarch then the reconciliations announced in the conclusion to this work to which "the Germanic peoples has been entrusted." And entrusted to the German peoples, he declares, is nothing less than the reconciliation of the state, nature, and the ideal world (PR:222–23).

We have refused to 'subtract' this overdetermination from Hegel's speculative articulation of modern law and what, following Gadamer, we might call its lingering "prejudice of completeness." Heidegger, who, recall, had claimed (at least at one point) that the multiplicity of thought need not conflict with the strictness of interpretation (and analysis), doubtless saw this better. Here he remained perhaps still in line with Hegel's insight outlined in the above text, even if the mythemes that overdetermine Hegel's position in the end rendered it impossible for Hegel himself. On the other hand, we have refused to see in such overdeterminations the motivation for a simple return to an event or nature antecedent to law for its meaning or value.

Doubtless, as will become evident, such issues will further complicate the question (and the history) of meaning and value themselves and again overdetermine their theoretics from within. In the above text, at least, Hegel uses the plural, 'peoples', for the 'Germans', who would participate in the grand reconciliation between the state, nature, and the ideal world. But this reconciliation, it must be insisted, is possessed 'titularly' by no such community: it lies always 'between' us: hence the 'interplay' between interpretation and law. Indeed in the very interplay of universality itself we have found, once more, the rationality and the historical differentiation(s) of traditionality at stake—and the fertility of Hegel's account to have posited the question of legal recognition [*gesetzliche Anerkennung*] in their midst (PR:140). Here doubtless, without denying the violence at the origin of modern law, legal hermeneutics can find its 'clue' for extending Hegel's shortcomings within the Hegelian thesis itself. For the fertility of the Hegelian conception in the end lies precisely in the complexity it outlines and relies on for the care for law (rightly construed 'civility') in delineating the links between universality, completeness, and recognition, the latter in turn articulated doubtless through the modern narratives of law and freedom, contingency and necessity themselves. Recalling once more the complicated syntax of the hermeneutic circle, we can say that incompleteness "need not" prevent the legitimacy of law, and indeterminacy "need not" prevent the just rule of law, if both will always venture and require the supplement of recognition and care. But both will require that the link between history and meaning, truth and narrative, being and time be constantly reinterpreted.

# 3. On Levinas, the Ethics of Deconstruction, and the Reinterpretations of the Sublime

# 1. Deconstruction, the Requisites of Reason, and the Morality of Obligation

The project of "deconstructing" and of "overcoming" the tradition has always concerned itself with the question of alterity, the question of the deferral of the other within the regulations of philosophy.[1] In one sense to attempt to delimit a domain of the rational that would escape the violence of theory and the accompanying antinomies between the same and the other is as old as the title 'ethics' itself. Still, that this "other" should find determination (*Bestimmung*) precisely in human guise, that is, the appearance of a *visage*, a "face" which *en effet* forces pure reason to turn practical, has always troubled it. The persistent appearance of Emmanuel Levinas's 'concept' of the face within the text of deconstruction is, then, to use a word Jean-Luc Nancy invokes in describing the categorical imperative, a "strange" or uncanny event—in fact, that "than which nothing is more strange," as he put it, waxing perhaps both onto-and-theological.[2] Moreover, recognizing this hinge between the appearance of the moral law within the Kantian text and its Levinasian counterpart may be essential to coming to grips with issues (and hesitations) concerning the ethical in the texts of deconstructive theory.

As has become evident such claims will immediately encounter the ruins of sympathy and sympathetic understanding (*synesis, sygnome*), the problem of the will and the remainder of 'goodwill' itself. The problems surrounding the notion of 'sympathy' itself will be complex. As Max Scheler put it in his classical treatise on this matter, in delusive empathy, the problems at stake will likewise be interpretive:

> The medieval writers were often given to reading their own thought or those of their own time into the sources and documents of classical antiquity, thereby fathering Christian modes of thought upon Aristotle for example. Whereas the tendency in modern times has been to take up ideas which have been unconsciously acquired and thought a thousand times, and put them forward as new and original, the older (medieval) habit was to extract ideas which were actually new and original from such authors as were invested with special authority.[3]

Such auricular investments will indeed be overdetermined. Thus Freud's peculiar pairing of transcendental metaphysics with paranoia, both of which "draw conclusions from insignificant signs which others give to them"—and now both in turn he claimed "destined to be changed again by science into psychology of the unconscious."[4] And nothing will be more complicated granted such an economics and its claims to have mined "the

intensively tilled soil from which our virtues proudly emerge" than to confront the uncanny issue of obligation itself,[5] particularly granted its modern
manifestations; divided, that is, between theory and practice, self and other,
conscience and recognition.

As a result, the problem of tracing the event of obligation within the play
of theoretical difference, the underdetermination of the moral, and the antinomies of transcendental dialectic has always run deep, persistently and
perhaps suspiciously eluding demonstration. In fact the initial move licens-
ing an extension that granted "primacy" to the practical in the transcendental text perhaps already precariously derived from the *Aufhebung*, (or even
the "will to power") of metaphysics. Kant himself announced the question
of this extension's deferral and elevation in the preface to the 1787 version
of the *Critique of Pure Reason*: "I have therefore found it necessary to deny
knowledge (*Ich musste also das Wissen aufheben*) in order to make room for
faith" (Bxxx). And the question of the status of this event, the sole *Faktum*
of reason, as Kant called it (CPR:31), has always seemed problematic within
the texts of "deconstruction," perhaps wholly in accord with their Heideggerian ancestry and the ontological *Destruktion* by which the *Kantbuch* had
itself committed the phenomenon of 'respect' to the "strangeness and ob-
scurity of the transcendental imagination."[6] The play of interpretation
which resulted almost inevitably forced a certain "demythologizing" of the
classical account of the ethical person.[7] And thus, the appearance of the
Levinasian "claim" to the contrary, privileging the ethical against its withdrawal, must appear equally "strange" to assert.

In one respect that appearance, as the historian of ideas would insist, is a
simple empirical fact. At the very least it can be said that Levinas's trace precedes its appearance in the text of deconstruction by at least two decades, as
Jacques Derrida has acknowledged in appealing to it as a model of deconstruction itself. And, if the trace precedes conceptual articulation, the Levinasian claim is precisely that this trace, *pace* all attempts to mark its
withdrawal, also re-mains after the concept: neither this nor any other "mediation" might limit it, since the trace remains precisely an-archical with respect to all "textuality," an *empeiria* that *cannot* be regulated within the
economics of simple deferral.

This event eludes all ontologics and all de-ontologics; it opens a "metaphysics" that institutes the denial of the privilege of ontology. The relation
involved, and perhaps even the proportionality (*analogia*) of its elements,
occludes classical solutions to the *aporia* of the same and the other, undercutting the priority of the 'subject' in its relation to 'Being'. Instead it is
claimed, "the absolutely other is the Other" (TI:39). And thus, this "other"

metaphysics would arise only in breach (*rupture*), a detotalization which marks the failure of theory before an event which cannot be encompassed. The positivity of 'theory' would be discovered in respect for exteriority (TI:43), an 'outside' that exceeds the grasp of the speculative, confronted with an "idea" whose *ideatum* occurs only as an event, a "nature" excessive to all theory in the strict sense. The exteriority of this trace would mark instead the risk of a certain "communality" unencompassable within the unity and the subsumption of the concept and devoid of any algorithmic criterion, a *Masstab* of unity for its grasp—it being precisely a matter of the *Masslösigkeit* that is in question; or, as Hegel put it in the *Logic*, a "vanishing," a "dispersing" of the finite in the beyond, the failure of all quanta (WdL:371ff.).

Still, as Nancy rightly realized early on, the discourse of this other "nature" which spurs on the ethical, and the transition or *Übergänge* beyond the speculative, pivots on a Kantian effect. "Pure philosophy," Kant claimed, "is all at sea when it seeks through a priori concepts to obtain insight in regard to the natural world" (A725/B753). And, this was an "insight" with portentous consequences concerning our learning, but none more portentous perhaps than those issuing with regard to the failure of its exemplar, *mathesis* itself. While Kant was willing to say that mathematics constituted, indeed constructed, our most perfect reflection of the divine *intellectus originarius,* "the most splendid example of the successful extension of pure reason" (A716/B740), it could not assist in the ultimate closure of pure reason. Being ultimately escaped the certainty of *mathesis.* "Theory," discursive knowledge, was at best finite. Even though "examples are contagious," mathematics could not furnish the paradigm of reason (A716/B740). Hence the failure of philosophical modernism, if not the eschatology of philosophy itself.

> It therefore becomes necessary to cut away the last anchor of these fantastic hopes, that is, to show that the pursuit of the mathematical method cannot be of the least advantage in this kind of knowledge (unless it be in exhibiting more plainly the limitations of the method); and that mathematics (*Messkunst*) and philosophy, although in natural science they do, indeed, go hand in hand, are none the less so completely different, that the procedure of the one can never be imitated by the other. (A726/B754)

Kant's distinction saved the appearances as well as his own examples (Newton and Galileo), making them by a kind of Pythagorean leap certain in themselves. And if likewise, he thereby opened up a famous *agon* between the natural and the human sciences, those examples had their own skeptical returns which at the limit could be, he realized, both "dangerous" and "destructive" (A768/B797). Nature (as a totality) escaped—escaped measure, escaped mathematics, escaped the concept. Concepts instead were partial, furnishing at best, Kant claimed, a point of view: "Every concept may be regarded as a point which, as the station for an observer (als einen Punkt ansehen, der, als der Standpunkt eines Zuschauers), has its horizon, that is, a variety of things which can be represented, and, as it were, surveyed from that standpoint" (A658/B686).

But this Standpunkt and its Ansehen, too, is overdetermined, and, perhaps equally "dangerous," schematized still in fact within the figure of a mathematical analog. On the one hand, on its basis Kant postulated a series of horizons, a variety of perspectives which by subsumption and "ascent" would yield a "highest of all genera, and so . . . the universal and true horizon," a god's-eye view from which "the plane of knowledge," as he called it, would be complete (A759/B787). And, this conceptual optics would perhaps likewise provide the fulfillment of the modernist account of experience, the complete saturation of the epistemic tabula rasa as re-presentation, a plane by which even Leonardo had attempted to reconstitute the painterly image: "The plane surface has its complete image in another plane surface which is the object opposite it."[8] This perspective, perspectivism itself, formed the basis for modern rationality and the aesthetic. Kant, too, viewed not only concepts but works of art as Aussichten with horizons which provoke thought into reflection. Nonetheless, he denied with regard to both the epistemic as well as the aesthetic that a horizon and its perspective could find closure, that the "image," to speak as both Kant and Leonardo did, could find "completeness." To attain this plane is to find a horizon that "in its sweep comprehends it all, and which has been entitled by us the idea of unconditioned totality, [t]o reach this concept is impossible" (A759/B787). This idea is a mere focus imaginarius whose function is, at best, heuristic, the site of a certain transcendence which could never strictly be made "transcendental."

Still, notwithstanding Kant's condemnation of finite intellect to the realm of the discursive, it would be incorrect to claim that we have no "experience" of this failure or of what escapes both representation (Vorstellung) and the discursive or strictly categorical. Indeed much more in Kant's thought perhaps depends on it than is usually thought.

> This world presents to us so immeasurable a stage of variety, order, purposiveness, and beauty, as displayed alike in its infinite extent and in the unlimited divisibility of its parts, that even with such knowledge as our weak under-

standing can acquire of it, we are brought face to face with so many marvels immeasurably great, that all speech loses its force, all numbers their power to measure, our thoughts themselves all definiteness, and that our judgment of the whole resolves itself into an amazement which is speechless, and only the more eloquent on that account. (A622/B650)

In the third *Critique* this withdrawal and negation was positively denominated (in accord with a tradition that went at least as far back as Longinus) by the "concept" of the "sublime"—that is, an experience which was not simply a regress from the conditioned to the conditions but precisely—again to use Longinus's term—an *elevation* (*diarmati*) beyond condition:[9]

The satisfaction in the sublime of nature is then only negative (while in the beautiful it is positive) viz. a feeling that the imagination is depriving itself of its freedom, while it is purposively determined according to a different law from that of its empirical employment. It thus acquires an extension and a might greater than sacrifice—the ground of which, however is concealed from itself. . . . (CJ:109)

The straining of the imagination before this "different law" and its inadequacy to an event and an intensive "magnitude" that "overflows" its extensive correlate revealed, indeed symbolized, another horizon, that of the moral imperative and the mind's susceptibility to practical ideas, refiguring by a certain disavowal the ancient relation between the Beautiful and the Good.[10] While the architectonic of the principles of pure reason in the first *Critique* had been instituted on the grounds of modern *mathesis,* the sublime arose precisely on the grounds of the latter's failure, or the limit of the category of quantity—a failure which, moreover, unleashed the possibility of the moral sphere and a radiance which would still enlighten even if it had never been "measured." And hence, this "straining of the imagination" remained "attractive [because] reason exerts a domination over sensibility in order to extend it in conformity with its proper realm (the practical) and to make it look out [*hinaussehen*] into the infinite, which is for it an abyss [*Abgrund*]" (CPR:104–5). The sublime thus serves as a 'schematism' for the ethical.

In one sense this was not new. Before Kant, Edmund Burke had made the unlimited expanse of extension a source of the sublime, seeing as well "the appearance of infinity" in disorder.[11] Moreover, he claimed that the ensuing experience of astonishment so filled the mind that it could not entertain any other object, "nor by consequence reason on that object which employs it."[12] It took those most troubled by reason's lapse before the sublime to see what had been accomplished thereby. As Strauss rightly saw, in all this

Burke remains "in explicit opposition to the classics: Burke denies that there is a connection between beauty, on the one hand, and perfection, proportion, virtue, convenience, order, fitness, and any other such 'creatures of the understanding', on the other."[13]

As a result, however, the appeal to the sublime seemed only to reinstitute the failure of the ethical within theoretical modernity, culminating for Strauss at least in the loss of any object as basis for moral judgement. Nonetheless, while Kant also saw a shattering of understanding's harmony in the event of obligation, the latter became precisely thereby the condition of the emergence of *another* reason, the emergence, that is, of the ethical.[14] Burke had similarly recoiled from the experience of individual judgment in the political realm, of course. While society may rest on consent, "old custom is the great support of all the governments in the world. The excess of speculation would only give rise to discontent and the spirit of litigation."[15] Kant's commitments regarding individual experience and the sublime and the other order of reasons they indicated obviously could not have disagreed more.

## 2. Phenomenology, the Horizons of Intentionality, and the "Rationality [That] Gleams Forth in the Face to Face"

While Levinas came to similar conclusions concerning the exteriority of the ethical—appealing to "the first rationality [that] gleams forth in the face to face" (TI:208)—he initially confronted the problem of the horizonal and its excess through the work of Edmund Husserl. Husserl increasingly came to rethink the evidence of his phenomenological investigations through its complex matrix of intentionality and fulfillment, that is, a strategy of regulative ideas that bridges the abyss between the evidence of lived experience and the ideal iterability required for a pure science of essence. From the outset of his work with Husserl, beginning as early as his 1930 work, *The Theory of Intuition in Husserl's Phenomenology*, Levinas claimed that Husserl's evidential commitments to concrete life as the ultimate source of evidence could only be rightfully grasped on the basis of "the affirmation of the intentional character of practical and axiological life."[16] The difficulties of this affirmation, however, were equally unsurpassable. Husserl's commitment to lived experience and the departure from it instituted by transcendental phenomenology was decisive, making "possible this passage from ethics to metaphysical exteriority" (TI:20); but it equally reduced Being and all "relations into correlatives of a gaze." And, thereby, it leveled off the overdetermination on the Kantian horizon.

> Since Husserl the whole of phenomenology is the promotion of the idea of *horizon*, which for it plays a role equivalent to that of the *concept* in classical idealism; the existent arises upon a ground that extends (*dépasse*) beyond it, as the individual arises from the concept. But what commands the non-coinciding of thought with the existent—the Being of the existent, which guarantees the independence and the extraneity of the existent—is a phosphorescence, a luminosity, a generous effulgence. The existing of the existent is converted into intelligibility; its independence is a surrender in radiation (*une reddition par rayonnement*). To breach the existent from Being is simultaneously to let it be and to comprehend it. Reason seizes upon the existent through the void and nothingness of existing—wholly light and phosphorescence. Approached from Being, from the luminous horizon where it has a silhouette, but has lost its face, the existent is the very appeal (*l'appel*) that is addressed to comprehension. (TI:44–45)[17]

It is a passage that twists and tropes in what is itself a kind of withdrawal of meaning from the concept, refusing to attach the radiance in question to a rhetorics of simple clarity or adequation. Levinas's "claim" is, nonetheless, that the reduction of Being to *Evidenz* and idea ultimately precluded the appearing of what transcended or over-flowed the *ideatum*. Kant had also claimed that the "transcendence" of the regulative idea itself was confirmed by a kind of "strong evidence" (A661/B689) acknowledging that this evidence nonetheless underdetermined the Ideas and could not prevent conflict over their interpretation—one which was, consequently, "impossible to decide" (A501/B529).[18] Moreover, since knowledge had been bound to the "decidability" conditions of his Analytic, the best that could be said of this "evidence" concerned its "utility" in extending but not demonstrating the grounds of those conditions. But that meant as well that Kant would need to "bar" the "experience" of the sublime—in all its implications, ethical and aesthetic—from the realm of the cognitive (CJ:133). What the sublime ultimately disclosed was not a question of the empirical, but the limits of the empirical and the necessity of surpassing, if not overcoming it.

If Husserl's phenomenological extension equally opened up a domain of experience beyond the empirical, the experience of the "meant as meant," as he called it, Being as such, it did so only on the foundation of the original phenomenon, the gaze of consciousness, a "luminosity," or a clearing before the intentional arc. Phenomenological evidence was precisely a matter of "showing," a matter of clarification or enlightenment—*Aufklärung*, as Husserl put it.[19] Hence, it called forth the question of its verification, the question of its own strictness, and thus, the ontological difference that in principle separated the meant from the meant *as* meant. The primordial instance of "obligation," accordingly, would concern the problem of finitude and what 'always already' escaped the distance which separates Being from its "meaning," a "transcendence" that escaped the foundations of comprehension and the unity of the concept.

Still, even Heidegger's account of the *ex-stasis* of Being and the articulation of its withdrawal perhaps also restricted the ethical event that might exceed Being altogether by a certain over-taking, a *sur-prise*, as an evidence which differs from that adhering to the cognitive gaze. Rather, Levinas claimed, this attempt to found Being by the spontaneity of an epistemic grasp, constituting it on the basis of its own luminosity, must undergo a certain reversal before an event, again Kant's *Faktum*, which calls spontaneity itself into question—a phenomenon that not only transcends but exceeds, a phenomenon (*phanestaton*), that is, which compels instead simply on the basis of its radiance (*ekphanestaton*). In fact, whether or not it has ever taken place, this moral "law" still commands out of radiance, like a jewel *für sich selbst glänzen.*[20]

But the "reversal" Levinas discerns is still not a simple reversal that would substitute the will for a concept in the *realization* of the speculative, as readings of the second *Critique* from Fichte onward had decreed, nor one which might simply substitute heuristic utility for truth, as had Kant in the Transcendental Dialectic in the wake of the failure concerning decidability. Rather, Levinas's reversal enforces a passivity before an event which overtakes by what remains (within the calculus of probability) merely a "silhouette," allowing it to emerge *en face,* despite the undecidability of its modal license.

Levinas appeals in fact to an evidence which, if it began with the "phenomen-ological," still escaped all phenomenology, an evidence which, to speak Kantian, remained "abyssal," an-archical and undeniable—"a philosophical evidence (which) refers from itself to a situation that can no longer be stated in terms of 'totality'" (TI:24). The origin of this concept doubtless finds schematic outline in classical phenomenological glosses on intersubjectivity or "the problem of other minds." In these accounts the other is viewed precisely as a certain nonprimordiality that appears in transcendental or reflective immanence—that is, the evidence of a transcendence, an 'other' which is not I.[21] However, like all evidence which is not fully present, or that is inadequate, the other here is construed as a transcendence only in the negative sense. For Levinas, however, the 'evidence' in question is not negative; instead, it is an event which escapes the schematics of finitude and the economics of negative transcendence. It is the up-surge of an ideatum that ruptures theoretical unity, a "reason which has no ground" and yet which cannot simply be rejected as irrational. This event of separation which defies the concept is described by Levinas as the encounter with the "face" of the Other (TI:29):

> The way in which the other presents himself, exceeding *the idea of the other in me,* we here name face. This mode does not consist in figuring as a theme under my gaze, in spreading itself forth as a set of qualities forming an image. The face of the Other at each moment destroys and overflows the plastic image it leaves me, the idea existing to my own measure (*mesure*) and to the measure of its *ideatum*—the adequate idea. It does not manifest itself by these qualities. . . . It expresses itself. (TI:50–51)[22]

And this expression beyond all figure and metaphor, "the deformalization or concretization of the infinite" (TI:50), immediately surpasses the realm of the epistemic by a transition or *Übergänge* that engenders the height of the ethical as an "expression" that equally "commands" in delimiting both the *ex-stasis* and the fragility of the finite.

> This gaze that supplicates and demands, that can supplicate only because it demands, deprived of everything because entitled to everything, and which one recognize in giving . . . this gaze is precisely the epiphany of the face as a face. The nakedness of the face is destituteness. To recognize the Other is to recognize a hunger. To recognize the Other is to give. (TI:75)

This 'figuring' is to be liberated from the archive of metaphysics which would reduce the encounter with the Other, the "face" of the Other, to mere "clarity" and the intersubjective to the "neutrally" interpersonal. And if Levinas liberates the discourse of the sacred in this retrieval—which, as he insists, is not to say that he simply turns "theo-logical," he insists (TI:75)— it is equally a retrieval of the sublime from the metaphysics of the beautiful. The latter, instead, substituted "an image for the troubling depth of the future," resulting in "a beautiful form reduced to itself in flight, deprived of its depth" (TI:263). As such it substituted a foundation, a demonstration, a form, a clarity, and a security for the ungraspable "height" revealed in an "existence unfounded for without foundation," the "grace" and the "radiance" that had fought metaphysics throughout the *agon* that marked its encounter with the sublime. As Plotinus realized before Kant, in accord with Longinus (and by means of "evidence" equally as shocking), the beauty of the "face" owes nothing to form, or at least to proportion, to a *mesure,* but rather to "a remoter principle," a splendor as sublime as ever, which "floods with awe and gladness, stricken by a salutary terror."[23]

The (relational) concept of the face-to-face indicates an event beyond the violence of history, but it is still not a 'concept' without a history—a history, as will be seen, that requires further attention for its adjudication. It suffices to note provisionally that Levinas's account of the event of the face also emerges from the figures and narrative of the tradition, as well as, it should be insisted, from the phenomenological, and even literary narratives that had preceded him—for example, Sartre and his own invocation of the narratives of Faulkner, where the link between the flesh and transcendence had been intimately explored.[24] Doubtless, moreover, it is the narrative of tradition that first offers such a 'revelation', as God spoke to Abraham face-to-face, like a friend: a 'person' and not a figure—and this concept too, as will become evident, betrays its own logic.[25] But what Levinas insists on in demarcating the excess of the face before representation is its rupture with all figure and all tradition. It is precisely the sublimity demarcated in the face that removes it from the frozen appearance of form, figure, and concept.

Still, with the sublime it is perhaps always a question of heights and depths, assents and elevations, of radiance across the abyss—and, Jacques Derrida had initially worried, an economics which guarantees, even if *per analogia* and figuration. By this economics Levinas's face, even as the zero degree of signification, reflects still a height, a transcendence. Even in its "utter nudity," even within a destitution which summons, it remains: "the body is a figure of speech," a figure whose reference escapes totality—absolutely—precisely by troping the finite.

> Infinity (as infinitely other) cannot be violent as is totality (which is thus always *defined* by Levinas, always determined by an option, that is, an initial decision of his discourse, as *finite totality*): totality for Levinas means a finite totality. This functions as a silent axiom. This is why God alone keeps Levinas's world from being a world of the pure and worst violence, a world of immorality itself. The structures of living and naked experience described by Levinas are the very structures of a world in which war would rage—strange conditional—if the infinitely other were not infinity, if there were, by chance, one naked man, finite and alone. (VM:107)

This "counterfactual" by which the solitary in a kind of sublime reversal would *not* transcend involves the simplicity of abandonment and oblivion, the state of nature as an absolute state of war. It involves, if you will, the incursion of the Hobbesian nightmare that has always accompanied the modern rejection of tradition—the history and nightmare, to use the Joycean figure, from which we are trying to awake.[26] As the Joycean figure itself denotes, the problem of interpreting (and adjudicating) the Levinasian event is as much linguistic as it is epistemic or metaphysical, as Derrida had indicated from the beginning by pairing the iterable univocity of Husserl with the *contrepoids* of Joycean equivocity.[27] There was always the hope, as Hobbes put it in opposing "vain and fabulous tradition," that we might remember what the original names stood for (Lev:687). Even Heidegger's hope "to preserve the *force of the most elemental words*" could not be simply detached from the levelings in this inheritance (BT:262; Heidegger's emphasis).

For Derrida the question initially was whether Levinas can forbid the unutterable violence that threatens his account—and what possibility has been regulated. "Language is indeed the possibility of the face to face and of being-upright, but it does not exclude inferiority . . . " (VM:107). The discourse on the other itself could not rule out the possibility that, far from being a summoning based on destitution and fragility, the other might command out of simple mastery; thereby, the discourse of the other and exteriority would succumb to the economics of power and the ultimate dissolution of respect within assertion. Given this alternative, Levinas's claim would always be infinitely questionable. Hence the consistency, and perhaps even the necessity of the phenomenologist's demurring before the Levinasian axiom and its "evidence," which could never be fully adequated. And, if not out of commitment to phenomenology's intuitions, then at least to its rigor, Derrida would never be closer to Husserl.

Even if phenomenological intentionality is infinitely deferred in the process of reiteration and confirmation, and even if, consequently (as Husserl himself eventually realized), no evidence however apodictic is unrevisable—if, that is, "intentional incompleteness" is endemic to phenomenology from its first breath—it remains the case that the logic of phenomenology likewise *forbids* the affirmation of the *infinitely* other (VM:120–21). For Levinas this "surpassing of intention" that results from its being submitted to its horizons brings about "the ruins of representation" thereby opening up the possibility of "an ethical *Sinngebung*," an essential relation "respectful of the Other." But Husserl could only refuse its transcendence:[28] "reason" could not simply hand itself over to whatever an infinitely *unknowable*—an event, that is—beyond adequation might "command." Such a move would involve nothing less than the decapitation of reason itself, to use a figure Husserl employs elsewhere. And the strictness of the philosopher's text here should not be underestimated, as the following text—Husserl's Stoic version of the *Euthyphro*, which Derrida did not fail to cite—reveals:

[T]he subjective a priori precedes the being of God and world, the being of
everything, individually and collectively, for me the thinking subject. Even
God is for me what he is in consequence of my productivity of consciousness;
here too I must not look aside lest I commit blasphemy, rather I must see the
problem. (FTL:251)[29]

It was a conclusion whose "monstrous" consequences did not shake Husserl. Even if as a result we are consigned to "the darkened corner haunted by
the spectres of solipsism, and, perhaps, of psychologism, of relativism," Husserl declared, "The true philosopher, instead of running away, will prefer to
fill the dark corner with light."[30] Any other claim would open up the interminable possibility of terror and irrationality. And it was a doubt and a corresponding need for demonstration, for grounds and adequation, that blocked
up all "transcendence," all "elevation," and ultimately all rational "ascent."

## 3. The Legacy of the Divided Subject and a Good beyond the *Eidos* of the Beautiful

Still, Levinas himself claimed in *Totality and Infinity* that what broaches the
exteriority of the ethical remained an *Evidenz,* one which equally refused
the reduction of being to power. For this claim he ironically invokes the
name of Nietzsche:

> We come upon events that cannot be described as noeses aiming at noemata,
> nor as active interventions realizing projects, nor, of course, as physical forces
> being discharged into masses. They are conjunctures in being for which perhaps the term "drama" would be most suitable, in the sense that Nietzsche
> would have liked to use it when, at the end of *The Case of Wagner,* he regrets
> that it has always been wrongly translated by action. (TI:28n)

What was in question, Nietzsche claimed, was wholly a matter of pathos,
a Dionysian *mimeisthai* anterior to the Apollonian image, which, by being
transformed into an "act," dissolved the decisive connection it had with
narrative, with "legend" and "sacred history."[31] That is, drama lost its connection with a pathos undergone, and specifically, a passivity which unveils, *apocalypsis.* Jean-François Lyotard, whose earlier *Économie libidinale*
(1974) attempted to exhibit a Dionysian theater of intensities, was ultimately forced to take note. And, thus, that work, constructed on the post-
Deleuzean notion of the affirmation of intensities and the discharge of
forces, failed as an experiment to capture *pathos.*[32]

If it were the case, as Lyotard claimed already in 1970, that art and the sacred have been leveled off "because we are in a system that doesn't give a rap about sacredness," but only about "what can be sold," it is true nonetheless that the problems of the ethical and the phenomenon of injustice remain.[33] And, while in the aesthetic we may be satisfied with the principle of pleasure and pain, "with justice we have to do with the regulation (*la régulation*) of something else." That is, instead of dealing with "differences of intensity and velocities" as his tract on the libidinal had, the question of justice invokes a "difference" in the will itself—one before which "the faculty of willing needs to regulate itself (*se réguler*)."[34] As Kant put it after defining pleasure or happiness in the first *Critique* in terms of "the degree of intensity," desire is "checked" by obligation (CPR:77).

While for Levinas this "checking" was described in terms of a summons, Kant was perhaps more direct concerning its effect. This checking marked the humiliation (*Demütigung*) of desire, in which the latter undergoes "elevation" (*Erhebung*), an event which is not an incentive for morality, but the experience of morality itself. This "humiliation," in other words, is at the same time an event of elevation and respect, a determination (*Be-stimmung*) which "we cannot help feeling," and a feeling (*Stimmung*), moreover, that can be represented only through a kind of *pathos* (CPR:80–81) and a dispossession from oneself that divided the subject from within. Its occurrence is not one that 'man' brings forth and possesses, but one that instead "possesses man"; an elevation, a *Zu-stimmung*, one in which we are quite literally beyond our senses, in the *ex-stasis* of the finite, a Good beyond all ontic goods.[35]

The categorical imperative in one sense belonged wholly to modernism, or wholly to its "elevation" of *mathesis universalis* in the claim that there was an algorithm for strict, univocal adjudication of the ethical, a kind of heteronomy of the demonstrative. But if, consequently, this algorithm provided necessary and sufficient conditions for this adjudication, it was not the case that it could be applied to just anything. And, *if* in this regard it were the case that its commitment to *mathesis universalis,* to the mathematically formalizable, ultimately fell short—opening the door for the calculability which afflicted the dangers of act-utilitarianism and the bureaucratic rationalizations of *Zweckrationalität*—the categorical imperative's resources, indeed grounds, were not simply thereby exhausted. Rather, it rested on its own 'axiom' of "relevance," or application, a hermeneutics and symbolization that explicated a 'topic' for respect—as writers such as Schopenhauer and Scheler realized in advance of Levinas:

> Respect always applies to persons never to things. The latter can awaken inclinations, and even love, if they are animals, or fear, as does the sea, a volcano, or a beast of prey, but they never arouse respect. (CPR:79)[36]

Nonetheless, with Kant too it was in a sense a matter of an idea whose time would never come, whose assertion would never find determinate evidence for such narratives, which never, consequently, could be free from the question as to whether it has taken place (*arrive-t-il*). As Lyotard put it, then, its transcendence would always remain "empty"[37]—echoing in fact, to use Lefort's term, the "empty place" of transcendence within political modernity. Even Kant realized that his account of the moral event was based on a principle, that of our freedom from incentives (autonomy), which could not itself be established, nor simply thereby be free from the conflict of interpretations.

Thus, in the foundation of 'morality' there would always be an abyss and an inextricable dispute—first concerning its possibility (which Kant, apparently, fully realized), but equally, Lyotard claims, a debate about its character, its type (which Kant, explicitly, in any case did not). The latter involved precisely the character of its *topos*—its domain or *régime*. Under what description had injustice taken place, and under what description is it to be rectified? This was, of course, precisely the problem of the interpretation of justice.[38] Put negatively or counterfactually, injustice would always involve an event, an *Ereignis* whose determinacy, whose *propre* escapes us, and which, consequently, could always be denied within a particular "universe" of sentences. But that was in a sense Levinas's claim about the ethical, its "safe-guard," as Lyotard put it.[39] Far from it being the case that too many ethical theories could lay claim to legitimation in the ethical, it was precisely the case that strictly taken—and in the absolute sense obligation seemed to require—*none* could. Every description, every idea remained inadequate before this breach, thereby opening up the problem of de-totalization and the possibility of an exclusion, a tort, or in Lyotard's word, a *différend*.

> Each sentence is in principle the setting into play of a differend between the genres of discourse, whatever be its domain. The differend proceeds from the question: How does one enchain? which accompanies a sentence. And this question proceeds from the nothingness which accompanies this sentence with the "following." There are differends because, or like, there is *Ereignis*. But the latter forgets more than is possible: the genres of discourse are modes of forgetting of the nothingness of the occurrence, they combine the void between sentences.[40]

This *différend* will always spring forth from an abyss and its agonistic, an agonistic in which the prescriptive takes place in exclusion and in which an injustice "has occurred."

On Lyotard's reading, however, if Levinas preserves the difference within assertion in recognizing the ethical, it did not occur to him to break with the notion of evidence, truth, and what he called "positive transcendence." On this view the "propositions" of *Totality and Infinity* are perhaps so concerned with the problem of "irrationality" in confronting the event of originary obligation which overflows all adequacy that they are still couched in the declarative and ornamented with the truth predicate, thus losing hold of the exteriority of the ethical to all and any schematics of the speculative. For Lyotard the point is that here, at least, "truth" is not the problem; rather the problem again is the "terror of theory,"[41] as he put it. In other words, the problem is exclusion, and thus, ultimately injustice.

We are confronted with injustice, the agonistics of *theory* notwithstanding. As Kant put it, the *Faktum* of the "ought" remains whether or not its possibility has been theoretically admitted or verified. Adorno equally saw this summons in a statement that has continually provoked Lyotard, a statement that imports with full irony the destiny of the quantitatively sublime:

> After Auschwitz. . . . our metaphysical faculty is paralyzed because actual events have shattered the basis on which speculative metaphysical thought could be reconciled with experience. Once again, the dialectical motif of quantity recoiling into quality scores an unspeakable triumph.[42]

The question then, as Lyotard claimed, was how to bring the unexpressed, the unheard, within the realm of the expressed: "To give the differend its due is to institute new addresses, new addressers, new significations, and new referents in order that the injustice find an expression."[43]

Still Derrida questioned Lyotard's *Faktum* as he did that of Levinas before him, questioning, that is, whether this provocation did not really surrender to the impossibility of empiricism, the simple exchange of philosophy for nonphilosophy, and the critical for the precritical, attempting to force the necessity of grounds upon a unique event (and a characterization) which always remained contingent, fallible, and open to conflict. As he replied to Lyotard in the colloquium at Cerisy in 1980 ("The Ends of Man Starting from the Work of Jacques Derrida"), there is a sense in which even the invocation of "After Auschwitz" remains nostalgic: bound, (hinged between evidence and idea), a presumptive discourse "centered" on an event and its tragedy for occidental rationality, to be adjudicated by an "us."[44] If Derrida remains entirely "sympathetic" to Lyotard, he refuses nonetheless to give "assent." Rather, Lyotard's question was one to which one could not provide an answer within the genre of the philosophical, as he had said to Levinas in 1964.[45]

Rather than "enchaining differently" in ways that would bring the exclusion or *différend* to expression, Derrida, at the beginning at least, had seemingly been involved in articulating the groundlessness which haunts all assertion. *Différance* was from the outset a logic of undecidability, a logic of deferral which not only underdetermined but also undercut the play of evidence and idea, whose failed relation the strategies of Kantian regulation made manageable by the concept of a horizon. *Différance* was, in short, a "deregulation" of all strategies, an economics 'without reserve'. And its task became the inexorable tracing of the "episyllogisms" and "prosyllogisms," the "ascents" and "descents," to speak Kantian (A 336/B 394), which lead to everywhere and to nowhere. From its emergence in the commentaries on Husserl the account of *différance* turned on the failure of extension facilitated in the notion of the Kantian idea:

> Phenomenology would thus be *stretched* between the *finitizing* consciousness of its principle and the *infinitizing* consciousness of its final *institution*, the *Endstiftung* indefinitely deferred (*déférée*) in its content but always evident in its regulative value.[46]

In all this, Derrida would still claim decades later that Kant can be recognized to be "marking a limit, indeed the end of a certain type of metaphysics."[47] Still this advance occurred only insofar as it also likewise

> freed another wave of eschatological discourses in philosophy. His progressivism, his belief in the future of a certain philosophy, indeed of another metaphysics, is not contradictory to this proclamation of end and of the end.[48]

Throughout, Derrida denied the viability of this alternative, which claimed to appropriate horizons and to grasp the totality *in progressus*. Moreover, Levinas himself claimed that Derrida's denial opens up the possibility of thinking beyond Kant and the critique of metaphysics for the first time, and thus the possibility of moving beyond ontology—though he wondered, if metaphysics was really at an end, if it was thereby without issue, and if the moral "ought" and the exteriority of the ethical had thereby been dissolved.[49]

Derrida thinks like neither Kant nor Husserl here. While deconstruction is not simply critique, it nonetheless responds to the unwieldy 'synthesis' of critique, responding on the one hand to internal critique (or criteriologically fixed analysis) and at the same time to the question of its underdeterminacy and suspicion—namely that all analysis presupposes synthesis. If all analysis is then schema-specific this does not imply simple relativism: "First of all because, as Husserl has shown better than anyone else, relativism, like all its derivates, remains a philosophical position in contradiction with itself."[50] The goal instead is to recognize the complication of synthesis itself: "However stabilized, complex, and overdetermined it may be, there is a context and one that is only relatively firm, neither absolutely solid [*fermeté*] nor entirely closed [*fermeture*], without being purely and simply identical to itself."[51] If contextual schemata are open to analysis and are not simply indeterminate, they are not thereby closed to question and void of underdeterminacy: nor even, then, to the analysis of the concept of the good-will and the ought with respect to them.

## 4. The 'Ought', the Unpresentable, and the Difference That a Voice Makes

It was perhaps inevitable, however, that this "ought" too would be submitted to the trace of *différance*. In one sense, as has been seen, it has been so from the beginning. Even Kant acknowledged its withdrawal from cognitive apperception. The categorical imperative occurs within a "subject" that is "divided against itself" (A464/B493), dispersed in a conflict which from the "standpoint of the theoretical"[52] remains precisely "undecided," making this imperative, theoretically, dialectical and illusory—a mere silhouette, as Levinas would say. And yet, Kant acknowledges, the problem of the law remains, announced from an abyss which "shines" in itself even though it may itself never have taken place without name, causal history, or proper identity. As has become clear, to think that the law can only be thought as exclusion, limitation, and the simple wielding of power remains insufficient to the question of its 'positivity', constitution, norm, and difference. But what is the nature of this event and how is it differentiated within these extensions? Paralleling a question Derrida once posed upon the phenomenological text, is it that "this difference calls for a voice"[53] for its resolutions, that is, the voice of auto-affection and the metaphysical whisper, or is there a voice which "calls" *différance*? And more to the point, as Jean-Luc Nancy quite properly asked: "What speaks this sublime voice (is *archi-écriture* a sublime voice)?"[54]

Still, Kant provided an index: "Reason" calls (*erfordert*) (A649/B677).[55] But that is the paradox: for Kant, for Derrida, and perhaps for "Reason" itself. If Kant is correct that in the final analysis "there can be but one reason," it "must," even he acknowledges, "be differentiated (*unterschieden*)." Is this the call of "dialectical" reason, the call of rational "extension," which "calls upon us to bring about such unity as completely as possible" in hopes that there might be what even Kant called a "hidden identity" to the extensions, the appearance, and even the faculties (A649/ B577)? It is precisely this call of which Adorno aptly said, "Something whispers into reason's ear that the totality of things in being converges with it after all."[56] But on Kantian grounds this voice would be mad, fully paranoid, to use Freud's term, a siren which ultimately undercuts reason's search for grounds, and dissolves freedom itself. "We know only a small part of this world" and all that exceeds our horizon mitigates against this totality, as the experience of the sublime revealed. Instead the sublime forced Kant to recognize that it involved "no extension of knowledge of theoretical reason and of its knowledge of given supersensuous objects, but still an extension of theoretical reason and of its knowledge with respect to the supersensuous in general" (CPR:140). And yet this extension was no mere "extension," and its "ascent" was no mere inference. In fact this other law, apodictically certain, as Kant claimed, is neither inductively nor deductively "fixed," but "fixed of itself alone (für sich selbst fest)" (CPR:48). This other law involves an extension without deductive "ascent," an *elevation,* to a height that is equally an abyss which "must be assumed by the theoretical as something offered *from outside* and not grown in its own soil" (CPR:126; my emphasis).

It was, in the first instance, the "voice" of all that Kant attributed still to the sublime, neither merely deductive extension, nor merely a deferral, a voice which the *Religion* characterized as the "call of the divine," and the first *Critique* (stoically) as "the divine man within us."[57] And, it was perhaps the remainder, thereby, of an ancient "call" within the text of philosophy, a *hermeneia* for which philosophy could provide no ultimate discipline, neither by *techne* nor *episteme,* nor even "divination."[58] All philosophical characterization of it could then at best be tropes, never simple denominations or denotations, never simple 'literal' (non-narratival) interpretation, demanding instead an extension beyond any such simple or single interpretation. The sublime—and all that adheres to it—deals with what "literally taken and logically considered . . . cannot be given" (CJ:108). Hence, as Nancy rightly claimed, the condition for the possibility of the "divine call" remains contingent upon the categorical imperative as a *Faktum,* a unique unschematized appearance within us. In the critical system "God exists," as he put it, only "because the categorical imperative exists."[59] And yet, in the same sublime instant this abyss of the *Faktum* marked, as Jean-François Lyotard has put it, Kant's most "hebraic moment," an ethic in which "representation is forbidden, the eye closes, the ear opens in order to hear the father's word."[60] But he added, it would take an atheist—or better, a meta-physical atheist—to hear this word, beyond the seduction of the speculative and metaphysical whisper in which one might instead hear the "splitting" in the voice(s) of reason and its inevitable submission to "differentiation."[61] This submission, as Nancy has said, with all the force of rational extension, is as inevitable as it is unavoidable:

> Thus and by a syllogistic view that is quite simple, if the ought appears essen-tially to finitude, the ought submits (if I may say so) essentially to difference. Which means on the one hand, and most simply and most manifestly, that the telos of the ought (the being of having to be in general) differs or differentiates itself, but also that difference creates the ought, by itself. Or that *différance* obligates. . . . [62]

But, as such, the 'ought' also seemed to mark the emergence of a danger beyond all regulation, beyond, that is, the danger which Kant thought could be avoided by judicious legislation. For if *différance* obligates, if it calls, what "call" is it? Is it the call which merely extends, the after-image of a silhouette, which simply defers its own disillusion and ultimate paralysis; is it as much simple dis-tension as ascent? Or is it that other call, the voice which Nancy still "calls" sublime, which is undecidable, ungroundable, nei-ther simply true nor false, but rather, as Levinas put it, an overflowing of the idea by the *ideatum* in a form of essential violence which sustains the act (TI:27)? The problem in these early debates is how deconstruction's com-mitment regarding the failure of theoretical constructivism, the transcen-dental illusions that accompany the reductions (and exclusions) of formal semantics, might at the same time reveal the event of the ethical. An ethics of obligation, an ethics based simply on the limitation of the will—or even its failure in tragic mourning—would not in the end suffice: in fact neither the pure syntactics of law nor the pure semantics of presence (or absence) will suffice. The account of 'différance', after all, neither concept nor intu-ition, had acknowledged it from the outset. The question was the complex-ity of their synthesis, the problem of law and its interpretation. And yet as the Kantian terminology attests, just this 'double gesture' had accompanied Kantian thought from the outset. The point in one sense was that decon-struction continually attempted to articulate such an encounter, always aware of the fragility that accompanies it.

To raise such questions, to delineate the risk of the ought is by no means simply to deny the effect of the ethical within the play of "*différance*," how-ever. Rather, it is to truncate, perhaps as Lacoue-Labarthe and Nancy did in concluding the 1980 Cerisy colloquium on the ends of man, the extent to which the question of this "end" and its retreat must be seen as a question that more directly concerns the interpretation of human "dignity"—even though this *différance* itself seemingly marked the withdrawal and the *retrait* of all values (*Werte*).[63] Delimiting the limits of 'theoretical' possibility—indeed in confronting what was from within the constraints of a certain theoretics an impossibility—thus had a portentous effect. And the question of this 'impossibility' and its promise would increasingly come to the forefront in these writings, as shall be seen. The question, as always, was how to interpret it. Initially, however, it is critical to grasp its historical effect. For tracing the withdrawal of value and the calculation of the evaluative was, after all, likewise the condition for the possibility of the interrogation of a being which, to speak Kantian, "is not to be valued as a means to an end . . . nor even to his own ends, but is to be valued as an end in himself."[64] And, precisely in this regard the deconstruction of 'value' doubtless spurs the question of ethics within the text of all "deconstructionism," the question, that is, of the *ethos* of the withdrawal, liberating in its wake what remains 'unpresentable'.[65]

The connection between the ethical, its passage beyond the unpresentable, and this in turn to the appearance of obligation, accompanied post-Kantian transcendentalism from the outset. Moreover, it haunted this tradition's problematic link with discourse, the public sphere and communicability—or in short, its connection with the canons of truth as objectivity. In his *Sittenlehre*, Fichte directly relates this event of the unpresentable to the problem of moral consciousness and its certainty, still within the framework of what he called "moral impulse." He assigns the "difficult question" concerning the confirmation (*Bestätigung*) of "theoretical judgment concerning duty" to the realm of reflective judgment—that is, he acknowledges the strict indemonstrability of claims because the categorical imperative could not provide an "external" or "objective criterion" for moral judgment. Yet he claimed nonetheless that the *Ich stehe hier* of the imperative was satisfied by a criterion which was "intrinsic" and necessary, one "beyond which no other consciousness can test or correct" and one which is, moreover, disclosed precisely through the imagination's interplay of determination.

> So long as the power of judgment (*Urteilskraft*) is still searching for the cognition, the free power of imagination (*freie Einbildungsvermögen*) floats between opposites, and there arises—from the fact that the search is undertaken at the instigation of an impulse (*Trieb*), which has, therefore, not yet been satisfied—

a feeling of doubt. . . . As soon as the power of judgment discovers the required cognition, the fact that it is the condition which was required appears from a feeling of agreement which manifests itself. The power of imagination (*Einbildungskraft*) is now necessitated through all reality; I cannot view the matter in any other way (*Ich kann nicht anders*).[66]

Moreover, notwithstanding Fichte's commitments to impulse and desire, the primacy of the will, and the incorrigibility of conscience, it is precisely the encounter with the other that announces our "passivity," which is the content of this event of obligation, as Fichte demonstrates in approvingly citing Schelling, the experience of recognition.

In the present instance, however, there is not merely a limitation of our *being*, but also of our *becoming;* we feel our acting repelled internally; there is even limitation of our desire to act (*Trieb nach Handeln*) and hence we assume *freedom* outside us. (Mr. Schelling expresses this excellently in the *Philosophical Journal*, Vol. IV, p. 281: "Wherever my moral power finds resistance, there cannot be mere *nature*. Shudderingly I stop. 'Here is man!' speaks a voice to me. I *must* not go further.")[67]

The itinerary of this logic, its *Wechsel* and its withdrawal is, obviously, not absent in contemporary thought, linking the play of transcendental difference, the *arche* of a certain *syn-thesis* that precedes and withdraws from all re-presentation, and an event that blocks reason's advance. Heidegger was merely asking the most traditional and central issue concerning the problem of the ethical (and with an equally overdetermined force that did not leave his own text unscathed in the wake of the sublime) when he wrote: "The desire for an ethics presses ever more ardently for fulfillment as the obviousness no less than the hidden perplexity of man soars to immeasurable heights."[68]

The legacy of Heideggerian interpretation, as has become evident, also insisted on committing this *Faktum* concerning the ethical to the play of transcendental imagination and the play of ontological difference. As Derrida has recently reemphasized, the contrast between Levinas and Heidegger (versus, for·example, that between Levinas and Schmitt) cannot be a strict opposition (Adieu:161n). But the *Faktum* itself also remained unsurpassable, the opening of an excess in the practical realm would be at one and the same time both the institution and the risk of community,[69] illustrated by Dasein's precarious relation to, as always already being with, others (*Mitsein*). Indeed if the end of 'metaphysics', as Heidegger glossed it, involved the possibility of Dasein's "abandon" within the proliferation of difference[70]—

and consequently, that all claims to immediacy were naive, even perhaps *pace* Levinas, claims to the ethical immediacy of a "face," it did force the recognition that all difference could not simply thereby be leveled off or reduced to "indifferent determinateness"—quantitative difference, again to speak Hegelian.[71] And, in this regard, if claims regarding the appearance of the "Other" and its "summons" seemed in Heidegger's wake inextricably 'metaphysical', here too the claim in question did not preclude 'ethical' retrieval, and ultimately responsibility, and, finally, care.[72] Indeed that was its point: that all such questions rested upon grasping such care as the fundamentally unifying structure of Dasein's very existence.

But we should not omit the historical complications attending Heidegger's articulemes for this call of conscience. While his earlier rendering of conscience followed a medieval tradition of translating Aristotle's *phronesis* by means of conscience (*synderesis*), we should recall, in the first place, that even the call of conscience was admittedly 'dialogical' at least insofar as "hearing constitutes the primary and authentic way in which Dasein is open for its ownmost potentiality-for-Being. Moreover, all this must be affirmed without denying the importance of Heidegger's (lingering Thomistic) gloss on *phronesis* as conscience, its (Kierkegaardian) emphasis on Dasein's singularity here, nor the lingering significance that death has for all these matters. All in fact reemerged in *Being and Time*'s explicit refiguration of the *convenientia* of Dasein's 'between': this 'refiguration' in turn becomes articulated in the relationality which adjoins Dasein and its world (BT:172), the equiprimordiality of Being and Truth (BT:215, 217), and last but not least, Dasein and *Mitsein*—in all cases an equiprimordiality shorn of a primordial ground (*Urgrund*) (BT:170). The question (and the implications) of this 'between' or '*convenientia*', especially as it pertains to 'intersubjectivity' or to friendship, is one to which we shall again return later. For now it is important not to lose the present context of their emergence.

Section 34 of *Being and Time* remains an explication of Dasein and language, prepared by Heidegger's elaboration of the interpretive *als Struktur* in the attempt to "liberate grammar from logic" (B7:209). Here communication in the broad sense, which includes both "hearing and keeping silent" (BT:204), is articulated as an *existentiale* of Dasein, which he calls discourse (*Rede*). If such discourse is broader than assertion, indeed broader than the publicly communicable, it remains inextricably bound to both in a very Aristotelian sense: "Being-with develops in listening to one another [*Aufeinanderhören*] . . ." (BT: 206). This *Rede* always already involves the historicity of *Mitsein*. But what is also incontestable for Heidegger is how such listening-to-one-another has proximally and for the most part broken down, dispersed in the failure of modern everyday practice, dispersed in "the privative modes of not-hearing, resisting, defying, and turning away [*die privativen Modi des Nicht-Hörens, des Widersetzens, der Trotzens, der Abkehr*]" (BT:207). Discourse has decayed into the deficient modes of 'idle talk'. Hence Heidegger's critical demand for an enquiry that surpasses the privative obviousness of the ontic. It is in just this sense that we will need to see that the hermeneutics of empathy and the hermeneutics of Being were of a piece (cf. BT:163).

## 5. 'Discrete Fraternity', Pluralism, and the Complications of an Unresolved History

Still, if the remainder of obligation had been figured in the relation of conscience to *Mitsein*, it remained, as has been seen, ambiguous in Heidegger's text, divided between Dasein's ownmost call to authenticity and its *Mitsein*, an event neither simply ontic nor ontological, neither simply subjective nor 'intersubjective', but precisely the 'between' in which both emerge as *existentialen* of the 'care' structure itself. Now in one sense it was precisely this articulation of such a 'between' with ontological overtones that formed the object of Levinas's critique: ontology remains figured in the reduction of plurality into totality, even (and perhaps especially) in its figure of the *pros hen*. What Levinas would call the "voice [that] interrupts the saying of the already said" (OBBE:183) is not Dasein's call to itself or that of Being beyond it, nor merely the ontic voice of a friend but more "the voice of the friend whom every Dasein carries with it" in its ownmost potentiality for Being (BT:206). But while such an event is 'mentioned' in *Being and Time*, it is not much 'used'. Hence Buber's early charge that it remained a 'monological' work. And to the extent that it has missed this 'transcendence', Levinas insists, ontology as first philosophy has always been a metaphysics of power, a claim that refers to Aristotle's *energia* doubtless in the same moment that it refuses to forget Hobbes's war of each against all. Still, Levinas's relation to 'ontology' remains equally unwieldy. Such a critique of ontology is not simply its negation, or its *simple* negation in any case. Hence the positive resources of transcendence that Levinas finds in the tradition, "a being separate from infinity which nonetheless relates to it" (TI:80).

Indeed, in the culmination of *Totality and Infinity*'s discussion of separation and discourse, Levinas himself provides fragments for a history of this 'concept', a history with three 'waves' or permutations. The first is Plato's invocation of the Good as preceding the true, an event giving being to being and that on which all mortals rely in venturing their (fallible) accounts (*logoi*). The second, in the medievals' account of analogous attributes, maintains this relation between transcendence and (under)determinacy. Finally, Levinas recurs to Descartes's third *Meditation,* exposing this transcendence in the midst of transcendental meditation itself, articulating an event which exceeds representation as its positive extension. Yet are there really no 'ontological' implications to this history? Levinas states that this 'transcendence' "should have served as a foundation for a pluralist philosophy in which the plurality of being would not disappear into the unity of number nor be integrated into a totality" (TI:80). Here of course he rejoins Kant's criticisms of such extensions as improper totalization: such totalities result in precisely transcendental illusions—first, qua totality, in reason's inevitable search for the ultimate unity or the ground for all grounds, and second, in an intrinsically dangerous appeal beyond the mediations of ratiocination itself. And this danger is doubtless as present in the Levinasian text as in any other ratiocinative text, especially in its internal critique and appeals beyond theory. Levinas's gestures to the past, however, do suggest at the very least that the conceptual history from which his position emerges is a complicated one, its 'surpassings' or 'refigurations' never an all-or-nothing matter.

Despite his appeals to pluralism, however, Levinas left the discussion of plurality too much unexplicated—as both Heidegger and Derrida themselves did perhaps. And, this 'absence' too perhaps remains symptomatic: we must remain baffled by the interface between ethics and ontology in the end. No more than reason can simply be dissolved, whatever its differences, can ontology simply be said to be absent from ethics, not even from its explication of the 'face'. Recall that "the immediacy of the face-to-face" itself is supposed to be not simply an ontic event, but the revelation of a height— indeed one which, as will become further evident, separates Levinas's account from simple personalism by a complexity that tries to meet the tensions in the very tradition that Levinas invokes. Far from it being the case that "the immediate is the face to face" *simpliciter* (TI:52), the immediacy is, again, unfathomable, hidden not only by the height in which the face 'withdraws' precisely "the relation between the being here below and the transcendent being that results in no community of concept or totality" (TI:80), but also by a 'relation without relation' for which Levinas reserves the link between ethics and the *religare* of religion. This community 'otherwise' is not itself then simply a matter of the *Darstellung* of the face. Indeed later in *Totality and Infinity* Levinas further sets forth the 'ontological' and epistemic 'conditions' for the presentation of the face:

Because my position as an I is *effectuated* already in fraternity the face can present itself to me as a face. (TI:280; Levinas's emphasis)

Such a *fraternité* or incommensurable co-mmunity would be divided between 'generosity' and 'reciprocity', 'power' and 'knowledge', and, granted the critical requisites of modernity, even the Good and the True—and we might wonder whether it has been sufficiently explicated. We might, for example, already wonder not only about the link Levinas draws to the positive infinity of Descartes's third *Meditation,* but also its link to the ethical mirror image of this infinity—precisely the virtue of generosity that so complicates theoretical modernity. For Descartes, after all, generosity was to "provide the key to all the other virtues," but, unlike classical virtue, it remained devoid of 'fixed' reference—and thus remained endangered by the Hobbesian threat that afflicted all 'subjectivity'.[73] Subjectivity would always in a sense be this unstable 'exception', and intersubjectivity similarly 'ex-cepted'. If the immediate is the face-to-face, it is so always already within the withdrawal of *fraternité,* or to speak classically once more, friendship, and "the reference of every dialogue to the third party" (TI:280). For Levinas, however, at stake was an event beyond all appropriation—an event that remains in its transcendence appropriable by "neither knowledge nor power" (TI:276). And what is crucial is to sufficiently grasp this event that escapes the 'bonds' of both only by rearticulating those bonds from within. 'Ethics' after all will be 'related' to the historical contingencies of knowledge and power by default; the question is how to understand the rational complexity of its excess. And, as Levinas's histories have provisionally articulated, the complexities of this history will be both conceptual as well as real.

Now this complexity is too often missed—if not in his own work, then surely often enough in Levinas's commentators. In a rereading of dialogism and Levinas's work in particular, Francis Jacques, for example, claimed that while Levinas's descriptions may be highly accurate for ethical purposes, they are highly errant for any other account of relationality.[74] The objection has become almost standard: still Jacques articulates it with a perspicuity usually lacking. "Like Kant," Jacques claims, Levinas "decides to replace knowledge by respect. Instead of founding this respect on a universal morality of which the self is the agent," Jacques continues, "he bases it directly on the solitude and individual transcendence of the other."[75] But, of course, both Kant's 'replacement' and the problem of individual 'transcendence' are not mere theoretical placeholders in the construction of moral theory but equally historical in effect. They are not pure concepts but equally the effect of historical refiguration of narrative, concept, and event. Beyond the (modern) conceptual necessity of universality Levinas still remembers both the conceptual recourses such requisites replaced as well as the exclusions which accompanied them. Here objectivity and the violence of ideology need not be opposed.

Still, the result, as Jacques sees it, is the lack of reciprocity characteristic of standard accounts of such 'intersubjective' relationality. Indeed lacking such resources Levinas's self simply becomes held *hostage* in its relation to the other.[76] We have already confronted the problem. This 'relation' both is and is not a relation in the metaphysical sense; it is based on an irretrievable asymmetry and an infinite distance which it shares, Jacques again claims, not with transcendence but simple egoism—and hence remains always one step from barbarism. And here he is direct: even if what is at stake is the *primum relationis,* "the best we can do is agree on a description, but without forgetting that beneath the description lies an inalienable well of experience that analysis must seek to explain."[77] Again we have witnessed the complexity of Kant's account of obligation and the problem of its inevitable symbolization of the law: Jacques—like others who make such assertions—is quick in his own lingering 'Averroist' claim that the self is instead to be taken as an 'agent' of universal morality. Still, beyond this, Jacques doubtless does speak to a more ancient (and at the same time more critical) concern: the extent to which Levinas has lost the notion of reciprocity (or 'equivocity' internal to Aristotle's claim that "the friend is another self")—and hence the 'communicability' that might still link friends beyond the reduction of relationality to transitivity, calculability, iteration, and law. In this respect the 'call' of the other, which is continually in *question* in these debates, does not answer to a definite description or fixed reference, but is instead a certain rational dispossession that is 'interlocutory' from the start; its 'between' is always both transcendentally symmetrical and likewise transcendentally 'ventured' (i.e., asymmetrical).[78] Hence the continuing appearance of apparently contradictory markers in the *'more'* that ensues (e.g., respect for a relation 'that is not a relation', a duty which acknowledges universal law *and* the singular it excludes, etc.).[79]

What rational dialogue doubtless attests to, and ethics 'responds' to, is precisely this 'symmetrical asymmetry', a reciprocative rationality that, precisely in its own internal dispossession, both extends and articulates the disequilibrium of the event. Again, neither the 'saying' nor the 'said' are reducible to (or conceptualizable apart from) one another. On the other hand, on Jacques's (more modern, indeed postphenomenological) view, all such reciprocity antedates the self and constitutes personal identity only in the relation.[80] Identity (transcendental or otherwise) on this view becomes 'reified', only a socialized product. Hence the refusal to encompass the 'other' within the communitarian universal would be viewed as an (outdated) artifact of subject-centered rationality, a refusal that has perhaps troubled modern accounts of 'personhood' from the outset.

Historically, in any case, the concept of person remained accompanied by an excess or '*transcendens*' irreducible to conceptual demonstration and ontic norm. It is just this history, moreover, that is at stake in the concept of person, which Jacques himself (like others) acknowledges descends through the complex (theological) history of 'interpersonal relations' from Augustine and Boethius to Aquinas, from Kant to Hegel and onward. It is, again, a complex history in which transcendence, singularity, relation, and personhood are similarly impacted—by negation, finitude, asymmetry, representation, and the violence of a certain (modern) histrionics of the persona as role. This history, moreover, attends both the attempts of deconstruction of the tradition 'after Hegel' and those that would again overcome Hegel by a successor theory (e.g., of discourse rationality): while Habermas, for example, has attempted to provide an account of political rationality modeled on the Hegelian objective spirit, Nancy has recently found in its account of the inquietude of the selfsame, the recognition of the fugitive and rhythmic event in which the absolute, always 'between' us, is never possessed.[81] While we may well ultimately need to demur from such extremes, if we are to adjudicate the Levinasian account of the ethical event, here, as will become evident, the analysis will need to be specific. If previously we have found the archive of friendship intransigent to the issue surrounding the concept of community, the problem of the 'other', doubtless complicated in its reference to Hegel, remains in its modern guise inextricably linked to the origins (and history) of personhood. That is, again to invoke Gadamer's term, the question of the other in this respect remains connected to (even while disrupting) the *Begriffstradition* of personhood.[82] As in most such conceptual genealogies, however, the issue is *not* simply the truth value of a certain narrative, theory, or theological dogma, but rather the exposition of the interrelation (and intelligibility) of the concepts at stake.

Like all such *Erwiderungen*, this reinterpretation both interfaces and exceeds its origins, originating, as Levinas's work attests, both out of a specific history or traditionality, but also out of a certain distance, a certain violence, rupture, and dispersion that remains always 'untimely' with respect to it. If all conceptual transformations cannot be readily disjoined from institutions, both institutions of power and knowledge, even in exceeding those constraints, such transformations always already respond to a specific conceptual problematic. Doubtless then without being reducible to this 'ontic' history, even Levinasian interpretation, as we have seen, remains unintelligible apart from it (the historically 'said'), and thus thereby complicated again in the relation between history and being. The result forms a complex interface between rational contingency and necessity.

Derrida said perhaps nothing else in his 1967 "Violence and Metaphysics," insisting that by making "the origin of language, meaning, and difference the relation to the infinitely other, Levinas is resigned to betraying his own intentions in his philosophical discourse" (VM:151). Trading on a logic Derrida had already discovered at the heart of the Husserlian *logos*, this 'origin' becomes subject to a certain inner equivocity:[83] in contesting the resolution and coherence of the *logos* (philosophy) Levinas's account also became articulated through a history that links "both the philosophers and the prophets" (TI:24). Doubtless, in this regard, as Derrida aptly notes, the discourse of the other becomes subjected to an equivocal history and its equivocal narratives, where, as Derrida puts it in citing Joyce ("the most Hegelian of modern novelists"), "Jew greek is greek jew" (VM:153).[84] Still, if the encounter with the other rationally (or conceptually) descends out of this uncanny '*combinatoire*', it likewise presupposes, as both Hegel and Joyce exemplify, the mythemes of a specific conceptual history, which Francis Jacques still terms, perhaps even more uncannily, granted the mythemes at stake, 'Trinitarian' personhood. It is perhaps no accident (nor is it incorrect) that Jacques himself still finds therein the paradigm of interpersonal relationality, one which, as we have said, from the outset precedes the narratives of its Hegelian past.[85] But here the 'departure' that the Levinasian account institutes becomes even more uncannily evident, both further articulating the logic of its own internal rupture and what has been termed elsewhere the dispersion of the theological-political across the landscape of theoretical modernity.[86]

# 4. Person and E-vent

*On Fragmented Transcendence*

The friend is another self.

—Aristotle, *Nicomachean Ethics*

The negative description of transcendence as the impossibility for the transcendent being and the being that is separated from it to participate in the same concept also comes from Descartes. For he affirms that the term being is applied to God and to creation in an equivocal sense. Across the theology of the analogous attributes of the Middle Ages this thesis goes back to the conception of the only analogical unity of being in Aristotle. In Plato it is found in the transcendence of the Good with respect to being. It should have served as a foundation for a pluralistic philosophy in which the plurality of being would not disappear into the unity of number nor be integrated into totality.

—Levinas, *Totality and Infinity*

I shall pause here to consider the ideas which previously arose naturally and of themselves in my mind whenever I considered what I was. I thought of myself as having a face. . . .

—Descartes, *Meditations*

[I]f instead man experiences the look, in unreflected letting-be-encountered, as the looking at him of the person who is encountering him, then the look of the encountering person shows itself as that in which someone awaits the other as counter, i.e. appears to the other and is.

—Heidegger, *Parmenides*

*Philia*, which for the Greeks and even the Romans remains the model of what is excellent in human relations (with the enigmatic character it receives from opposite imperatives at once reciprocity and unrequited generosity) can be received as a heritage always capable of being enriched.

—Blanchot, *Michel Foucault as I Imagine Him*

# 1. Personalism, the Closure of Moral Theory, and the Remnants of the Sacred

The persistence of the issue of 'personalism' in twentieth-century thought perhaps confounds even our best theoretical analyses. The reasons for this are complex: historical, moral, doubtless political—as well as conceptual. Even the concept of 'person' itself has been a contentious one, however.

Moreover, such contentiousness has persisted even in the wake of recent criticism, 'deconstructive' or otherwise. Early on, in fact, discussions of the ethical in the wake of deconstruction and the perceived failure of moral theory frequently pivoted—implicitly or explicitly—around the question of renewing (or discarding) various accounts of personhood.[1] Many also agreed, however, that, granted the tragedies (real and conceptual) that accompanied Western metaphysics, this concept, the locus of both agency and right, corporality and dignity, was not up to its task and could not be reinvoked without alteration. Even these views were not without precedent, however.

Hegel already claimed that talk about personhood remained substantially insufficient before the play of forces in which all 'persons' stood at risk, always threatening the recognition of their autonomous individuality. Indeed, as he pointed out, the logic of such recognition only repeats the dispersion internal to power or force itself. Doubtless this too was a claim that was modern (or at least 'Hobbesian') enough.[2] Still, Hegel also articulated this dispersion (or 'dialectic') in terms—as will become further evident—that have troubled both the logic and the descent of personhood, those of master and slave. And yet, as both history and reason seemed to dictate, any deduction that would hope to readily resolve such dispersion risked becoming one-sided or simply strategic, indeed calculated—and to use Hegel's term "useless [unnütz]" (PS:112). But, as has already become evident, recent accounts have remained no less unconvinced concerning the usefulness of Hegel's own strategies for the resolution of this dialectic, questioning both the voluntarist metaphysics of the desire for recognition and Hegel's claim to have provided an epistemically adequate science for calculating its cognition.

Neither appeal to law, nor reason, nor even the phenomenology of recognition itself seemed up to the task before such threats from history or power, nor for providing an account for completing (or salvaging) the 'logic' of personhood. Indeed the complicated result (to use Hegel's term, its double meaning [Doppelsinnung], divided between concept and experience, self and other) is that we still may not know what 'person' means.

Accordingly, apparently discarding the traditional language of personhood, more recent appeals have been made—as indeed many of their existential ancestors had—to an 'encounter', a 'relationality', or an 'event' that departs both from the substantialist orbit of traditional metaphysics and from requisites of modern moral theory. Yet, following the Heideggerian criticisms of scientific reason (ratio) that often provided protocols for their strategies, such accounts of the person (or its conceptual remainder) seemed almost destined to depart from the orbit of the rational altogether. The result risked invoking a domain, not without a certain perduring angst, seemingly beyond all rational warrant, helpless before reason, as Adorno said of the work of art—a claim which, its critics declared, betrayed a certain uncomfortable proximity to emotivism. Indeed like Heidegger himself, in his refiguration of personhood in a Dasein analysis, Adorno was equally adamant in declaring himself simply "against personalism."[3]

Again, without denying the force of such strategies, even were the contemporary effects of 'personalism' restricted to minimal claims—and invocations seemingly beyond the force of theory and law—even this result would not be uncontroversial. After all, even classical moral 'theory' too could find no easy place for such concepts, nor do current replacements simply overcome its invocation through a reduction that would make all meaning parasitic upon practices and demonstrable convention. The history of the semantic clusters to which the term 'person' was attached—its *Begriffstradition*—seems aporetic before such reductions. If the concept (or role) of a self remains parasitic for its intelligibility upon the goals and problematics of a given (historical) practice, the concept of person would remain (transcendentally) exceptional before all this, summoning respect regardless of its 'intelligibility'. To use Kant's terms, terms that were always figured and refigured within the regulation of law, at stake was not simply 'purposive', but an event that revealed itself to moral conscience as an 'end in itself'. In fact those arguing out of the 'personalist' or humanist tradition had continually claimed that at stake was less the effect of demonstrable necessity than the trace of a 'thou' whose summons trades upon conscience and the announcement of an inner voice (*hermeneuein*) belying all strict interpretation.[4]

But again, such 'dialogical' claims (not only concerning the self's dialogue with itself, but the self's dialogue with the 'other') appeared to be only anachronistic juxtapositions that seemed 'out of joint'—if not simply out of place. When, as has been seen, Dante's "On Eloquence in the Vernacular" declared that the natural language originated as a response to an unspoken question or 'call' from God, the coalescence of narrative and belief (or *mythos* and *logos*) remained at least mythically (or perhaps theologically) minimally understandable. Now such appeals as those regarding the 'call' of 'Being' or of the 'other' seemed (theoretically) simply unintelligible, linked inevitably to a mourning for what is now a world well lost.

It is also understandable, however, why even in post-Kantian Continental philosophy, where reductions of the self or of consciousness have always been contested, the invocation of the concept of person itself has been

controversial. Descending from Scheler to Heidegger and beyond, the claim
has been made that this persona—originally (or at least etymologically) the
mask (*persona*) through which the tragic actor related his or her dramatic
tale—has always been nascently the mask of Being. Indeed that was the objection: invocations of this term were always precritically linked to already
prejudiced ontic commitments, without sufficiently raising (or 'encountering') the question of 'personal' Being, *die Frage nach dem Personsein*.[5] If not
always, at least often enough it seems, Jean-Luc Nancy would be right to
claim that such personalism never "managed to do anything more than coat
the most classical individual-subject with a moral or sociological paste."[6]
Adorno had similarly raged—ironically, directly at Heidegger's own treatment—not only that accounts of the dialogical, I-thou relation "have assumed the oily tone of unbelieved theology," but even that Heidegger's
account of authenticity founded on the resoluteness of Dasein remained ultimately a "personalist manifesto"—in a time when, *pace* claims to the substantial dignity of the person, confronted with the play of force or power
itself "this substantiality does not exist."[7] The truth of the person seen, as
Adorno put it, from "the philosophy of history" was declared to be a schizo-
phrenic split between the inside and the outside, the particular and the universal, albeit one poststructuralists too would occasionally have declared to
be a happy, if revolutionary result.[8] But granted such divisions, it is not
clear at all how to understand 'personhood', let alone what 'personal' dignity would entail. And here—*pace* Adorno's arguments that it remained
mystified—the history of philosophy perhaps again becomes critical.

In this regard, it has been said that the terms of our ethical theories remain only fragments detached from the contexts in which they gained
significance.[9] It might be said, too, that, as a result, the term 'person' is one
of those cases in which, to follow Wittgenstein, "sometimes an expression
has to be withdrawn from language and sent for cleaning—then it can be
put back into circulation."[10] Not unaware of the problem, Levinas stated
that his work "does not seek to restore any ruined concept" (OBBE:185),
doubtless the concept of person included. Yet perhaps nowhere else do we
find a thinker so explicitly grappling with our conceptual ruins—and what
still breaks forth "during some flashes" in "the history of philosophy," precisely in the lapse in which "being and time fall into ruins" (OBBE:8–9).
What would be required, however, as Levinas put it, would be "a new way
of reading the history of philosophy."[11] The latter requires "an entire work
of interpretation to accomplish in order to make [the past] current."

Such 'currency' however could not be limited to the mere circulation of
concepts—any more than had Wittgenstein's. What was at stake was as

much ethical as it was conceptual, a history as much unnarratable (*inénarrable*) as it was yet to be (propositionally, in any case) narrated. The problem was grasping—doubtless narrating—what could not be strictly narrated, thematized without reduction (OBBE:166). Indeed many who acknowledged it were led to change their theoretic strategies in order to confront the exclusions (and dangers) involved. Acknowledging that such a sociological concept as role "sanctions the bad, perverted depersonalizations of today," thinkers like Adorno and Foucault would still have us exchange for the empirical analyses of the institutions of power, the "microanalysis of persons."[12] But even in their case it is often enough not clear either what makes such analyses significant, since it is unclear what is at stake, or what remnant of dignity is to be gained, and, moreover, whether the whole question of *dignitas* can be salvaged at all.

Again, without simply denying such analyses, any reexamination of the concept of personhood—or what is figured thereby, both within and beyond law and person—will need to trace out what is at stake in the past narratives out of which such 'pastings' may be the leveled-off remainder: if not as an "unbelieved theology" then a "religion without religion." If the extension of 'person' in these polemics was not limited (or limitable) to a finite sequence of permutations within theological and moral doctrines, it has been inextricably linked with sacred narratives—and the question of its status, consequently, inextricably complicated thereby. Even Kant's apparently innocent discussion of person in terms of its perdurance through time links it to the idea of (and the narratives articulating) holiness (*Heiligkeit*)—albeit only by a certain dialectical illusion which demonstrably involves a "perpetual circle" that can never be relinquished (CPR:126; A346/B404). Even here, consequently, the emergence of this persona becomes contested, articulated only within a field of antinomies between the theological and philosophical.

It could be argued that if the intelligibility of the concept of person inextricably links this figure to a certain play and "fragmented transcendence," exactly what makes this link irreducible likewise bars 'personhood' from being reduced to any bound variable, any empirical semantic field, or any particular doctrine.[13] In this regard, as inextricably linked with narratives concerning the sacred, the concept of person must also rupture and fragment its own archive as much as it complicates the generation of moral theory. The point for reasons now evident has a certain Benjaminian edge: doubtless concepts, too, have their own 'aura'.[14] The point, moreover, may also have a certain Wittgensteinian edge: "What is good is also divine. Queer as it sounds, that sums up my ethics. Only something supernatural (*über-*

*natürliche*) can express the Supernatural."[15] But equally, Wittgenstein realized, all that links such an ethics with more substantial or objectivist accounts here would be endlessly complicated thereby. And doubtless it will not be until we have unraveled that linkage that we can adjudicate its effect, requiring inter alia that we face the hinge between personhood, the sacred, and the modern institutions of law more directly.

Here, however, we are likewise confronted with an archive that is both usually absent from contemporary discourses and yet, strangely, not simply dissonant from them. This history, to use Gadamer's characterization, may indeed remain "extremely instructive" for grasping the problem of the other and intersubjectivity. Surely, in its light, claims like Manfred Frank's that a more substantial sense of individuality remains requisite for our talk about the ethical and the political become further intelligible.[16] And, as he reminds us, it is Habermas who has claimed that "among modern societies only those that manage to integrate into the realm of the profane essential features of their religious traditions, i.e. elements that transcend the merely human, will be able to preserve what is substantially humane."[17] We recur to such historical antecedents, consequently, neither to endorse them nor ultimately to discard them so much as to confront the figurations of tradition in the heart of their contemporary remainder. It is not that the link between the sacred and such 'phenomenologies' resolves the conflicts in the ethics of personhood. Unlike other 'theological' turns in phenomenology that would jeopardize the role of evidence through appeal to *mythos* or sacred narrative, here we will insist neither on the relationship of substitution or progression, nor resolution and conflict but on the specificity of the theoretical history or genealogy which overdetermines the concept of personhood and, consequently, the question of transcendence (or, alternately, the empty place) in our midst.[18] The issue nonetheless is a philosophical one. As Levinas himself realized, "[t]he Place of the Good above every essence is the most profound teaching, the definitive teaching, not of theology, but of philosophy" (TI:103). At stake perhaps is a certain paradox that has accompanied philosophy from the outset. On the other hand, the problem of its articulation is not similarly simply logical or 'philosophical' (or 'religious') but 'hermeneutic': hence, for example, the significance, for Levinas, of the 'figure' of multiplicity expressed in the idea of creation *ex nihilo* and an existence which does indeed depend on another, but not as a part of a totality that is separate from it (TI:104).

Any attempt to simply undertake 'transcendental explication' here will inevitably confront, as a result, the limits of analysis. Like all conceptual histories or genealogies we inevitably confront the problem of the present, of our contemporaneity. Doubtless, as Levinas would argue, this becomes especially pronounced in the question of personhood, where it becomes obvious that "to wish to escape dissolution into the Neuter, to posit knowing as a welcoming of the Other, is not a pious attempt to maintain the spiritualism of a personal God, but is the condition for language, without which philosophical discourse is but an abortive act, a pretext for an unintermitting psychoanalysis or philology or sociology, in which the appearance of a discourse vanishes in the Whole" (TI:88). At stake can be neither 'fideism' nor 'demythologizing'[19]—but the question of their intelligibility, narrative, and conceptual history. Obviously we cannot hope to trace this history in full detail; we can only indicate, by tracing one of its moments, the overdetermined past from which the concept (and the problem) of personhood emerges. Such an analysis should by no means be taken to be exhaustive— nor even exemplary—but rather attests to the theoretical complications at work in its past.

## 2. On the Origins of the Concept of Person

It is enough to take even a cursory glance at significant documents of this past to engage its complexity. For example, question 29 of Thomas Aquinas's *Summa theologiae* (I-Ia)—a text to which Jacques too makes brief reference—reveals the dialectic articulated in the philosophical and theological archive from which the concept of the person emerged. Boethius's definition that a person is "an individual substance of a rational nature" had already been flagged by Aquinas as having origins in Greek tragedy, recognizing that the word originally signified 'mask'. Moreover, the origins of this archive remain mimetically expressive, "for 'person' comes from 'sounding through' [*personando*], since a greater volume of sound is produced through the cavity in the mask" (ST:I.29.3). A Greek (conceptual) past too is invoked, since a person as an individual substance of rational nature is claimed to underlie a thing, a nature (*physis*), and, in particular, since it is claimed to be that which underlies accidents, hypostasis, or substance. 'Person' is in fact defined by 'what these three names signify in common in the genus of rational substances" (ST:I.29.2) and "hypostasis and person add the individual principles to the notion of essence"—precisely in this sense that "soul, flesh and bone belong to the nature of man whereas this soul, this flesh and this bone (qua hypostasis and individuating) belong to the nature of this man" (ST:I.29.3).

As Aquinas already realized, however, the logic underlying the concept of person was by no means simple, and it threatened the logic of definition itself insofar as the person is that rational substance which is "individuated through itself." Rational substances, that is, "have dominion over their own actions" (ST:I.29.1)—and incidentally, not tyrannically, but politically, as he put it elsewhere, invoking Aristotle (ST:II.9.2). Throughout in fact, Aquinas's account maintains links with ancient legal institutions and the legal roles of persons—to which it will be necessary to return.[20] Nonetheless, what remains even more significant is his recognition that the transference at stake concerning individualization will belie the logic of genus and species, an exception evidenced in their being signified by a special term: "individuals of a rational nature even have a special name among other substances; and this name is person." But the definition is already problematic on its own terms since to add the word 'individual' to 'essence' is to seemingly conflate genus and species.

Aquinas's treatment of this special signification of the unity of person is likewise a subtle one spurred by the *aporiae* that had been encountered in sacred doctrine concerning the Trinity of divine 'persons'. As a result the semantics at stake would be sufficiently complex that they belied the standard logic of terms, requiring a certain theoretical change of paradigm. If, as Umberto Eco has rightly argued, Aquinas was categorical in limiting "profane poetry and allegory," he likewise realized that it had to be quite otherwise with the Sacred.[21] The separation between *ens creatum* and the creator forced, if not the abandonment of Aristotelian logic and its rhetorics, then at least their extension through the figurative. The question of *mimesis* and *poiesis* thus becomes more than a matter of edification, but instead the irreplaceable means for elevation beyond the finite. "Poetry makes use of metaphors to produce a representation, for it is natural to man to be pleased with representations. But sacred doctrine makes use of metaphors as both necessary and useful" (ST:I.1.9). Moreover, Aquinas allows that to the extent that this 'special name' of person had been "used just as any other absolute term," it had been misunderstood in a way that facilitated attack by heretics (especially regarding the doctrine of the Trinity). Since nothing in the strict sense can be applied equally to God and creatures, the word 'person' must not be used univocally (ST:I.29.4)—yet neither was the meaning so equivocal that it could not still be used doctrinally. The creed of Athanasius, after all, had spoken of the Trinity as three persons. We have, it seems, ventured into the complex logic of analogy.

Even Aquinas realized, however, that this was anything but an obvious solution. This theological usage, taken literally in any case, marked a departure from scripture insofar as the term 'person' itself does not occur in either the Old or the New Testament. Moreover, insofar as the term had originally meant a specific thing (that is, a mask), he openly acknowledges its metaphorical status (ST:I.29.3). Hence the special—or metaphysical—usage of the term will involve a certain theoretical novelty, even if Aquinas (consistent with his poetics) restricts his consideration to theological coherence:

> Although the term person is not found applied to God in Scripture, either in the Old or New Testament, nevertheless what the term signifies is found to be affirmed of God in many places of Scripture. . . . If we could speak of God only in the very terms themselves of Scripture, it would follow that no one could speak about God in any but the original languages of the Old or New Testament. The urgency of confuting heretics made it necessary to find new words to express the ancient faith about God. Nor is such a kind of novelty to be shunned, since it is by no means profane, for it does not lead us astray from the sense of scripture. (ST:I.29.3)

If the 'absolute' sense could—albeit uneasily—depend on the logic of substance, the concept of person even departs from this index, becoming an openly theoretical construction, a figure, or even a certain play on words—and granted its genre, a philosopheme. From the opening of the *Summa*, as Umberto Eco saw, Aquinas's semiotics deftly authorized but limited this move—only Dante would generalize such theoretical inventions, which would invoke the difference at stake as universal. In the same moment, Dante had correlatively allotted a perfection or virtue commonly restricted to 'infused' or 'sacred virtue' to the secular domain, a realization of human (possible) intellect in the earthly community (*humanitas civilitas*). And, from the outset, as has become evident, this flirted with the charge of Averroism.[22]

Aquinas himself intended to strictly confine the figural to providing a necessary (and not, as with the poetic, a merely pleasing) extension for a finite intellect in matters which exceeded its conceptual grasp (ST:I.1.9). Aquinas provides us directly in this regard with an example: a trope concerning its 'self-realization': "person means as it were by itself one [*per se una*]" (ST:I.29.4). Still, the figure here was not simply a play on words; it served to amplify the extension of the concept, or to reconstruct it. What he added to vouchsafe the 'logical syntax' of the Trinity against the charges of the heretics still belied indexical simplicity insofar as it is the logic of relations (and not substance) that articulates the intelligibility of the Trinity. Aquinas takes this from Boethius, who had, Aquinas recalls, recognized in inventing the new concept that "every term that refers to the Persons signifies relation."[23]

What distinguished the special sense of person from the outset was its figured connection to the logic of relations (or roles) regarding definition, it being both invoked and extended by means of analogy. While, as has been seen, theological implications were present throughout the concept's past—and Christian ones at least as early as Tertullian's 'solution' in the third century—it is Boethius's reinterpretation in terms of relation that opens the dialectics of its semantic field. In fact, Boethius himself begins the discussion of relations by invoking a certain dialectic in this respect:

> Let us now consider relationships to which all the foregoing remarks have been preliminary; for these especially, which are clearly seen to exist because of something else coming in, do not seem to produce predication by themselves. For instance, since master and slave are relative terms, let us see whether either of them is such that is a predication by itself or not. But if you suppressed the term slave you would simultaneously suppress the term master (*Atqui si auferas servum, abstuleris et dominum*). . . . [24]

It is the relation which maintains the relative identity of the terms, an identity 'suppressed', to use Hegel's term, in the 'sublation' of the relation. Applying the logic of relations to the question of persons, Boethius, bound equally by the logic of the Trinity, is then led directly to consider the relationality of persons.

> Wherefore if father and son are predicates of relation, and, as we have said, have no difference without that of relation, but relation is not predicated with reference to that of which it is predicated as if it were the thing itself, it will not imply an otherness of the things of which it is said, but, in a phrase which aims at interpreting what we could hardly understand, an otherness of persons (*non faciet alteritatem rerum de qua dicitur, sed, si dici potest, quo quidem modo id quod vix intelligi potuit interpretatum est, personarum*).[25]

The *alteritas personarum* is, as has been seen, in one sense a figure, an *interpretans*. It is in any case the difference of persons, nothing outside the relation itself, a difference which we are constantly liable to substitute for a thing. Wholly constituted in transcendence this difference remains without a fixed or 'Absolute' (predicable) referent, a *Sinn* without strictly univocal *Bedeutung;* in other words, it is wholly figured within the play of 'analogy', the play of relation itself, "existence towards something," as Aquinas put it (ST:I.40.1). Theologically embedded, then, it remains, one might suspect, recalcitrantly anthropomorphic—as allegorical as it is analogical. Indeed Aquinas again furnishes us with an example of its etymological antecedent:

"Although this name person may not belong to God as regards the origin of the term, nevertheless we can extend this term perfectly well for our present purpose. For as famous men were represented in comedies and tragedies, the name person was given to signify those who held high dignity (*dignitatem*)" (ST:I.29.3).

But by the same logic it would be wrong—even in fact restricting one's discussion to Aquinas—to assume that the special sense of 'person' had been circumscribed for a domain of nonfinite reference. The relational trope which furnished the articuleme of Trinitarian logic was not simply theological: the logic of analogy, as the moderns would realize, always overdetermines as much as it underdetermines. The 'logic' of analogy is as much dialectical as demonstrative, its rationality as much figure as proof, its origin as much imaginative as intellective to use Boethian terms: in short its intelligibility is as much 'human' as it is 'divine'.[26] Accordingly, the trope depended upon in its theological invention in the usage of 'person' perhaps equally haunts the diacritics of ordinary 'sense'. Even in the realm of human affairs the logic of extensional identity breaks down: 'person' names neither simply a genus nor a species, neither simply a universal nor a mere particular, but perhaps a 'between' denominable by neither *singularitas*. For Aquinas, it is always the difference of this flesh and bone, but it likewise denotes the subsistent reality in that nature, the 'transcendent' nature which *is* precisely as this composite—precisely, it might be said, insofar as the transcendence of the human soul is already figured in its relation to something higher in the order of the intelligible, by an analogy already effective, the analogy of *pros hen*. Accordingly: "Even in human affairs this name person is common by a community of idea, not as a genus or species, but as a vague individual thing" (ST:I.30.4). 'Community' here belies both by essence and existence—and as the specificity of their relation it transforms the *per se–per participationem* metaphysical hierarchy. And as such, as Aquinas puts it, "this is common in idea to the divine person, that each of them subsists distinctly from the other in the divine nature." While Aquinas could affirm Richard of St. Victor's definition of person as "an incommunicable existence of an intellectual nature," he could not endorse the inference that a community of persons so construed is to be understood as "a community of exclusion." Instead, "although person is incommunicable, yet the mode itself of incommunicable existence can be common to many"—and this too he held to be a common idea that obtains between human affairs and divine (ST:I.30.4). And yet the difference that obtained between the two realms—and doubtless the emergence of such a congruence—had always been problematic.

## 3. The Declension of the Person, the Figures of the Self, and the Absolute of Self-Certainty

From the beginning, even from the opening texts of *Genesis*, the problem of images interfered by a kind of inter-reference and would always be articulated by narratives which inter-vened between the finite and the infinite. Kant would in a sense only reinvoke the dangers, accompanying the figuration of the Absolute under the guise of the moral law. The being of the human was from the outset the site of a certain defracted 'radiance'. Augustine (following Ambrose and Theodorus) endorsed the transfer in reinscribing the Old Testament within the Christian narrative. The human soul is the closest entity in all creation to God.[27] If not simply divine as the heretics thought, the human soul remains still close enough to the divine to warrant the transfer—in any case, that is, still a person.

The problem, which Boethius's premodern articulation already acknowledges to be beyond comprehension, is thus related to a disequilibrium in the transfer itself, the disequilibrium in the relations through which 'person' becomes constituted. Suspicions concerning the status and the complicity of dominion then inevitably became relevant. The possibility could no longer be avoided that the invocation of 'person', far from being a site of refracted transcendence, provided the mask for the actualization of power, as Hobbes (and later Nietzsche) would insist in retrieving the archive of persona as mask.[28] This disequilibrium anticipates the development of the 'person' in philosophical modernism, in which it is either reduced to a rational faculty, in accord with the concept of human soul as specifically discursive, or it is transformed into a power of the will, consistent with its capacity to be individuated through itself—that is, insofar as rational substance has dominion over itself, to use Aquinas's term. Doubtless the problem echoes directly in the epistemic issue of certainty and reflective 'equilibrium'. The problem likewise has political overtones. The problem of political representation introduced the disequilibrium in which history and virtue would be risked: inter alia whether such representatives should derive from a 'natural aristocracy' in order to insure the 'natural' link between power and nature or whether such representation should be limited granted the fallibility of representation and power itself. Retrospectively, it is clear that either reduction—political or metaphysical—risks losing the disequilibrium constitutive of the composite (and the recognition) of the person both as figure and event: as both the eruption of transcendence and as "this flesh and this bone." Strict demands for demonstration would replace the event of reason for psychologism, either in Hobbes's case 'from below' in the search for power, or 'from above' by turning reason into a (universal) faculty or rational agency. Hence the inevitable insight of Kant's paralogisms, which identified the failure at issue, in Boethius's terms, in taking relation (phenomenal appearance before the subject) as if it were the thing believed.

Only Hegel, who in the analysis of recognition can still be seen to be responding to Hobbes, perhaps would again emphasize the disequilibrium in question.[29] It is forgotten in many recent discussions of the problem of recognition that Hegel's *Erwiderung* with respect to the relational past of personhood trades once more upon the figure of analogy and dialectics—ultimately only to treat this 'excess' as a figure of proof, consequently confusing the path of withdrawal with that of the *more geometrico*. The preface to the second edition of the *Encyclopedia* openly asserted what was at stake, claiming that theologians of the day had abandoned the metaphysical speculations at stake in the Trinity.[30] Recall, however, that for Hegel such relational 'trinities' would not be confined to any specific religion, ultimately—indeed he found such speculations not only in Christianity but in both Indian and Greek "religion" (HP:I:135). Doubtless such 'relationality', as will become evident, reveals as much about speculation as it does about personhood. It was, in any case, Hegel insisted, time to rethink these matters once more. The result, however—for better or worse—was less a reiteration than another refiguration of the concept of the Trinity, an exposition whose account of the relational provides another one of those moments in which, as Findlay said, Hegel becomes our Aristotle.

Still, the point here as elsewhere is not a simple one, and certainly not a matter of adjudicating Hegel's refiguration from a theological standpoint—in which it doubtless involves (albeit intentionally) a fundamental departure from existing doctrine. From the outset, Hegel had sought to unlock—to transfer (and refigure)—the theoretical fertility surrounding the logic of relationality contained within the concept of the Trinity, by grasping the logical syntax of the Absolute as one which was not simply conceptual but a 'living unity', not simply a numerical but a living essence, a unity in being.[31] His mature *Lectures on the Philosophy of Religion* only reaffirm it in their definition of the absolute as Spirit:

> Spirit is for spirit and of course not merely in an external, contingent manner. Instead it is spirit only insofar as it is for spirit.[32]

And such a self-relating relation involves openly the rationality of its speculative extension:

> The Trinity is called the mystery of God; its content is mystical, i.e. specula-
> tive. But what is for reason is not a secret. In the Christian religion one knows,
> and this is a secret only for the finite understanding.[33]

In all this "Being a person is the highest intensity of being-for-self," but no
longer simply as transcendent with respect to difference but instead as articulating—and actualizing—itself across this diversity.[34] Far from being
precluded from the excess of *transcendens,* reason is ushered into it by phenomenology and dialectic, the exposition of which is the opening of the Absolute as Revelation.[35]

It would be hasty to charge, as did Sartre for example, that Hegel was an
epistemological optimist who simply lost sight of the problem of evil (or the
phenomenon of shame).[36] Nor can their differences, granted the archive we
have traced, be attributed simply to Sartre's avowed 'atheism'. For Sartre too
it was a question of the contingency—and the unwieldiness—of transcendence (and the violence it portends). It is important first off, however, to recall the status of the retrieval at stake. The problem of Absolute knowledge
for the medievals—if not the moderns—had been solved with Boethius's
tack: the Absolute would be grasped only relationally in transcendence. For
Hegel, however, building on the analogy involved in all relational exposition, the articulation would now be brought into accord with the epistemic
and demonstrative demands of philosophical modernism. And the synthesis of the *Scientia Dei* would be exchanged for the demonstrative (and immanent) demands of *Wissenschaftstheorie.*

Within the articulation of Spirit, the intertwining of finite and infinite
that was once conceptualized through the 'unicity' of transcendental analogy
now became articulated through an oscillation (*Wechsel*) which extended
through the rationality of the self. This "I" became the transcendental indexical of epistemic possibility, articulating the demonstrative unfolding (*explicatio*) of the One as the exposition of consciousness. As *The Lectures on Religion* put it, again fully synthesizing ancient and modern demands for ad-
joining the finite and the infinite:

> I am the relation of the two sides: these two extremes are each just me, who con-
> nect them. The holding together, the connecting, is itself this conflict of self
> within the unity, this uniting of self in the conflict. In other words, *I am the
> conflict,* for the conflict is precisely this clash, which is not an indifference of the
> two (as) distinct but is their bonding together. I am not one of the parties caught
> up in the conflict but am both of the combatants and the conflict itself. I am the
> fire and water that touch each other, the contact (now separated and ruptured,
> now reconciled and united) and union of what utterly flies apart; and it is just
> this contact that is itself this double, clashing relation as relation.[37]

The opening of this relation as relation, however, became for Hegel a revelation of the Absolute which truncates the significance of the 'clashing'. The latter resonates doubtless both with a certain retrieval of medieval poetics and the epistemic demands of philosophical modernism.[38] However, the resulting importation of the divine attribute in epistemic subjectivity was, as even Hegel warns us, mythical from the outset—and perhaps even the return of the specter of Averroes. Ethical life is "a living and independent spirit which like a Briareus appears with myriads of eyes, arms, and other limbs, each of which is an absolute individual."[39] Granted the corresponding reconciliation of the substance of Spirit, the concept of the person throughout Hegel's works would be definable only as individual, as "formal abstraction" or "the supreme indifference of the single individual," or as pure relation to itself as absolute.[40]

Yet, Hegel himself denied that subjectivity could finally be conceptualized by this indifference. His criticism of Kant's account, accordingly, focused precisely on the lack of relation in Kantian personhood: not only in its account of the person as simple substance (which Aquinas in a sense had already proposed, since even a person as *ens creatum* is figured in the *pros hen* of the Creator) but also in Kant's treatment of the ego as simple 'identity'. In effect, Hegel retrieves the concept of the link of '*persona*' with legal and historical institutions—and in particular the modern institutions of civil society. From the outset, in fact, the issue of mediation between transcendence and institution, the divine and the human, natural law and positive law, was entwined with the concept of the person. In medieval political theology, as has been seen, this problem came to the fore in an instantiation of mediation, the problem of the interstice of the king's two bodies, the interstice between incarnation and incorporation.[41] This difference underlies the figure of the king, but equally the figurative investment of political identity itself—which is consequently never simply a matter of community and substance nor devoid of analogy. Nor is this mediation absent in those who come after Hegel, even if the bulk of modern political theory seemed intent on denying it in the 'ideology' of contract and consensus. Kant had nascently recognized the issue (not only in the question of the interpretation of law itself, but also) in the *Kritik*'s exposition of intersubjectivity, insofar as identity presupposes synthesis, the 'joining' of time to time—and perhaps then the specificity of my time to yours. Still, again, the unicity of time intersubjectivity articulated—as Kant likewise recognized—is not the unicity of substance. 'Spirit' is never simply denominated and its 'theory' never simply constructible (nor consequently, simply 'deconstructible')—and it is doubtless just here that Hegel's own attempt simply turned 'mythic'.

Here Fichte had seemingly prepared Hegel's path. Indeed the 1794 "Vocation of the Scholar" had already—in a gesture that points back to Aristotle's *eudaimonia* as much as it does forward to Heidegger's 'leveling'—declared that "it contradicts [man's] own being, if he live in a state of isolation." Individuality is instead parasitic upon society (*Gesellschaft*), a community pervaded by design in which "the agreement of many things in one end, freely fulfilled, is the sure and infallible characteristic of rationality as manifested in its results."[42] Still, Fichte refused to make such a community simply determinate, articulating it still, as he put it, "in Kantian terminology [as] a free reciprocal activity founded on ideas (*seine Wechselwirkung nach Begriffen*)."[43] His *Rechtslehre*, again venturing to capture the unicity of right and nature, would similarly presuppose such community without fully developing its consequences. Those consequences perhaps became only fully articulated in Hegel's phenomenology of recognition, where the difference of egological perspective and the ethics of egoism meet head-on in the dialectics of self-consciousness. Here the relational event of consciousness of self and consciousness of other is specifically explicated, neither as a simply 'external' relation (relation of self and other), nor simply as a unification based on love or reconciliation or conflict and struggle—neither simply Hölderlin nor Hobbes. Hegel's phenomenology is a venture of the possibilities of reciprocal relation—and, as possibility, a venture of the transcendence that figures the *alteritas personarum* from within a reconciliation based both on recognition and generosity.

And yet, Hegel's account of the natural 'law' of spirit, as has become apparent too, ultimately abandons the withdrawal of the noumenon—or perhaps takes Fichte's pronouncement about actualization and free fulfillment at his word—in asserting a movement—a science and a voluntarist metaphysics—which becomes again substantialized through realization. The modern dialectic of recognition in this regard still looks more like a method than a 'reconciliation', more like a procedure to decide between possibilities than the venture of possibility itself. The dialectic of self-certainty was never far from the problem (and infinite task) of mutual self-consciousness, or Aristotle converted into Descartes's Archimedean point, the transcendence of Being exchanged for the proof of the real and realization. Hence Boethius's exemplar for the category of substance (or predication through itself) becomes in Hegel the effective realization of self-individuality—even if in Aquinas's gloss on persons as entities *qui habent dominum sui actus* and which *per se agunt* there is a certain antecedent. But a person now involves not simply an entity, "individuated through itself," to use Aquinas's term, but—one scientifically defined by itself—an event which in exchanging transcendence for certainty, wears its modern (and Hobbesian) moment on its sleeve.[44]

Doubtless Hegel's move, *pace* his nascent 'Aristotelianism', is one that reflects historical necessities: to be precise, the development of civil society—"the system of the ethical order, split into its extremes and lost," an event in which historical practices, far from being the origin of virtue, turn out instead to be opposed to it. The elevation of the individual involves many things, but certainly this "diremption" must itself be part of any factorial analysis. Significantly, although the word 'recognition' can be traced to Hobbes's time, major English lexicons contain no entries for 'individualism' or 'individualist' prior to the nineteenth century—nor it should be added, 'personalism' or 'personalist'. Even in the richest accounts, both of these terms remained conceptually undifferentiated: the former as the final element of analysis, the *individuum*; the latter as its nonmaterial exemplification. What remains of Aristotle in Hegel is perhaps most effectively seen in the *self-sufficiency* of the individual now *as universalized*, by which it was disconnected not only from the social practices which nourish it, but equally from the transcendence at stake. But the result will be problematic. As Levinas put it:

> The true human subjectivity is indiscernable, according to Leibniz's expression, and consequently it is not as the individuals of a genus that men are together. One has always known this in speaking of the secrecy of subjectivity; but this secrecy has been ridiculed by Hegel: speaking thus was good for romantic thought. . . .[45]

As we have seen, Manfred Frank has argued that it is in virtue of an *esse commune* that the Thomistic semantics is regulated (as Leibniz's after it) through the Divine *pros hen*, an economics which assures the continuity of genus and species across the hierarchy of substances. Against it he opposes a 'heretical tradition' that culminates in Schleiermacher's emphasis on the individual, in which the individual is not simply derivable from a common essence. Here instead:

> It [the familiarity of an existing individual with itself] 'supplies' and 'supplements' the 'missing unity' of that movement in which the individual self-consciousness attempts to represent the *universal* condition of truth in itself. . . . In other words, the absence of natural signification that would define it in its essence once and for all forces the individual to turn to interpretation; it has to project its meaning anew in every moment and will never dissolve the alternative perspectives, in which its own Being and the Being of the world present themselves to it, 'into an identical thinking and eliminate all differences'.[46]

We have seen that the continuity at stake in the medieval (and Thomistic) *esse commune*, however, also already remains 'figured' through *transcendens*—and doubtless as writers like Eco and Sollers have insisted, it was even more openly figured in Dante's wake, a figuring explicitly absent in the demonstrative pretensions of the moderns. It is just this lack of appeal to transcendence that led Heidegger to claim that Descartes's refusal of this issue was "an evasion [that] is tantamount to his failing to discuss the meaning of Being"—in short, the *Seinsfrage*. Hence, "Descartes is always far behind the Schoolmen" (BT:126). As such the question of analogy already attests to the ontological difference itself, and already anticipates, rightly construed, the ineliminable difference of individuality. We have confronted it again in the ineliminability of the *alteritas personarum*. In a sense Heidegger's 'Dasein', like Schleiermacher's individuality, is precisely in this regard the refiguration of modern subjectivity: "the transcendence of Dasein's Being is distinctive in that it implies the possibility and the necessity of the most radical individuation" (BT:62).

Consistent then with his medieval protocols, while Aquinas invoked the language of person as instantiation in providing an exposition of the relational account of personhood, he also disconnected it from—or at least figured it within—the problem of substance. Individualization, to put it simply, remained conceptually linked with the articulation of a law which transcends individuality and to which individuals are always already "substantially attuned." The logic of relations was applicable here only in recognizing a certain stray ground. As Aquinas recognized in invoking the extension of 'person' before the transcendence of the Trinity—even in acknowledging its indefinite 'community'—this semantic 'excess' is just what prevents simple transfer back into the realm of individual 'substance'. What the modern emphasis on certainty attests to is the problem of this 'inter-reference', to use Michel Serres's term, and to use terms Heidegger had invoked before Lefort, the problem of the "empty place [*Stelle*]" denoted by the absence of a primal ground or *primum analogatum* (BP:81).[47] Doubtless, at least since *Being and Time*, Heidegger's refusal to trace ontology back to a primal ground attests to his (postphenomenological) attempt to think individuality and transcendence together (BT:170).

Before him, Scheler on a number of occasions openly grappled with this remainder. In his book *The Nature of Sympathy*, for example, having dismissed both Averroist and pantheist ('logonomical') attempts to congeal the essence of persons, he likewise grappled with the Thomistic account of the event of personhood as *singularitas*. Ultimately Scheler dismisses the unspecified particularity of the Thomistic account for the sake of a true essence: personhood, for Scheler, would denominate a spiritual entity where difference in plurality would indeed be difference in kind.[48] Still echoing Humboldt and Schleiermacher (and anticipating Wittgenstein, as will be seen) Scheler explicated the 'phenomenological' predicates such a view would imply: "the more deeply we penetrate into a human being . . . the more unmistakable, individual, unique, irreplaceable, and indispensable does he become." But what he did not see, and surely Sartre did, was the potential for epistemic conflict which such a uniqueness entailed (i.e., difference in epistemic 'kinds'). What the Thomist could assume theologically, the modern epistemologist could not: the benevolence that attaches to '*transcendens*'. While Sartre would still invoke Cartesian *generosité* as fundamental to ethics, the methodical doubt that underwrites Cartesian 'experience' leaves its profound effect on his account of the encounter with the other and the issue of recognition. Sartre nonetheless would openly acknowledge the 'Thomistic' moment in "Existentialism Is a Humanism," in responding to the objection that there are signs given to guide moral judgment.[49] There are signs, Sartre replied, but they must be decided, deciphered in an underdetermined and intersubjective field. As a result, the Cartesian meditations on phenomenology would be divided from within, inter alia transforming its 'monologue' into dialogue. Recall that Descartes himself in the second meditation had already raised the danger that accompanied the experience of doubt for 'knowledge of other minds': from the semblance of appearance the other might be an instrument, an automaton, and the other of argumentation an evil *génie*. The evidence of the other is never simply an iteration, but at most an 'analogon' of myself, an 'iterability' always ventured in difference: neither similarity nor difference can simply be asserted in this relation. But then neither could the modern phenomenologist simply assume such 'qualitative difference'.

## 4. *Alteritas Personarum*

Bluntly stated, then, the logic of relations will not be (either theoretically or practically) possessed as a 'property'. No 'person' will exhaust the 'differential' of *alteritas personarum*; no analogy here will find its simple or absolute index or ground. To speak Wittgensteinian, 'personhood' will not be 'circumscribed'. Such relational personhood, that is, will not find simple predication; its 'use' instead will be articulated within the (ontological) difference and fragmentation of analogy itself; the difference, as Gadamer too put it, at stake between the human and the divine Word.[50] Moreover, here again we can find Wittgenstein's analyses provide interesting confirmation. In the *Investigations* theology was coupled with the problem of grammar and the issue of the divine was a matter of a 'form of life' and the syntactic *Spiel* of language games (*Sprachspiele*). But Wittgenstein was, as always, conscious of the limits this theory implied and the imperative which resulted: "Don't play with what lies deep in another person (*Spiele nicht mit den Tiefen des Andern*)."[51] Rather than a set of predicates rigorously encompassing its specificity, the grammar of 'person' required that this 'term' be characterized precisely in terms of the specificity of a relation which exceeds such circumscription.[52] It is this which Hegel, ever relying on Boethius's example, had seen from the outset: at stake "is a not a conceptual unity (as, for instance, a unity or harmony of disposition, similarity of principles, etc.). A unity which is only a unity in thought is abstracted from life. On the contrary, it is a living relation of living beings, a likeness of life."[53] The risk, as Levinas fully saw, was that this account of personhood, "free and for itself" (OBBE:127), would simply collapse into self-contained unity, the identity of subject and substance. Instead, its identity (and 'substance') would always be ventured, at risk, and before the other.

The dignity of persons, as has been seen, further always remains linked to the institution and subversion of power; doubtless in this respect (conceptually) modern, the question of dignity opens precisely in tracing this overdetermined irreducibility and fecundity (the 'nonsubsumability') of this difference, which belies even our best attempts at theoretical or scientific reduction. Even those approaches most openly committed to the fecundity of the archive of analogical reasoning as a model for scientific analysis failed to provide a determinate concept of personhood.[54] It will be inevitably and inextricably shorn of predication in the absolute sense, its indexical desubstantialized. For the same reason, however, it must also be insisted that even 'Heideggerian' critiques 'demythologizing' the metaphysical or ontotheological status of 'person' must tread carefully.

To invoke the conceptuality of personhood, I have been arguing, is not simply to invoke a substance but also to engage a 'relationality' which emerges through certain conceptual (and causal) history. To claim this is neither to dissolve or exhaust the 'concept' but to confront the complexity of the venture it involves. Nor could Heidegger himself refrain from entering its complex chain. Indeed, the link with that past was also clear from the outset. As Heidegger put it, already articulating the question of personality in his 1916 *Habilitationsschrift* on Duns Scotus:

> The concepts of the "personality" (*Persönlichkeit*), of the spiritual individual, are not, it is true, entirely foreign to Scholasticism (one thinks of the teachings of the Trinity and of angels, of the anthropology). Yet, the complexity of the historical personality, its specific character, its contingency and manifold effects, its interconnections with its surroundings, the idea of historical development and of problems tied to this are present to medieval life only in inadequate conceptual form. (FS:206)

Against the 'inadequacies' of the premodern concept of personality, however, in 1916 Heidegger likewise emphasized the richness of its conceptual heritage, precisely in connection with the problem of analogy and transcendence. As a result, "the conceptual expression of the unity and diversity" becomes in the intensity of its lived experience, the qualitatively differentiation of "this side and the beyond . . . the richest experience in the individual life of the immanent personality (*Lebens des immanent persönlichen Einzellebens*)"—which would be leveled off in modern attempts to articulate the rational. Heidegger himself doubtless struggled with such attempts in the compositions leading up to and including *Being and Time* (FS:331).

Grasping what was at stake in the remnants of historical 'personalhood' would require, as Heidegger already realized, both theoretical and historical amplification—beyond, but (as has become evident) not simply despite, its sacred origins. Both find effect in *Being and Time*. Theoretically the theological problem of analogy would be returned to its ancient roots in the question of being. Historically, the matter became even further complicated, however, requiring a twofold transformation. First, the horizons of Dasein's transcendence would be articulated in terms of lived temporality, its 'historicity'. Factically, however, as the critique of 'civil society' in Division One already made apparent, clarifying historical 'personality' required, in contradistinction to the vertical transcendence of the medievals, grappling with, to use Walter Benjamin's term (who too was equally aware of the relevance of this archive in this regard), the historical "catastrophes" which loomed in the history of the twentieth century.[55] The resulting analysis would pair the emergence of individuality with both an increased sense of its 'dignity' and equally its tragedy, its historical fate. And both would be fraught with the difficulties in conceptualizing 'Dasein's' origins.

Dasein's Being-in-the-world is wholly relational and Heidegger's account of the relationality of Being-in from the outset was construed in terms of the resources of relation as 'dwelling', which was intended to escape both traditional ontological categories and their modern mathematical and functional counterparts. Still, Gadamer was not simply off the mark (nor those like Foucault in challenging it) in claiming of this relation that it occurred through the singularity of Dasein's attending to an inner *Verbum*, an 'excess' which both depends on and extends beyond the words of language, exhibiting then "something in common between the process of the divine person and the process of thought."⁵⁶ And yet (likewise irreducibly) the critical enquiry of Heidegger's *Seinsfrage* separated itself and its interrogation of the person from any such 'theological' basis, which would be an investigation of entities proscribed by the difference that underwrote all ontological enquiry. The transcendence of Being is not simply identifiable with the transcendence of the divine, any more than it is identifiable with any other ontic substance or entity. If God is an entity, even the *ens summum*, the 'Being' at issue in Heidegger's *Seinsfrage* is a critical (ontological) interrogation of Being which, in accord with the most ancient of archives, could be bound by no specifiable index, no (ontic) entity in particular, the 'highest' included. Doubtless it should be insisted that, while the 'relationality' at stake in Heidegger's Dasein analysis is not simply opposed to enquiry concerning 'personhood', then it is also not simply identical with it. Indeed that was the point: insofar as transcendence in personalism was always already (and traditionally) linked to an ontic 'indexical', being had not explicitly become a problem (BT:74). Nor, it should be added, had the problem of its figuration, interpretation, or refiguration.

It would be remiss to see this relationality of disclosure (*aletheia*) as merely a categorial matter, separable from the 'ontic' instantiation through which it became an issue—the instantiation, as he described it elsewhere, which is the remainder of the *personalitas transcendentalis*, the differentiation of nature and spirit, substance and subject (BT:125). Hence, too, as we have noted previously, Heidegger's own explicit refiguration of Aquinas's account of the *transcendens* of *verum* in the soul, in its Being properly suited to come together (*convenire*) with entities of any sort whatsoever, in the figure of Dasein (BT:34). Indeed the problem of this *convenientia* is just the problem of the "between," belying a relation of things present-to-hand (BT:170). Likewise, in the very problem of its being the relationality of this 'between' disrupts the assurance of such transcendentality and the continuity of the *esse commune*. Dasein is itself the (historical) differentiation of this between of ontic-ontological differences, the being in whom 'Being' is an issue—and doubtless this *convenire* affects the 'between' not only of Dasein and Being, but *Dasein* and *Mitsein*.

This problematic index of Dasein's 'personhood' is likewise, then, worn on its sleeve. For all his criticism of 'personalism', Heidegger's radicalized ontology of Dasein remains too irreducibly 'personalized' (i.e., 'individual') to simply dissolve the difference at stake: "Because Dasein has in each case mineness [*Jemeinigkeit*], one must always use a personal pronoun when one addresses it: 'I am', 'you are'."[57] By placing itself in simple opposition to personalism, *Being and Time* inevitably emphasized a further complication in the complex grammar of personhood. The Greeks had already transferred the concept of role and person from dramatic and legal contexts to linguistic structure itself. Dionysius Thrax's grammar defines '*persona*' thus: "the first, by whom the word; the second, to whom the word; the third, of whom the word."[58] Heidegger's claim extends beyond this, articulating the emergence of this event, the intertwining of Being and *logos*. Here too we lack "above all, the 'grammar'" (BT:63). The locative personal designation, "'I here' does not mean a certain privileged point—that of an I-Thing" but is to be understood in terms of its *ethos*—"the 'yonder' which is the dwelling-place of Dasein as *concern* [*Besorgen*]" (BT:159). Still, for reasons now evident— neither myself as I-thing nor others are encountered "as person-Things present at hand" (BT:156). Both emerge as relational (and constitutive) 'characteristics' of Dasein's primordial being-in-the-world. And, as a result, rationality remains inevitably bound to this event in which all meaning, or the articulation of intelligibility, emerges. Still, articulating his position in 1927 against the backdrop of Natorp and Rickert, Heidegger claimed that "Philosophy must perhaps start from the 'subject' in its ultimate questions, and yet for all that it may not pose its questions in a one-sidedly subjectivistic manner."[59] In *Being and Time*, accordingly, if Dasein is essentially *Mitsein*, it is also true that Dasein in its singularity remains 'excessive' to *Mitsein*: "the expression 'Dasein', however, shows plainly that 'in the first instance' this entity is unrelated to Others" (BT:156). Hence, the still valid 'cartesianism' of the phenomenological model.

Intentionality—far from being a faculty—or a substantive property of the soul—must be also in this regard a question (indeed an opening) of such relations. Intentionality "belongs to the ontological constitution of the subject itself," the difference, that is, which in the end exceeds Dasein; it is not the reduction of 'revelation' but the e-vent of its opening.[60] Thereby, Heidegger could rightfully claim that Dasein's ontological foundations were "overlooked" by personalism, which precritically reinvoked the semantic complexes uniting 'body', 'soul', or 'spirit' without raising the question of 'personal Being'. But he realized, too, that any attempt to reduce what is at stake, substituting objects or theoretical entities for its event, was tantamount to depersonalization (*Entpersonalisierung*)—a depersonalization, he realized, likely to have terrifying historical consequences (BT:73).[61] History, after all, is on Heidegger's account both the condition of and the threat to human identity and authenticity. And *pace* his critics at this point (e.g.,

Adorno) the full effect of this threat could not be articulated without Heidegger's foray into its genealogy, both real and conceptual—hence again the relevance of the history of philosophy.

Recent theoretical accounts of recognition that model identity as the correlate of discursive competence—not as 'originating' but as the effect of social practice—would miss this point. The social constitution of identity misses the problem of 'constitution' itself—the problem, to use Hobbes's term, of the passage from the 'natural' person to the feigned or artificial, the slippage or transferal from the 'I' to the 'we'. Hobbes's original account of the 'face' in its modern guise, as has been noted, already linked the persona to the problem of representation, to the conflict of masks and a surpassing of person by its personate or representative (Lev:217). Such reductions of 'person' to objective 'role', for reasons now evident, would always risk the 'I' that exceeds such representation, such social 'identity': without it the problem (and the phenomenology) of the passage (or 'transference', to use Hobbes's term) from the I to another, or the 'I' to a 'We' cannot even arise. In this regard, even the 'critical' question, when figured through the question of 'Dasein', amounts, not simply to a focusing on the individual soul, a matter of "deuniversalization," to use Hegel's term, but the venture of reason through the interplay of self and other within the contingent 'prose' of history.[62]

The *alteritas personarum* in this historicity would again remain irreducible; the 'personal relation' in question will not be strictly 'parsed'. Neither defined, nor ascertained, nor quantified, nor subsumed: it will instead involve an event in which the person as 'being toward another' is ventured, both in theoretical and practical contexts. It is just this fragmentation at stake in the *alteritas personarum*, as has been seen, that would find its contemporary remainder precisely in the question of friendship. Here the relationship would be neither transcended, nor dissolved, nor made *Aufgehoben*, but affirmed, ex-posed, ex-plicated, and acknowledged explicitly as relation, a relationship neither defined nor dominated by its polarities—in this respect perhaps implicitly (and profoundly) democratic.[63] And 'friendship' as has become apparent, the *ethos* in which such relationality might still flourish, itself will be the affirmation of this 'between' by which we all are separate, and yet are 'subjects', only in relation—the relation, as Levinas has emphasized perhaps more than anyone else, of the face-to-face.

Invoking this ancient word 'friendship' for the relationship between subjects however, not only, again, glosses its ancient inheritance, but shows how much is contested in the Hegelian and Hobbesian explanation of recognition in terms of will to power. It is friendship, as opposed to egoism, which separates the discourse of persons from both the abstractions of *eros* and the impersonal metaphysics of faculties. There is after all no faculty—nor strict demonstration—of friendship. Doubtless the concept of friendship prima facie seems as foreign within modern discourses as recognition is within the ancients'. Still, recognition was nascently at stake in what Aristotle termed friendship's 'step beyond' love, the latter being not only both ontic and ontological but a matter of mutual 'recognition' and goodwill.[64] Moreover, this 'reciprocity', this *Wechsel* of friendship, precisely that of such relationality itself, it might be argued, was at stake as what constituted community for Aristotle, ultimately a question of the 'between':

> Friendship and justice seem as we have said at the outset of our discussion, to be concerned with the same objects and exhibited between the same persons. For in every community there is thought to be some form of justice and some friendship too. . . . And the extent of their association is the extent of their friendship, as it is the extent to which justice exists between them. And the proverb, what friends have is common 'property', expresses the truth; for friendship depends upon community.[65]

This common 'property' however cannot simply be the identity of a common *substance,* nor does it exist without the relation itself, although it is never reducible to it. It is the figured difference of 'persons' itself that is at stake and not simply their common identity; it is the 'commonality' by which that difference that is to be preserved arises. The difference of persons is not that of concrete substances of the same 'species'. This 'difference' questions the simple logic of natural kinds. Likewise, however (and doubtless in the wake of the question of recognition), in the relation of Aristotelian friends, we can understand the theoretical risks of Aristotle's own 'reification' in claiming that the friend, insofar as each is related to "the other as to himself," is "another self."[66] The other is not the 'same' as myself but the other him-or-her-self, the difference of the other as person, the *alteritas personarum*. Justice, as Aristotle realized, is most completely justice in relation to the other (*pros heteron*) and not simply relation to oneself (*pros hauton*) [1129b26f.]. Consequently, in this sense friendship is nascently a 'personal' relation, not an abstract one, and such 'communities' are not abstract entities but concrete relations: the relations in which the *alteritas personarum* itself becomes ventured, risked, recognized, and reciprocated—or corrupted and dissolved. But what has equally become evident is that the relations between 'ethics' and 'ontology' will be complicated and not simply exclusive.

## 5. The Sublime and the Ordinary:
## On Dialogue, Narrativity, and Plurality

Notwithstanding Levinas's charges against ontology—that ontological 'imperialism' neutralizes the otherness of the other—Heidegger himself, as adamant as he was about the nonpriority of the question of the I-thou relation, was not simply desensitized to the encounter upon which Levinas insisted. Indeed, the account of this encounter is facilitated by his own overcoming of modern transcendentalism and the anonymity and 'splitting' of the subject as autoaffection, opening precisely in the ruins of transcendental 'logic'.

> If however man does not experience his own looking, i.e. the human look, in "reflection" on himself as the one who represents himself as looking, but if instead man experiences the look, in unreflected letting-be-encountered, as the looking at him of the person who is encountering him, the look of the encountering person shows itself as that in which someone awaits the other as counter, i.e. appears to the other and is. The looking that awaits the other and the human look thus experienced disclose the encountering person himself in the ground of his essence. (Par:103)

The event of this encounter is doubtless portentous, its implications overdetermined: epistemic, ontological, and finally ontic and ethical in import. It is an event, to use Heidegger's term, which arises from the archive of the sublime that is fully 'uncanny' (*unheimlich*). Beyond the archive of the tragic virtues which had often accompanied his account, those such as fortitude, sacrifice, and resolute shattering, Heidegger now insists that this word *unheimlich* will have "nothing in common with its banal sense as 'impressive' and 'moving'" (Par:106)—in short, the violence which accompanied the Burkean legacy that attends the modern itinerary of the sublime. Instead, this uncanniness must be sought not beyond but precisely within the ordinary or the near. Here as elsewhere, Heidegger would attribute it to an encounter beyond tradition in the Greek beginnings from which the West has declined, thus attempting to get beyond illusion and figure. Moreover, he connects it, here as elsewhere, to the eschatology and destiny of Being's withdrawal (and, most primordially, to man's being "looked upon")—and here more tragically to the destiny of the German people (Par:100). As has become apparent, however, one must wonder whether it is a question of 'getting beyond' anything so much as a question of seeing tradition and the encounter with its effect within the ordinary, of looking past its exclusions or leveling—a matter of 'seeing otherwise'. It becomes a question, then, of discerning the complexity of the uncanny and the suspicious, the excluded and the transcendent, perhaps even the 'universal' and the singular in the ordinary itself: not as the 'beyond' that orders the destiny of a people but of the extraordinary that is 'ordinarily' articulated and differentiated in its midst, precisely again in the multifariousness of its voices. Nowhere perhaps is the claim made by Dominique Janicaud, that it is not ontology but the destinal that interferes with the ethical in Heidegger's thought, more justified.[67] Rightly understood, the 'ontological' plane sustains the ethical in the same sense—as Levinas puts it, that subjectivity in general emerges from "a place both presupposing and transcending the epiphany of the Other in the face. . . . this plane is that of love and fecundity" (TI:253).

This 'plane' is reducible neither to a play of forces that might underlie it nor to a form that might 'transcend' it—not even the "eschatology of Being."[68] Again, to invoke Heidegger's term, in either case such a reduction would amount to a 'depersonalization'. The 'one' of intersubjectivity will be neither divine nor immanent, not even 'triune': its 'plurality' will always remain unresolved, always open beyond itself, always in need of interpretation, always 'human'. In fact, we can say of the latter precisely what we found earlier in the Thomistic account of language. Reason requires imagination and language just to the extent that reason is human. Hence Aquinas's claim that the angels have no use for imagination: unlike humans, having no acquaintance with unencumbered particulars, they have no need for imagination (i.e., no need to interpret) (ST:I.89.1). And doubtless this 'hermeneutic' dimension also must accompany the question and the history (and realities) of personhood; thus understood, as Heidegger's account of depersonalization originally acknowledged, history must be understood without recourse to transcendental abstraction.

The conceptual history of such 'personalism', not to speak of the hermeneutic issues raised thereby, still might seem foreign to Levinas's project (both conceptually and theologically); but we should proceed carefully here. Quite apart from (or perhaps just because of) the differences in sacred archives at stake, it might be said, Levinas was able to bring to light the resources which had been contested and slowly eroded in the descent of the concept of the person. Here Levinas's 'Jewish' past becomes less a 'dogmatic' hermeneutic that might overdetermine this event than a protocol for the discovery of what may remain continuously overlooked in the omissions and reductions which continuously threatened it. Precisely in discussing revelation in the Jewish tradition, Levinas has reaffirmed the matter in these terms, first with respect to hermeneutics itself.

> The Revelation is this continual process of hermeneutics, discovering new landscapes in the written or oral word, uncovering problems and truths locked within each other. As such, it is not only a source of wisdom, the path of deliverance and elevation; it is also the food of the life of knowledge, and the object of the enjoyment (*jouissance*) which goes with it. Thus Maimonides, in the twelfth century, could attach the same pleasure and happiness to the hermeneutics of Revelation that Aristotle attaches to the contemplation of pure essences in Book X of the *Nicomachean Ethics*.[69]

Moreover, it is the event of this traditionality itself, that is, the handing down of its past as this present, that underscores Levinas's point and rejoins the conceptual series we have traced:

> The Revelation has a particular way of producing meaning, which lies in its calling upon the unique in me. It is as if a multiplicity of persons—and it is this multiplicity, surely, that gives the notion of 'person' its sense—were the condition for the plenitude of 'absolute truth', as if each person, by virtue of his own uniqueness, were able to guarantee the revelation of one unique aspect of the truth, so that some of its facets would never have been revealed if certain people had been absent from mankind. I do not mean that truth is anonymously produced within History, where it finds its own supporters! On the contrary, I am suggesting that the totality of truth is made out of the contributions of the multiplicity of people: the uniqueness of each act of listening carries the secret of the text; the voice of Revelation, in precisely the inflection lent by each person's ear, is necessary for the truth of the Whole.[70]

Here Levinas again stands perhaps in close proximity to Gadamer and his account of tradition as a multifariousness of voices, a *dialegein*, which, as the welcoming of difference, is "the tradition in which we want to share and have a part" (TM:284). To Levinas's multiplicity of persons, a multiplicity already apparent from the problem of the *alteritas personarum* itself, it is necessary in the end to add the multiplicity of interpretations and their narratives. Indeed we have witnessed this in what Heidegger (ultimately) sought in the Greeks, Hegel in the Trinity, Levinas in the Torah and the Talmud, all of them perhaps obliquely in the issue of Aristotle's relevance, perhaps even in the ruins of the logic on which Brentano's *intendit significare* depended. With the event of obligation that emerged from the encounter with the other and the question of the *alteritas personarum*, there likewise emerged both the problem of the multiplicity of persons and co-mmunity, and doubtless then the multiplicity of narratives—and then the problem of interpretation. Notwithstanding concerns with the theoretization and re-duction of the person—concerns the person not be equated with any figure, to use Levinas's term—it remains true too that respect for the other also in-evitably arises from and in relation with the problem of narrative and inter-pretation. It is in just this sense that the problem of respect for the other internally broaches the question of an expression irreducible to the apo-phantic representation of the said—and, to the extent that phenomenology remains correlated with the latter, "a plot [*intrigue*] that is not reducible to phenomenology" (OBBE:46).[71]

Like all appeals (or denials) of tradition, as we have seen, here Levinas's too must articulate a certain *Erwiderung*. And here it emerges again:

> For the veritable tradition (*tradition vénérable*) to which Hegel refers, the ego is an equality with itself, and consequently the return of being to itself is a concrete universality, being having separated itself from itself in the univer-sality of the concept and death. But viewed out of the obsession of passivity, of itself anarchical, there is brought out, behind the equality of consciousness, an inequality. The inequality does not signify an inadequation of the apparent be-ing with the profound or sublime being, nor a return to an original innocence.
> . . . It signifies an inequality in the oneself due to substitution, an effort to es-cape concepts without any future but attempted anew the next day. It signifies a uniqueness, under assignation of responsibility, and because of this assigna-tion not finding any rest in itself. (OBBE:115)

Even in this attempt to escape such concepts, however, Levinas's account cannot be removed from the question of tradition. Indeed, against the total-ization of Hegel's return to self, it is a matter of distinguishing the "good Cartesian tradition [*bonne tradition cartesienne*], where the clear and dis-tinct ideas still receive light from Plato's intelligible sun" (OBBE:133). Such a tradition precludes Hegel's (Leibnization) inversion of 'illuminated' or transcendent identity. Indeed, as has become evident, in one sense Hegel simply (speculatively) completes the functional totalization of the *mathesis universalis*, founding its (totalized) identity in an absolute cognitive subjec-tivity, the *Ich* = *Ich*.

Here if Hegel becomes our Aristotle, he does so precisely through a cer-tain 'inverted world' which, again to use Joyce's term, outlines the "night-mare from which we are trying to awake," completing Western philosophy's "refutation of transcendence" (OBBE:169). Indeed against 'Hegelian' identity, in fact Levinas traces an inverted identity in which, rather than a return to self, the I attains its identity only in its venture before the other. Invoking an argument that dates from his early analyses of Husserl—but claiming that the latter too simply remains "in conformity with the whole tradition of the West [in which] knowing remains the norm of the spiritual" (OBBE:96)—Levinas claims, "such formalist or mathematical visions of intelligibility" lead us back to a teleology of cognition—and ultimately to the ethics which might make such a teleology possible (OBBE:96).[72] But the 'conditionality' of such a reliance would call into question the very protocols of phenomenology that strictly correlate subjectivity and the knowable (OBBE:17).

As has also become evident, however, it is clear that for Levinas, the 'Western tradition' is not univocal—even if it is true that "the main tradition" (OBBE:95) of the West, divided between the totalization of ontological finality and mathematical functionalism, continuously threatens the tradition of the Good. Here, moreover, it is clear that Levinas's typification of 'Western thought', in which "the subject is at service of the system," is also 'Hegelian'—a Hegel who is 'systematic' (i.e., a formalist) and whose suspicions of the proximity of human appearances "weigh on human identity" (OBBE:59). Indeed it is in just this sense that, in the ethical moment, through "substitution . . . identity is inverted" (OBBE:115). No longer ecstatic with respect to a sublime or inadequate being, in acknowledging the Good itself (i.e., in being obligated), the self is 'held hostage' by the other, the face of the other in proximity. All meaning, all signification would emerge in this opening—indeed for Levinas proximity is signification.

Still we have seen that the attempt to simply equate transcendence and concept is 'angelic'; Levinas himself evoked the term with regard to the 'equations' of modern apophantics, "however sublime it be" (OBBE:6). He admits, further, that one can proceed 'ontotheologically' "by starting with the supreme efficacity of God," but only at risk of losing transcendence. Against it Levinas had traced "the very inordinateness [démesure] of infinity" where equivocation is never dissipated" and whose very insight depends on acknowledging that "the transcendent does not let itself be assembled" (OBBE:94, 161). Yet the fecundity of this account demands that we not lose sight of this 'ambiguity' and the resources which continue to furnish its intelligibility—whether they be Plato's 'One without being', or Husserl's pure Ego, transcendent in immanence, or the Nietzschean laughter which (anarchically) refuses language (OBBE:8). All doubtless have been refigured in Levinas's own 'narrative' of the ambiguity of 'diachronous' or 'dia-logical' relation beyond simple reciprocity and agreement (OBBE:25). As such, however, the "truth of the whole," by which Levinas links revelation to the multiplicity of persons, will similarly be 'equivocally' plural—as he openly argued concerning the medieval account of analogy.

At stake in the question of the other (and the question of its interpretation) is the opening (and the problem) of transcendence—and, as has been seen, for Heidegger, 'personalism' had always missed it (BT:74f.). What Levinas again adds to Heidegger here, as he put it in an article on dialogue, is the recognition that the 'between' of ontological difference is also the between or opening of the 'dialogue' itself: indeed that the 'dia-logue' at stake in both just "is transcendence."[73] Levinas himself also saw that the "depth semantics" of the personal pronouns 'I' and 'thou' at stake in both are decipherable only from—but equally beyond—"a phenomenology of Relation."[74] Indeed, appealing to the archive we have traced, Levinas claims, "the [first person] pronoun already dissimulates the unique one that is speaking, subsumes it under a concept. But it designates only the mask or the person of the unique one, the mask that leaves the I evading concepts, the I involved in saying the first person, absolutely uncontrovertible into a noun" (OBBE:56). For that very reason the relation at stake will escape the logic of indexical and fixed reference.

But as has likewise been seen, the concept of the person itself is already figured 'relationally' and the very concepts of obligation and respect already broach a logical syntax *figured* by narratives of revelation and unconcealment. And doubtless—albeit blinkingly—this too had been Kant's claim about respect for the law: the logical syntax of obligation is inextricably accompanied by and identified through such narratives of identity and transcendence. To respect the other is surely to respect such narratives and, as Kant too had demonstrated, not simply to hope to escape from such traditions but to encounter them in their uncanniness, an uncanniness which both sustains and threatens in the figure of traditionality itself. Such 'respect' became especially apparent—and problematic—in Kant's symbolization of the law; a symbolization that in acknowledging the underdeterminacy at stake, likewise refused all fanaticism. Hence the problem of law or right (*droit*)—and the question, to speak Hobbesian, of a "unity" among the "plurality of voices," one less revealed than "instituted."

As Hobbes acknowledged "the true God may be Personated [a]s he was; first by *Moses*" and "[s]econdly by the Son of man" (Lev:I:16; Hobbes's emphasis). The multitude of men, however, are surely made One person only problematically, if ever—and even if only figuratively. It is doubtless then "not without importance to know if the egalitarian and just State in which man is fulfilled (and which is to be set up, and especially to be maintained) proceeds from a war of all against all, or from the irreducible responsibility of the one for all, and if it can do without friendship and faces" (OBBE:159–60). But as such the transcendence (and the identity) at stake is less 'beyond' us than "between us," a matter less of our being 'mutually' held hostage by one another (the premises remain Hobbesian) than a matter of this between and "the extraordinarily everydayness of my [and our] responsibility" (OBBE:141).

Granted the ambiguity of the everyday, the history of interpretation cannot be simply equated with the history of revelation: the multiplicity of interpretations need not coalesce; none is endowed in advance with the keys to certainty. 'Revelation' always requires both interpretation and critique. Hence the problem (to use Heidegger's term) of a "hermeneutics of empathy" (BT:163), dividing both adjudication and interpretation from within. Doubtless this division complicates the requisites of its legitimation from the outset. Only briefly perhaps in confronting the problem of witness and sincerity does Levinas 'attest' to this 'contamination' of the said upon the 'saying', removing it from angelic immanence.

> Thematization is then inevitable, so that signification itself shows itself, but does so in the sophism with which philosophy begins, in the betrayal which philosophy is called upon to reduce. This reduction always has to be attempted, because of the trace of sincerity which the words themselves bear and which they owe to saying as witness, even when the said dissimulates the saying in the correlation set up between the saying and the said. Saying always seeks to unsay that dissimulation, and this is its very veracity. (OBBE:152)

Such 'saying' emerges again only out of ambiguity; its prophesy therefore "is not the makeshift of clumsy revelation" (OBBE:152), but instead requires ambiguity, equivocity, and limit—and thereby requires both interpretation and critique. If thematization is inevitable—and surely in this regard it is—the hope that the relation to transcendence at stake might be said—angelically—must be foregone: the immanence of significance breaks up. Levinas clearly recognized the paradox of this 'depiction': "transcendence owes it to itself to interrupt its own demonstration" (OBBE:152). But this 'interruption' and the problem of legitimacy it inaugurates is doubtless intrinsic to signification itself—or surely has been from the outset of the 'detraditionalization' out of which modernity and even the 'good Cartesian tradition' itself already emerged.

## 6. Beyond Obligationism, the Venture of Generosity, and the "Exposure to Critique"

At the beginning of modern thought, just before giving up the most ancient of philosophical understandings of humanity as the rational animal for the sake of thinking substance, Descartes's meditation was momentarily arrested: "I shall pause here to consider the ideas which previously arose naturally and of themselves in my mind whenever I considered what I was. I thought of myself as having a face. . . ."[75] Granted the problematic through which theoretical modernity in the wake of Descartes and Locke linked personhood and self-awareness, Descartes's 'thought' was a portentous one. But this 'thought' occurs problematically, only within a fundamental absence, like the withdrawal of the other before my mind. "The trouble is," as Sartre stated, "I don't see my face."[76] Nor would the face that I see, the face of the other, ever simply be a direct 'analogy' of my own. Does the other ever present an image like myself—even in the pairing of our bodies, to use Husserl's word? There is a transcendental subreption working in such appeals: I then have a 'face' like the other, since he or she has a body like mine. The inference in fact may well go the other way: if not simply proceeding from the other, at least a relation whose 'between' is nonreflexive and irrecuperable, that defies re-presentation. The other remains in all this an event that escapes *mimesis*, an irreducible appearance that never will become an object. As Edith Stein put it in her classic description of empathy, at stake is "a primordial experience of what is given non-primordially" which "announces the foreign individual" and which therefore defies "inner perception."[77] Hence originates Levinas's point, or to speak Sartrean, the necessity of 'conversion' before such an encounter—a 'call' in which it opens.

On the other hand, Cartesian generosity—like the Stoic singularity of the *cogito* in general—likewise seemed always to confound. Having noted the positivity of the third Meditation's encounter with transcendence, Levinas himself still construed the modern ethic of generosity as merely egoistic (OBBE:118). Strauss had concurred, claiming that dependent simply on an intention, 'Cartesian' morality had now lost its objective basis—that indeed it was "Hobbes' system of morality [that] corresponds to Descartes' deepest intentions."[78] Even Gadamer had concurred this much. Gadamer too condemned Descartes's discussion of morality for its merely provisional status, claiming that Descartes had left morality to the side, granted his commitments to science—and his radical distrust of authority (TM:273). Instead, Gadamer countered, not only must morality not be so radically coupled

with distrust of authority, but "the real force of morality . . . is based on tradition" (TM:280). Moreover, as thus dependent on the classical, ethics
needed to be distinguished from the 'shock' of the sublime: the classical
concerns less what "surpasses all conscious expectations" than the recognition of something "enduring" (TM:288).

Again, however, we will need to be more cautious: 'tradition', as has become evident, is neither so univocal nor so immanently authoritative. Here
Gadamer sounds close to the very 'traditionism' he has rejected. Even the
truth of tradition must be 'wrestled away' from its failure, as Heidegger put
it. The (Aristotelian) reliance on (past) practice has been rendered problematic. Elsewhere Gadamer claimed that the sublime also "elevates" us and
that, in this regard, precisely what is significant about the aesthetics of the
sublime is that it overcomes egoism. Doubtless his account of the perdurance of tradition depended on such sublimity, connecting hermeneutics itself as "the event of genuine experience" to the ancient account of radiance
(*ekphanestaton*) of the beautiful in which the Good itself appears (TM:
480f.). Heidegger's construals of phenomenology itself were not far from
this, the encounter with an event that always exceeded the limitations of
transcendental presentation. At stake was an event which ruptured all
forms of simple 'subjectivism'—epistemic, ontologic, and ethical. 'Cartesian' generosity in this sense, as Jean-Luc Marion has insisted, is less about
egoistic autoaffection than it is about the acknowledgment or *esteem* for
what transcends within oneself.[79] Here too we should not forget Levinas's
'three waves'. In the same way that Levinas articulates the Cartesian 'idea of
infinity' that erupts in the ruins of representation, so equally generosity
erupts the constraints of modern egoism. Doubtless—and as has already
become apparent in our discussion of civility—we shall need to confront a
history of the passions that accompanies the history of 'Being'. Here, beyond
Aristotle, Levinas and Gadamer (following Heidegger) concurred, there lingers the problematic character of the (Platonic) Good: the good that lies
problematically beyond the (ontically) true.[80]

As has become evident, Gadamer realized that the problem of the Good
hovers in the background of even Aristotle's criticism of Plato, beyond
even the shared practices of the *polis:* we must, Aristotle realized, when all
is said and done, honor the Good even more than the past. Neither thinking nor ethics can be simply reduced to the time of the past nor even the
task of remembering: at stake will be an event that exceeds both, not reducible "to the interiority of memory," as Levinas reminds us (TI:51).
Moreover, its intelligibility will again be differential and 'lateral', tied nei-

ther simply to the *arche* or *telos* of classical culture (*Bildung*)—nor the discourse of enculturation—but like the logic of personhood that it refigures and transforms, remains irreducible to either a genus or a 'generation'. At stake again is more "the transitivity of teaching and not the interiority of reminiscence" (TI:101). Beyond the historicism of reliance upon received or 'inherited' practice, the 'between' of hermeneutics will always be linked to the problem of the Good and more anciently, in the question of Being, the between that incites the articulations of analogy 'otherwise' (TM:295).

Still, the *inference* of analogy fails—and (before Levinas) Scheler, Husserl, and Sartre seemingly acknowledged it as much as any modern following Hobbes. As Levinas reaffirmed, we should not lose track of "all the abysses of transcendence, all the intervals that cut across 'analogical unity'" (OBBE:94). Analogy always involved a rational appeal that failed the logic of demonstration: not because the articulation of analogical interpretation fails outright, but because it is not an *inference* at all, but the interplay of experience and idea, reason and fact.

Wherever such remnants become renarrated, they do so always more as a venture than a proof, divided between narration and the unnarratable (*l'inénarrable*)—and the event in which "the unnarratable other loses his face as a neighbor in narration" (OBBE:166). The 'tales' (*fables*) that emerge 'analogically' remain always problematic, the opening of a semantic field irreducible to a simple index. This was what Gadamer had spelled out vis-à-vis the problem of the "old story" of the Good—and it is doubtless what had incited Heidegger's own reading of the *Seinsfrage*.[81]

Gadamer at one point claimed that he had learned the complicated relation between narrative and interpretation from Lacan (PH:41). Here, however, we can see what he must add to Lacan's account, based on the elusive drama of psychoanalytical unconscious. Recall that this is a dramatics, or at least its Nietzschean antecedent, that Levinas had also affirmed at the outset of *Totality and Infinity* (TI:28n). In particular, Lacan had criticized Aristotle's account of the Good as overly Parmenidean, *identifying* the Good and one's own happiness—and tacitly thought and Being. Lacan had declared that "Parmenides was wrong and Heraclitus right" in proclaiming that "[the Lord] neither speaks out, nor conceals . . . but gives a sign."[82] What Gadamer saw, following Heidegger's *Seinsfrage*, was that the Good would not be simply divorced from this Heraclitean moment. The point is that no more than 'Being' can be identified as 'thought' can it be identified with an 'unthought' or an 'unconscious'—any more than 'Being' can be identified with anything at all. Neither 'Being' nor the 'Good' can be denominated by a simple index, or a posited identity, articulating an event (and a semantics, strictly, i.e., demonstrably unnarratable) that exceeds both. Here the 'analogy' of being would always indicate more a problem than a solution.[83]

Levinas, of course, says the same about the "extraordinary" word 'God'— "an overwhelming semantic event" irreducible to the said (OBBE:151). None of these semantic 'excesses' can be reduced to a proposition, to an ontic indexical, to the simple reference of a noun. But nor, I have insisted, can they assume the certainty, immanence, or proof of the latter. These 'old stories' will not replace theory nor the task of theorizing: this is what makes them 'narratives' of the 'unnarratable'. This is what renders them 'ambiguous', 'equivocal', and problematic—and in the wake of modern systematics a venture beyond the 'universal' that remains provisional.

In a sense this too is what makes the ethical in general, like the Cartesian ethic of generosity in particular, a venture that is always 'provisional'. But even Kant acknowledged that, granted the requisites of theory, the grounds of morality remain indemonstrable. Hence, it will be objected, we will need to say more about the modernity of Levinas's "good Cartesian tradition" unless we are to miss its transformation from its traditional past—and without reducing the 'reciprocity' it opens up to indifferent equity or a simple quantitative quid pro quo.[84] But it may well be just this provisionality that also marks the distinctly modern legacy of Cartesian generosity—or at least the acknowledgment of transcendence in its midst, the detraditionalization of transcendental authority notwithstanding. Devoid of traditional authority, the ethic of generosity is Descartes's acknowledgment that such *esteem* exceeds calculative or egoistic reduction. What the Cogito (stoically) attests to, its theoretical reductions notwithstanding, is both the problem of difference, or 'dispersion' to use Hobbes's term and, in the problem of *générosité*, the question of recognition it entails. Hence the requisites of assertion are equally unsurpassable: Gadamer himself realized that, as we have seen, dialogue is explicitly connected with judgment. But recognition—and the dialogue it entails—will be understood deficiently if it is simply understood as calculation, as a means to an end, even the end of consensus. Both are part of a "putting into question of all affirmation for oneself" (OBBE:111). At stake is less a matter of being "on the watch for recognition" (OBBE:119) than an openness to the other and "the very exposure to critique" (OBBE:122).

Granted such 'exposure to critique', however, no more than the recognition of the other can be reduced to an immediate (eschatological) revelation can the other's 'unapproachability' or 'nonsubstitutability' either provide or force the end of all moral theory. Here, to recur to Derrida's earlier articulation, the "eschatological discourses" that are "freed" in Kant's wake will also encounter their own limit—doubtless Levinas's eschatological 'narratives' included, as has been seen.[85] If the event of the face-to-face escapes all moral theory (if all saying emerges in relation to the other, irreducible to the said), this other is still what all moral theory was 'trying to say'—even of course in the recognition that 'it' cannot be said. We might say, now deliberately invoking Wittgenstein, that other troublesome 'moral' theorist of the twentieth century, that at stake is the silence at the limit of the sayable, the silence of ethics—and of the Good and of Being and "if there is a value which is of value," the inexpressible that lies beyond the said. Strictly speaking, then, as the *Tractatus* claimed, "there can be no ethical propositions."[86]

Later Wittgenstein would repeat the assertion to the Vienna Circle, but augment it by claiming that the failure to articulate a satisfactory definition of the Good not only brings us to the limits of language, but itself likewise "points to something" (WLE:13). As such it is clear why Wittgenstein could 'say' what seemed the utterly unsayable within the constraints of the positivist picture—that he understood what Heidegger meant by silence (or Kierkegaard, by the Paradox).[87] But the claim that metaphysics (or theory) is now at an end is precisely what the various positivisms—logical, empirical, and phenomenological—all shared in common. There will be a history of 'theory' just as there is a history of truth. If in encountering the event of the ethical we are beyond propositional representation, we are not simply 'without' it, even if the ethical remains never simply picturable by representational means. These are the silences that philosophy both expresses and interprets—as books like Levinas's attest. Indeed, as Pierre Hadot has declared, this 'mysticism' (and the theoretical stoicism that is its performative) is what books like the *Tractatus* and *Totality and Infinity* share in common.[88] All language arises out of and returns to such silence, appealing beyond propositional space to a silence in which, qua 'transcendence', "ethics is transcendental."[89]

Still, this also explains why the theological narrative cannot, as Francis Jacques thought, simply furnish a paradigm for interpersonal relation: the simple immanence and transparency of the theological is lacking. What Jacques calls its 'eminently valuable' heuristic standpoint has equally proven 'transcendentally subreptive', taken as a system of immanent propositional truths. As perhaps no one more than Hegel exemplifies, Jacques's explicit hypothesis concerning the theological paradigm has furnished the protocols for classical theories of personhood. Such immanence as Levinas claimed must remain 'angelic', confronted with a relationality that is "only mediating" (OBBE:6). It is precisely in denying such immanence that "(m)odern antihumanism, which denies the primacy that the human person, free and for itself, would have for the significance of being, is true over and beyond the reason it gives itself" (OBBE:127). Nor can the latter's withdrawal be overcome through appeal to language as communication. Indeed, as we have also seen, the emergence of language is concomitant with *finite* rationality, a rationality that renders such immanence problematic (i.e., hermeneutic), an interplay of language and 'transcendence', word and silence. Aquinas's account of transcendence, that is, of 'communicative substance', might consistently claim that "it belongs to the essence of Goodness to communicate itself" (ST:III.1). Devoid of such a metaphysics, however, modern accounts immanently linking the rational to such 'communicability' (or consciousness to shared rather than 'secret' thoughts, as Hobbes put it) would remain both reductive and dangerous. It is no accident that Levinas still defends such 'secrecy' or that he connected it to freedom and its conceptual articulation to 'romantic thought'.[90] But such a defense is not a return to immanence: it cannot simply escape the finite or what Hobbes called "the authority of man" (Lev:I:7).

As Derrida has rightly pointed out, even Levinas's invocation of the *visage* is not a simple return to a theological tradition; 'visage', after all, is both a (modern) translation and "reinvention" (Adieu:VI). But as both translation and reinvention (or refiguration) such a 'visage' emerges from a complicated history: it has been, after all, not simply the 'power' of God but the violence of humanity that is at stake in Levinas's thought since the opening pages of *Totality and Infinity*—and hence, the question of how to grapple with the 'interval' that separates them. If Levinas hoped to "disengage this holiness, not in order to preach some way of salvation . . . [but] in order to account for the impossible indifference with regard to the human," he did so fully in acknowledging both the equivocity, the ambiguity, and the silence at its origin.[91]

## 7. Ethics as Transcendental

We will need to see this silence and its 'transcendental' dispersed (and interpreted) in our midst. In the *Wechsel* of this silence (the *Wechsel* of the implicit and the explicit, the expressible and the inexpressible) we can also trace the fragmented transcendence of 'transcendental' personhood, divided between individual and universal, the I and the thou, self and other—

and finally, Being and the Good. Moreover, as we have seen, this fragmentation equally reinvokes the question of imagination that has always haunted modern transcendentalism, whether it be in the relation between ethics and aesthetics (which Wittgenstein, for example, still claimed to be inseparable)—or the question of friendship or the alter ego at its heart. The predicates indeed seemed to circulate from one domain into the other. While Levinas's 'descriptions' of the face seemed always to invoke the sublime, thinkers saw the work of art in moral terms: indeed, as has been seen, Adorno claimed works of art were similarly "a priori helpless."[92] And the issues of politics (or of peace) were never far removed—whether as the community of God or the community of artists. Throughout, Levinas hoped to strictly distinguish the question of the Good from that of the Beautiful and argued at times on behalf of "a life other than friendship (*l'amitié*)," as he vigorously argued against Buber's idealism (TI:69). We are beginning to see these oppositions fragmented. It is in just this sense, too, of course, that the question of theoretical 'priority' or 'first philosophy' is in turn fragmented.

As Lyotard insisted, the *polemos* of theory, both interpretive and underdetermined, is inescapable: knowing that, however, does not condemn us outright to theoretical illusion, let alone falsity or 'terror'. Nor, on the other hand, does it condemn the 'saying' of the ethical to the unsaid, the ineffable. Knowing that reason will inevitably be schema-specific neither simply dissolves objectivity nor simply condemns us to relativism. Lyotard's 'hope' that Levinas should have broken with the notions of evidence, truth, and transcendence remained too 'pagan', too naive; pragmatics cannot replace or escape the vagaries of judgment (and theory). Lyotard's appeals to the strict 'incommensurability' of the sublime (or enthusiasm) remained always parasitic upon Kantian restrictions on cognitive demonstrability.

It is true: the concept of the 'ought' delimits the domain of the (demonstrably) rational without simply encompassing or defining it. The question of law doubtless always remains figured, its necessities underdetermined—and potentially overdetermined thereby. But none of this implies, as we have seen, that law is simply a matter of the imposition of force, nor without legitimation. If the rational inevitably requires judgment, execution, and act, it likewise requires iterability, plurality, and recognition. Here, however, the individual becomes twice unsurpassable; as both the articuleme of 'Being' and the excess before which all judgment goes silent, the remainder of the 'sublime' always-to-be articulated, acknowledged—and respected. But recognition, consequently, must be more than the face-to-face; it must articulate the 'reciprocity' of right and the ideality of judgment, while judgment in turn must yield to the summons of the other, without simply dissolving into anonymous iterability. Hence again the symmetrical dissymmetry or the *Wechsel* of dialogue.

These terms, evidently, still remain idealistic—indeed Fichtean. And they seem only to reinforce old antagonisms. Derrida's earlier "Violence and Metaphysics" had noted the proximity of Schelling to Levinas in the issue of an 'empiricism' beyond philosophy (VM:152). Fichte, as we have seen, had already introduced (surely without solving) both the problems of recognition and the importance of moral imagination in post-Kantian continental thought. If Levinas condemned Fichte for the subsumption of the other beneath the posting acts of consciousness, specifically railing against Fichte's voluntarism, he repeated the latter's dialectic of recognition without perhaps acknowledging its full complexity. Fichte's dialectic between the asymmetry of the *Aufforderung* and the reciprocity of recognition provides the conceptual outline of the problem of the other.[93] While Levinas had argued that the Fichtean free ego could not undergo the passivity of suffering from the non-ego (OBBE:123), Fichte himself, as we have seen, had acknowledged this encounter in which "shudderingly I stop" before an "object" which "cannot be mere *nature*." It is anything but accidental, however, that this statement is also included in the origins of Buber's "History of the Dialogical Principle."[94] The origin of intersubjective relationality opens not in a free *act* but in a summons, a 'passivity' between freedoms: such a summons, however, does not preclude but requires institutional and juridical articulation. Indeed it is just the latter that codifies the task (and the *Wechsel*) of recognition. Neither, however, can simply be founded in a lifeless act, requiring a deeper understanding of the relationality at stake and the care—or to use Fichte's latter terms, the distinction between Being (*Sein*) and existence (Da-sein)—through which separation, distinction, and difference arise and are reconciled.[95] Far from precluding ontology, 'ethics' here would require it. Indeed, notwithstanding his own focusing on the founding *acts* of the self, even Fichte had seen, in the later works, the need for a "profound (*tiefste*) metaphysics and ontology."[96] Here 'ethical' theory would seem to reencounter the Heideggerian project of a 'profound' or 'fundamental' ontology. Perhaps it is neither ontology nor theory that threatens ethics so much as an ontology and theory which are insufficient to the task.

If Heidegger himself seemed in the end to subsume the question of the Good not only beneath interpretations of ontology but Being's destinal withdrawal, such interpretation could proceed only by acknowledging a certain 'pre-ontological' Good that 'nurtured' it. This was, recall, precisely his claim about the logic of the hermeneutic circle: "interpretation . . . operates in that which is understood and it must draw its nurture from this [*und aus ihm her sich nahren muss*]" (BT:152). In such hermeneutic 'circles' we should also acknowledge the fragmented remainder of *Naturrecht* and the complicated bond that unites words and deeds, self and other, and finally the *alteritas personarum* itself. Such circularity is both fragmented and ventured in the sublimity of this 'between'—and by the hermeneutic of 'friendship' and 'befriending', the event of 'facing', to use Levinas's term (TI:209). But as has become evident, in Levinas there is friendship and there is friendship: while the event of facing is conjoined to friendship (OBBE:160), apart from such concrete relationality, friendship (e.g., in Buber's I-thou) is said to be abstract. But one might wonder about the 'reciprocal' as well.

To emphasize these terms for the relation is not at all accidental. As we have seen, thinkers as diverse as Gadamer and Derrida have also recurred to the concept of 'friendship' of late to articulate the relation at stake—and Heidegger for the consonance that joining (*Fuge*) that made the relation possible, without simply returning to the 'cosmological' friendship that had puzzled Aristotle at the outset of his treatise on friendship.[97] The latter will be more complicated than this: an event that answers neither simply to Aristotle's *philia*, nor to the *philein* that might predate it, nor simply to the rational (communitarian) practices which may have conjoined both. None of these sufficiently captures the transcendence at stake nor the *Wechsel* articulated in the relation, nor the singularities conjoined therein—nor finally the modern problem of legitimation and interpretation (or authority) that accompanies this. If, as Derrida too has pointed out, "there is Aristotle and there is Aristotle"—the Aristotle of unity, substance, and nature which underlies both and thereby justice—the latter depends always on the friendship in which it becomes articulated in relation to the other self, and which, in the problem of the relation between virtue and the Good, also outlines the relation between 'ethics' and 'ontology'.[98] Justice, however, does not reduce to the mere encounter between singularities, nor the problem of finitude, nor to the figuration that exceeds them: all this descends from other conceptual 'traditions' and other thoughts and would end in Levinas's caveat concerning the subreptions of totality and danger of substitution of ideas for persons.[99]

Still, we should deny the claim that too often links this substitution to simple negation. Rightly construed, the ethics of recognition surely does not require that one simply be held hostage by the other. Nor does an account of the ethical relation require that the Good be disconnected from all reciprocity. It is in this respect, as has become evident, that claims regarding virtue must be limited in order to avoid the vices of 'slavishness'—or, with

Hegel (and Boethius before him), in order to avoid resolving relationality into the fixed polarities of the master-slave dialectic. If the ambiguity of the ethical relation will always necessitate critical interpretation—if both the possibility and the 'violence' that threatens the ethical will always necessitate an endless interrogation concerning whether it has taken place (Lyotard's "*Arrive-t-il?*"), this does not preclude—but requires—a justice or decency whose equivocity flourishes precisely as this 'good ambiguity'.[100] The very interrogation that opens the possibility of ethical interpretation here must preclude dogmatic resolution: this too is the legacy of its 'undecidability'.

We might still question whether, despite Levinas's claim to the contrary, he has not privileged the position of the slave (OBBE:105); whether the simple obsession with persecution, to speak Freudian, still flirts with its own 'paranoia of speculation'—perhaps even the dream of totality.[101] For example, Levinas states, "To be oneself, otherwise than being, to be dis-interested, is to bear wretchedness and bankruptcy of the other, and even the responsibility that the other can have for me" (OBBE:117). But how can that be, without a return to self, without the dissolution of difference, and without tacitly re-assuming the position (i.e., the identity of the master)—and in any case the Hegelian spirit in which "I am the relation of the two sides"? Doesn't such an assumption undo the difference of singular responsibility itself, to be itself and *not* the other and hence, 'similarly', both *needful* of the other as other and 'equally' in peril?

In all strictness, and for all its fecundity, Levinas's hope for peace in such moments still seemed committed to the very *egoistic,* perhaps even Hobbesian premises he sought to surmount. As has been seen, Derrida in a 1967 article had articulated 'God alone' as the only possibility which precludes the violence against which Levinas rails (VM:107). But this too much precludes the possibility in which 'we' might intervene on violence, the possibility in which 'peace' might depend not simply on the responsibility of singular conscience but more on the 'authority' that lies between us. Here 'friendship' could not simply be opposed to politics as peace is to war—but would still, unlike Hobbes, require a politics that (without succumbing to violence or the conjunctions of violence and metaphysics) might sustain it. Here however Levinas, on the one hand, remained staunchly linked to the 'foundation' of the separated ego—and, on the other hand, to justice as abstract anonymous universality. And his solution remains, correspondingly, bound to the requisites of obligationism. While this is doubtless part of the Kantian legacy to which Levinas refers, Kant's 'hermeneutics', especially in articulating foundations for a metaphysics of virtue, also sought explicitly to surpass the subjectivist antimony to which Levinas remains bound. And, despite its limitations, such a 'surpassing' was even more explicit in post-Kantian accounts of recognition beginning with Fichte. It is true that, for Levinas, Fichte too restricted the relation at stake to "the act that would effect it" (OBBE:101), and his account of reciprocity, accordingly, remains similarly restricted. Rightly understood, however, the summons of the other (*Aufforderung*) does not preclude but instead institutes the *Wechsel* of freedom and individuality—without being reducible to either *relata* of the self and other polarity. In a sense, though, it might be objected, Aristotle had said nothing else (NE:1125a).

## 8. A Final Vis-à-vis with Aristotle: On the (Im)possibility of Reciprocity and the *Aporiae* of Recognition

I have insisted on the 'exception' of Aristotle's account of friendship, as have others in this context. As Blanchot has put it, specifically noting the enigmatic intertwining of reciprocity and unrequited generosity, "*philia* . . . can be received as a heritage always capable of being enriched."[102] It is doubtless just the enigma of this heritage we have been tracing. Still, it is just this "Greek heritage" to which many (e.g., Derrida) have objected, challenging its metaphysics, the exemplariness of its essentialism, its exclusiveness, and its latent egoism and 'utilitarianism'—for all of which the appeal to reciprocity is the purported proof. But, as has also been seen, Derrida has (along with Blanchot and Deguy) also insisted on a certain irony in the 'heritage' of Aristotle's accounts, citing a fragment attributed to Aristotle according to a "certain latin tradition" which lamented, "Oh, my friends, there is no friend." The latter, according to this tradition, was to be construed as Aristotle's most direct response to Plato—and to Platonism. We should wonder at the oppositions in the account. We have in any case refused the correlation of reciprocity construed simply as a quid pro quo or its sign (in which reciprocity is the expression of friendship) reduced, as Derrida puts it, to a "proof"—and denied (as had Heidegger) that the 'accord' related in the *analogia* at stake could be reduced to extrinsic 'proportion'.

It may be instead that it is the antinomies of egoism and altruism that must be rejected. Moreover, it is the latter rejection that may enable us to grasp the 'friendship' of democracy, and even the democratic contract itself, which Derrida hopes friendship, properly 'deconstructed', can sustain. When Hobbes declared that "the affection wherewith men many times bestow their benefits on strangers is not to be called charity, but either

contract, whereby they seek to purchase friendship, or fear, which maketh
them purchase peace," he had in a sense already seen this.[103] It is not fear of
death which sustains the contract—even if the picture we have is that such
fear motivates it. Rather it is the promise of a mutually sustained peace, of
"counter-assurance" (Lev:I.16), doubtless constituted only in the internal
regulations of law itself: the friendship of 'contract' and 'law' belies simple
utility and suspicion, where both the rational and generosity might coalesce. Here if Strauss saw Hobbes as the true author of Cartesian ethics we
should acknowledge the extent to which both Descartes and Hobbes mutually 'enlighten' one another in the interplay of generosity and promise. This
interplay allows us to recognize what Levinas termed "the surplus of my du-
ties over my rights" (OBBE:159) without reducing its complexity to either
polarity—and hence to a politics either without the ethics to sustain it or an
ethics that would dissolve rights into obligations. Indeed in this light, far
from dissolving the question of 'reciprocity', the problem would be one of
rightly interpreting the 'reciprocity' at stake in such relationality.

In this, however, it becomes clear that rightly construed, rather than being
a *privilège mutualiste*, such reciprocity is the 'eventing' of friendship.[104] Reciprocity—like recognition—is less the condition or the 'proof' of friendship
than its expression, the sign (*semeion*) of friendship, as Aristotle literally put
it. As has become evident, we will need to see the (hermeneutic) problem of
the Good—its sublimity—at stake here as well.[105] The 'question' of Aristotelian *philia* may well lie beyond egoism and altruism, in the same way that it
lies beyond the categories of the active and the passive. It is in demanding
that it be either/or that such claims would remain held hostage by Hobbesian
premises. Here again it is not a matter of a return to Aristotle so much as
grasping the aftereffects of its default, where 'nature' and community have
been rendered problematic. In the end, no more than 'obligation' can be correlated with the (personally) singular, can law be correlated with the (impersonal) anonymous universal: both will be 'ours' in precisely the sense that
they lie 'between' us. The problem as always—indeed as has become evident—the human problem par excellence—is how to interpret this.

Confronted with the failures of modern systematics, the obligation privileging the needs of the other to be irreducible will rightly remain unsurpassable—any other claim, it will be objected, will just as inevitably render
the other a dependent variable of a function (and a destiny) that belies it.
The question is whether this recognition is enough. Against such premises
ethics must be the denial of 'theory'. But the question is whether theory itself must instead be understood 'otherwise'. And unless and until theory
(and its 'life') is otherwise construed, Levinas's account of the 'excess' of the

other must hold. More than this, however, we must also articulate such 'transcendence' in particular. We must calculate (and adjudicate) and we must acknowledge the excess that escapes the limitations of calculation. This, is after all, just the 'theory' of the Good. But it is just this conjunction of the calculable and the incalculable, analysis and synthesis, principle and transcendence that is required: the hope to disjoin these elements is what underlies the Platonist attempt to *possess* the Good. It is Plato after all, as the *Symposium* attests, who had linked human relations to possession, the desire to obtain totality (or completeness)—and thereby the need to escape striving itself.

Aristotle's account of friendship, rightly construed, remains human, differentiated, and indeed ordinary—and in any case spellbound neither by the opposition between violence and the sacred nor that between 'transcendence' and justice. As 'human' it remains not divine, tied to the appearances, to motion, to desiring—in this regard to Heidegger's *physis*—but equally to a care for the other in him or herself (*kath'hauto*). Moreover, while such accounts seemed to hold only of 'private' individuals, it did not preclude Aristotle from recognizing the political import of friendship: friendship, in particular the friendship of the citizen, always supplants justice. Indeed if Hobbes would claim that it is not friendship but contract that is the *vis vivendi* of politics, he had in a sense missed Aristotle here too. Without simply disagreeing with Hobbes, Aristotle had already seen—even if he had not confronted the problem of conflict—that were there no friendship at all, the promise (the 'civility') that underlies the contract would be impossible. Even here the flourishing of institutions is not simply distinct from the care, 'reciprocal' relation, and mutual independence of individuals who "go through time together" (*syndiagein*). It is doubtless this 'excess' that all theory, ethical and political, must acknowledge.

In this sense the insistence on dialogue 'beyond theory' must be affirmed. *Pace* claims like those by Jacques (or Habermas), the premises of 'phenomenology', in stoically refusing to distinguish singularity and subjectivity, refuse thereby to make it a discursive effect; the originary dialogue beyond theory cannot simply be augmented by a successor theory.[106] Indeed, the link between the transcendental and the singular cannot be surmounted without reduction. This is not to claim that this link is intrinsically veridical, but only that it is irreducible. Doubtless it is true: "The 'communication' of ideas, the reciprocity of dialogue, already hide the profound essence of language" (TI:101). But, on the other hand, neither communication nor dialogue—any more than analysis—simply falsifies, let alone dissolves, the question of transcendence. If neither Being nor the Other are reducible to

'meanings', if our grasp is always 'partial', neither are they intelligible apart
from them. The sublimity and the excess such *transcendens* may announce
cannot simply exceed idea, interpretation, and explanation; to speak Derridean, the calculable and the incalculable cannot be simply opposed.
Rather it is precisely in the encounter with the other—which is not reducible to distinct 'effects' or obligations—that both become possible: it is in
just this sense that Dasein and *Mitsein*, like Being-in-the-World itself, might
again become intelligible as "an equiprimordiality of constitutive items."
The latter, Heidegger claimed, is a phenomenon that "has often been disre-
garded in ontology, because of a methodologically unrestrained tendency to
derive anything and everything from some 'primal ground'" (BT:170).[107] I
should add, moreover, *pace* Lacan's claims that Aristotle simply identified
*logos* or Being (or desire and happiness), that in the figure of equiprimordiality itself Heidegger articulated not the identity, but the problematic
belonging-together, the con-junction in the remainder of analogics of same
and other (BT:34), one inevitably broached through heterogeneity and (ontological) difference.[108] Such 'heterogeneity' doubtless affects the articulations of ethics as much as ontology, the other as much as the self, the past
as much as the present—articulating, beyond "homoiotical interpretation"
a certain relation to the other, doubtless a certain "(in)articulation" in its
midst.[109]

Granted the vagaries of modern theoretics, it will be said the 'face-to-face'
has perhaps never fully taken place. Indeed Kant's own venture had worried
as much, doubtless confronted with a history, a sublimity, and experience
whose complexities remained nondefeasible.[110] We have not been granted a
priori 'intuitions' regarding such difference any more than we have overcome the snares of passion and power. Neither sensibility nor understanding
have been 'well grounded', let alone ultimately adequated. The 'solution' to
the dialectics of self-consciousness, the matrices of power, or the master-
slave dialectics of conceptual personhood can be neither simply ethical nor
ontological. This is doubtless the complex inheritance of the theoretics and
the 'theologics' of personhood—and the care that must now attend it. Moreover, it does not follow that a metaphysical or theological sympathy, or even
generosity either dissolves or overcomes these antinomies. Hobbes surely
had seen this as much as Sartre, whose account as a result would always
verge upon, if not utilitarianism, at least an estranged egoism.[111] Generosity
becomes instead (and was perhaps always already in its Cartesian guise) a
venture beyond such antinomies, beyond the abstractions of personalism—
and perhaps the lingering possibility thereby of a 'discrete fraternity', to again
use Lacan's term.[112]

Responding both to Sartre and to Heidegger, Merleau-Ponty early on wrote that I live "not for death" and "not for myself alone but with other people."[113] He did so, however, not out of naiveté, but precisely in acknowledging the complications of our belonging to history. Writing about the same time as Levinas was composing *Totality and Infinity*, still responding to Sartre, and not without the remainder of such friendship in mind, Merleau-Ponty wrote:

> Freedom and invention are in the minority, the opposition. Man is well hidden, and this time we must make no mistake about it: this does not mean that he is there beneath a mask, ready to appear. Alienation is not simply privation of what was our own by natural right, and to bring it to an end, it will not suffice to steal what has been stolen, to give us back our due. The situation is far more serious: there are no faces underneath the masks, historical man has never been human, and yet no man is alone.[114]

# 5. On the Dispensation of the Good

Anything it could contain must be either good to it or not good; but in the supremely and primally Good there can be nothing not good; nor can the Absolute Good be a container to the Good; containing then neither the good nor the not-good it contains nothing and, containing nothing it is alone; it is void of all but itself.

—Plotinus, *Enneads*

6.371 At the basis of the whole modern view of the world lies the illusion that the so-called laws of nature are the explanation of natural phenomena.

—Wittgenstein [TLP]

The imperfection of languages consists in their plurality, the supreme one is lacking.

—Mallarmé

But what does law mean here?

—Heidegger, Davos debate with Cassirer

I can readily think what Heidegger means by Being and Dread.

—Wittgenstein

[T]alk about an "analogical function" possessed by natural meanings for the predicative explication of transcendental complexes of matters has simply become an *expression that causes a predicament.*

—Fink, *Sixth Cartesian Meditation*

Transcendence owes it to itself to interrupt its own demonstration.

—Levinas, *Otherwise than Being*


## 1. The Paradox of the Good

The paradox of the Good, as Plotinus saw every bit as much as Heidegger, Sartre, or Wittgenstein, is that it emerges only within a certain nothingness. The Good emerges as a question, that is, already ruptured with the time of the present, institution, ontic instantiation, or 'value', and one to which both etymologically and theoretically the problem of interpretation—the question of this 'between' (*inter*), of what is near (*proti*) and its value (*pretium*)—has always been 'archaically' linked. Both syntactically and semantically the 'appearance' of the Good is as extraordinary as the nothingness of its 'being'. As has become evident, it was just for this reason that Levinas called "the place of the Good above every essence . . . the most profound teaching, the definitive teaching, not of theology, but philosophy" (TI:103). If, as has been claimed, in modernity the bond between the right and the Good has ruptured, the problem, as we have seen, is the 'empty place' which characterizes the withdrawal which such a lapse in bonds opens up. Hence Levinas's gloss: in all this talk of finitude what is at issue is "society." This issue, this lapse or separation which limits all such 'talk', however, is always already the issue of the Good, its rupture beyond 'being'. Yet, as Plotinus observed:

> Thus we rob it of its very being as the Absolute Good if we ascribe anything to it, existence of intellect or goodness. The only way is to make every denial and no assertion, to feign no quality or content but to permit only the 'It is' in which we pretend to no affirmation of non-existent attribute. (E:V.5.13)

The point is in the first instance a logical one, as not only Levinas but both Heidegger and Wittgenstein saw in Kant's wake. Being is not a predicate. The Good is not a set, nor simply a container; it is surely not contained, nor (Plotinus was specific) can it be classified in the same order as other goods, whereby it would become not unity but a duality: a 'combination' of what it is and what it is not. Heidegger had directly invoked it, decisively in his argument against Nietzsche, and was fully aware of the modern 'transformations', whereby Being had been transformed into a play of forces extrinsically and extensionally determined. "[T]he celebrated 'universal' sense of 'Being' is not the reified emptiness of a huge receptacle, into which everything capable of transformation can be thrown."[1] In one sense the status of the Good, its remainder in contemporary thought, would depend on grasping the complex 'procedures'—radically nonprocedural in the methodological sense—by which the ancients had articulated it, dianoietic, dialectical, intuitional, and so on. Doubtless this 'remainder' in one sense had been articulated through the path of hermeneutics itself. Heidegger himself had openly signaled the ancient legacy of this Plotinian and neo-Plotinian past, articulating the relationality of the rational as divided between *ens a se* and *ens a ablio*.[2] The 'relationality' at stake was, too, as Kristeva has noted, foundational among the Western 'tales of love', if always threatened by its own collapse into narcissism.[3] This *convenientia* was not simply the (conceptual) unity of multiple particulars but, still reflecting "the mystical tradition of Dionysius," a union of "the ontological differences that separate me from other" in his or her singularity. As has been seen, Heidegger's *Being and Time* had internally acknowledged the legacy of this *convenientia* inherent to our Being-in-the-world (BT:170). And Gadamer devoted the whole of an appendix in *Truth and Method* to retrieving the notion of expression as *explication*, where "multiplicity... is not a mere fall from true unity" to serve as "the basis of our critique both of 'art of experience [*Erlebnis*]' and of romantic hermeneutics" (TM:435). The problem would be, however, articulating such an account within the constraints generated by the lapse in transcendental 'harmonics'.[4]

Plotinus had also furnished Hegel with a model of the Absolute, of a Reason which is in and for itself, albeit a model which, devoid of the "anxiety to explain and to interpret," verged upon fanaticism (HP:II:407). Ironically this fanaticism is explained by Hegel as based on confusing "the thought of the essence of God being Thought itself and present in Thought," whereas "God is doubtless a Beyond [*ein Jenseits*]"—a difference that "to certain extent . . . is Nature which is beyond thought" (HP:II:411). Still, Hegel claims that Plotinus leaves the development of reason in and for itself (both "philosophically" and "dialectically") undeveloped: "for Plotinus the Good is said to be without resolution and will; for will has in it the distinction of itself and the Good" (HP:II:414–15). Hegel himself in any case was by no means ambiguous in his own attempt to explicate the development of the Absolute as will.

If Hegel became the most celebrated (or decried) of speculative metaphysicians, he construed the Good by strict syllogism—doubtless a certain modern refiguration of the 'practical syllogism'. Indeed, *pace* the charges of irrationalism leveled against him, he did so openly, both rationalistically and logistically—to the extent that he articulated the idea of the Good as "the urge to give itself objectivity and to realize itself in the objective world" (WdL:818). The result, as we have seen, even where Hegel attempted most strongly to defend both right and law, by a certain 'implosion', simply equated truth, norm, social practice, and 'ego-formation'. Consequently the idea of the Good as such, for Hegel, still remained a (subjective) idea and thereby lacking the moment of science or theoretical idea, the latter in turn to be accomplished through realization itself—that is, action (WdL:821). But the point, of course, was that neither the account nor the desire for the Good was a 'syllogism', nor were either graspable by deductive inference: the result was indeed the inverted world whereby the true would supervene on the Good. The point, moreover, has implications not initially foreseen. While Hegel's harshest critics, beginning with Bolzano, condemned him in all rigor for confusing dialectical and logical necessity, doubtless the problem returns in the question of the relation between 'logic' and Being. It would not suffice to posit 'being'—or any substitute thereof—as an objective correlate of our knowledge: this is precisely the failure of classical 'Wissenschaftslehre', Bolzano's included. Such correlations instead always remain nascently rational 'theodicies', as the very theoretical language that accompanies such debates continually attested. Only a Wittgenstein could perhaps directly formulate the paradox for such Bolzanoan constraints informing the views not only of Frege, but Husserl and both their 'analytic' followers.

Having said that logic is transcendental, that what cannot be perspicuously set forth cannot be said, Wittgenstein, in what must have seemed like the stare of Thrasymachus to his Platonist colleagues in Vienna, still declared that the inadequacy that surrounds notions like the Good "points to something" (WLE:13). The Good, instead, "has nothing to do with facts" and "cannot be explained (*erklärt*) by any proposition." One cannot rationally proceed "as if what is good could still be given some foundation." The 'argument' would be repeated in Wittgenstein's response to Moore in *On Certainty,* where the structure of language game as life-form itself would receive a similar gloss; no less than Heidegger's *In-der-Welt-Sein,* the event in question was one defying explanation, ultimate foundation, and proposition.[5]

For both Wittgenstein and Heidegger, the question of the Good 'pointed beyond to something'. In the first place, of course, it pointed beyond bad theories. If Wittgenstein's path took him far beyond the early forms of early 'analytic' philosophy, so similarly had Heidegger's beyond the classical forms of phenomenology. It was not accidental that Scheler had found Moore's account of the Good similar to his own: 'analytic philosophy' and 'analytic phenomenology' were of a piece in their narratives concerning the given and in their 'myths' regarding analysis itself. The history of theory would be no kinder to them than would be the real history both had omitted from their accounts. Hence Gadamer's claim, that "today it seems to us that the dispute between Husserl and the Vienna Circle regarding the true positivism would have gone against both sides" (PH:173).

The Good remains always ironical with respect to such order, to the ontic order of such factual 'observability', opening to what lies beyond such instances. While Heidegger's *Being and Time* glossed '*phainomenon*' as an "emanation [*Ausstrahlung*] of something that hides itself in the appearance" (BT:54), its gloss on authenticity had in fact connected the question of the Good to the issue of traditionality, to the handing down of a heritage which makes authentic existence possible and "the existential possibility of being 'good,'" to "wanting to have conscience" of such possibility (BT:334). We have traced the historical articulemes accompanying the concept of tradition that lie behind this gloss: the notion of a heritage or treasure (*Erb*) that is handed down (*überliefern*) and taken over (BT:435). The semantics of Wittgenstein's characterization of the Good, like his articulation of the 'holiness' of the person, is surely no less 'traditional': "if any proposition expresses just what I mean, it is: good is what God orders" (WLE:15). But of course no proposition suffices here—and certainly not (as Schlick's positivist construal had thought) the voluntarist (or conventionalist) one—that the Good is good 'because' God orders it. Indeed, Wittgenstein rightly construed the latter to be simply an attempt again to provide a foundation, a propositional explanation for what has none: the attempt to provide a frame or to 'classify' the Good, to use Plotinus's term, whereas the former, lacking a 'because', "cuts off the path to any and every explanation" (WLE:15). And that just is the paradox of the frame, of the propositional 'picture', which Wittgenstein had seen as much as Duchamps. We are of course left with the obliqueness of such 'talk' regarding the 'Good' and the 'Holy', where "ethics if it is anything, is supernatural, and our words will only express facts" (WLE:7). We have not forgotten that this is just how Wittgenstein spoke of 'persons'. But also, not having fully forgotten Nietzsche—surely Wittgenstein did not—we might ask, does Wittgenstein speak literally or figuratively here? Well, not figuratively, "for else (such words) should be also expressible in prose" (WLE:16). But not literally either, for no 'fact' is pictured in the case of the Good. But surely this discourse is not without meaning. And what correspondingly are we to say of the 'life' of life-forms?

The corresponding problem doubtless reoccurs in Heidegger's account of truth as unconcealment (*aletheia*) and not simply in the problem of the opposition between the literal and the figural, or the poetic and the philosophical, *mythos* and *logos*—albeit by a certain "depicturization," as Heidegger put it in 1925 (HCT:44). Here too, however, the problem of the 'frame' was not absent. Hence Heidegger's own (critical) gloss that tradition as "taken over"—and perhaps especially as *explicitly* taken over—is so "not necessarily as having thus come down" (BT:435). Indeed one might say *never, 'as such'*. To cite Gadamer's gloss, to understand is to understand differently. On the one hand, the separation this difference entailed made possible its critical moment, the possibility of adjudication, appropriation, or disavowal. And yet, it will be replied, for Heidegger what seemingly added necessity to contingency was nothing more than resoluteness. "The more authentically Dasein resolves . . . the less it does so by accident" (BT:435). But of course resoluteness does not make truth, but Being does, the *es gibt,* or 'It is', to again cite Plotinus's gloss. In the end it is less decision than 'perception' that will be at stake in the question of the Good. This emphasis on silence, or perception, the 'this is how I see it' in which, as Wittgenstein put it, 'reason comes to an end' is not, as has been charged, and surely not intrinsically, the entrance of all that is irrational or simple mysticism in the twentieth century. But what is it?

We are still reminded of Levinas's demurral on 'ontology', which doubtless would include appeals to *Lebensformen*—and, with regard to the most philosophical of truths, even Plotinus's attempts to surmount the 'separation' involved by descent and emanation rather than deduction (TI:103). Here we might wonder whether the 'empty place' of the Good had been adequately confronted, even if *sur rature*, to use the terms of Heidegger's deconstructionist followers. It is true, as Nancy has claimed, that Heidegger's construal of hermeneutics (and its limits) "certainly has something essential in common with the Benjaminian idea of translation as well as with the Wittgensteinian theme of showing as opposed to saying."[6] And, we have affirmed this throughout. The question is how to think what lies between them and how to articulate its rationality. Further, replying to those who had returned to Kant by demanding the abandonment of 'ontology' for transcendental semantics and the question of meaning, Nancy had insisted instead on the question of what exceeds presentation, essence, communicability, a 'meaning' irreducible to a fixed *Sinn*. But such insistences had raised standard objections to Heidegger, and those like Renault and Ferry had explicitly relied on it (in referring to Tugendhat).[7] Truth does not (or does not simply) mean unconcealment but also (and surely 'critically') the truth of assertion; the recognition of the problem of the noumenon in transcendental analytics is, accordingly, claimed to be of a piece with the move from ontology to transcendental semantics. But Kant himself had acknowledged the limitations of such an analytic in the recognition that we have an understanding that extends further than such limits—and neither Wittgenstein nor Heidegger had missed it. This understanding, doubtless, depends on an expressivist archive antecedent and excessive to the constraints of the frame of analysis and representation. Indeed its 'antecedence' as a meaning, as Nancy still construed it, is more 'lived' than 'posited', an 'opening' more historical than calculable.[8] At the same time he likewise insisted on the essentially 'intersubjective' character of such an 'experience'. The relations that constitute *Mitsein* in the end are 'without determinate syntax' and beyond essence;[9] what Heidegger has emphasized is the problem of grasping the opening (*das Offenheit*) from which they emerge. Not only, that is, did the question of the Good point beyond bad theories but equally to the event

(*Ereignis*) of 'opening' itself, an opening from which the frame of representation and its analysis emerged, and not vice versa.

Here we encounter the 'transcendental' difficulties over which much of poststructuralism had labored. The question of such an opening and a *semiosis* antecedent to representation, in fact is still connected by Nancy to semiotics, and a 'significance' which reason both mines and is undermined by in its attempt to equate the world with "everything that is the case." What remains uncontained in this formula, as Plotinus had already seen, is the paradox of such containment, the 'play of the world' itself. These terms, inevitably cited by the logical analyses of deconstruction, are in the first place, Fink's.[10] Both Derrida and Gadamer have affirmed these terms in the context of their grappling with the issue of semantic or semiotic considerations. The later Wittgenstein's emphasis on the play of language is not far removed from such terms, an emphasis that equally contains both formal and aesthetic components. For all these thinkers it is the play of imagination, 'semantic or semiotic', that lies at issue. Levinas, on the other hand, contrasted such views with his own "way of the infinite," where, beyond the indeterminacy of 'free play', the (ethical) relation in which "proximity is the very signifying of signification" is claimed to be "more determinate" (OBBE:116, 85). It is in just this sense that (even 'beyond' the political) Levinas would claim that the ethical relation revealed "the Rome to which all roads lead"[11]—and thereby perhaps beyond the entanglements of sovereignty that has accompanied discourses on the power (or transcendent 'sovereignty') of the Good. This view will surely be a complicated one, then. The 'terms' of this 'play' that Levinas would reject are equally complicated—and, inter alia, exhibit the affinity (if not dependence) between such deconstruction and the thought of Plotinus.[12]

Beyond such 'containment', antecedent to the totalities of propositional space(s)—and thus never fully sayable—classical 'transcendental logic' encounters the problem of origins. In this excess the question of genesis, that is, encounters a 'transcendental' history such transcendental logics omit through a certain 'blind spot' intrinsic to representation: the impossibility of fully presenting the frame itself—and equally, in the problem of its own origins, perhaps the possibility of a certain intrinsic 'narcissism'. Moreover, to the extent that such representation had been intrinsically (and problematically) the logic of transcendental consciousness, as Schelling first saw, reason confronts, thereby, the 'unconsciousness' from which it emerged— to speak Sartrean, *l'irréfléchi* at the heart of transcendental genesis. Such a genesis, beyond simple propositional space, links reason intrinsically to the withdrawal of 'Being' understood as a totality of objects—and to time.

Aware of both the logical and historical complications at stake, Merleau-Ponty had also articulated this event through reference both to the inadequacies of transcendental logic and the question regarding the link between reason and history it opens up—openly reinvoking Hegel's (Baconian) terms we have encountered along the way, the question of the 'prose of the world'. The question is what we should make of the remainder.

## 2. The Permutations of Law, the Voice of Conscience, and the Limitations of the Said

The problem, it will be objected, is that 'talk' about the limits, or contingency, or finitude of reason (and the significance of its 'beyond'), even if 'phrased' in a domain 'otherwise' than the said, is simply unable to account for our involvement with language. It dissolves our dependence on language as discourse (e.g., Benveniste), misses linguistic meaning as an event, not of the expressive phoneme, but of the sentence (Frege), and forgets that the speech act is less 'constitutive' of language than it is its function (Searle). Such talk, in short, cannot account for discourse as a construction that is both convention and norm. Such views, it will be objected, are precisely what 'deconstruction' purported to undo, in 'loosening up' commitments to the 'metaphysics of presence': questioning the priority of form over content, the literal over the figurative, constraint over transformation, the synchronic over the diachronic, the received over the possible, and so on. Still, we should proceed carefully before such analyses. The relevance of deconstruction doubtless equally depends on a view of theory as construction. Even if the dominant thematics of 'Western' metaphysics have been Platonist and 'constructive' (this is, as Heidegger claimed, what makes possible the affinity between the ancient account of *episteme* and the modern account of theory as construction), it does not follow that all of philosophy must be 'metaphysical' or even that it always has been: witness (as Derrida acknowledged) Plotinus himself, for example.[13] Our histories will doubtless be more complicated; deconstruction should not be taken to be the whole of philosophy. Hence the standard objection: always appealing to the insufficient conditions of analysis, 'deconstructive' claims are unable to account for their own epistemic and logical necessity.

Without attempting internally to adjudicate these debates we will widen their scope, as Heidegger already in fact had, in claiming that what is at stake cannot be confined to the theoretically circumscribed domain of the philosophy of language (*Sprachphilosophie*); indeed such containment is precisely what is in question (BT:209). But nor, it will be objected, can what is at stake in our accounts of meaning or rationality be based on a simple 'retrieval', say a return to the canons of Aristotle's *Rhetoric,* or Augustine's encounter with time, or to the *grammatica speculativa* of the medievals, all of which attracted Heidegger at different moves in his analyses. No more than the conflicts of modern politics could be overcome by such regressions could the conflict at stake in accounts of language—as inter alia Wittgenstein's rejection of Augustine's account of prelinguistic (and preconventional) reference had revealed (PI:1ff.). Similarly, the appeal to a prelinguistic or extralinguistic (i.e., conventional) "saying without the said" (OBBE:45ff.) seems as mythic as "the Rome to which all roads lead"—a simple abstraction from the constitutive conventions, the labyrinth of language (PI:203). If there is a 'saying' that always exceeds the said it relies on the said for its very coherence. Levinas, after all, concurred with Wittgenstein at least this much: he too claimed that the order of the Good "does not contradict but goes beyond the rules of formal logic" (TI:104). But in the issue which concerns us here, the interpretation of the Good itself, it will be claimed, such issues have direct impact, impacting, that is, both the limits of intelligibility—and the 'sayable'. Here again it is the complication of 'laws' beyond mere notions of domination or subsumption, immanence and act, excess and 'transcendence' that seems to weigh heavily on such accounts.

The question of law, it should first be replied, doubtless still remains critical to all this—and in particular, its 'modern' conception, less a wielding of than the internal constitution and articulation of 'force', as we have seen. With regard to the question of the Good, nowhere is this more initially poignant than in the debate surrounding Kant's legacy, not least of which, in retrospect, that between Cassirer and Heidegger in Davos—and those most strongly Heideggerian have again pointed to its significance. While Cassirer had made the relation between law and autonomy crucial to his account, Heidegger, in accord with what he perceived to be the hermeneutics of Kant's schematism, had in fact demurred, wondering what law can mean in this context—how, that is, it is to be interpreted. Here too it will be objected that Heidegger insufficiently accounts for the positivity of law itself: time and again he dissolves any link between conscience, law, and authenticity.

It is true, as Heidegger saw, that Kant's Interpretation of conscience "was suggested . . . by the idea of moral law" (BT:339). This was not accidental: indeed it spoke to a transformation in the rational, in which, detraditionalized, reason would be 'internally' differentiated. On the other hand, Heidegger himself had come dangerously close to being denied such 'ontic' recourse in the end. Granted the default in the everyday, Heidegger himself had been left questioning whether conscience can ever become accessible within the everyday experience of conscience (BT:339). Of course, in one sense, just as in the case of the Good, it cannot. On the other hand, Heidegger's whole phenomenology of this default of the everyday presupposed that there remained a possibility of authentic *Mitsein,* beyond 'domination', whose path was indicated through the phenomenology of anxiety, the nullity revealed in such inauthenticity—with the possibility, through care, of a transformation within the authentic possibility of the everyday itself. Indeed, since Heidegger had construed Dasein's authentic existence to be one in which "existence can even gain the mastery over the everyday" (BT:371), one might wonder whether he ever relinquished the notion of such a 'law' construed as domination. In any case, one must wonder at the totalizing characterization and exclusion in Heidegger's account of the everyday. We might wonder whether Heidegger had precluded himself thereby from responding to what Levinas would call—doubtless intentionally—"the extraordinary everydayness of my responsibility for other men" (OBBE:141). As a result, for Heidegger even Kantian "respect means responsibility toward oneself" (BP:141). Granted such levelings it almost seems inevitable, as Lyotard charged, that "Heidegger had to completely miss the intelligence of the Kantian ethics."[14]

We might wonder, instead, whether the everyday simply 'levels', whether the Good only appears by default (or by negative dialectic, for that matter). And we might wonder, accordingly, whether Heidegger himself had been fooled by the 'counterfactual' indicated in its failure, and which in turn impelled the fantasies of destinal or fated eschatologies—that the Good must appear always (and only) 'elsewhere'. As a result, the Good would be engaged less in the everyday relations (and legal bonds) of Dasein's 'unifying' care than in the agonistic of *Kampf,* the shattering of death and the ritualistic repetition of heroes that have gone before us or poets who prophesy beyond us: and hence the tragic destiny of a people, a *Mitsein* wholly 'specular'. In all this we are left wondering whether the *Evidenz* of the everyday itself had been entirely overlooked, if not annihilated: Aristotle having been simply abandoned for Kierkegaard and Nietzsche, whose political shortcomings Heidegger seemed destined to repeat in the grand style.

It is not that we will not need the *phronemos* and the wisdom of the past. But nor can thinking merely be a matter of remembering (or *mimesis*). The prophet, intuition, and imagination are equally inextricable from the rational, which doubtless is divided in their midst, between retention and pretention, the past and the future, retrieval and invention. Hence, as we have seen, emerges the importance of Heidegger's account of the reciprocal rejoinder—and the irony that accompanies all repetition, distinguishing it from simple iteration. Rightly understood, this is the 'critical consciousness' Tugendhat sought in the 'open region', where neither the truth of assertion, nor of the thing itself have been abandoned but rather historically articulated: "evidential certainty," that is, would indeed be surmounted without *ceding* to a precritical concept of the immediacy of truth (thus losing the evidential itself).[15]

Heidegger in all this was perhaps too oblivious to the ironies in his own repetition of Kant's claim: even were we to lack demonstrable ontic exemplars, the Good still appears in the 'heart' of the *sensus communis*. Phenomenology (and precisely Heidegger's version) was supposed to overcome—without dissolving—the phenomenal/noumenal distinction. The 'prose' of the everyday could not be as leveled as he left it. Its intelligibility in the end remained irreducible both to the poetics of tragedy and comedy, resolute heroes and visionary poets, Sophocles and Aristophanes. If ultimately lacking in sufficiency, the 'conventions' of the everyday remain, to use the Kantian term, 'inextricable' and in this sense normative, precisely as the source of coherence: "This everyday way in which things have been interpreted is one into which Dasein has grown in the first instance, with never a possibility of extrication. In it, out of it, and against it, all genuine understanding, interpreting, and communication, all rediscovery and appropriating anew are performed" (BT:213). In this sense, against all Platonizing attempts to exchange the everyday public realm for a more profound 'elsewhere', both Heidegger and Wittgenstein must ultimately concur, notwithstanding the 'silence' to which both appealed: "Ordinary language is alright."[16] If the ordinary still requires interpretation, what is clear is that it neither simply prevents authenticity nor fully occludes authenticity, requiring that the dispersions in its midst be better authentically deciphered rather than simply 'mastered', as Heidegger had hoped (BT:422).

As he would later see, against such 'catastrophic' alternatives, "the ordinary is extraordinary."[17] This is by no means to exchange Heidegger's acknowledgment of the Good's withdrawal for immanence (the dogma of convention) but to recognize this opening as the 'prose' of ontological difference itself: to articulate being is to encounter its withdrawal—and reciprocally, to encounter its withdrawal is to confront the problem of its frame, a frame always already articulated, even if as unspeakable or silent (BT:208). Nancy has argued that Being and *Mitsein* cannot be divided, that intelligibility and authenticity are inherently related and 'dialogical'. Equally, however—and without at all simply succumbing to the 'fates' of conventionalism—such 'bonds' are not simply 'ontological' but (as such) intrinsically and internally institutional, rational, and legal. This is not at all to simply reduce the meaning of Being to a critical tribunal. Again, to invoke Nancy's terms, the withdrawal of the political does not signify its disappearance.[18] It will be a question of grasping both the 'transcendence' of the political and adjudicating its ontic institution.

Kant was obviously aware of law as 'internal' or 'formal' differentiation. Still, the second *Critique* articulates the moral law as an occurrence that in itself neither fully nor sufficiently constitutes the rationality of conscience; hence the acknowledgment of the inevitable supplement, or 'dialectic' of Reason—or as Heidegger rightly says, its 'Interpretation'.[19] Thus it is doubtless not quite right simply to claim that Kant represented the conscience as a 'court of justice'. It was his trope after all, a 'figure' for what could not simply be reduced to what is "available and calculable" (BT:340). Freedom is not simply calculable and surely not available as a presentation; it remains, even when 'codified', a 'phenomenon' fully hermeneutic in character. In construing the categorical imperative through the figure of the court of justice, Kant took the latter not simply to be a model for deliberation or a simple decision procedure, but also a model of 'jurisprudence'. Moreover, the appeal to objectivity in such requisites fully acknowledges the suspicions of power, the possibility of their internal regulation, and the hope for a 'peace' that might surmount their conflicts. I am not suggesting that Kant saw this but that we see it retrospectively through Kant. On the other hand, I am not denying that Heidegger saw it, only that he ever saw it sufficiently.

Granted the internal articulation of law itself, divided not only between the 'ontic' and the 'ontological' but likewise determination and indeterminacy, the faculty of ontological synthesis, transcendental imagination will be further complicated both semantically and syntactically—in ways Heidegger's own deferral of the question of law would not sufficiently grasp. This is not simply what Cavaillès called "the revenge of technique"; it is rather to grasp the complicated forms in which interpretation and reinterpretation, identity and difference would emerge. All of this still echoes the complicated emergence of poststructuralist thought from the shortfalls of transcendental logic concerning formal notions of determinability, completeness, saturability—all terms that hauntingly remained part of the lexicon of deconstruction.[20] As is the case with all phenomenology, it bespeaks an 'origin' for which no determinate transcendental logic would suffice, 'phenomeno-logical' included: the task is to think the opening of this difference itself without immanence or method, beyond the simple wielding of the Good or the diaphanous play of difference. But this too accompanies, I have suggested, the opening of the modern problem of law and those (like Heidegger's) attempts to grapple with its 'phenomenology'.

Here, perhaps, we can make further sense of Heidegger's account of the crisis of foundations of mathematics in the disputes between formalism and intuitionism (HCT:31; BT:25). In retrospect it appears that he thought Brouwer (whose 1929 lecture has been said to be decisive for the later Wittgenstein) and Weyl were closer to his considerations than they were to Husserl (HCT:3). Husserl's own nomological 'axiomatics', in this respect, remained more consonant, as he affirmed, with the axiomatic systematics of Hilbert.[21] It is not, however, as though there were no inferential links at all at stake in Heidegger's 'explications' of fundamental ontology. Indeed *Being and Time*'s account of science as "the totality established through an interconnection of true propositions"—albeit incomplete apart from Dasein's interconnection in them (or whose "manner of being which this entity— man himself—possesses") perhaps still shows the influence of these debates (BT:32). Heidegger surely could agree with Weyl that the complications of modern theoretics implied that we must "renounce the mystical error of ever expecting the transcendent to fall within the lighted circle of intuition."[22] To lose sight of this question, moreover, is, in the end—notwithstanding all talk of Being's withdrawal—to render the event of meaning immanent; it is, to use Chrétien's term, still to render the intellect 'angelic' (and as we have seen, Heidegger's analysis of the *Scotusbuch* had not missed it), untroubled by the difference between self and other, meaning and language.[23] Of course, as becomes equally troubling, there is a sense in which for Heidegger it is precisely the poets (or alternately, as we have seen, *Being and Time*'s heroes) who may be just such 'angels' (BT:437).[24] But to lack a hermeneutics for decipherment and redecipherment is to fail to give an account of the rational, which is by contrast, precisely nonimmanent. And to simply construe such necessities as decline, a decline from *Logos* to *Ratio,* is both to succumb to the nostalgia of historicism and to miss the critical transformations at stake in this history. The same ambiguity—or perhaps failure to confront ambiguity itself otherwise than as simple 'leveling'— doubtless proves a fatal flaw in Heidegger's inability to grasp the rationality of democracy. It is not enough, after all, to simply say that the law is dispatched from beyond us when it is likewise 'dispatched' between us, the discourse (*Rede*) always already articulated in the between of dialogue—and which in turn, as we have seen, Gadamer had in fact explicitly linked to the problem of assertion (TM:261n). Here it becomes clear that the notion of truth as critical or evidential assertion or "critical consciousness," that concerned Tugendhat so much, might indeed have been able to find its proper place in what he called Heidegger's "metatranscendental position" and its advance over Husserl's Platonist foundationalism. But it would do so of course, not by remaining 'transcendental', but by finding resources beyond (and antecedent to) classical transcendentalism.[25]

Neither the notion of institutional (Hegel) nor logical norm (Frege) had been usurped or dissolved by the 'excess' of *aletheia* and the *Mitsein* which sustains it (by 'hermeneutic virtue', as Gadamer put it). These rational limits would be, of necessity, always already augmented—both epistemically in acknowledging the difference out of which judgment emerges and ethically in acknowledging what Habermas has called the distortions, Strauss the persecutions, Foucault the costs—the problem of "how much it costs to tell the truth"—that obtrude judgment. Post-Hegelian attempts to identify (if not reify) the rational with objectivity, the norms of social practice or 'objectification', would thus inevitably confront their own transcendental illusion. If the question of certainty and objectivity arose precisely in the failure of social practice, in the 'dangers', to use Hobbes's term, in the past— and hence the problem of detraditionalization—no new tradition, not even the tradition of science itself, would escape the problem (and exclusions) of power. The complex relations between the sayable and the said, the frame of representation and the silence of its exclusions, will be complicated indeed—framed between, if not the unknown and the unknowable, then surely the not yet known and the exclusions of the already 'known' but not said. Hence the 'violence of theory', as those like Levinas worried. Neither objectivity nor truth nor theory, however, have been simply dissolved thereby. Instead, *pace* Wittgenstein's attempts to strictly distinguish them, the Good and theory are not without history and not without connection to real events, even if both remain irreducible to such events.

In one sense what Wittgenstein and Heidegger share is this distinction of ontic fact and 'transcendence'. Or, to put it another way, what both share, as is well known, is Kierkegaard, whose account of the ethical as (both ironically and paradoxically) transcending the universal survives in both thinkers and their attempts to insist on its silence beyond the said. But equally, both (as a matter of course) had again insisted on the importance of the link between passion and the Good, and correspondingly, their paradox within the 'said'. The question was what to make of it. For Wittgenstein, any attempt to further articulate the relation involved a return to explanation.

Heidegger, in denying the hope of a reduction to a primordial ground, was also fully cognizant of the need for an articulation that belied the framework of explanation. In articulating Dasein as an 'equiprimordiality of constitutive items', he sought to provide an account of Dasein's attunement (*Stimmung*) that transcends the pulverization of the passions by efficient causality—thus belying the illusion that the 'laws' of human existence are the natural laws of explanation, to use Wittgenstein's terms. Here the passions would not be simply an epiphenomenon of facts but originally disclosive, originally attuned to Being and the Good, as they had been for the ancients. Indeed Heidegger himself says as much in claiming that the account in Aristotle's *Rhetoric* "must be taken as the first systematic hermeneutic of the everydayness of Being with one another" (BT:178). But equally the juxtaposition of this account of everydayness, as has become evident, for Heidegger also revealed the historicity of the failure of our "being with one another."

Here, without succumbing to the claim that all 'knowledge' is (false) 'power' (which Bacon's original conjunction of these terms had ironically denied[26] at the outset), we will need to augment the history of such concepts by the history of events—of which Levinas as much as Adorno surely points to one, in the name of Auschwitz, and to another insofar as sexual difference is to provide an "example" of the 'pluralism' Levinas has in mind (TI:121).[27] Another history, the history of exclusion undertaken under the name of truth, is written at the heart of such concepts. Here it is not quite the case, as MacIntyre put it in relation to Gadamer, that "the history of ideas turns out to be the queen of the sciences"—a claim that, taken literally, would succumb to Husserl's objections to historicism in the end.[28] Rather it would be a question of articulating and adjudicating the history of the narratives, metaphors, and forces (exclusionary or otherwise) that facilitate and disrupt, nurture and destroy human flourishing. Neither Being nor certainty simply succumb to their ontic or factual 'history'.

It is not an accident that such concerns have arisen from the task and the theories of phenomenology—and doubtless this too has both historical and theoretical motivations—even when what is at stake in this withdrawal is a 'plot' [*intrigue*], to use Levinas's term, that escapes the transcendental presence of phenomenology. Doubtless, moreover, the conjunction of the term 'phenomenology' in thinkers as diverse as Wittgenstein and Heidegger continues to perplex us, especially granted their construals. While Heidegger took the task of phenomenology to be fundamental ontology, Wittgenstein used the term to articulate the characteristics of a philosophical grammar of use. Granted the problem of the Good, divided between the event, appearance, and the limitations of the said—the problem of the disequilibrium of 'phenomenology' itself—can no longer be avoided.

### 3. Saving the Appearances: Phenomenology, the Conflict of Interpretation, and the Ruins of the Ordinary

The complications of the term 'phenomenology' in modern philosophy are notorious, divided between semiotics, characteristic (and thus grammar), and appearance (or alternatively illusion [*Schein*])—and after Lambert, divided as much between Kant and Goethe or Hegel as Husserl and Heidegger (or Mach and Wittgenstein).[29] Phenomenology was always an enquiry divided between the modern ideals of "strict science" or the science of the Absolute as pure Being encased in the necessity of deductive exemplars—and, as the science of appearance, the histories, genealogies, and crises— empirical, real, and violent—that accompanied such demands.[30] Hence the irony of even Wittgenstein's apparently logical pronouncement that "ordinary language is alright." The ideal of pure science always emerged, as Derrida had put it directly of Husserl's phenomenology, "a warp and woof not its own."[31] On the one hand—and Derrida's own account simply repeats it—phenomenology itself seemed to be never quite up to such ideals, always transforming the theoretical status of such purity from determinate to indeterminate, its ideals from the constitutive to the regulative. On the other hand, however, the virtue of phenomenology was not simply to abandon such appearance; instead it stoically appealed to the evidence of appearance itself against the abstraction (or separation) of such pure forms. Doubtless this is what made Aristotle the fellow traveler of all phenomenologists: the claim that, before such 'separateness', the venture of "the particular is more true" (NE:1107a). Moreover, clearly this is why the phenomenology of perception remained critical to its accounts, even when the notion of decision seemed to intervene to underdetermine them, divided between retention and protention, past and future, memory and imagination, recollection and expectation. Even in the midst of appeals to resoluteness, as Nancy saw, what remained critical was precisely perception of the *es gibt* itself, the account of perception as a truth-taking (*Wahr-nehmung*).[32] Such 'appeals', however, are not simply true 'de facto', hence the disequilibrium of the stoic *epoché*. The problem of history, domination, and the descent from origins continually interrupts such appeals, affecting not least of all the relation between individuality and *determinatio* that the very concept of 'Dasein' was invoked to figure.

The instability of such accounts, the phenomenological antinomies that attend the modern failure of objectified individuality, and the conflicts of much of twentieth-century theory which they represent, have been evident throughout this itinerary. Scheler's ethic of sympathy, one whose debts to "the profound chapter on Friendship in his *Nicomachean Ethics*" is openly acknowledged,[33] deplored the detraditionalization of modern civil society as decline.

> Under the sway of the principle of solidarity, everyone knows and feels that the community as a whole is inherent in him—he feels that his blood is the blood which circulates in the community, that his values are part of the values which permeate the community. Here all values are based on solidarity of feeling and willing. . . . [In modern civil society] the "community" and its structure is replaced by "society," in which men are arbitrarily and artificially united by promise and contract. In fact, "society" is not the inclusive concept, designating all the "communities" which are united by blood, tradition, and history. On the contrary, it is only the remnant, the rubbish, left by the inner decomposition of communities.[34]

Against Scheler's lingering (albeit romantic) reading of the classical, the twentieth century would quickly counter with the narratives of high modernity and its condemnation, to use Baudelaire's term, of "the funeral cortege of tradition." Among phenomenologists, Sartre would doubtless be most radical in his defense of freedom against the alienations of tradition. In many respects such narratives would epitomize the conflict of ancient and modern aesthetics, a conflict for example between Winckelemannian classicism and the rise of the avant-garde, a term political in origin.[35] Again, for a case in point we can cite Sartre's *Saint Genet,* a text both indebted to Scheler and radically at odds with him.

> Action, whatever it be, modifies that which is in the name of that which is not yet. Since it cannot be carried out without breaking up the old order, it is a permanent revolution. It demolishes in order to build and dissembles in order to resemble. From morning to night we heap up shavings, ashes, scraps. All construction entails an at least equal amount of destruction. Our unstable societies fear lest a false movement cause them to lose their balance. They therefore ignore the negative moment of their activities. . . . The fear of knocking down the edifice is so great that we even take from ourselves our power of creating: we say that man does not invent, that he discovers. We reduce the new to the old. Upkeep, maintenance, preservation, restoration, renewal—these are the actions that are permitted. They all fall under the heading of repetition. Everything is full, everything hangs together, everything is in order, everything has always existed, the world is a museum of which we are the curators. (SG:24)

Again, for Sartre such a determinate repetition would amount to an automatism of the Good in bad faith through which praxis would be subordinated to ontology. The *Notebooks on Ethics* accordingly identify "the Everyday, Order, Repetition, Alienation" as the "other than man," and "Festival, apocalypse, permanent revolution, generosity," on the other hand, as "the moment of man" (NB:414). Now it is not that Sartre argues for or wills simple negation or destruction—a will to destruction and projection that *Saint Genet*, after all, argues is the exemplification of (perhaps radical predisposition toward) evil itself. Nor does he argue for a simple matrix of destruction.

A certain 'surrealism' is evident in such claims, as is Sartre's recognition of the sacred horizon which subtends all reality, still attesting to the problem of *transcendens* and Scheler's 'essential experiences of divinity'. Hence the emergence of the lingering remnant of the ancient link between the sacred and *l'imaginaire*. Still, if the account of *transcendens* has now been thought from within atheism, it could not be replaced by surrealist experience of the *merveilleux* and its religion of Beauty or Bataille's *Summa atheologique*. The latter, like Genet, Sartre openly declares, still remains a "secular disguise" (SG:246). Moreover, Sartre condemns Breton (here and elsewhere) for searching for surreal truth in destruction—or in a unity beyond the dichotomy (and disequilibrium) of construction and destruction (SG:244). The aesthete's vision—the simple substitution of value for reality—is condemned as evil itself in the destruction of Being. Neither the aesthete nor *l'homme de bien* can feel the surprise of reality—the beauty of nature, an "evident finality" and the real-historical "manifestation of value" (SG:372). Similarly, granted both the reality and the disequilibrium at stake, Sartre condemns even Nietzsche's doctrine of the eternal recurrence for missing the difference that intervenes between reality and invention, or, more to the point, the real and its imaginary analogon (SG:347). If we rely on the analogons of *l'imaginaire* for invention, Sartre condemns (as strongly as Foucault after him) the metamorphoses of "the medieval clerk" in which "every apparent analogy is a sign of deep identity" (SG:471). Against such a hermeneutics, as has been seen, the *Notebooks* demanded that we ask "what is the structure of our society that provokes the appearance of this emphasis on hermeneutics?" (N:435). The difference that intervenes in Sartrean repetition is both qualitative and real—if always subject to a (quantitative) exteriority, or the dispersion in the passage from *quantum* to *quantitas* that Kant had discovered at the heart of transcendental temporality.

Instead it again is the *Wechsel* itself—the 'detotalized totality' that accompanies *praxis* and *theoreia*—that Sartre articulates. The effect is not 'beyond good and evil' but a Hegelian '*Aufhebung*', as he puts it—albeit one whose synthesis is never fully achieved. Hence the radicalization of the Sartrean claim: "the fact remains that, in the historical institution, this situation cannot be achieved. Thus any Ethic which does not express that it is impossible today contributes to the bamboozling and alienation of man" (SG:186n). Both history and critique deny any simple 'convertibility' between Being and the Good. Rather it is their complication that must be thought: "I am far too convinced that *any* ethic is both impossible and necessary" (SG:224; Sartre's emphasis). Here we meet the antinomy with Scheler again.

At one point in his *Formalism*, Scheler would argue that the question of justification connected with moral theory is the result of such historical collapse: "Its origin is always connected with the processes of disintegration in an existing ethos."[36] But Scheler himself already seems to speak directly to the experiences of detraditionalization *itself*, in asserting that the "essence of maturity lies in the immediate *being-able* to differentiate." Moreover, such maturity is thwarted "as long as (a person) simply *coexecutes* the experiential intentions of his environment *without* first understanding them, and as long as the forms of *contagion*, plain cooperation, and tradition in a wide sense are the basic forms of the transference of his own mental state to others."[37] Still, Scheler remained resolutely and abstractly communitarian about its implication.

Divided in these accounts is the question of adjudication and the problem of the laws that might still bind community. Even the poststructuralist commitment to difference acknowledges this effect of detraditionalization. If difference everywhere underlies the rational, then, if "difference is articulation,"[38] it is not the case after all, as Plotinus's benevolent or generous One might assure, that "difference everywhere is good" (E:V.7.3). If the Good everywhere exceeds instantiation, that is, if the Good is everywhere different, it does not follow that difference everywhere is good, nor of course that all exclusions are simply evil, *pace* Sartre: the regulation of law excludes every bit as much as difference articulates. To simply identify difference and the Good, after all, belies both difference and "the generosity of the Good itself" in its being 'beyond' such distinction—even in giving what it cannot 'contain', as Plotinus again puts it, paradoxically (E:VI.7.42).[39] But this paradox, this circularity, as Plotinus already schematized it, is of course precisely both its paradox and the possibility of its reliability—as Heidegger will say of Being (or later the earth) or discursively the possibility that 'nurtures' the hermeneutic circle.

If we have traced the archive of obligation through the 'aesthetics' of the sublime, in the ruins of transcendental logic the requisites of hermeneutics,

it would seem, still gain their intelligibility from that of the Good. Ironically, while Levinas had sought to separate his own debts here—correlating
the Beautiful with the said, to determinate reference (to the noun) and
hence with 'ontology'—the 'genealogy' of such concepts surely again complicates such attempts. As Plotinus put it, "the Good is gentle and friendly
and tender, and we have it present when we but will. Beauty is all violence
and stupefication" (E:V.5.12). Repeating in fact a logic we have found internal to Aristotle's account of friendship itself, Plotinus declares: "The Good
has no need of the Beautiful, while the Beautiful does need the Good"
(E:V.5.12). While both proceed from a common source, he states, it is precisely the inadequacy of intellection which divides them, the internal dissonance of difference itself. Construed both epistemically and ethically this
dissonance returns the 'sublime' dissonance of the Beautiful to promi-
nence—and one whose internal conflicts would await modern articulation
for their grasp, doubtless affecting the 'ontological' difference at stake in
their 'modern' hermeneutics. And yet, the 'separation' or difference at stake
in recent accounts of friendship is perhaps less 'postmodern' than an articulation of the 'distance' which accompanies the figure of the Good itself—
arising then not simply out of a critique of 'identity' or the fear of egoism
and hence the obligations of respect. Even the 'humiliations' of Kantian respect could make sense only if the Good were more than mere categorial iterability. Indeed, if as Heidegger thought, Kant's analysis of respect
"remains but an attempt, even though immensely successful, to shake off
unconsciously the burden of the traditional ontology" (BP:147), it did so
precisely in articulating the 'disjunctive synthesis' between categoriality
and its 'beyond', a realm beyond agonistic, still "at the disposition of whom
ever desires it"—albeit only insofar as each "has become other himself"
(E:V.5.12; VI.9.10). And, it is just here, as Hadot saw, that Plotinus, not again
without attempting to transform narcissism from within, passes beyond ar-
rogance.[40]

## 4. Beyond the *Theatrum Philosophicum*:
## The "Mixed Message" of Modern Systematics

This 'beyond' would not appear in the theater of representation. The rules of
such articulation are conventional, as Wittgenstein (increasingly) insisted,
not explanations of nature; if the 'world' is itself (transcendentally) reducible
to a matrix of propositional equivalence, the extension that accompanies the

'concept' of the Good could not be. But this recognition does not imply—indeed it makes possible, he insisted—that such propositions have no connection with the Good, even if they are never simply identifiable with the Good. This is just what Sartre referred to as the 'impossibility' of politics and ethics. Here too the claim of impossibility remained ironical, demanding a task devoid of immanence. But as Plotinus put it, "we can admit the possibility" without identifying intellection and the Good itself (E:VI.7.42). This separation is the opening of critique, without dissolving the identity of the thing itself. Rather, 'being' tolerates a plurality of such conventions, as Aristotle knew—again without dissolving justice (NE:1134b ff.). And yet such laws must be articulated without ultimate guarantees. Nothing, granted the play of plurality at stake, precludes the 'exclusions' of law from being subreptive, false in the extreme. Against Aristotle's claim that the opposition between the universal and the particular does not imply that "the law is not correct" here the question of the legitimacy of law ("which law?") is unavoidable. Neither mere calculability nor the simple invocation of nature will suffice. In both respects, as Husserl put it, "a one-sided rationality can certainly become an evil."[41] Instead we will need to consider, to use Heidegger's characterization of *in-der-Welt-sein* itself, the "equiprimordiality of constitutive items" at stake within the rational: representation and transcendence, assertion and reliability, evidence and interpretation. None of this undercuts our dependence on convention, norm, or law, but rather underscores the difference out of which we speak and an event (*Ereignis*) whose ultimate foundations escape us.

As others have recognized—Vincent Descombes for one—such claims concerning our inevitable dependence on conventions whose ultimate warrant escapes us, still sounds like poststructuralism.[42] And this much, doubtless, was what was right about poststructuralism: its radical critique of immanentism and its talk of the 'metaphysics of presence'—rightly raising anew the problem of language before classical transcendentalism. Equally, we have noted (and Descombes also does) that we depend on such conventions for our intelligibility. It is, after all, the very stuff of objectivity. Hence emerges the demand for construing the requisites of consensus as the paradigm of political rationality. But if we should not take objectivity lightly, we should not take this concept of objectivity itself, any more than any other, to have escaped the vagaries of its own history, tied both to paradigms of deductive necessity and an account of judgment purged of tradition, paradigm, and practice—nor should we preclude the transformation of such constraints, as the later Wittgenstein would see.

At the end of his book on Wittgenstein and the invention of necessity (a book Descombes cites in his critique of poststructuralism) Jacques Bouveresse returns to what Wittgenstein's transformations imply for phenomenology. These transformations, he admits, are ambiguous because of the difficult problem of determining "the exact position of Wittgenstein in relation to phenomenology."[43] In the first place, as Descombes put it elsewhere (a statement that Lyotard would later accuse of nostalgia or at least disappointment), "We will not be able to say everything."[44] While apparently innocent, this claim entails an abandonment of the principle of expressibility, as it was called, that animated Platonist and logicist thought from Frege and Husserl onward. Semantic (or, for Wittgenstein, 'phenomenological' or 'grammatical') necessity will be conventional. Phenomenological necessity thus construed will be limited by conceptual use. Hence in some sense, a distinctly 'nonlogical' sense with which Wittgenstein contrasts it, 'phenomenological' or semantic necessity will be historically contingent—and thereby malleable. If we did not invent speech—any more than we invented walking on two legs, he reminds us—Wittgenstein likewise acknowledges that successful practitioners can alter the rules. There are, after all, "countless kinds" of sentences and the "multiplicity is not something fixed, given once for all" (PI:§23). Still, assertability will be (factually) bound in any case by constraints—such was part of the heritage bequeathed by Kant. As Wittgenstein put it:

> The limit of language is shown by its being impossible to describe the fact which corresponds to (is the translation of) a sentence, without simply repeating the sentence. (This has to do with the Kantian solution of the problem of philosophy.) (CV:10)

But in Kant's solution we also confront what Alberto Coffa has aptly termed Kant's "mixed message."[45] At stake in this mixed message is the conflict between Husserl and Frege—and perhaps, it should be added, those in their wake. In recurring from ontology to transcendental analysis Kant had depended on (and transferred) the success of the mathematical applications of natural sciences into a transcendental account. About this transcendental science, it seemed that, like all sciences Kant had declared, there would be just as much science as there is mathematics in it.[46] Indeed those in the semantic tradition from Bolzano to Carnap and beyond sought to systematically formalize the analytical or structural characteristics of meaning, consistent with Kant's claim that the transcendental categories were a kind of grammar of the rational.[47] At the same time, however, Kant was clear that such analysis would at most assist in delineating the limits of thought, without exhaustively providing a formalization of its content, since philosophy and mathematics are heterogeneous disciplines: unlike the strict constructions of mathematics, philosophy lacks both ultimate definitions and demonstrations. The experiment of the Copernican turn had originated as he put it, in an "analogy" based on one "species of rational knowledge" (B:xvi).

As we have seen, for Kant philosophy remained achromatic and dialogical. Meaning remained parasitic upon the conditions of transcendental consciousness. While semanticists could find only psychologism in the latter, Husserl, doubting all that Kant had committed to analyticity, saw in Kant's transcendental claim the need to provide an account of the background conditions of the rational, at the risk of dissolving the achievement (and the validity) of the rational.[48] The latter for Husserl could be achieved only in a phenomenology of the structural characteristics of consciousness, articulated in the judgments of intentional thought. Here, like Brentano before him, Husserl had recourse to the medieval account of consciousness as intentional, rendering the account of meaning parasitic upon the *intendit significare,* the significative act. The latter however differs from the medieval's faculty psychology and lies beyond the agonistic of its metaphysics. As J. N. Findlay put it: "while the scholastic 'intention' was a strange piece of machinery designed to carry out a strange task, on which it threw not the slightest light, Brentano substituted the task for the machinery, the performance for the instrument, so that an intention ceased to be something that explained mental transcendence, and simply became a case of mental transcendence itself."[49]

Here we must confront something further about Kant's mixed message. Again to cite Coffa: "Kant's doctrine of pure intuition had multiple origins."[50] The point is less psychologistic than it is epistemic. What Husserl (following Kant and Fichte) had found in the 'Thomistic' event in which "the intellect knows that it possesses the truth by reflecting on itself" was the necessity of providing an account of the epistemic foundations of analysis: not in the sense of the primitive building blocks of semantics (though often enough he made that claim too), but in the sense of providing an account of the latter's 'ciphering'—in the Kantian sense, its adjudication.[51] Hence for Husserl there emerges the necessity of recurring to a phenomenology of reason at the risk of turning 'consciousness' itself into an extensional feature simply reducible to ontic or semantic analysis.

Frege had vigorously denied Husserl's move, and denied it again on formal grounds. Far from it being the case that semantics ultimately relied on such phenomenological lived experiences for the basis of judgments, here Frege could only see the Aristotelian limitations inherent in its ancestry.[52] As Frege had put it, articulating his own contribution to semantics, the concept of logical function, rather than logical 'primitives', at the basis of judgment there are only more judgments—not more and more privileged contents or primitive concepts, the concept of 'consciousness' included. From Husserl's standpoint, on the other hand, and without denying the logical point, the origins of such concepts remained obfuscated, an obfuscation Frege's own followers would mask in positivism and the reemergence of what Kant called dogmatism.

The resulting dialectic appeared to indicate something of a double bind in Kant's mixed message. Semantic analysis seemed to require an account of origins that was not dogmatically invested in a mythic or positivist given. On the other hand, any account of 'transcendental' origins always required conceptual exposition.[53] If analysis would not suffice, neither would the simple phenomenological description of intuitional synthesis. The appeal to the foundations of intentional judgment, lacking external criteria for univocal exposition (let alone explanation) seemed always problematic, or 'hermeneutic'. Indeed (as Heidegger would remark) in this regard the appeal to intentionality was always more a problem than a solution. Against the 'Thomistic' reflective self-grasp through which Husserl had refigured Kant, Heidegger accordingly invoked its 'Augustinian' alternative, in which the self has become an *aenigma* unto itself. In fact, it could be claimed that Kant himself had grasped the point in his peculiar formulation of the self as an "indeterminate empirical intuition" (B422). Couched in this impossible figure was Kant's recognition of the limitations of any strict phenomenological exposition, in other words, the limitation of the noumenon (B344).

Here too, however the hermeneutic of Kant's mixed message remains, to use his term, "inextricable": while acknowledging such constraints on assertability—and strictly taken phenomenology understood as a descriptive science, to be negative, devoid of extrinsic criterion[54]—Kant likewise acknowledged that we have an understanding and hence a meaning which *problematically* extends further (A255/B256). And, just here, in confronting the problematic sense of the noumenon is where Heidegger's *Seinsfrage* emerged. This other sense of 'phenomenology', never simply dismissable, was doubtless equally troublesome to Wittgenstein: in response to James's charge that before experience (e.g., the aroma of coffee) our grammar is inadequate, Wittgenstein replied, "Then why don't we introduce a new one?" (PI§610). Surely such claims reflect Wittgenstein's inclinations toward conventionalism, but they may also reflect the naive representationalism upon which such conventionalism is parasitic: a naiveté our finitude (and historicity) belies. Wittgenstein's phenomenology (a term he himself used in the early thirties) was a phenomenology not of the contents of consciousness but of the conventions that articulate its limits and would be equally bound by the history that exceeds and informs it.

While such conventionalism acknowledges the unlimited transformative capacities of language, it also verges upon the claim that all things can be 'said'—and that the 'sayable' and the well-formed formulae of the 'said' are simple correlates. But this assumes that the point is simply to render such experiences adequate, that what cannot be adequated is adequatable, and that what cannot be adequatable in this sense is again simply a 'symptom' of our illusion. Here, as thinkers like Levinas continually railed, 'Western' philosophy seemed simply, if not 'totalitarian', at least both reductive of difference and the continual refutation of transcendence—or at least what remained "unnarratable"—either as *visage* or as idea—within its formal or 'structuralist' enterprise (OBBE:169).

Kant himself, as we have seen, knew better in claiming that metaphysical ideas are not simply figments in the mind or without 'right'. As Wittgenstein too relented: "to use a word without justification does not mean to use it without right" (PI§289). The mistake would be to think that such ideas or their descriptions are simply true—or alternately false. It might be replied—and Wittgenstein did at one point—that "if only you do not try to utter what is unutterable then *nothing* gets lost."[55] Still, we are left with the problem of the 'nothing' itself, as Heidegger (and Plotinus) realized. And as the later Wittgenstein acknowledged, what was at stake belied conventionalism: a problem of running up against the limits of language that characterizes both the problem of ethics and the 'being' of the Good. Here we will need both 'phenomenologies', therefore. We will need both the conceptual phenomenology that Wittgenstein linked to assertability, to justification, and use, and the descriptive or 'experiential' phenomenology that belies the reduction of representation and fact, in which meaning, without being reducible to translation and interpretation, depends on the latter. We will require, moreover, two kinds of analysis and two kinds of 'analyticity', both again perhaps part of Kant's mixed message and divided legacy. We will need first the analyticity of Frege, early Wittgenstein, and their followers, that is, functional analyticity with respect to a language, a norm, and a practice. Second, however, we will need the analyticity of Husserl and his followers, 'predicative' analyticity, appealing to an object intentionally (or

'reflectively') 'posited', presupposed or not yet codified categorically or lin-
guistically 'named'. Both accounts, linking meaning to both institutional
'assertability' and intentional 'interpretation', arise perhaps in the breach of
detraditionalization that originates with modernity. The constant tendency of
'positivist' revisions of this history would always be either to dissolve the
question of translation and interpretation into its objective constraints, or
to mistake either to be simple assertions.

If interpretations by themselves do not determine meanings (PI:§198), in
this respect they are never very far from them. Indeed, in one sense, such
interpretations make up the whole of philosophy for Wittgenstein, the
sense in which "working in philosophy . . . is really a working on oneself,
on one's own interpretation."[56] And this too, clearly resonates with Plotinus's 'narcissistic' turn inward. Both have been confused with 'Augustinian'
subjectivism.[57] Wittgenstein's own turn inward was, equally as clearly, not a
simple passing beyond the 'conventional' but indicative of a more complex
account of the conventional and its beyond. And, inter alia it was indicative
of a more complex relation to the 'Good'—and the problem of interpretation—in our midst. Here, it might be said, there is a certain rapprochement
with Levinas, who was, but for quite different reasons, as troubled by Plotinus's metaphorics of the One's 'overflowing' as was Hegel himself. "How, in
Plotinus, would the One overflow with plenitude and be a source of emanation, if the One persevered in being, if it did not signify from before or beyond being, out of proximity, that is, out of disinterestedness, out of signification, out of the-one-for-the-other?" (OBBE:95). To be sure, this is a complicated
matter, one that has divided Plotinus's commentators.[58] What is true, in any
case, is that precisely in this 'beyond' in our midst Levinas found a relation
with the Other—and he may indeed be not far from Wittgenstein. But to reinvoke Wittgenstein's account of the sacred, the relation of the-one-for-the-
other (and its interpretation) are by no means reducible to the conventional: this was Schlick's mistake. Moreover—and without abandoning
Wittgenstein's account nor turning 'theological' any more than he did—it is
not accidental that the medievals understood the 'order' of this 'between' as
a 'friendship with God'. The point is that the order of this 'between' is neither reducible to the conventional nor simply to its 'beyond'. And the idea
that meaning could simply be reduced to communication or decision procedure seems simply spurious here.

What is highly questionable is whether consensus, rather than, say, intelligibility or recognition, should be taken to be the *telos* of rationality or even
communication. As neutral a bystander as Nicholas Rescher has rightly ob-

served in this regard that Habermas is "always overlooking the paramount role of interpretability (rather than cognitive agreement) in matters of communication."[59] If, as Frege and his followers saw, objectivity is not to be taken lightly (i.e., not to be taken as an abstraction), neither will it be uninterpreted.

Further, against conventionalism (and, as Descombes saw, such certain conventionalist tendencies of poststructuralism) neither meaning nor rationality are simply dissolved in convention and code in being dependent on conventions. Such 'objectivity' is not the mirror of nature. This is the illusion of modernity, as Wittgenstein clearly saw in the *Tractatus*. And, in still recognizing the question of the 'beyond' that accompanies such limits itself—to use Hegel's terms that still attest to the problem of the Good itself, the 'nonbeing' that accompanies the limit (WDL:126)—Wittgenstein saw this better than his conventionalist Viennese counterparts.[60] Such laws could neither be reduced to explanations of natural facts simply independent of them, nor (internally) reduced to the simple conventions through which they become 'meaningful'. This point, as I have made evident, has certain Hegelian overtones in its account of a real or 'concrete' necessity not simply distinguished from contingency.[61] Still, neither nature nor law could be reduced to such convention—nor certainly could the Good. This is not to say that they will be reduced to mere 'correlates' either. Talk about the Good will be grasped as little by semantic role, or 'use', than it had been by representation. As Wittgenstein declared, having in effect pondered both: "I want to impress on you that a certain characteristic misuse of our language runs through *all* ethical and religious expression. All these expressions *seem, prima facie,* to be just *similes*" (WLE:9; Wittgenstein's emphasis).

Indeed the so called 'similes' of the ethical and the religious shadow language in just the way that 'analogy' and interpretation always accompany it. Here Wittgenstein could have learned from Saussure, always less concerned about the propositional frame of language than linguistic history. Analogy, as Saussure put it, is both a means of innovation and change: the fact is that "language never stops interpreting and decomposing its units."[62]

This is not to say that there is no difference between the literal and the figurative, nor that there are no complications in the event of their intertwining, the appearing of the saying in the said, to use Levinas's terms. Something of this 'complication' is even perhaps at work in Levinas's accounts of my being held 'hostage' by the other—or my substitution vis-à-vis the other. Even if, as Levinas argues, "strictly speaking (*à la rigueur*) . . . I am a hostage" (OBBE:128), is this true, strictly speaking, *de dicto* or *de re*? Hence the charge that Levinas's account would be of little use to someone if they really *were* a hostage. But, surely Levinas's account eludes such distinctions. As Wittgenstein realized, if such expressions *were* simply similes, they could be rearticulated literally (WLE:16). Heidegger similarly had refused to reduce such talk to mere stories or figuration expressions (or 'ontic figuration', as he referred to the '*lumen naturale*' [BT:171]), even though, certainly aware of more ancient resources, he too realized that what was at stake precisely escaped ontic reference—also recognizing, again as Wittgenstein too asserted, that the "tendency" to "thrust against the limits of language . . . *points to something*" (WLE:13; Wittgenstein's emphasis). Indeed Derrida suggested, in relation to the problem of simile and analogy (and explicitly in relation to the *Enneads*), that it is only in "this war of language against itself that the sense and question of its origin will be thinkable"—precisely as the dispersion of limits and difference.[63]

Hegel, on the other hand (and doubtless 'Hegelian' readings of Wittgenstein), impelled simply to identify talk of the Good and objectivity, would miss it—and missed the complexity in Plotinus's account. Hegel claimed, recall, that what manifested itself in Plotinus was not an anxiety to explain and interpret what forces our attention as reality (HP:III:407). He acknowledged, moreover, that such concerns were not simply merely *Schwärmerei*, or religious fanaticism (Eastern or Western), since it is the idea, "doubtless a Beyond to individual self-consciousness," that is at stake (HP:III:410–11). Hence Plotinus is said to be beyond the demand for a criterion that divided stoicism (ancient and modern) from within (HP:III:408). And yet, devoid of the correlation of objectivity and idea, the mere particularity Hegel analyzed previously in the Stoics returns:

> With the Stoics right reason and the securing of it on its own account is the highest principle. But here, too, we immediately see that we are thereby merely led round in a circle in a manner altogether formal, because virtue, conformity to nature, and reason, are only determined through one another. Virtue consists in living conformably with nature, and what is conformable to nature is virtue. (HP:III:259)

Having equated the Good with Objectivity, having equated rational explication with *Erklärung,* and Being with presentation, Hegel in the end could have proceeded in no other way. Neither Wittgenstein nor Heidegger could join him in this gesture. We have seen Heidegger's invocation of the (neo-Plotinian) *implicatio-explicatio* doublet in the (conventional-historical) background of interpretation, (stoically) denying that such 'circularity' need be vicious. Such interpretation too would not be up to demands for criteria, but proceeds only on the basis of its "thrown possibility" (BT:183). Here too the encounter with Good would be a matter of 'running up against the limits'—and the necessity, in Wittgenstein, of a certain 'interpretation of oneself' or, in Heidegger, 'loyalty to oneself' (BT:443) that again exceeds the propositional equivalence of the said.

Still, we should not overestimate the convergence between Heidegger and Wittgenstein here too. However much Wittgenstein claimed to have understood Heidegger's 'Being' and 'Dread', his 'desubjectivized' account of meaning as representation and then use (and explicitly, the critique of Augustine) could not allow him ultimately to share such dread—nor could Heidegger's critique of *techne* allow a similar sharing of Wittgenstein's reduction of all meaning: if not ultimately to 'truth-functions', then at least to rules. It is up to us to parse the difference. It is striking, however, that in a 1912 letter to Russell, Wittgenstein relates that he is reading William James's "Varieties of religious experience," a book, he explains, that "helps me to get rid of *Sorge* (in the sense in which Goethe used the word in the second part of Faust)."[64] What is striking, that is, is that Heidegger himself provides a detailed account of the relation between Goethe's text and the "pre-ontological illustration of existential-ontological Interpretation of Dasein as care" (no. 220 of the Fables of Hyginus) in *Being and Time* (BT:492n). Heidegger provides further clarification by reference to Seneca's claim that while the good of God is fulfilled by his Nature, "man, is fulfilled by care [*cura*]" (BT:243). Doubtless these thinkers could not seem further apart. Whatever we are ultimately to make of this divergence, this much seems true: no more than Wittgenstein seemed in the end to rid himself of such *Sorge* (nor his conventionalism its own voluntarist limits) will we readily rid our accounts of the self of such *seme* and their alterity. Hence again the 'perdurance' of such narratives, their histories, and the problem of the reciprocal rejoinder they entail with the past. Doubtless this is a matter both conceptual and real. In the midst of our conventions the problem of the 'other' reasserts itself—and equally (and almost reciprocally) appeals to the 'other' or to 'transcendence' inevitably confront the problem of coherence, assertability, and justification. If those most directly influenced by the *Tractatus* had best articulated the limits of assertability, those in the wake of phenomenology had done a much better job at recognizing the complicated relations between 'history' and 'nature', the self and objectivity, even if too often or often enough they seemed to succeed by cutting off the 'appearances' from the problem—and the conventions—of objectivity itself, their repetitions of Plotinus's paradox almost unconscious.

## 5. On 'Humanism', the Aftereffects of Tradition, and the *Ethos* of Care

Here Heidegger's account of the *Nomos* as the 'dispensation' of Being, beyond the limit of such representation, directly announces another realm not contained in it. The latter again manifests the 'eventing' (*Ereignis*) of the Good as an "equiprimordiality of constitutive items." Moreover, it would do so by refiguring humanism beyond the antinomies that have always accompanied modern theoretics: if we are "to restore meaning to this word" (LH:224). Thereby Heidegger interrogated a realm beyond the limits of representation and (calculated) value, articulating a beyond in their midst, "a humanism that thinks the humanity of man from nearness to being" (LH:222).

I have argued of such humanism, however, that, rightly seen, precisely in emphasizing the question of the ordinary, the 'elevation' of the vernacular (in Heidegger's case, the speaking of language, *die Sprache spricht*) and the question of another order of 'transcendence' (or difference) in its midst, was also of a piece with the humanist emphasis on the rational as a question of translation. As such, 'humanism' had already 'deployed' itself 'beyond essence' (i.e., the presupposed index of *'ousia'*) and thereby against the irrationality of the *ratio* construed as representation, subjectivism, and calculative role. Heidegger himself had lamented the fact that

> Dasein has had its historicity so thoroughly uprooted by tradition that it confines its interest to the multiformity of possible types, directions, and standpoints of philosophical activity in the most exotic and alien of cultures; and by this very interest it seeks to veil the fact that it has no ground of its own to stand on. (BT:43)

Still it is also true that such a 'ground' emerges only in 'alterity', the play of (ontological) difference—even if he initially had limited the alterity in question to that between the past and the present.

Consistent with his more hegemonic view of history as decline from origins, Heidegger declared remembrance more important than 'cosmopolitanism' (LH:219). He proceeded thereby, or often enough, as if the truth of being as return to origins might provide a successor theory to the truth of representation, its 'new' narratives simply replacing the modern, in the demand for the recollection of a tradition before the 'hardened' and 'fallen' tradition we have received. But the contrast here between 'self' and 'other', hegemony and alterity, the 'homeland' and 'the foreign', may well be too strong. After the rupture of detraditionalization Heidegger describes, we will encounter 'ourselves' only in difference and before others: a matter not only of 'remembrance' but also recognition, disavowal and critique. This is why it has been claimed that not only 'ethically' but epistemically Levinas's characterization holds: "Paradoxically it is qua alienus—foreigner and other —that man is not alien" (OBBE:59). Precisely here is where the encounter with the 'near' might still become manifest. Thus the problem of assertability or certainty and the problem of Being (or the 'other') are of a piece in lacking ultimate ground—indeed such 'withdrawal' or detraditionalization, I have said, is what binds them together.[65] And, as I suggested, it is just this complicated logic, divided in the juncture, the between (*inter*) of the near (*proti*) and the 'otherwise', that has been at stake in interpretation from the outset.

It is clear too that this is how it is with tradition: as much interpretation as 'exegesis', as much invention as remembrance, as much refiguration as canon. Often enough, of course, Heidegger himself revealed such reweaving of the ancient 'stories' about Being through the modern narratives of freedom and liberation, explicitly recognizing the underdeterminacy of their interpretation. "Whether the realm of the truth of Being is a blind alley or whether it is the free space in which freedom conserves its essence is something each one may judge after he himself has tried to go the designated way, or even better, after he has gone a better way, that is, a way befitting the question" (LH:223). And yet, it will be said, here too Heidegger perhaps sounds still very 'egoistic'. He sounded perhaps too Kierkegaardian in any case—as though Dasein, a solitary person, and Abraham or some (solitary) people in some sense were fated to share a common path, and as if "the conflict of interpretation," as *Being and Time* put it, were simply thereby to be surmounted (or 'mastered'). In such solitude and especially before the solitude of death, the domination Heidegger had recoiled from in the analysis of *das Man* would be itself mastered—if only "for that moment" (BT:422).

Again, contested here is the problem (and history) of individuality itself: if the Good will be beyond 'the universal', unlike Kierkegaard's account of religious revelation (as Weyl, as we have seen, put it directly to Husserl), the Good will not be intelligible if simply detached from the universal. The problem is articulating the 'synthesis' of this separation—that is, how to make the nothingness of the Good not simply ineffable, or even worse, to make the Good, not simply no longer coextensive with the said, but with the simply unsayable. Here too, as Wittgenstein put it, "this entanglement [*Verfangen*—a term Heidegger equally uses for the everyday] in our rules is what we want to understand (i.e. get a clear view of)" [PI:§125]. And, he also recognized that "the civil status [*die bürgerliche Stellung*] of a contradiction, or its status in civil life," is at issue in the question of meaning, a recognition that doubtless also impacted the problem (and the limits) of talk about the Good. Moreover, as Wittgenstein equally saw, such 'limits' may make all talk of blindly following a rule symbolic or mythological (PI:221). But it is just in this sense that I have argued that the problem of interpretation and the problem of difference are less separate from, than essential to the rational—and essential, as we have seen, to what ever will be the remainder of humanism and its articulations between past and future. And it is precisely this "running up against the limits of language" that 'points toward' a realm both beyond theory and beyond science that is too often missed in nominalist or postmodern (or 'pagan') construals of Wittgenstein (e.g., Lyotard's).

But this event, the event in which justice requires care, discernment beyond the conventional—to cite Aristotle, the event in which justice requires 'friendship'—will be a complicated one. And, as has been argued, it will be especially complicated granted the detraditionalization of modernity. The demand for the universality of law may always remain necessary but insufficient, always 'ontic'. Still, the attempt to resolve this ambiguity by concentrating on the hermeneutics of application, while doubtless again necessary, always depends on the analogies that link the past and the present—precisely the unicity of tradition that modernity continually called into question. This was why, after all, Gadamer's own emphasis on application and precedent, even in invoking the model of Aristotelian *phronēsis*, could not simply affirm it. The transcendental unities that assured such *phronēsis*, the unity of the past, tradition, and nature had been called into question: hence in this 'posttraditional' *phronēsis*, "we understand in a *different way if we understand at all*" (TM:297; Gadamer's emphasis).

Against romantic attempts to align traditional precedence and law, custom and law in the end must go different ways.[66] Here as Levinas (and Kant) declared, the time of the ethical remains always ruptured, inordinate against the determinacies of the past, the opening of conscience always exceeding the contingency of human institution. If Gadamer had demurred from Heidegger's 'translation' of *phronēsis* into conscience (a translation that found its historical precedent in the medievals) surely the account reflects Heidegger's own historicity.[67] In this conceptual transformation of *phronēsis* Scheler had already worried about the elevation of "the subjective sources of cognition," describing it as "one of the many colors of the sunset of religious belief."[68] Still as the *das Man* analysis attests, Heidegger's "violent reading" explicitly reflects the "leveling" that had incited modern political theory. While *phronēsis* had explicitly linked human flourishing to practice, convention, community, and communitarian wisdom, human 'authenticity' could no longer reliably depend on the public world. Instead appeals to transcendent authority had become, if not strictly contestable, then factically contested, carried out under conditions in which both authority and legitimacy had become problematic—and indeed had been experienced as such from the outset of modern political theory. Hobbes's attempt to redefine conscience by turning it away from "secret facts" and reducing it to shared knowledge ('con-science') would surely be an attempt to turn such a problem into a pseudo problem, perhaps typically reductive (and protopositivist) (Lev:I.7). But this much remains true: 'transcendence' now would be as much a 'human' question as a 'sacred' one (Lev:I.7). Even Levinas would perhaps not be so far off from this recognition in claiming that theological terms must get their meaning not in the divine but in the ethical relation of the human face-to-face (TI:79). Indeed, notwithstanding the quarrels all these thinkers have with historical 'humanism', the problem of this default of transcendence is what they share in common.

The dialogue of I and thou and its intrinsic link to ordinary language, to which modern humanists continually appealed, remained, like the political institutions they sustained, similarly inevitably divided (i.e., democratic).[69] All three were extrinsically linked in Humboldt, for example. Doubtless such links attempting to reinstitute or refigure the positivity of transcendence in this 'between' would impact even accounts of meaning in general, binding all such assertion to convention, institution, and discourse. Even Levinasian attempts to reduce meaning to a saying prior to the said will thus always depend on irony: if the ethical always departs from historical institution, it never fully escapes it. Attempts to escape historicity in the end remain as internally ruptured as the very failures they seek to redress. In the end we require both: both the discernments of conscience and convention, civility and law, the 'saying' and the said, friendship and justice. But these conjunctions only betray the complex constructions and deconstructions in our concept of humanism.

We have wondered, accordingly, about the rational reductions in Heidegger's claim that all humanism, consistent with "the first humanism, Roman humanism, and every kind that has emerged from that time to the present, has presupposed the most universal 'essence' of man to be obvious" (LH:202). This, as is the case with the charge of 'metaphysics' in general, rules out not only the differences between them (Heidegger mentions Roman humanism, Renaissance and classical German thought, and privileges

Hölderlin over them all in the end). It also dissolves the ontological difference itself articulated only in their midst, not to speak of the humanism in
Heidegger's own past—and, of course, his own narrations.

In one sense, I have suggested, Heidegger's account of Dasein's being-in-
the-world wears its own modern refiguration of the ancient *Seinsfrage* on its
sleeve. This is true, not only insofar as such being-in-the-world articulates this
refiguration ('fundamentally') through 'Dasein', but also insofar as its "equiprimordiality of constitutive items," the remnant of the ancient's analogy—
now devoid of "primordial ground"—also articulates (as 'fundamental ontology') this 'beyond' precisely through an internal differentiation (BT:122).
Such an internal differentiation, after all, still reflects (while surpassing) the
modern account of systematics—the very systematics *Being and Time* described as "a totality established through an interconnection of true propositions" (BT:32). Hence, again, his 'affinities' in the debates between Weyl
and Brouwer, and Hilbert and Husserl. Internally, in any case, Heidegger
had already acknowledged the modern conception of law as iteratively and
internally constitutive. In condemning such formal notions outright to inauthenticity, he never simply denied them but denied their ultimate
sufficiency—hence the supplement of care. Rather than 'reducing' such 'in-
ternalist' connections—as had Husserl before him, always flirting with a notion of the given that reverted to 'externalism'—Heidegger articulated a
'beyond' that 'transcended', supplemented its constraints. The same could be
said of Levinas's critique of the "anonymous universally" of *droit* (TI:306).
While Levinas too identifies his account of 'fecundity' "outside the State,
even if the State reserves a framework for it," it is perhaps a matter of thinking both together and, in any case, neither reducible to, nor strictly taken
distinct from one another. Here too the contrast between Levinas and
Heidegger cannot be absolute. The point perhaps is to see the difference of
Being and the other and the question of transcendence in their midst.

For reasons that have become evident, Heidegger's gloss on 'Roman humanism' still rings true in one sense: a humanism simply understood as the
'wielding', mastering, or assertion of power could no more attend to the 'call'
or 'dispensation' of Being than its simple representative or calculative reduction could. The event of the rational—and the laws which internally articulate it—would be more complex, as will the judgment of being to which we
appeal. Reason will always be more than the 'faculty of principles' and law
will be more than simply the autochthonous wielding, perception, or subsumption of force. Still, if *Nomos* here "is not only law but more originally
the assignment contained in the dispensation [*die Schickung*] of Being," as
we have seen, it too will be divided in our midst, always more than mere sub-

sumption, whether by representation or appeal. If, that is, 'Nomos' is 'not only' law it will 'also' *be* law, precisely as divided in our 'midst'. The question is whether that is all it will be and whether, as so articulated, in acknowledging what it is not and what lies 'beyond' it, the Good will escape the figures (and of course the event) of domination and 'death', in what even Husserl in his drive for purity recognized as the evil of one-sided modern rationality.

Identification, constitution, and normative judgment remain essential to the interpretative complexities or constellations that accompany the rationality of the political and its ineluctable bond to time. We have seen that the problem (the synthesis) of identity and difference (norm and interpretation, law and application, determination and transcendence) is precisely what is at stake in the 'mixed message' of critical judgment. As we have also seen, however, this synthesis is equally characteristic of a problem that accompanies all traditionality, an event both critical and coherent at once, that emerges by a logic of *Erwiderung,* of 'reciprocal rejoinder'. It is just in this regard that Adorno claimed the fundamental questions of critical enquiry undergo *renovatione* before the question of how a "thinking obliged to relinquish tradition might preserve and transform tradition."[70] But the reciprocal rejoinder such a *renovatio* entailed divided its accounts—and the experience—of the *principium individuationis* from within, dividing reason between its origins and ends, even natality and demise. Hence the *Auseinandersetzung* between Arendt and Heidegger, *Eudaimonia antem mortem:* while Heidegger had (stoically) tied his meditation on human authenticity to the singularity (and inescapable determinacy) of death, Arendt appealed to 'natality' as the possibility for freedom and invention.[71] Doubtless this antimony is again too abstract—both in itself and for the purpose of capturing the fertility of Ardent and Heidegger's difference. But this difference itself attests to the extent to which the question of death itself had taken on monstrous proportions in the levelings of the modern everyday—the extent to which the latter had indeed become a certain "nightmare from which we are trying to awake," to use Joyce's characterization of this history.[72]

Even the Stoics themselves were perhaps not so conflicted: we are reminded of Seneca's admonitions on care (and death) on which Heidegger's articulation of Dasein's being as *cura* had relied: "I should prefer you to abandon grief, rather than have grief abandon you. . . . Let us enjoy our friends, because we do not know how long this privilege will be ours."[73] Seneca's point was that even the requisites of Stoic self-sufficiency, before the terrors of necessity, do not foreclose such bonds. This is, as we have seen, the driving force of Arendt's claim: "What saves the affairs of mortal men from their inherent futility is nothing but this incessant talk about them."[74] But, of course, Seneca still claimed (as Kant's metaphysics of morals did too) that it is not just 'talk', but the 'prompting' or 'predispositions' of nature (i.e., Being) that remained at stake 'between' individuals.[75] Indeed, Seneca claimed both that the self-sufficient person required friends and that the need for friendship had such a 'natural' basis—albeit one clearly non-egoistic in nature. The philosopher needs friends "not," as Epicurus claimed, "that 'there may be someone to sit by him when he is ill, to help him when he is in prison or in want'; but that he may have someone by whose sick-bed he himself may sit, someone a prisoner in hostile hands whom he himself may set free."[76] Here it may indeed be true, as Levinas states that "Stoic nobility of resignation to the logos already owes its energy to the openness to the *beyond* essence" (OBBE:178; Levinas's emphasis). But Seneca is also insistent that the self-sufficient person is explained away if he is explained by "withdrawing the wise man from the world."[77]

This much is also true, however: the world does not simply vouchsafe the 'connaturality' of friendship. Instead, Seneca is equally clear about its dangers, where the ruin brought about by humans upon one another is claimed to be worse than that of beasts and more frequent than accidents: "it is from his fellow man that a man's everyday danger (*cotidianum periculum*) comes."[78] And here, moreover, "the nearer the danger comes the more carefully it is concealed." Boethius of course would later be even stronger concerning the 'leveling'—or the lapse—at stake: "human perversity makes divisions of that which by nature is one."[79] Confronted with what Strauss called the "extreme case" of modernity, Hobbes would claim, precisely to the contrary, that nature itself disperses and humans—in default of contractual "counter-assurance"—only manifest its power. Nothing in Seneca could have prepared him in this regard for the calculations that would ultimately unite death and *techne,* nor the complications attending the *cura* that Heidegger would refigure in the face of them, nor the enormity of their cost.

In the problem of death Hobbes's legacy remains: linked on the one hand to the limit of what can be calculated from the standpoint of the agent (i.e., to what I can be certain of), and on the other to what cannot be re-presented— both my 'future', which can at best be anticipated, and the other, who can at best be analogized. In both respects, of course, death remains undeniable: my death cannot be calculated nor can I simply take the place of the other's death. Both singularities, both mine and the other's, are in this respect unsurpassable, unsubstitutable, and irreplaceable. And yet it is also true that neither the possibility of *eudaimonia* any more than justice (or *theoreia*) are simply dissolved in the limits of death.

As has become evident, many like Adorno recoiled at Heidegger's codification of depersonalized nullity in *Being and Time*'s meditation on death.[80] Still, it might be objected that Adorno himself remained almost spellbound by this 'shock' of thinking expressed, as he put it in a celebrated phrase, "after Auschwitz," a *syntagm* which was for him the philosopheme of pure identity as death.[81] Against the event expressed thereby, before which "our metaphysical faculty is paralyzed," it was a question for Adorno of preserving nonidentity, or what others call difference—a difference we have traced through the concept of friendship—in a time in which, as Adorno put it, "people are spellbound without exception and none of them are capable of love, which is why everyone feels loved so little."[82] To face all this, however, as Adorno too attests, we require still the right combination of the *humaniora,* or at least its remainder, "the right *désinvolture* and sympathy."[83] This combination, it might be said, still attests to the remnant of Aristotle's *synesis*—like the Good itself, now fragmented between its possibilities and its 'ghosts', not least of all the ancient legacy of generosity (*aphthonia*) itself. Here again ours may well be a time in which, to use Heidegger's terms, "all compassion and forbearance has been burnt out"[84] and in which it became conceivable that "the tragedies of Sophocles— provided such a comparison is at all permissible—preserve the *ēthos* in their sagas more primordially than Aristotle's lectures on 'ethics'" (LH:233). But we should not forget—surely at his best Heidegger did not—Aristotle's own *Erwiderung* with this past in an ethics of virtue and its appeal to community, nor Seneca's in the ethics of care in its default—nor the 'Being' that is at issue between them and the 'histories' (and transformation) that were, in turn, provoked and fragmented in their wake. And nothing perhaps would be more fragmented in these 'transmissions' (and hence of this tradition) than the concept of *humanitas* itself—as Kant was critically the first to acknowledge, in calling into question the possibility of both metaphysics and human 'nature' itself. As we have seen—from Heidegger to Carnap— here Kant's legacy remained overdetermined, as much the denial that 'metaphysics' could mean one thing as that it might be fulfilled. In question was as much the withdrawal as the dissolution of the science Aristotle sought to found in the wonder at being (*thaumazein*). Here too, however, Heidegger had found care (BT:215)[85]—albeit endangered by the failures that had accompanied traditionality, if only in its ruins.

We have traced the complexity of this event, complicated, that is, both by history and the requisites of reason through which it became manifest. It was left to Sartre (always more 'Plotinian' in his insistence on the nothingness at the 'heart of Being') to also insist on its agonies and the "ruins of sub-

jectivity" in the twentieth century. But he also recognized that the Good—
which was never a concept nor a convention, nor never 'was' (in the strict
sense) at all—need not similarly be thought to be in ruins. Indeed, this
precisely was "the language of evil: Good is only an illusion; Evil is a Nothingness which arises upon the ruins of Good" (SG:625). It is in just this
sense that Levinas similarly concluded *Otherwise than Being* in stating that
"this work . . . does not seek to restore any ruined concept" (OBBE:185).
But, if the Good is not 'in ruins', it will still need to be interpreted.

Confronted with the ambiguity of such interpretation, Levinas does not
hesitate before the limits of requisites of the said; there is another 'saying'
which doubtless shares something of the aesthetic but is not simply its
functional equivalent: *pace* Wittgenstein's claim, ethics and aesthetics are
not one (TLP:6.421). Moreover, the meaning at stake is not simply beyond
the world (TLP:6.41), nor is the silence at stake simply 'unsayable'. Rather,
precisely in breaking with the limits of the said, this saying would make articulate what lies in proximity 'otherwise'. Indeed Levinas's account insists
that "if there is a value which is of value" (TLP:6.41) it cannot be left in silence. Nor of course can such value (*Wert*) be reduced to a *Werttheorie*
whose calculations, as the history of the term attests, seemed all too inevitably to derive from mere economics.[86] Granted what is at stake with respect to the Good, whatever 'is of value' must be said—if never adequately
(OBBE:151). In such a 'discourse' and against "the propositions of negative
theology" there is a saying which bears witness to the interruption—and
the rupture—of the Good at the heart of the said.

Doubtless such a 'saying' beyond the said would be complicated—and
more complicated than Levinas allowed. "The extra-ordinary word *beyond*,"
on which such saying depends, neither escapes history nor remains simply
locked up in it. Neither ethics nor ontology comprises then the whole of 'first
philosophy': the Good, after all, is what lies between them. We recognize instead that justice is never simply an "ancillary or angelic order" of propositional equivalence (OBBE:161) nor is ethics simply beyond history. Instead
both are ventured, interpreted, justified, and at risk within it. Here, however,
we can put the result briefly, albeit without being able to elevate the result to
the status of an axiom or to demand its recognition by the force of a conclusion. By a 'we' divided in being, we live the fragments of tradition; by a judgment often enough underdetermined in warrant and overdetermined in
nature, we articulate the hermeneutics of the contemporary: a care divided
between past and future, contingency and hope, imagination and remembrance, the self and the other—venturing thereby the difference between
what we have become and what we will be.

## Introduction

1. I allude here to the internal complications of Husserl's account of time as analyzed by Shaun Gallagher, *The Inordinance of Time* (Evanston: Northwestern University Press, 1998). My point is that this 'inordinance'—the term is originally Levinasian—belongs to 'time', as much as a historical and conceptual effect as a metaphysical or epistemic problem. It is in this respect that Husserl recognized temporality as the most 'profound' of 'phenomenological' problems—and that the problem of tradition would ultimately openly erupt in Husserl's later work.

2. See Michel Foucault, *Madness and Civilization: A History of Insanity in the Age of Reason,* trans. Richard Howard (New York: Pantheon, 1965), p. 285. The importance of Hegel, who is always "insidiously close by" in our "attempting to flee Hegel," was further emphasized in Foucault's inaugural lecture at the College de France. Indeed, following Hyppolite, Foucault articulates Hegel as "a schema for the experience of modernity." See "The Discourse on Language," appendix to *The Archaeology of Knowledge* (AK:235–36).

3. See Nancy, *Hegel,* p. 5.

4. Hans-Georg Gadamer, *Hegel's Dialectic: Five Hermeneutical Studies,* trans. P. Christopher Smith (New Haven: Yale University Press, 1976), p. 7.

5. See F. W. J. Schelling, *System of Transcendental Idealism* [1800], trans. Peter Heath (Charlottesville: University Press of Virginia, 1978). For further analyses of this issue see my "On the Rights of Nature," in *Tradition(s)* (Bloomington, Indiana University Press, 1997) (hereafter, *Traditions I*), ch. 3.

6. In the *Nicomachean Ethics,* Aristotle refigures the word 'ēthos' from ethos (virtue of character from habit, and perhaps, more antecedently 'dwelling') (1103a). Later, Heidegger will question whether Sophocles had grasped its meaning better than Aristotle (LH:232–33), an issue to which we shall return.

7. See my "Hegel, Hermeneutics, and the Retrieval of the Sacred," in *Extensions: Essays on Interpretation, Rationality, and the Closure of Modernism* (Albany: SUNY Press, 1992), ch. 3.

8. See HP:I:134–35; likewise see Hegel, *Lectures on the Philosophy of Religion,* trans. R. F. Brown, P. C. Hodgson, J. M. Stewart, and H. S. Harris (Berkeley: University of California Press, 1987), vol. 2, p. 587n: "[T]o Europeans it must have been in the highest degree astonishing to encounter this lofty principle of the Christian religion here; we shall become acquainted with it in its truth later on, and we shall see the spirit as concrete must necessarily be grasped as 'triune'." The overdetermination of Hegel's 'figuration' of the concrete will become the subject of analysis in ch. 3, below.

9. See Bergson, *Duration and Simultaneity* [1922], trans. Leon Jacobson (Indianapolis: Bobbs-Merrill, 1965); and the discussion of Gilles Deleuze,

*Bergsonism,* trans. Hugh Tomlinson and Barbara Habberjam (New York: Zone Books, 1988), pp. 79f.

10. See Otto Pöggeler, "Heidegger, Nietzsche, and Politics," a paper originally presented in Chicago, Paris, and at Duquesne University and published in *The Heidegger Case,* ed. Tom Rockmore and Joseph Margolis (Philadelphia: Temple University Press, 1992), see p. 127. Inter alia, Pöggeler's claim here is that if "'Continental Philosophy' signifies a philosophy with speculative, existential, and hermeneutic elements" (117), it has also been more than that—as these considerations evidence, a point to which we shall return. Here, however, the point is not that such accounts emerge *because* of relativity theory, nor even that they are simply *analogues* of it; rather any account ('hermeneutic' or otherwise) that claims the meaning of concepts is in part determined diacritically or diachronically will not merely be able to dismiss this history.

11. See Claude Lefort, *The Political Forms of Modern Society,* ed. John B. Thompson (Cambridge, Mass.: MIT Press, 1986), p. 305. Lefort's emphasis.

12. See Maurice Merleau-Ponty, *Adventures of the Dialectic,* trans. Joseph Bien (Evanston: Northwestern University Press, 1973), p. 226.

13. Ibid., p. 200.

14. The problem of such 'contemporaneity' had indeed threatened 'everyday' phenomenological coherence from the outset—not only in the phenomenology of nature, where Husserl's student Oskar Becker had encountered it (in relation to Einstein) as early as 1923—but also in the coherence of the rational itself, where the 'aftereffects' of the past or sedimentation, which were initially articulated as the coherent background of phenomenological presence, became increasingly problematic. While Schutz focused explicitly on the aspect of simultaneity, it doubtless already informs the hermeneutic of Heidegger's *Being and Time,* whose considerations on the significance of Einstein's relativity date from as early as the former's 1924 lecture "The Concept of Time." There these issues are taken to provide a "provisional hint" for his analysis of Dasein and the question of time—albeit by acknowledging Einstein's affinity with Aristotle(!). His point, however, was that such considerations cannot be "forced one-sidedly into the field of the theory of science [*Wissenschaftstheorie*]" (BT:450). See Heidegger, CT:3. Also see Oskar Becker, "Beiträge zur phänomenologischen Begründung der Geometrie und ihrer physikalischen Anwendung," *Jahrbuch für Philosophie und phänomenologische Forschung* 6 (1923); and Alfred Schutz, *The Phenomenology of the Social World,* trans. George Walsh and Frederick Lehnert (Evanston: Northwestern University Press, 1967), pp. 143ff.

15. See Leibniz, *The Monadology,* §57, 84f.

16. See Jacques Derrida, *Edmund Husserl's Origin of Geometry, an Introduction,* trans. John P. Leavey (Stony Brook: Nicholas Hays, 1978). Here Derrida explicitly links the Husserlian problem of iterability to the threat of equivocity

posed by cultural memory, Hegelian memory and the Joycean 'nightmare' of history (102-3). In fact (like Foucault), Derrida's 'reengagement' with Hegel reoccurs throughout his work.

17. See Maurice Merleau-Ponty, "Phenomenology and Psychoanalysis, Preface to Hesnard's *L'oeuvre de Freud*" in *The Essential Writings of Merleau-Ponty,* ed. Alden Fisher (New York: Harcourt, Brace and World, 1969); *Notes de cours 1959-1961* (Paris: Gallimard, 1996), p. 388. For further discussion of this issue see Michel Henry, *The Genealogy of Psychoanalysis,* trans. Douglas Brick (Stanford: Stanford University Press, 1993).

18. See Hans-Georg Gadamer, afterword to Hermann Lang, *Language and the Unconscious: Lacan's Hermeneutics of Psychoanalysis,* trans. Thomas Brockelman (New Jersey: Humanities Press, 1997), p. 177.

19. See Jean-Luc Nancy, *L'imperatif catégorique* (Paris: Flammarion, 1983), p. 60.

20. See Jean-François Lyotard, "Philosophy and Painting in the Age of Their Experimentation: Contribution to an Idea of Postmodernity," trans. Maria Minich Brewer and David Brewer, in *The Lyotard Reader,* ed. Andrew Benjamin (Oxford: Blackwell, 1989), p. 190.

21. 'Conservative' accounts that would simply see Joyce or Proust to be 'deprived' of traditional identity would miss the (rational) refigurations at stake within them. Compare Paul Ricoeur, "Self as Ipse," in *Freedom and Interpretation: The Oxford Amnesty Lectures,* ed. Barbara Johnson (New York: Basic Books, 1993), p. 116. The importance of such interpretations for the ethical would be pivotal for Levinas's posttraditional account. See OBBE:166: We will return to the question of refiguration in its midst.

22. See Martin Heidegger, *Ontology: The Hermeneutics of Facticity,* trans. John van Buren (Bloomington: Indiana University Press, 1999), p. 83. Heidegger's emphasis.

23. See Hannah Arendt, "The Concept of History: Ancient and Modern," in *Between Past and Future* (New York: Penguin, 1968), pp. 41-90; and Jean-Luc Nancy, "Finite History," in *The Birth to Presence,* trans. Brian Holmes (Stanford: Stanford University Press, 1993), pp. 160ff., which discusses Arendt's account.

24. See Jacques Lacan, *The Four Fundamental Concepts of Psycho-Analysis,* ed. Jacques-Alain Miller, trans. Alan Sheridan (New York: Norton, 1978), p. 250.

25. Marcel Proust, interview with Élie-Joseph Bois, "Variétés littéraires: A la recherche du temps perdu," *Le Temps,* 13 (November 1913): 4, cited in Julia Kristeva, *Le temps sensible: Proust et l'expérience littéraire* (Paris: Gallimard, 1994), p. 384.

26. Ludwig Wittgenstein, "Conversations on Freud," *Lectures and Conversations on Aesthetics, Psychology, and Religious Belief,* ed. Cyril Barrett (Berkeley: University of California Press, 1967), p. 45.

27. See Søren Kierkegaard, *Fear and Trembling,* trans. Howard V. Hong and Edna H. Hong (Princeton: Princeton University Press, 1983), pp. 83f. Kierkegaard himself refers the issue to Aristotle's *Poetics,* ch. II. The implications of this 'Kierkegaardian moment' for ethics is discussed by Wittgenstein in his lecture and discussions with Schlick on ethics. See WLE:13.

28. See Eugen Fink, *Sixth Cartesian Meditation: The Idea of a Transcendental Theory of Method,* trans. Ronald Bruzina (Bloomington: Indiana University Press, 1995), p. 113.

29. Maurice Merleau-Ponty, "Eye and Mind," trans. Carleton Dallery, in *The Primacy of Perception,* ed. James M. Edie (Evanston: Northwestern University Press, 1964), p. 171. On Merleau-Ponty's late discussions of simultaneity see, for example, *Notes de cours* 1959–1961, pp. 198f.; on analogy (in Sartre, Husserl, and Heidegger), p. 124. Finally, on the interrelation between interpretation, analogy, the *Seinsfrage,* and the logic of traditionality, see my "Traditionis Traditio," *Tradition(s) I,* ch. 1.

30. Julia Kristeva, *Proust and the Sense of Time,* trans. Stephen Bann (New York: Columbia University Press, 1993), pp. 4–5.

31. See Julia Kristeva, "On Eccentric Seeming: Imagination as Process," in *Tales of Love,* trans. Léon Roudiez (New York: Columbia University Press, 1987), pp. 176ff., 378ff. As Kristeva elsewhere notes, in the encounter with the uncanny (and, I should add, the problematically or uncannily 'near') Freud and Heidegger 'merge' up with one another in the problem of *Kulturarbeit*—and its imaginary. See Julia Kristeva, *Strangers to Ourselves,* trans. Léon Roudiez (New York: Columbia University Press, 1991), p. 189. For further discussion of this issue see Jean-Luc Nancy and Philippe Lacoue-Labarthe, *The Title of the Letter: A Reading of Lacan,* trans. François Raffoul and David Pettigrew (Albany: SUNY Press, 1992), pp. 127–8; 133ff.

32. See Gianni Vattimo, *Beyond Interpretation,* trans. David Webb (Stanford: Stanford University Press, 1997), p. 1.

33. Martin Heidegger, "Phenomenological Interpretations with Respect to Aristotle: Indication of the Hermeneutical Situation," trans. Michael Baur, *Man and World,* 25 (1992): 361, 367.

34. See Friedrich Hölderlin, "Letter no. 236 to Casimir Ulrich Böhlendorf," in *Essays and Letters on Theory,* trans. Thomas Pfau (Albany: SUNY Press, 1988), p. 150.

35. Cicero, *De officiis,* I, 59. See the discussion of Albert R. Jonsen, Stephen Toulmin, *The Abuse of Casuistry: A History of Moral Reasoning* (Berkeley: University of California Press, 1988), ch. 3.

36. While classical hermeneuts had made this claim generally, moral theorists in a number of domains came steadily to similar conclusions about the relation between narrative and tradition. See, for example, Stanley Hauerwas's account of moral theology, "Casuistry as a Narrative Act," *Interpretation* 37 (1983): "So the prohibitions required by particular narratives are one of the

ways the narratives are tested against human experience. They are the way the narrative is challenged and renewed. . . . From this perspective casuistry is not simply the attempt to adjudicate difficult cases of conscience within a system of moral principles, but it is the form that a tradition must use to test its own commitments. For in fact a tradition often does not understand the implications of its basic convictions" (380).

37. Blaise Pascal, *The Provincial Letters*, trans. A. J. Krailsheimer (Baltimore: Penguin, 1967), VI:91.

38. For further discussion of this issue see my "On the Right to Interpret: Beyond the Copernican Turn," in *Extensions*, ch. 8.

39. See Gilles Deleuze, *Différence et répétition* (Paris: Presses Universitaires de France, 1972), p. 82. As Kant put it: "'I think' expresses an indeterminate empirical intuition"—and yet this does not mean "that the 'I' in this proposition is an empirical representation" (B423). It might be said, consequently, that what is 'denoted' (and "actually exists") is neither simply ontic nor ontological, but emerges in their difference—and what is expressed and 'signified' (*bezeichnet*) therein remains always 'hermeneutic'.

40. Friedrich Schlegel, "Critical Fragments," in *Philosophical Fragments*, trans. Peter Fichow (Minneapolis: University of Minnesota Press, 1991), p. 5.

41. Ibid., p. 6.

42. See Iris Murdoch, *The Sovereignty of Good* (London: Routledge and Kegan Paul, 1970).

43. See, for example, Stuart Hampshire, "'A Wonderful Life,'" review of *Ludwig Wittgenstein: The Duty of Genius*, by Ray Monk, *New York Review of Books* 38 (January 1991): 3–4.

44. See Plato, *Ion* (535f.). I have commented on the hermeneutic relevance of this text in "The Philosopher's Text," in *Extensions*, ch. 9.

45. Manfred Frank, *What Is Neostructuralism?* trans. Sabine Wilke and Richard Grey (Minneapolis: University of Minnesota Press, 1989), pp. 362–63.

46. Ibid., p. 448.

47. Here we may wonder, for example, about Ricoeur's continual overly 'noematic' reading of Merleau-Ponty's account of the *langagière* character of language and history, cited by Ricoeur in this text as well (TN:III:221). Compare Maurice Merleau-Ponty, "On the Phenomenology of Language," in *Signs*, trans. Richard C. McCleary (Evanston: Northwestern University Press, 1964), p. 88. Equally in this text, Merleau-Ponty argues for a lateral universal not opposed to "the diversity of languages" and an account of history understood not as a dialectical progression but a "logic in contingency," which informed his reading of "the prose of the world" from the outset. As a result, respect for the past as coherence does not entail respect for the past as a system of propositional truths or statements. Hence, as Merleau-Ponty states, the "classical" should not be taken to be the result of "miraculous adequation." Instead, "as obligatory steps for those who want to go further (*parlantes au delà*) (it) retain(s) an expressive power which exceeds state-

ments and propositions" (*Signs,* p. 11). The *Vorhabe* of tradition is not simply a "presumption of truth," as Ricoeur's formulation would have it, perhaps still too Burkean. See Ricoeur, TN:III:227.

48. TN:III:225.

49. Cf. TN:I:69f.

50. See my "Traditionis Traditio," in *Tradition(s) I,* ch. 1.

51. See Jean-François Lyotard, *The Postmodern Condition: A Report on Knowledge,* trans. Geoff Bennington and Brian Massumi (Minneapolis: University of Minnesota Press, 1984), pp. 60f. Also see Paul Ricoeur, *The Conflict of Interpretation,* ed. Don Ihde (Evanston: Northwestern University Press, 1974). Ricoeur's later work (especially TN) is largely an attempt to surmount this position, which subsumes interpretation beneath reference. See TN:I:77f. For further discussion of this issue see my "On the Rationality of the Fragment," in *Extensions,* ch. 10.

52. Seyla Benhabib, equally having pointed to the incoherence in Lyotard's account, similarly points to an account of narrative knowledge it presupposed that is not opposed to discursive knowledge, and which is, to use Bloch's phrase, "the 'non-contemporaneous contemporary' of discursive knowledge." See "Epistemology of Postmodernism: A Rejoinder to Jean-François Lyotard," *New German Critique* 33 (Fall, 1984): 118. She also questions Habermas's insufficiencies here: "Admittedly, whether a non-foundationalist justification of these commitments, which also avoids the metanarratives which Lyotard so effectively dismantles, is possible, need to be investigated" (123). In the end on, its own terms, Habermasian accounts still remain open to this question, though Benhabib's account of narrative doubtless headed in the right direction for rectifying their failure.

53. See *Tradition(s) I,* p. 32f.

54. See Claude Lefort, "The Permanence of the Theological Political?" in *Democracy and Political Theory,* trans. David Macey (Minneapolis: University of Minnesota Press, 1988), pp. 225ff. This is not, obviously, simply a matter of the "death of God." As Heidegger already realized in reference to this "empty place" in Nietzsche, the pronouncement "God is dead" does not mean simply "there is no God." See Martin Heidegger, "The Word of Nietzsche: God Is Dead," in *The Question Concerning Technology and Other Essays,* trans. William Lovett (New York: Harper and Row, 1977), pp. 100, 105. Still, granted the (universal) theoretical requisites of modernity, the question will, even granted such an acknowledgment, always be, Which God? Notwithstanding the shortcomings of his own account of meaning, here we can make sense of Levinas's claim that "it is our relations with men . . . that give to theological concepts the sole signification they admit of" (TI:79). As the medieval problem of the divine names already realized, any *theory* of the 'theological' will be 'plural' (i.e., interpretive)—and so will our politics as Lefort emphasized (and Heidegger, obviously, did not).

55. Standard lexicons in both German and English link the term 'rejoinder' to legal response. This use is instantiated at BT:50, where the verb '*erwidern*' is invoked with 'legal' or argumentative force, significantly enough, in Heidegger's 'historical' deepening of the term 'phenomenology': "Thus the term 'phenomenology' expresses a maxim which can be formulated as 'To the things themselves!' It is opposed to all free-floating constructions and accidental findings; it is opposed to taking over any conceptions which only seem to have been demonstrated; it is opposed to those pseudo-questions which parade themselves as 'problems', often for generations at a time. Yet this maxim, one may rejoin [*erwidern*] is abundantly self-evident, and it expresses, moreover, the underlying principle of any scientific discipline whatsoever. Why should anything so self-evident be taken up explicitly in giving a title to a branch of research? In point of fact, the issue here is a kind of 'self-evidence' which we should like to bring closer to us, so far as it is important to do so in casting light upon the procedure of our treatise. We shall expound only the preliminary conception [*Vorbegriff*] of phenomenology. This term has two components: 'phenomenon' and 'logos.'"

Heidegger proceeds to reinterpret the question in terms of the history of the concept "put together" in 'phenomenology'. A clearer exemplification of the argumentative status of *Being and Time,* its *Erwiderung,* and the argumentative (dialectically explicit) strategy through which it takes recourse to this history could not be more evident.

56. Roland Barthes, *Sade/Fourier/Loyola* [1971], trans. Richard Miller (New York: Hill and Wang, 1979), p. 10.

57. See my "On the Rationality of the Fragment," in *Extensions,* ch. 10.

58. See Roland Barthes, *S/Z,* trans. Richard Miller (New York: Hill and Wang, 1974), p. 61. On the problem of Heidegger's own relation to cubism, see Jean Beaufret, "Heidegger et la pensée du declin," in *Dialogue avec Heidegger* (Paris: Minuit, 1974), pp. 155ff. To the extent that such 'cubism' is articulated through the joining of analysis and synthesis, the first 'cubist' is, of course, Kant. See Martin Heidegger, *Kant and the Problem of Metaphysics,* trans. Richard Taft (Bloomington: Indiana University Press, 1990).

59. See Claude Lévi-Strauss, *The Savage Mind* (Chicago: University of Chicago Press, 1966), ch. 1.

60. See Walter Benjamin, "The Task of the Translator," in *Illuminations,* trans. Harry Zohn (New York: Schocken Books, 1969), pp. 72, 75–76. As Benjamin notes, the term 'irony' "here brings the Romanticists to mind" (77).

61. The claim that, confronted with the risk of becoming ungrounded "poetic images," hermeneutics "proves its own validity only by appealing to a historical process of which it proposes a reconstruction," is Vattimo's. Further, he rightly recognizes that such a "reconstruction of a hermeneutic notion of rationality is inseparable from a reconsideration of the relation between hermeneutics and modernity." Lacking such analysis, Vattimo claims, hermeneutics would simply

yield a "theory of multiplicity." As will become immediately evident, however, it will be both. See Vattimo, *Beyond Interpretation*, appendix ("The Reconstruction of Rationality"), pp. 98, 107. The claim that "(h)ermeneutics must therefore renounce its universalist claim if it is to preserve a regional legitimacy" is discussed in Ricoeur. See TN:III:225.

62. Kant's *Critique of Pure Reason* uses the word 'explication' (*Explikation*) only once, where (along with 'exposition', 'declaration', and 'definition') it is subsumed beneath 'explanation' [*Erklärung*] (A730/B758). At the same time, against this reduction, Kant's account of dialectic, especially evident in the second and third *Critiques*, depended on "extended" rational resources classically associated with these notions. The result is that Kant delivers what has been aptly termed a "mixed message" to those in his wake.

63. See Jacques Derrida, "The Time of the Thesis, Punctuations," trans. Kathleen McLaughlin, in *Philosophy in France Today*, ed. Alan Montefiore (Cambridge: Cambridge University Press, 1983), pp. 39–40. The problem of the "historicity or traditionality" that conjoins Joyce and Husserl is discussed as early as Derrida's *Edmund Husserl's Origin of Geometry*, p. 103.

64. See Aristotle, *Rhetorics* 1356a; Hobbes, Lev:105.

65. Leo Strauss, *Persecution and the Art of Writing* (Glencoe, Ill.: Free Press, 1952), p. 154.

66. Ibid., pp. 31f.

67. See Manfred Frank, "Two Centuries of Philosophical Critique of Reason and Its 'Postmodern' Radicalization," in *Reason and Its Other: Rationality in Modern German Philosophy and Culture*, ed. Dieter Freundlieb and Wayne Hudson (Oxford: Berg, 1993), pp. 67–83.

68. See Hans-Georg Gadamer, "Subjektivität und Intersubjektivität, Subjekt und Person," in *Gesammelte Werke*, vol. 10 (Tübingen: J. C. B. Mohr, 1995), pp. 98f.

69. See Jürgen Habermas, paper presented on the occasion of G. Scholem's eightieth birthday, *Merkur* 1 (1978), cited in Frank, "Two Centuries of Philosophical Critique," p. 79.

70. See Jean-Luc Nancy, *Être singulier pluriel* (Paris: Galilée, 1996), p. 84.

71. Ibid., pp. 84–85.

72. See Kristeva, *Proust and the Sense of Time*, pp. 4–5.

73. See Kristeva, *Tales of Love*, pp. 178–81.

74. Ibid., 179. Among the other things accomplished in Hannah Arendt's thesis is the link articulated between Heidegger's *Sorge* and the historical emergence of love as a Western tale. See Hannah Arendt, *Love and Saint Augustine* (Chicago: University of Chicago Press, 1996). While Kristeva herself questions whether Lacan is a Thomist without God as Marx was a Hegelian without Spirit (183), these issues, as Heidegger's own internal references to the Thomistic *convenientia* obviate, are tied to a complex history. Moreover, as Scheler's (romanticized) version of the Augustinian *ordo amoris* indicated, the issue of this

history has accompanied modern 'phenomenology' (and its 'ethics') from the outset, a point to which we shall return. See Max Scheler, "*Ordo amoris*," in *Selected Essays*, trans. David Lachterman (Evanston: Northwestern University Press, 1973).

75. See, for example, the texts on this topic compiled by Wladyslaw Tatarkiewicz, *History of Aesthetics*, vol. 1 (The Hague: Mouton, 1970), pp. 189ff. Clearly, if this hypothesis is correct, Heidegger's retrieval of *convenientia* also takes the effect of a certain retrieval (and deconstruction) of the history of ethics—one which accompanies his retrieval of the problem of Being and its correlated critique of modern, scientific rationality.

76. Arendt, "What is Authority?" p. 121.

77. See Kristeva, *Strangers to Ourselves*, pp. 191–92.

78. See Pierre Hadot, "Reflections on the Idea of the 'Cultivation of the Self'," in *Philosophy as a Way of Life*, trans. Michael Chase (Oxford: Blackwell, 1995), pp. 211–12.

79. See the discussion of these issues by P. Christopher Smith, *The Hermeneutics of Original Argument* (Evanston: Northwestern University Press, 1998), pp. 21ff.

80. See my "Transcendental Philosophy and the Return to Origins: On the Stoicism of the Transcendental Singular" (forthcoming), and "On the Right to Interpret: Beyond the Copernican Turn," *Extensions*, ch. 8.

81. Again see, for example, Jean-Luc Nancy, *Le sens du monde* (Paris: Galilée, 1993), pp. 13ff.

82. See, for example, Philippe Lacoue-Labarthe, "Transcendence Ends in Politics," trans. Peter Caws, in *Typography: Mimesis, Philosophy, Politics*, ed. Christopher Fynsk (Cambridge, Mass: Harvard University Press, 1989).

83. See Jacques Derrida, "Psyche: Inventions of the Other," in *Acts of Literature*, ed. D. Attridge (New York: Routledge, 1992), p. 337.

84. See Martin Heidegger, "Die Kategorien und Bedeutungslehre des Duns Scotus," in FS, conclusion. Compare Walter Benjamin, "Program of the Coming Philosophy," trans. Mark Ritter, *Philosophic Forum*, 15.1–2 (Fall-Winter 1983–84). "How the psychological concept is related to the concept of the sphere of pure knowledge remains a major problem of philosophy, one which perhaps can only be restored from the age of scholasticism. Here is the logical place for many problems that phenomenology has raised anew."

85. See Merleau-Ponty, *Signs*, p. 54. Again, both Ricoeur and Lyotard would reinvoke the term in Merleau-Ponty's wake in providing an 'expressivist' (*langagière*) semantics that both acknowledges the formal (rule-governed) background of expression and the indeterminate semantic resources that accompany and facilitate its transformation. See TN:I:69; Jean-François Lyotard, "Time Today," in *The Inhuman*, trans. Geoffrey Bennington and Rachel Bowlby (Stanford: Stanford University Press, 1991), p. 72.

86. Jean-François Lyotard, "A Bizarre Partner," in *Postmodern Fables,* trans. Georges Van den Abbeele (Minneapolis: University of Minnesota Press), p. 127.

## 1. Interpretation, Dialogue, and Friendship

1. See Lefort, "Permanence of the Theologico-Political?" As will become evident, on this account if democracy is the modern institution that interprets the symbolic order of the political without confusing it with the real, hermeneutics similarly interprets the rational beyond its (modern) technical manifestations, the remnant of the speculative similarly devoid of immanence and determinacy. For Lefort's own discussions in this regard, see part 6 ("L'oeuvre, l'idéologie, et l'interprétation") of his *Le travail de l'oeuvre machiavel* (Paris: Gallimard, 1972).

2. See Newton, *Opticks,* query 31. Thomas Hobbes, *Leviathan,* conclusion.

3. Michel Serres, *Jouvences sur Jules Verne* (Paris: Minuit, 1974), p. 241.

4. Mikhail Bakhtin, *The Dialogic Imagination,* trans. Caryl Emerson and Michael Holmquist (Austin: University of Texas Press, 1981), p. 31.

5. See A835/B863.

6. Hannah Arendt, "Tradition and the Modern Age," in *Between Past and Future* (New York: Penguin: 1977), pp. 27–28.

7. See Sigmund Freud, "The Uncanny," in *The Standard Edition of the Complete Psychological Works of Sigmund Freud,* 24 vols., ed. James Strachey (London: Hogarth Press, 1955), 17:219–56.

8. See for example Friedrich Schlegel, "Critical (Lyceum) Fragments," no. 25, in *Philosophical Fragments:* "The two main principles of the so-called historical criticism are the Postulate of Vulgarity and the Axiom of the Average. The Postulate of Vulgarity: everything great, good, and beautiful is improbable because it is extraordinary and, at the very least, suspicious. The Axiom of the Average: as we and our surroundings are, so must it have been always and everywhere, because that, after all, is so very natural" (p. 3).

9. See Giovanni Boccaccio, *De genealogia deorum* (Bari: G. Laterza, 1951). On the complex links here between renaissance humanism and Heidegger, see Ernesto Grassi, *Heidegger and the Question of Renaissance Humanism* (Binghamton, N.Y.: Center for Medieval and Early Renaissance Studies, 1983).

10. See Irenaeus, *Against the Heretics,* trans. John Keble (Oxford: James Parker & Co., 1872), book 3.

11. Plato, *Phaedrus* 274b-c.

12. Werner Marx, *Heidegger and the Tradition,* trans. Theodore Kisiel and Murray Green (Evanston: Northwestern University Press, 1971), p. 8.

13. Again, see Martin Heidegger, "Die Kategorien und Bedeutungslehre des Duns Scotus," in FS, conclusion. On Hegel's relation to Hobbes, see Jacques Taminiaux, "Hegel and Hobbes," in *Dialectic and Difference: Finitude in Modern*

*Thought,* ed. James Decker and Robert Crease (Atlantic Highlands, N.J.: Humanities Press, 1985). The *locus classicus* for such considerations is Ludwig Siep's "Der Kampf um Anerkennung: Zu Hegels Auseinandersetzung mit Hobbes in der Jenaer Schriften," *Hegel-Studien* 9 (1974): 155ff.

14. Martin Heidegger, *What Is Called Thinking?* trans. Fred D. Wieck and J. Glenn Gray (New York: Harper and Row, 1968), p. 178. Heidegger's emphasis.

15. See Friedrich Nietzsche, *The Will to Power,* trans. Walter Kaufmann and R. J. Hollingdale (New York: Random House, 1968), § 466.

16. See EPH, 129. Compare Merleau-Ponty's own gloss on Husserl: "Establishing a tradition means forgetting its origins . . ." (*Signs,* p. 159).

17. The importance of Hobbes in Heidegger's deliberations at this point are paramount—perhaps as important as his retrieval of Aristotle. Heidegger says that Hobbes's account of truth as the judgment of true propositions (not of things) is one-sided. Moreover, Heidegger adds that Hobbes's argument against the scholastics is critical, not only substituting 'equation' for 'convertibility' but computation for ratiocination. See *The English Works of Thomas Hobbes of Malmesbury,* ed. Sir William Molesworth, 11 vols. (London: John Bohn, 1839), vol. 1, *Elements of Philosophy,* pt. 1 "Logic," ch. 1. Hobbes's characterization of the scholastic doctrine as "childish babble" ("Logic," ch. 3, §7) will of course itself be subject to an inversion in the *Daseinanalytik* and its characterization of the leveling in everyday discourse and its superficial readings (*Angelesenen*) (BT:212) that neglect the primordial sources of truth. Thereby Hobbes account emerges as "cut off from its primary and primordially genuine relationships-of-Being towards the world, towards Dasein-with, and towards its very-Being-in" (BT:214).

18. Hobbes, "Logic," ch. 2, §4.

19. Ibid., §6.

20. See BP:190.

21. See TM:24; Marcus Aurelius, *Meditations* III 9; IV 4.

22. John Dewey, *Ethics,* pp. 364–65 cited in *The Moral Writings of John Dewey,* ed. James Gouinlock (New York: Hofner, 1976), p. 252. Compare Gadamer's own affirmation of the pragmatic dimension, TM:91.

23. F. W. S. Schelling, "Philosophical Letters on Dogmatism and Criticism" [1795], in *The Unconditional in Human Knowledge,* trans. Fritz Marti (Lewisburg, Pa.: Bucknell University Press, 1980), pp. 193, 189.

24. For further discussion of the dialogical 'decentering' of transcendental philosophy, see Bernhard Waldenfels's analysis, *Das Zwischenreich des Dialogs: Sozialphilosophische Untersuchungen in Anschluss an Edmund Husserl* (The Hague: Martinus Nijhoff, 1971), ch. 7.

25. Maurice Merleau-Ponty, *In Praise of Philosophy,* trans. John Wild and James M. Edie (Evanston: Northwestern University Press, 1963), p. 31. Likewise, as he realized, the continuing relevance of transcendental singularity to

dialogical accounts is precisely that, although the intersubjective passage is inextricably necessary, it is not sufficient. Hence the reciprocal inadequacies that underwrite dialogue: "But the real difficulty is that, if the true is not an idol, the others in turn are not gods. There is no truth without them, but it does not suffice to attain to the truth to be with them" (ibid.).

26. Michael Theunissen, *The Other: Studies in the Social Ontology of Husserl, Heidegger, Sartre, and Buber,* trans. Christopher Macann (Cambridge, Mass.: MIT Press, 1986).

27. Albrecht Wellmer, "Ethics and Dialogue," in *The Persistence of Modernity,* trans. David Midgley (Cambridge, Mass.: MIT Press, 1991). As will become evident, while this account endorses Wellmer's reading (which follows Silber) of Kant's ethics as implicitly an ethics of dialogue, we will deny that the classical account of 'dialogic ethics', on the other hand, was ever intended simply to be 'substituted' for moral principles (p. 142). Rather, rightly read, both precepts and dialogue converge in an account that is both hermeneutic and principled. Likewise, it will become apparent that the distinction between traditional, communitarian, and posttraditional theory at stake in Honneth's reading of Hegel is similarly abstract.

28. Ibid., p. 345.

29. Ibid.

30. Ibid., p. 227.

31. Axel Honneth, "Atomism and Ethical Life: On Hegel's Critique of the French Revolution," *Philosophy and Social Criticism* 14.4 (1988): 366. Likewise see Axel Honneth, *The Struggle for Recognition,* trans. Joel Anderson (Cambridge, Mass.: Polity Press, 1995). I have further traced the archive of recognition in my "The Face of the Hibakusha: Levinas and the Trace of Apocalypse," in *Writing the Future,* ed. David Wood (New York: Routledge, 1990).

32. Ibid.

33. Rudolf Carnap, *The Logical Syntax of Language* (London: Routledge and Kegan Paul, 1967), p. 52.

34. Axel Honneth, "Communication and Reconciliation: Habermas contra Adorno," *Telos* 39 (Spring 1979): 60–61.

35. Ibid., p. 47.

36. Ibid., p. 49.

37. Wellmer, *Persistence of Modernity,* p. 141.

38. Ibid., pp. 68–69. Wellmer's emphasis.

39. Immanuel Kant, *Religion within the Limits of Reason Alone,* trans. Theodore M. Greene and Hoyt H. Hudson (New York: Harper and Row, 1960), p. 62. Cf. Wellmer, *Persistence of Modernity,* p. 142. Wellmer's emphasis.

40. Theunissen, *The Other,* p. 132.

41. Franz Rosenzweig, *The Star of Redemption,* trans. William W. Hallo (Notre Dame, Ind.: University of Notre Dame Press, 1985), pp. 261–62.

42. Honneth, "Atomism and Ethical Life," p. 132.

43. See Martin Buber, *Between Man and Man,* trans. Ronald Gregory Smith (New York: Macmillan, 1965), pp. 1–33.

44. See Edmund Husserl, *The Crisis of European Sciences and Transcendental Phenomenology,* trans. David Carr (Evanston: Northwestern University Press, 1970), §53.

45. J. G. Fichte, *The Science of Ethics,* trans. A. E. Kroeger (New York: Harper and Row, 1970), pp. 260, 254.

46. See Edmund Husserl, "The Origin of Geometry" (K:360f.).

47. Heidegger's criticism of the primacy of the I-thou relation (as derivative with respect to ontological claims) occurs in a number of contexts. See, for example, BP:297–98.

48. See Leo Strauss, "Restatement on Xenophon's Hiero," in *On Tyranny,* ed. Victor Gourevitch and Michel S. Roth (New York: Free Press, 1991), pp. 194f.

49. See Kant's own gloss on the *sensus communis* in CJ:§40.

50. Theunissen, *The Other,* p. 362.

51. See Hans-Georg Gadamer, "The Diversity of Europe: Inheritance and Future," in EPH:235.

52. Emmanuel Levinas, "Le dialogue: Conscience de soi et proximité du prochain," in *Esistenza, mito, ermeneutica: Scritti per Enrico Castelli, vol. 2, Archivo di Filosofia,* no. 2: (Padua: Edam, 1980), p. 356.

53. As Montesquieu put it, then, "even virtue itself stands in need of limitation." See *The Spirit of the Laws* in *Selected Political Writings,* trans. Melvin Richter (Indianapolis: Hackett, 1990), book 11, ch. 4, p. 179; and the analysis by Hannah Arendt, *On Revolution* (New York: Penguin, 1986), pp. 152f.

54. Doubtless here *Truth and Method's* interface with the work of Leo Strauss becomes most complex—as can be seen even from Gadamer's footnotes. See, for example, TM:319n255. While his critique of the Enlightenment concept of prejudice and tradition had initially been footnoted to Strauss's *Spinoza* book, his account of natural law cites Helmut Kuhn's (critical) review of *Natural Right and History* in articulating the "hermeneutical problem" associated with it. In one sense, of course, what differentiates Gadamer's account here is his refusal (in the wake of Hegel) to simply jettison Hobbes's onslaught against the ancient account of natural law—even in fact while he appeals to Aristotle for precedent. Strauss had already acknowledged Aristotle's variance from the later (Thomistic) account of *synderesis* and its insight into the immutable Divine Law. See Leo Strauss, *Natural Right and History* (Chicago: University of Chicago Press, 1953), pp. 156f. When Gadamer cites the *Magna Moralia's* line, "Do not suppose that if things change owing to our use, there is not therefore a natural justice; because there is" (1194b-f), he has perhaps fully integrated it with his own project. Recall, in this respect, that the section on the hermeneutic relevance of Aristotle in *Truth and Method* began by acknowledging "that Aristotle is not concerned with the hermeneutical problem and certainly not with its historical problem"

(TM:312). I have more fully explored the complexity of the relationship be-tween Strauss and Gadamer elsewhere: see *Extensions,* pp. 160ff.

55. Adolf Reinach, *Über die apriorischen Grundlagen des bürgerlichen Rechts, Jahrbuch für Philosophie und phänomenologischen Forschung,* vol. 1, 1913. Hus-serl's comments on this work can be found in Edmund Husserl, "Adolf Reinach: In memoriam," trans. Frederick Elliston and Theadore Plantinga, in *Husserl: Shorter Works,* ed. Peter McCormick and Frederick Elliston (Notre Dame, Ind.: University of Notre Dame Press, 1981), p. 355.

56. Marcus Aurelius, *Meditations,* VIII.59.

57. Ibid., IV.12. The faculty of opinion itself, after all, he claims, "incline[s] us towards freedom from hasty judgment, friendship towards men, and obedi-ence to the gods" (III.9).

58. I allude here to Heidegger's own hermeneutics of care and its internal reference to Seneca. See BT:243; TM:24. As is evident by now, such historical 'retrievals' cannot amount to simple reinstatements. Rather, we must recognize that the history of the ethico-political (or the theologico-political, to use Le-fort's term) in such matters is no less significant than the history of 'ontology' is to the question of Being.

59. See Pierre Hadot, *La citadelle intérieure: introduction aux pensées de Marc Aurélie* (Paris: Fayard, 1992), pp. 206f. It is a mistake, then, "to represent stoi-cism as a philosophy of certainty and intellectual assurance" (p. 208).

60. Marcus Aurelius, *Meditations,* IV.3.

61. Walter Benjamin, *The Origin of German Tragic Drama,* trans. John Os-borne (New York: Verso, 1977), p. 224.

62. Hans-Georg Gadamer, "The Hermeneutics of Suspicion," *Man and World,* 17 (1984), p. 322.

63. See Francis Bacon, "Of Friendship," vol. 6 of *The Works of Francis Ba-con,* ed. James Spedding, Robert Ellis, and Douglas Heath (Cambridge: Cam-bridge University Press, 1863), pp. 323, 441.

64. Immanuel Kant, *Lectures on Ethics,* trans. Louis Infield (Indianapolis: Hackett, 1963), p. 207.

65. TM:322f. Cf. Aristotle, NE:1143a ff.

66. Significantly, Hobbes retains the Roman sense of 'tradition' here, defining it as "the transference or delivery of the thing itself," while to contract is to promise mutually in the transference of right, a transference which is not mutual but occurs "in hope to gain thereby friendship, or service from an-other"—a matter of gifts, "free gift or grace" (Lev:193). It is Fichte who trans-lates the language of 'transference' into the field of intersubjectivity: "To something posited in the first positing as an it, a mere object or thing outside us, the concept of selfhood discovered within us is transferred (*übertragen*), and synthetically united there-with; and through this conditioned synthesis there first arises for us a Thou (*Du*)." See Fichte, "Second Introduction to the

Science of Knowledge," in *Science of Knowledge,* trans. Peter Heath and John Lachs (New York: Appleton-Century-Crofts, 1970), p. 72.

67. Immanuel Kant, *The Metaphysical Principles of Virtue,* trans. James Ellington (Indianapolis: Bobbs-Merrill, 1964), p. 139.

68. As Jean Grondin has pointed out, the sections on Aristotle were appended in the later part of the composition process of *Truth and Method,* a manuscript originally focused upon the defense of the humanities. See "On the Sources of *Truth and Method,*" in *Sources of Hermeneutics* (Albany: SUNY Press, 1995), pp. 83–98.

69. Hans-Georg Gadamer, "Freundschaft und Selbsterkenntnis: Zur Rolle der Freundschaft in der griechischen Ethik," in *Gesammelte Werke,* vol. 7 (Tübingen: J. C. B. Mohr, 1991), pp. 404–5.

70. Gadamer, "Hermeneutics of Suspicion," p. 317.

71. See Kant, CJ:230.

72. See Paul Ricoeur, *Oneself as Another,* trans. Kathleen Blamey (Chicago: University of Chicago Press, 1992), p. 177.

73. Cf. Jean Paul Sartre, "Faces," in *The Writings of Jean-Paul Sartre,* ed. Michel Contat, trans. Richard McCleary (Evanston: Northwestern University Press, 1970), vol. 2. Aristotle himself recurs to the figure of the mirror in *Magna Moralia* 1213a: "when we wish to see our own face we do so by looking into the mirror, in the same way when we wish to know ourselves we can obtain that knowledge by looking at our friend."

74. George H. Mead, *Mind, Self, and Society* (Chicago: University of Chicago Press, 1934), p. 174.

75. Ibid., p. 62.

76. See Hans-Georg Gadamer, *The Idea of the Good in Platonic-Aristotelian Philosophy,* trans. P. Christopher Smith (New Haven: Yale University Press, 1986), pp. 151f.

77. See Hans-Georg Gadamer, "Hermeneutics and Deconstruction," in *Dialogue and Deconstruction,* ed. Diane P. Michelfelder and Richard E. Palmer (Albany: SUNY Press, 1989), p. 115.

78. For further discussion of this issue see my *Extensions,* suppl. to ch. 6, "Quarreling between the Ancients and the Moderns: Gadamer and Strauss."

79. Martin Buber, "Dialogue," in *Between Man and Man,* p. 36. In a 1938 work reviewing Heidegger, Buber already asserted, on the other hand, that "Heidegger's 'existence' is monological" ("What is Man?," ibid., p. 168). Finally it should be noted, in his "History of the Dialogical Principle," which appears as the afterword to *Between Man and Man,* Buber also relates the I-thou dialogue to post-Kantian thought, specifying Jacobi, Fichte, and Feuerbach. "Dialogue" itself, however, refers to Wilhelm von Humboldt's 1827 "Über den Dualismus" (p. 27). Of these thinkers, in any case, it is Humboldt who explicitly links the I-thou relation to the human flourishing of friendship—further indication of

his importance at the origins of hermeneutics. See Wilhelm von Humboldt, "Über den Dualismus," *Gesammelte Schriften* (Berlin: Preussische Akademier der Wissenschaften, 1903), vol. 6, pp. 24–27.

80. See Cornelius Castoriadis, "The Greek Polis and the Creation of Democracy" in *Philosophy, Politics, and Autonomy,* ed. David Ames Curtis (New York: Oxford University Press, 1991).

81. See Jacques Derrida, "The Mystical Foundation of Authority," trans. Mary Quaintance, *Cardozo Law Review* 2.56 (1990), p. 945. In one sense the logic here is quite ancient—justice exceeds all constructibility as its *pros hen:* "justice exceeds law and calculation" (p. 971). Yet Derrida too acknowledges the 'Hobbesian' moment: this fact cannot "serve as an alibi for staying out of juridico-political battles." Justice must be interpreted: "And so incalculable justice requires us to calculate" (p. 971).

82. This was of course Nietzsche's point. See *The Gay Science,* trans. Walter Kaufmann (New York: Vintage Books, 1974), book 1, §14. Here Nietzsche argued for a 'higher love' beyond what we call love and the need to possess. "Its right name is friendship." The step beyond *eros* however, is likewise acknowledged by Aristotle. Indeed what 'friendship' adds to *eros* in his account is in a sense recognition (NE:1155b ff.). For Derrida's discussion of these matters, see *Politique de l'amitié: Suivi de l'oreille de Heidegger* (Paris: Galilée, 1994), ch. 3.

83. See Jacques Derrida, "The Politics of Friendship," *Journal of Philosophy* 25.11 (November 1988): 682.

84. Claude Lefort, "The Question of Democracy," in *Democracy and Political Theory,* p. 19.

85. See Mikhail Bakhtin, *Problems of Dostoevsky's Poetics,* trans. Caryl Emerson (Minneapolis: University of Minnesota Press, 1984), ch. 3.

86. Maurice Blanchot, *The Infinite Conversation,* trans. Susan Hanson (Minneapolis: University of Minnesota Press, 1993), p. 81. See Julia Kristeva's essay on Phillippe Sollers, "The Novel as Polylogue," in *Desire in Language,* ed. Léon S. Roudiez (New York: Columbia University Press, 1980).

87. Charles Taylor, *Multiculturalism and "The Politics of Recognition"* (Princeton: Princeton University Press, 1993), pp. 50–51. Compare, at the other extreme with such modernist formalizations, Blanchot's attempts to delineate a "strange relation which consists in there being no relation." Blanchot, *Infinite Conversation,* p. 51.

88. Marcus Aurelius, *Meditations* IV.31.

89. Hence Heidegger's claim: "Hobbes necessarily has to be blind to the fundamental significance of the transcendentals" (BP:190). For Hobbes's denial of the Summum Bonum, see Lev:160.

90. See Mikhail Bakhtin, "Discourse in the Novel," in *Dialogic Imagination.* Again, however, we will need to grasp the complex interaction between law, history, and recognition. Compare Honneth, "Love, Rights, and Solidarity" in

*Struggle for Recognition,* ch. 3. The point, however, is that the idea of "post-traditional democratic ethical life" cannot simply (and surely need not) force a choice between a universalist or a substantive—ancient or modern—ethics.

91. See Kant, CJ:§60. Aristotle doubtless did not explicitly articulate the critical relation between communication and friendship. He did so to an extent, however, in claiming that friends need to spend time together (*syndiagein*), citing the traditional proverb that "Lack of conversation has dissolved many a friendship" (NE:1157b).

92. Hans-Georg Gadamer, *Plato's Dialectical Ethics,* trans. Robert M. Wallace (New Haven: Yale University Press, 1991), p. 218.

## 2. The Respect for Law

1. See Jacques Lacan, "Kant with Sade," trans. James B. Swenson Jr., *October* 51 (Winter 1989).

2. See PR: §209ff., 357f.

3. Blandine Barret-Kriegel, *The State and the Rule of Law,* trans. Marc A. Le-Pain and Jeffrey C. Cohen (Princeton: Princeton University Press, 1995), p. 57. It should be noted that while Kriegel's work in the end champions Hegel over against the Romantics—and perhaps especially Fichte—in this cause (and especially in being able to "reinject" the Kantian morality of law into his thinking [127]), as I have argued elsewhere, this confronts neither Hegel's own dissolutions of the modern conception of law nor the fertility of Fichte's extensions within the Kantian system. Kriegel argues that in the latter the nation takes the place of the state, education the place of justice, faith the place of law. Instead, we will need to think this nexus of principle and transcendence together, precisely in order to avoid the antinomies of (legal) positivism and organic romanticism.

4. Ibid., p. 58. It would be unfair to say, as Michel Serres does, analyzing the account of Romulus and Remus, that the very "concept of Rome" includes violence in its foundation, that this violence is recurrent, and that "the multitude is formed around the unity of the corpse." See *Rome: The Book of Foundations,* trans. Felicia McCarren (Stanford: Stanford University Press, 1991), p. 232. Such an account can surely be contested by positive readings of Roman foundation, for example by Eliot or Arendt. I have further analyzed these differences in *Tradition(s) I,* ch. 1. Still it remains true that the problem of violence, incorporation, and foundation would remain unresolved in its legacy. The hope that Serres holds out for ("Let the multiple graze in peace; tragedy disappears" [280]) becomes intelligible only within the modern account of law, whose syntactics, after all, formally articulated the possibility of multiplicity itself. This however, raises the problem of divided interpretation anew: dividing all interpretation from simple exegesis of past ideas or substantial or pre-predicative truth: its truth, that is, will be hermeneutic.

5. Ibid., p. 56.

6. Blandine Kriegel, "Rights and Natural Law," trans. Marc A. LePain, in *New French Thought,* ed. Mark Lilla (Princeton: Princeton University Press, 1994), p. 162.

7. Ibid.

8. See Leo Strauss, "How to Study Spinoza's Theologico-Political Treatise," in *Persecution and the Art of Writing* (Glencoe, Ill.: Free Press, 1952). Gadamer pointed out the relevance of this text to these issues in his comments on an oral version of this paper, delivered in July 1997.

9. Kriegel, *State and the Rule of Law,* p. 56.

10. See Francis Bacon, "Report of the First Day's Conference," in *Works* 10: 240–46. See the discussion of these issues, especially concerning the common law, to which we shall return, in Rose-Mary Sargent, *The Diffident Naturalist* (Chicago: University of Chicago Press, 1955), ch. 2.

11. Aquinas, *Summa theologiae* IaIIae, q. 92f.

12. Kriegel, *State and the Rule of Law,* p. 57.

13. Luc Ferry and Alain Renault, *Political Philosophy,* vol. 3, *From the Rights of Man to the Republican Idea,* trans. Franklin Philip (Chicago: University of Chicago Press, 1992), p. 31.

14. See Maurice Merleau-Ponty, *Sense and Non-Sense,* trans. Hubert L. Dreyfus, Patricia Allen Dreyfus (Evanston: Northwestern University Press, 1964), p. 63.

15. See my "On the Right to Interpret: Beyond the Copernican Turn," in *Extensions,* ch. 8.

16. See Manfred Frank, *Das individuelle Allgemeine: Texstrukturierung und-Interpretation nach Schleiermacher* (Frankfurt: Suhrkamp, 1977); and Vattimo, *Beyond Interpretation.*

17. See Jean Quillien, *L'anthropologie philosophique de G. de Humboldt* (Lille: Presses Universitaires de Lille, 1991), pp. 404f.

18. See Wilhelm von Humboldt, *The Limits of State Action,* ed. J. W. Burrow (Cambridge University Press, 1969), ch. 2 ("Of the Individual Man, and the Highest Ends of His Existence"). This chapter first appeared in Schiller's *Neue Thalia* in 1792. I use the Aristotelian term 'flourishing' intentionally: while Humboldt's liberalism in this text is manifest (it was cited by Mill in *On Liberty*), it is equally overdetermined, depending on ancient models of teleology for its accounts and openly citing (as Hegel would after him) ancient examples of Greece and Rome for its models (19). The result was to provide the flourishing of individuality and diversity, a "many-sided and vigorous character" that liberates "the uncommon, the marvellous," and "the original" (24, 20). Humboldt here already sets the stage for post-Kantian concerns over individual virtue and the law. See my "Hegel, the 'Plasticity' of Character, and the Prose of the World," in *Tradition(s) I,* ch. 4. In particular, Hegel's discussion of the many-sidedness of character occurs at pp. 245ff. At the same time,

however, it likewise manifests the blind spot that complicated romantic connections between voluntarism and naturalism. Hence Humboldt's conclusion: "reason cannot desire for man any other condition than that in which each individual not only enjoys the most absolute freedom of developing himself by his own energies, in his perfect individuality, but in which external nature itself is left unfashioned by any human agency, but only receives the impress given to it by each individual by himself and of his own free will, according to the measure of his wants and instincts, and restricted only by the limits of his powers and rights" (20–21). However, not without a certain irony, if not contradiction, Humboldt used such premises concerning 'care' or 'respect' for individuality not only to argue against state interference with individuality but also to claim that "the state is to abstain from all solicitude for the positive welfare of the citizens" (37) since this too would prevent the full development of individuality.

19. See Friedrich Schlegel, Athenaeum Fragments §118; *Lectures on Transcendental Philosophy* in *The Early Political Writings of the German Romantics*, ed. Frederick C. Beiser (Cambridge: Cambridge University Press, 1996), pp. 116, 154.

20. Humboldt, *Limits of State Action*, pp. 32, 17.

21. See for example, Pierre Manent, *An Intellectual History of Liberalism*, trans. Rebecca Balinki (Princeton: Princeton University Press, 1994), ch. 1.

22. Frank, *What Is Neostructuralism?* pp. 363–64.

23. Gadamer, *Reflections*, p. 41.

24. Heidegger, *Plato's Sophist*, trans. Richard Rojcewicz and André Schuwer (Bloomington: Indiana University Press, 1997), p. 286.

25. See Michel Serres, *L'interférence: Hermes II* (Paris: Minuit, 1972).

26. See my "'Between Tradition and Oblivion': Foucault, the Complications of Form, the Literature of Reason, and the Aesthetics of Existence," in *The Cambridge Companion to Foucault*, ed. Gary Gutting (Cambridge University Press, 1994), ch. 10.

27. Umberto Eco, *Interpretation and Overinterpretation* (Cambridge University Press, 1992), p. 16.

28. See Umberto Eco, *The Limits of Interpretation* (Bloomington: Indiana University Press, 1990), pp. 16ff.; *The Aesthetics of Thomas Aquinas*, trans. Hugh Bredin (Cambridge, Mass: Harvard University Press, 1988), p. 160.

29. Eco, *Interpretation and Overinterpretation*, p. 48.

30. See Leo Strauss, *The Political Philosophy of Hobbes: Its Basis and Its Genesis* (Chicago: University of Chicago Press, 1963), p. 88; See Bacon, *Works*, 3:435.

31. See Eco *Interpretation and Overinterpretation*, ch. 2.

32. See Eco, *Limits of Interpretation*, pp. 16f.; *The Aesthetics of Thomas Aquinas*, pp. 160f. On Dante's account of the polysemous and his self-interpretation

of the *Divine Comedy* through Aristotle's *Metaphysics,* see "The Letter to Can Grande," in *Literary Criticism of Dante Alighieri,* trans. Robert S. Haller (Lincoln: University of Nebraska Press, 1973), p. 99.

33. The complications attending the Boethian concept of person will be the subject of analysis elsewhere. See ch. 4.

34. As has been widely recognized, the question of analogy accompanies and overdetermines Heidegger's thought from the outset. The problem of Being's *Doppelgesicht,* its *Zweideutigkeit,* its *Zweifältigkeit,* its *Auseinandersetzung,* and finally the problem of its *Differenz* all doubtless emerge from (while radicalizing and calling into question) this topic—and recoil on the critique of modernity and its conception of rationality as *determinatio, definitio,* and *certitudo.*

35. Philippe Sollers, "Dante and the Transversal of Writing," in *Writing and the Experience of Limits,* trans. Philip Barnard and David Hayman (New York: Columbia University Press, 1983), p. 30.

36. See my "The Philosopher's Text," in *Extensions,* ch. 9.

37. Eco, *Limits of Interpretation,* p. 20.

38. Jacques Derrida, *Dissemination,* trans. Barbara Johnson (Chicago: University of Chicago Press, 1981), p. 296.

39. Eco, *Limits of Interpretation,* p. 20.

40. Derrida, *Dissemination,* pp. 296–97.

41. See Samuel Beckett, "Dante . . . Bruno . . . Vico . . . Joyce," *Our Exagmination round His Factification for Incamination of Work in Progress* (Paris: Shakespeare and Company, 1929). In thus relating Joyce to the rhetorical tradition Beckett realized in advance what Habermas did not, namely, the link between the ruptures and deconstructions of modernity and the history of the rhetorical tradition. The division between Gadamer and Derrida cannot be as wide as Habermas suggests. See Jürgen Habermas, *The Philosophical Discourse of Modernity: Twelve Lectures,* trans. Frederick Lawrence (Cambridge, Mass: MIT Press, 1987), pp. 187f.

42. See Jean-Louis Chrétien, "Le langage des anges selon la scolastique," in *La voix nue: Phénoménologie de la promesse* (Paris: Minuit, 1990), pp. 82, 97f. Likewise see Dante, "On Eloquence in the Vernacular," in *Literary Criticism of Dante Alighieri* (Lincoln: University of Nebraska Press, 1977), p. 4.

43. See Dante, "Eloquence in the Vernacular," p. 7.

44. Ibid., p. 10.

45. Jean-François Lyotard, "Philosophy and Painting in the Age of their Experimentation: Contribution to an Idea of Postmodernity," trans. D. Brewer, *Camera obscura* 12 (1984): 121.

46. Chrétien, "Le Langage des anges," p. 97.

47. See Dante, "Banquet," in *Literary Criticism of Dante Alighieri,* p. 65: ". . . my vernacular had a part in my generation, and so was one of the causes of my coming into being."

48. Serres, *Jouvences sur Jules Verne,* p. 241.

49. The Renaissance would thus increasingly articulate this separation from (and loss before) the past. For further discussion of the implications of this question in relation to Gadamer's hermeneutics, see Susan Nokes, *Timely Reading* (Ithaca: Cornell University Press, 1988), ch. 3.

50. This is not to suggest that interpretation is simply 'novelistic' fiction. As Wittgenstein put it regarding narrative, "we have quite different attitudes even to different species of what we call fiction" (CV:32). The narratives of reason and fiction, however, differ less by category than degree: hence the 'between' they equally cipher. See my "The Philosopher's Text," in *Extensions,* ch. 9.

51. Eco, *Aesthetics of Thomas Aquinas,* pp. 161–2. See Dante, "Letter to Can Grande," p. 100.

52. See Jaroslav Pelikan, *The Christian Tradition: A History of the Development of Doctrine,* Vol. III (Chicago: University of Chicago Press, 1978).

53. See *Tradition(s) I,* pp. 51f.

54. See Jaroslav Pelikan, *Mary through the Ages* (Chicago: University of Chicago Press, 1996), p. 45.

55. See Walter Benjamin, *German Tragic Drama:* "It may well be that the ground of antiquity was prepared for the reception of allegory by these religious impoverizations; but allegory itself was sown by Christianity. For it was absolutely decisive that not only transitoriness, but also guilt should seem evidently to have its home in the providence of idols and of the flesh. The allegorically significant is prevented by guilt from finding fulfillment of its meaning itself" (p. 224).

56. As Anthony Kemp has seen, invoking Foucault's terms, medieval 'historicism' beginning with Eusebius constituted a continuous and total history: "Medieval historical thought made substantialism and traditionalism identical. The tradition can be defined as everything that a present generation receives from the past. This constitutes the valid and true, the substantial body of knowledge. Everything, therefore, that it is possible to know is already known, and all knowledge is available by the method of consulting the tradition." Kemp, *The Estrangement of the Past: A Study in the Origins of Modern Historical Consciousness* (New York: Oxford University Press, 1991), p. 79. As I have made evident elsewhere, these are the major predicates of 'tradition' as it became conceptually exposited by Irenaeus and Tertullian. See *Tradition(s) I,* ch. 1. Dante in effect has already begun to refigure the link between truth, time, and the already known. Indeed, as Thomas M. Greene rightly caught, as a result, "Most texts since Dante do in varying degrees construct implicit versions of history." See *The Light in Troy: Imitation and Discovery in Renaissance Poetry* (New Haven: Yale University Press, 1982), p. 18.

57. Jacques Derrida, "Force of Law: The 'Mystical Foundation of Authority,'" trans. Mary Quaintance, *Cordozo Law Review,* Vol. 11, no. 5–6, July/Aug. 1990,

p. 971. Compare Heidegger's ". . . Poetically Man Dwells . . ." in *Poetry, Language, Thought,* trans. Albert Hofstadter (New York: Harper and Row, 1971), which concerns itself precisely with the status of such measuring and meting out, one that Heidegger attempts to refigure beyond simple quantitative reduction: "But the nature of measure is no more a quantum than is the nature of number" (224). Instead, beyond such reductionism, what measures must be interpreted: "The taking of measure is what is poetic in dwelling" (221).

58. Kriegel, *State and the Rule of Law,* p. 119.

59. Ibid., p. 121.

60. See Hegel, PS:§540; PR:218.

61. See Jean-Luc Nancy, "The Jurisdiction of the Hegelian Monarch," in *The Birth to Presence,* ed. Werner Hamacher and David E. Wellbery, trans. Mary Ann Caws and Peter Caws (Stanford: Stanford University Press, 1993).

62. See Boccaccio, *De genealogia deorum,* bk. xvi.

63. See Max Scheler, *Formalism in Ethics and Non-Formal Ethics of Value,* trans. Manfred Frings and Roger Funk (Evanston: Northwestern University Press, 1973); Etienne Gilson, *Dante the Philosopher,* trans. David Moore (New York: Sheed and Ward, 1949), pp. 166f.

64. Ernst H. Kantorowicz, *The King's Two Bodies: A Study in Medieval Political Theology* (Princeton: Princeton University Press, 1957).

65. Ibid., p. 468.

66. Ibid., p. 479.

67. Ibid., p. 474.

68. Immanuel Kant, "Ideas for a Universal History from a Cosmopolitan Point of View," in *On History,* ed. Lewis White Beck (Indianapolis: Bobbs-Merrill, 1963).

69. Ibid., p. 25, 20.

70. Ibid., p. 506.

71. See Jacques Derrida, *Limited Inc.,* ed. Gerald Graff, trans. Samuel Weber (Evanston: Northwestern University Press, 1988). For our purposes here what is crucial to these debates is the role of the paradigm of strict science with regard to contextual conceptual analysis—and regarding the issue of incorporation, political institution, and community. The lack of strict demonstration and the need consequently to deconstruct theoretical construction for Derrida (and notwithstanding his acknowledgment of the need to calculate, as we have seen) leads inherently to the question of exclusion. Searle, committed neither to the demand for strict demonstration (which he equates with logical positivism) nor the problem of power in contextual determination, defends the adequacy of reason in these matters. Again, for our purposes we will need both: beyond the naiveté of legal positivism, simple contextualism, and the suspicions of law as simple exclusion, we will require an account of rational adequacy and analysis and an acknowledgment of their limits. Eco's description of Derrida's *jeu de massacre* is to be found in *Interpretation and Overinterpretation,* p. 67.

72. Kriegel, "Rights and Natural Law," p. 158, citing Pufendorf, *On the Duty of Man and Citizen,* book 2, ch. 1.

73. Wilfred Sellars, *Science and Metaphysics: Variations on Kantian Themes* (New York: Humanities Press, 1968), p. 18.

74. Deleuze, *Différence et répétition,* p. 56.

75. Even the most deductive attempts to formalize legal reasoning admit it. Beyond legal positivism the rules of evidence of Roman law remained modeled on deductive models, requiring complete proof (*probatio plena*) before a verdict could be reached, based on predetermined numerical values. Common law, by comparison, was much more open-ended.

76. See Hobbes, "Dialogue between a Philosopher and a Student of the Common Laws of England," in *English Works,* 6:1–160.

77. See Hobbes, *The English Works,* 7:184 "Geometry . . . is demonstrable, for the lines and figures from which we reason are drawn and described by ourselves; and civil philosophy is demonstrable, because we make the commonwealth ourselves."

78. See TM:23. It may not be unrelated that Bacon invoked the necessity of historical considerations in moral questions and composed a treatise on the common law. In recognizing the context specificity of legal reasoning, again, nonetheless, we have not escaped the problem of its exclusions.

79. Heidegger, *What Is Called Thinking?* p. 71.

80. See "Thinking Life as Relation: An Interview with Luce Irigaray," *Man and World* 29.4 (October 1996): 353. As will become apparent, the history of such relational identity that "considers the concrete identity which is always identity in relation" (353) emerges not simply from a critique of the universal subject but in fact accompanies the history of the concept of personhood.

81. See Max Scheler, "Reality and Resistance [On Being and Time, Section 43]" trans. Thomas J. Sheehan, *Listening,* vol. 12, No. 3, 1977, pp. 61–73.

82. Compare for example Jean-Luc Nancy's analysis of 'being with' which explicitly connects it to the '*partes ex partes*'—though not to the modern (internally regulative) conception of law in *Être singulier pluriel,* p. 107. The conception of the law, rightly understood as withdrawal of the political, still remains without ontic specification, though not the accord of being-with, which is its 'term'. If plurality requires "another syntax" (56–57) surely that is not without connection to the forms of law—one whose (as the partes expartes denotes) transformations have their own history and prefigurations in modernity.

83. See Henry James, *The American Scene* (New York: Penguin, 1994), p. 11.

84. I have traced the transformation in *Tradition(s) I,* "Hegel, the 'Plasticity' of Character and the Prose of the World," ch. 4.

85. The OED thus finds medieval English, French (*civilité*), Latin (*civilitas*), and ultimately Greek (*politikè*) sources for *civility*: the point again, however, is the permutations which not only interconnect these terms but

transform and disconnect such terms. Even Kant's own commitments (surely acknowledging Rousseau's impact) were not unambiguous. The 1784 "Idea for a Universal History from a Cosmopolitan Point of View" insists here too on the requisites of critique: "We are *civilized*—perhaps too much for our own good—in all sorts of grace and decorum. But to consider ourselves as having reached *morality*—for that, much is lacking." See *On History*, p. 21 (Kant's emphasis).

86. I take these terms from Lewis Mumford's classic defense of humanism, written a few years before Heidegger's treatise. See *Faith for Living* (New York: Harcourt, Brace, 1940), ch. 19.

87. See Strauss, *Political Philosophy of Hobbes*, pp. 51f., 127–28.

88. See Desiderius Erasmus, "On Good Manners for Boys" [*De civilitate morum puerilium*], trans. Brian McGregor, in *Collected Works of Erasmus* (Toronto: University of Toronto Press, 1974), vol. 25. This work continued to influence humanistic studies well into the nineteenth century. See the classic study of this text: Norbert Elias, *The History of Manners*, trans. Edmund Jephcott (New York: Pantheon Books, 1978). As Elias also sees, it is crucial to see the transformation, the detraditionalization out of which *civilité* emerges: "The concept of *civilité* acquired its meaning for Western society at a time when chivalrous society and the unity of the Catholic church were disintegrating" (53). Elias further notes that the transition this treatise represents involves both a further differentiation of 'individuality' and an increased tendency for interpersonal scrutiny—and thus constraint (79). Even here, however, Elias attributes Erasmus's humanism to a personal character that emerges in a "relatively brief phase of relaxation between two great epochs characterized by more inflexible social hierarchies" (77). Nonetheless, precisely in appealing to the 'nobility' of humanistic enquiry, the unstable precursor to eighteenth-century *Kultur und Bildung*, as Elias notes, enables its practitioner "to keep his distance even from ruling strata and their opinions however bound to them he may be" (74). Precisely this 'distance', its dialogue and its interpretation, doubtless remain at stake in humanistic enquiry, contestations, and 'identity' from Erasmus to Fichte to Sartre and beyond. This is why such identity remains both 'personal', singular, and irreducible to objective accounts of 'socialization' or ego formation. Hence, I concur with Vattimo's discussion of the importance of Norbert (along with Weber and Girard) for accounts of modernization relevant for hermeneutics. Still, Vattimo misses here (and doubtless misses it as well in the other authors) the 'positivity' of the modern, the transformation of detraditionalization, construing it, again as merely a matter of 'secularization' and 'emptying'. See Gianni Vattimo, "Myth Rediscovered," in *The Transparent Society*, trans. David Webb (Baltimore: Johns Hopkins, 1992), pp. 41f.

89. Ibid., p. 289.

90. Ibid., p. 274.

91. See Montesquieu, *The Spirit of the Laws*, in *Selected Political Writings*, trans. Melvin Richter (Indianapolis: Hackett, 1990), pp. 126–28.

92. For further discussion of this issue see *Tradition(s) I*, ch. 4.

93. See Michael Oakeshott, *On Human Conduct* (Oxford: Clarendon Press, 1975), pp. 128–29, 257f. (on Hegel).

94. See my analysis of this interplay in "Kant, the Architectonics of Reason, and the Ruins of the Ancient Systems: On the Symbolics of Law," in *Tradition(s) I*, ch. 2.

95. See Friedrich Schlegel, "Philosophical Lectures: Transcendental Philosophy," in *The Early Political Writings of the German Romantics*, ed. Frederick C. Beiser (Cambridge University Press, 1996), p. 157. Again on Castiglione's ironical 'subversion' of Aristotle, see Strauss, *Political Philosophy of Hobbes*, p. 46.

96. I take this formulation from Alasdair MacIntyre's "Contexts of Interpretation: Reflections on Hans-Georg Gadamer's *Truth and Method*," Boston University *Journal*, 24.1 (1976). He too concluded that "We inhabit an interpreted world in which reinterpretation is the most fundamental form of change" (46). Everything perhaps hangs on the *implications* of the *mimesis* of the interpretive schematism—and "mimesis always claims truth" (43)—and the *complications* of the refigurations in its midst.

97. Schlegel, "Critical Fragments," §42, in *Philosophical Fragments*, p. 5.

98. See Immanuel Kant, *Logic*, trans. Robert S. Hartman and Wolfgang Schwarz (Indianapolis: Bobbs-Merrill, 1974), §119.

99. See Jürgen Habermas, *Between Facts and Norms*, trans. William Rehg (Cambridge, Mass. MIT Press, 1996), p. 115.

100. Ibid., p. 123.

101. See Leo Strauss and Hans-Georg Gadamer, "Correspondence Concerning *Wahrheit und Methode*," *Independent Journal of Philosophy* 2 (1978): 10. While admitting the position to be conservative, here we can see its positive gloss. For further discussion of this issue see my *Extensions*, pp. 157f.

102. See my "On the Right to Interpret: Beyond the Copernican Turn," in *Extensions*, ch. 8.

103. These terms are Lyotard's: here Lyotard's romanticism and Habermas's positivism, divided between 'excess' and principle, were very often of a piece. See my "Jürgen Habermas and Jean-François Lyotard: Postmodernism and the Crisis of Rationality," in *Philosophy and Social Criticism*, Fall 1984, no. 2; also see my "The Adventures of the Narrative: Lyotard and the Passage of the Phantasm," in *Philosophy and Non-Philosophy since Merleau-Ponty*, Continental Philosophy, no. 1 (New York: Routledge, 1988).

104. Manent, *Intellectual History of Liberalism*, p. 117.

105. Gadamer, *Reflections*, p. 48.

### 3. On Levinas, the Ethics of Deconstruction, and
### the Reinterpretations of the Sublime

1. See, for example, Jacques Derrida, "Tympan," in *Margins of Philosophy*, trans. Alan Bass (Chicago: University of Chicago Press, 1982). In this text Derrida "extracts" the problem of this other and its limit from "the infinity of quantum in the great *Logic* [of Hegel], and the critique of the Kantian antinomies" (p. xi)—matters which will serve as protocols here as well.

2. Nancy, *L'impérative catégorique*, p. 8.

3. Max Scheler, *The Nature of Sympathy*, trans. Peter Heath (New Haven: Yale University Press, 1954), pp. 245–46.

4. Sigmund Freud, *The Psychopathology of Everyday Life*, in *The Basic Writings of Sigmund Freud*, ed. A. A. Brill (New York: Random House, 1938), pp. 164–65.

5. Sigmund Freud, *The Interpretation of Dreams*, in *Basic Writings*, p. 548.

6. See Martin Heidegger, *Kant and the Problem of Metaphysics*, trans. James Churchill (Bloomington: Indiana University Press, 1962), pp. 30–31. For further discussion of this issue see H. Decleve's account of the exchange with Cassirer in *Heidegger et Kant* (The Hague: Martinus Nijhoff, 1970).

7. The question of this difference is one which Heidegger traces through the ontic and ontological split in Kant's treatment of the concept of personality in the first *Critique*'s Antinomies. See BT:366ff. Likewise in that work (and elsewhere) he reinstates the argument against Husserl, who, he claims, follows the secular tradition of the metaphysics of *animale rationale*, and Scheler, who still follows its sacred interpretation (74). Even in relation to Kant, Heidegger's treatment remains overdetermined, however—both in *Being and Time* and elsewhere. In the lectures on *The Basic Problems of Phenomenology*, especially with regard to the analysis of respect and the moral person, Kant is credited with having taken a step that was "immensely successful to shake off unconsciously the burden of the traditional ontology." In HCT, Heidegger claims that "Kant, in defining the rational person of man in his own fashion adopted the old Christian definition of man, detheologized only to some extent." See BP:147 and HCT:131. This doubtless should be compared with characterizations of Kant's 'Jewishness', such as those of Lyotard. Without adjudicating this difference, it suffices to note that the question of the sacred (and its narratives)—and the remainder in contemporary discourse—will never be far away in such issues.

8. See Leonardo da Vinci, *Treatise on Painting*, trans. A. Phillips McMahon (Princeton: Princeton University Press, 1956), p. 4.

9. See Longinus, "On the Sublime," trans. W. Hamilton Fyfe, in *Aristotle, The Poetics*; "*Longinus*," *On the Sublime*; *Demetrius, On Style* (Cambridge, Mass.: Harvard University Press, 1960), p. 139: "For the true sublime, by some virtue of its nature, elevates us: uplifted with a sense of proud possession, we

are filled with joyful pride, as if we had ourselves produced the very thing we heard." Compare Jean-François Lyotard's discussion of the sublime in "Presenting the Unpresentable: The Sublime," trans. Lisa Leibman, *Artforum* 20 (April 1982); as well as Jean-Luc Nancy's account of the sublime as an abyss between art and reason in *Le discours de la syncope* (Paris: Aubier Flammarion, 1976), p. 71.

10. See the analysis of my *Tradition(s) I*, ch. 2, pp. 19ff.

11. Edmund Burke, *A Philosophical Enquiry into the Origin of Our Ideas of the Sublime and Beautiful* (Notre Dame: University of Notre Dame Press, 1968), pp. 78–79.

12. Ibid., p. 57.

13. Strauss, *Natural Right and History,* p. 312.

14. For Burke the passion of the sublime was originally that of "astonishment" and only its "inferior effect" included "admiration, reverence, and respect." See Burke, *Philosophical Enquiry,* p. 57. Hence, there was a certain reversal in Kant's ordering.

15. See Strauss, *Natural Right and History,* p. 311.

16. Emmanuel Levinas, *The Theory of Intuition in Husserl's Phenomenology,* trans. André Orianne (Evanston: Northwestern University Press, 1973), p. 158.

17. A similar leveling-off has been recognized by Heidegger in his reading of Nietzsche: "[M]an has risen up into the I-ness of the ego-cogito. Through this uprising all that is, is transformed into the immanence of subjectivity. The horizon no longer emits light of itself. It is now nothing but the point-of-view posited in the value-positing of the will to power." Heidegger, "Word of Nietzsche," p. 107.

18. Cf. Levinas's criticism of representation claiming that "the world does not result from a postponement *decided* in abstract thought" (TI:157; Levinas's emphasis).

19. See Husserl, LI I:264.

20. Immanuel Kant, *Foundations of the Metaphysics of Morals,* trans. Lewis White Beck (Indianapolis: Bobbs-Merrill, 1974), p. 10.

21. For a more classical treatment of this topic see, for example, Edith Stein, *On the Problem of Empathy,* trans. Waltraut Stein (Washington, D.C.: ICS Publications, 1989).

22. Levinas's emphasis. I have further described Levinas's 'retrieval' of the classical aesthetic archive in my "Reason and the Face of the Other," *Journal of the American Academy of Religion* 54.1 (1986).

23. Plotinus, *The Enneads* I; I.6.7.

24. See Jean-Paul Sartre, *Being and Nothingness,* trans. Hazel E. Barnes (New York: Washington Square Press, 1966), part 3, ch. 3.

25. In this regard, see Emmanuel Levinas, "Persons or Figures," in *Difficult Freedom: Essays on Judaism,* trans. Sean Hand (Baltimore: Johns Hopkins University

Press, 1990); and the analysis by Jill Robbins, "Facing Figures: Levinas and the Claims of Figural Representation," in *Transitions in Continental Philosophy,* ed. Arleen B. Dallery and Stephen H. Watson (Albany: SUNY Press, 1994), pp. 283–91.

26. See James Joyce, *Ulysses* (New York: Vintage Books, 1961), p. 34.

27. See Derrida, *Edmund Husserl's Origin of Geometry,* pp. 102f.

28. See Emmanuel Levinas, "La ruine de la représentation," in *En découvrant l'existence avec Husserl et Heidegger* (Paris: Vrin, 1967), p. 135.

29. See Derrida, VM:132.

30. Ibid., p. 237.

31. Friedrich Nietzsche, *The Case of Wagner,* trans. J. M. Kennedy (New York: Russell and Russell, 1964), p. 26.

32. See Jean-François Lyotard, *Économie libidinale* (Paris: Minuit, 1974).

33. Jean-François Lyotard, "On Theory," in *Driftworks,* trans. Roger McKean (New York: Semiotext(e), 1984), p. 27.

34. Jean-François Lyotard, *Just Gaming,* trans. Wlad B. Godzich (Minneapolis: University of Minnesota Press, 1985), pp. 90–91.

35. See Kant, *Metaphysical Principles of Virtue,* p. 65: "Virtue in its whole is therefore to be represented not as if man possessed virtue, but as if virtue possessed man, since in the former case it would look as if he still had an option. . . ." Compare Longinus's account of the "possession" of the sublime.

36. See Arthur Schopenhauer, *On the Basis of Morality,* trans. E. F. J. Payne (Indianapolis: Bobbs-Merrill, 1965); and Scheler, *Formalism in Ethics.* It should be noted that at a critical point in his discussion of practical reason in the *Kantbuch,* Heidegger too submits this text to analysis with very different results, claiming that it involves not respect for the other person but rather that "[i]n having respect for the law, I submit to myself" (p. 165).

37. Lyotard, *Just Gaming,* p. 69.

38. Elsewhere I will more fully elaborate the 'missing' question of interpretation in Lyotard's account.

39. Lyotard, *Le différend* (Paris: Minuit, 1983), p. 184; my translation.

40. Ibid., p. 200.

41. See Lyotard, "Apathie dans la théorie," in *Rudiments païens* (Paris: Union Générale d'Éditions, 10/18, 1977), p. 9.

42. Theodor W. Adorno, *Negative Dialectics,* trans. E. B. Ashton (New York: Continuum, 1973), p. 361.

43. Lyotard, *Différend,* p. 29.

44. See "Debat" to "Discussions, ou: phraser 'Après Auschwitz,'" in *Les fins de l'homme,* ed. Philippe Lacoue-Labarthe and Jean-Luc Nancy (Paris: Galilée, 1981), pp. 311ff.

45. See Derrida: "Philosophy (in general) can only open itself to the question, within it and by it. It can only *let itself be questioned*" (VM:131).

46. Derrida, *Edmund Husserl's Origin of Geometry*, p. 138 (Derrida's emphasis).

47. Jacques Derrida, "Of an Apocalyptic Tone Recently Adopted in Philosophy," trans. John Leavey, *Semeia*, no. 23 (1982): 80.

48. Ibid.

49. Emmanuel Levinas, "Tout autrement," *L'arc* 54 (1973): 36.

50. Jacques Derrida, "Toward an Ethic of Discussion," afterword to *Limited Inc.*, p. 137.

51. Ibid., p. 151.

52. Compare Kant's attempt to make the horizons of the "standpoints" at work in this "undecidable conflict" harmonious in the closing sections of the *Foundations*, pp. 69ff.

53. Jacques Derrida, *Speech and Phenomena*, trans. David B. Allison (Evanston: Northwestern University Press, 1973), p. 15.

54. Nancy, *L'impérative catégorique,* p. 137.

55. For further discussion of this issue, see my "Regulations: Kant and Derrida at the End of Metaphysics" in *Philosophy and Deconstruction*, ed. John Sallis (Chicago: University of Chicago Press, 1987).

56. Adorno, *Negative Dialectics*, p. 246. Concerns regarding this voice of reason, its "vocation," and the transition from *Vernehmen* to *Vernunft* which afflicts its etymological and perhaps metaphysical past can be found as early as Schopenhauer's criticism of Kant, who condemned Kant's metaphorics as a "miserable witticism" and countered with his own, asking whether Kant's *Wissenschaftslehre* was not precisely *devoid* of science (*Wissenschaftsleere*). See Schopenhauer, *Basis of Morality*, pp. 80–81, 115. For a more recent analysis, see Jacques Lacan's pairing of the voices of reason and those of psychosis in his "Kant avec Sade," in *Ecrits*, pp. 772ff.

57. See Kant, *Religion within the Limits*, p. 133. Also see A569/B597.

58. See Jean-Luc Nancy, *Le partage des voix* (Paris: Galilée, 1982), pp. 60f.

59. Nancy, *L'impérative catégorique*, p. 28. As Nancy himself notes, this recognition only repeats Heidegger's claims regarding the primacy of the question of transcendental imagination and the emphasis on the finite in the analysis of the ethical.

60. Jean-François Lyotard, "Jewish Oedipus," in *Driftworks*, p. 42. Likewise see the treatment of Kant and Levinas in *Différend*, pp. 159ff. Finally, compare Kant's analysis concerning the unpresentability of the ethical in *Critique of Judgment*: "Perhaps there is no sublimer passage in the Jewish law than the command, 'Thou shalt not make to thyself any graven image, nor the likeness of anything which is in heaven or in the earth or under the earth,' etc. This command alone can explain the enthusiasm that the Jewish people in their moral period felt for their religion, when they compared themselves with other people, or explain the pride which Mohammedanism inspired. The same is true of the

moral law and of the tendency to morality in us. It is quite erroneous to fear that, if we deprive this tendency of all that can recommend it to sense, it will only involve a cold, lifeless assent and no moving force or emotion" (CJ:115).

61. Lyotard, "Jewish Oedipus," p. 53. In fact Lyotard's early intention was different, as this text demonstrates. In reference to Freud he claims in fact that "it was necessary that this Jew be an atheist in order that the renounced desire to see could change into a desire to know. . . . " Still, this transformation from the "desire to see" to the "desire to know" was not itself unproblematic, and, taken literally, perhaps self-defeating, as the later Lyotard perhaps would acknowledge.

62. Nancy, *L'impérative catégorique,* p. 131. Derrida's response to Nancy at that point, however, was no less strict than it had been to Lyotard and Levinas in the end. The *als ob* always demands the recognition of its own groundlessness, always posits its own illusory character and hence: "The structure itself of the law obliges its own transgression" (183). The logical paradox of this structure would be more fully emphasized in the Cerisy colloquium on Lyotard's work in relation to Kafka (1983). See Derrida, "Préjugés: Devant la loi," in *La faculté de juger,* ed. J-F Lyotard (Paris: Minuit, 1985).

63. Lacoue-Labarthe and Nancy, conclusion to *Fins de l'homme,* p. 691.

64. Kant, *Metaphysical Principles of Virtue,* p. 97.

65. Compare Fichte's remarks written in Kant's wake: "Man, insofar as the predicate of freedom is applicable to him, that is, insofar as he is an absolute and not a presented or presentable [*nicht vorgestelltes noch vorgestellbares*] subject, has nothing whatever in common with natural beings, and hence is not contrasted to them either." See Fichte, *Science of Ethics,* p. 115. Moreover, while we have noted the Fichtean precedent concerning the problem of "respect" in Heidegger's *Being and Time,* we should also note in this regard the problem of the *ex-stasis* of the ethical that results from its commitment to the transcendental imagination. Of interest here is Fichte's description of the emergence of the sublime in the "wavering" and the "interplay" at work in the transcendental imagination's synthesis of the difference between self and non-self: "It is this wavering of imagination between irreconcilables, this conflict with itself, which . . . extends the condition of the self therein to a moment of *time* . . . The imagination does not sustain this long—no longer that is, than a moment (except in the feeling of the sublime, where there comes upon us an *amazement,* a suspension of the interplay in time . . . [194; Fichte's emphasis]."

66. Fichte, *Science of Ethics,* p. 177.

67. Ibid., p. 236 (Fichte's emphasis). Fichte's reference to Schelling is from "New Deduction of Natural Right" (1976), a translation of which appears in Schelling, *Unconditional in Human Knowledge.*

68. Martin Heidegger, "Letter on Humanism," trans. F. Capuzzi and J. Gray, in *Basic Writings,* ed. D. Krell (New York: Harper and Row, 1977), p. 221.

69. Cf. Jean-Luc Nancy, *La communauté désoeuvrée* (Paris: Christian Bourgois, 1986), p. 23.

70. See Nancy, "L'être abandonné" in *L'impérative catégorique,* pp. 141ff. See *Being and Time*'s discussion of Dasein's having "been abandoned to its own null basis," p. 400.

71. See Hegel, WdL:350ff.

72. For a discussion of the interrelation between the corresponding terms as treated by Heidegger in BT (*Be-sorge, Fürsorge,* and *Sorge*), see §41, pp. 235ff.

73. See René Descartes, *The Passions of the Soul,* in *The Philosophical Works of Descartes,* vol. 1, trans. Elizabeth S. Haldane and G. R. T. Ross (Cambridge: University Press, 1972), art. 161, p. 406. On Descartes's relation to Hobbes's moral theory see, for example, Strauss, *Political Philosophy of Hobbes,* pp. 56f.

74. Francis Jacques, *Difference and Subjectivity: Dialogue and Personal Identity* (New Haven: Yale University Press, 1991), p. 141.

75. Ibid., p. 129.

76. Ibid., p. 143.

77. Ibid., p. 125.

78. I take these terms from Jean-Luc Marion. See *L'interloqué, Topoi* 7 (1988): 179.

79. See, for example, Jacques Derrida, *The Other Heading,* trans. Pascale-Anne Brault and Michael B. Nass (Bloomington: Indiana University Press, 1992), pp. 78f.

80. Jacques, *Difference and Subjectivity,* p. 124. Jacques is clear about his theoretical motivation in bypassing the phenomenology of the individual subject: granted the instability of transcendental singularity, and daring to admit that the emperor has no clothes, "we are obliged to change strategy and begin with the relations between persons, accepting that this roundabout approach will give back to subjectivity a certain consistency" (p. 162). The strategy which in turn makes individuality such an effect is surely not a new one. The question is what is gained at the cost of stability.

81. See Jean-Luc Nancy, *Hegel, l'inquiétude du négatif* (Paris: Hachette, 1997).

82. See Gadamer, "Subjektivität und Intersubjektivität," 10:98.

83. See Derrida, *Husserl's Origin of Geometry,* pp. 102ff. Significantly, a 1982 text on Joyce again returns to this discussion described as being "at the very centre of the book" and then proceeds to articulate the Joycean overtones of his itinerary since the early sixties. See Jacques Derrida, "Two Words for Joyce," trans. Geoff Bennington, in *Post-Structuralist Joyce,* ed. Derek Attridge and Daniel Ferrer (Cambridge: Cambridge University Press, 1984), pp. 149f.

84. What becomes evident then in such a history is the specificity in Derrida's demand that Levinas account for the "historical coupling of Judaism and Hellenism," thereby confronting his concluding question: "And what is the

legitimacy, what is the meaning of the *copula* in this proposition from perhaps the most Hegelian of modern novelists: 'Jewgreek is greekjew. Extremes meet' (VM:153; Derrida's emphasis). Prima facie, it would be ironic to say the least, to insist on articulating this history through the emergence of modern personalism and explicitly out of an initial refiguration of Christianity. The latter, however, surely provides both the theoretics and the mythemes for both Hegel's and Joyce's account. At the same time, in thus complicating the thematics of the end of metaphysics we can make further sense of what has been called Heidegger's "sins of omission"—namely his neglect of medieval prefiguration of modernity —a neglect on closer inspection that is not nearly so evident in Levinas's own account. Indeed his account explicitly confronts Heidegger here perhaps more than anywhere else in this history. As I have pointed out, Levinas's own 'history of metaphysics' discusses the plurality which the medieval doctrine of analogy should have made possible (TI:80). Here we can explicitly attend the complicity between this account and the account of relational personhood, one, as will become evident, which not only provides an explicit model for Hegel's account but underlies the account of recognition he develops—and which Levinas in turn transforms.

85. Jacques, *Difference and Subjectivity*, p. 69.

86. Here again I have in mind the investigations on this topic by Claude Lefort, "Permanence of the Theological Political?" in *Democracy and Political Theory*. Also, see *Tradition(s) I*, p. 118.

## 4. Person and E-vent

1. Simply to cite two examples: in her book *Saints and Postmodernism*, Edith Wyschogrod called for a renewed discussion of personalism and the saintly, while beginning with *Radical Hermeneutics* John Caputo similarly pointed to an account of the person outside the antihumanist critiques of thinkers like Heidegger and Derrida and their followers. See Wyschogrod, *Saints and Postmodernism: Revisioning Moral Philosophy* (Chicago: University of Chicago Press, 1990); John Caputo, *Radical Hermeneutics* (Bloomington: Indiana University Press, 1988), pp. 289–90. The issue, however, as will become evident, was widespread.

2. See Siep, "Kampf um Anerkennung." For further discussion of Hegel's attempt to overcome this *Auseinandersetzung*, see my "Hegel, the 'Plasticity' of Character, and the Prose of the World," in *Tradition(s) I*, ch. 4.

3. See Adorno, *Negative Dialectics*, p. 276.

4. Compare TM:358. See Heidegger's description of the claim of the *hermeneuein*, which both calls forth and withdraws from interpretation as hermeneutic in DL:28f.

5. See Heidegger, *What Is Called Thinking?* p. 62. Compare Scheler, *Formalism in Ethics*, p. 371.

6. Jean-Luc Nancy, *The Inoperative Community,* trans. Peter Connor (Minneapolis: University of Minnesota Press, 1991), p. 4.

7. See Adorno, *Negative Dialectics,* pp. 277–79.

8. Ibid., p. 281. See Gilles Deleuze and Félix Guattari, *Anti-Oedipus,* trans. Robert Harley, Mark Seem, and Helen R. Lane (New York: Viking, 1977).

9. See in this regard the analyses of Alasdair MacIntyre, *After Virtue* (Notre Dame, Ind.: University of Notre Dame Press, 1981), ch. 1.

10. Ludwig Wittgenstein, *Culture and Value,* trans. Peter Winch (Chicago: University of Chicago Press, 1980), p. 39.

11. See Emmanuel Levinas, *Ethics and Infinity,* trans. Richard A. Cohen (Pittsburgh: Duquesne University Press, 1985), pp. 43–44.

12. See Adorno, *Negative Dialectics,* pp. 280–81.

13. I borrow the term 'fragmented transcendence' (*abgebrochene Transzendenz*) itself from Adorno. See for example his *Aesthetic Theory,* trans. C. Lenhardt (London: Routledge and Kegan Paul, 1984), p. 184.

14. See Walter Benjamin, "The Work of Art in the Age of Mechanical Reproduction," in *Illuminations,* trans. Harvey Zohn (New York: Schocken Books, 1969), pp. 221ff.

15. Wittgenstein, *Culture and Value,* p. 3.

16. See Frank, "Two Centuries of Philosophical Critique," p. 79.

17. See Jürgen Habermas, paper presented on the occasion of G. Scholem's eightieth birthday, *Merkur* 1 (1978); cited in Frank, "Two Centuries of Philosophical Critique," p. 79.

18. Compare the criticisms of more recent elevations of the sacred over the phenomenological by Dominique Janicaud in *Le tournant théologique de la phénoménologie française* (Combas: Editions de l'Éclat, 1991). In advance, in focusing on the text of Thomas Aquinas, I gratefully acknowledge the comments on my analysis by leading scholars on Heidegger and Aquinas (John Caputo) and Wittgenstein and Aquinas (David Burrell). Still, the analyses that follow are not intended to enter into the debate concerning the 'ontological' character of Aquinas's thought. Jean-Luc Marion has indicated the complexity of such debates concerning the "metaphysical tradition" of the *ens commune,* the 'objective concept of Being' and Aquinas's refiguration of the Divine names (substituting *esse* for the good [*bonum*]), a substitution already complicated by what Levinas calls the "definitive philosophical—onto theological—teaching of the Good." See Jean-Luc Marion, preface to the English edition of *God without Being,* trans. Thomas A. Carlson (Chicago: University of Chicago Press, 1991).

19. Again, Levinas himself may be perceived to come close to the latter in claiming, "It is our relations with men . . . that gives to theological concepts the sole significance they admit of" (TI:79).

20. See for example, Gaius, *Institutiones,* IV, §86: "He who pleads in another's name (as a cognitor [attorney] or procurator [agent]) takes the accusation indeed

from the person of his employer *ex persona domini* but turns the condemation on himself."

21. See Umberto Eco, "Two Models of Interpretation" in *The Limits of Interpretation,* p. 14. Likewise see his *Aesthetics of Thomas Aquinas,* 160ff.

22. See Dante, *De monarchia* I.3–4. See the previous analysis of this text in ch. 2.

23. Boethius, *De trinitate* IV (as cited by Aquinas, ST:I.29.4).

24. See Boethius, *The Theological Tractates,* trans. H. F. Stewart, K. R. Rand, and S. J. Tester (Cambridge, Mass.: Harvard University Press, 1978); *De trinitate* V, p. 25.

25. Ibid., pp. 27–29.

26. See Boethius, *The Consolation of Philosophy.* It is just this complexity that led the moderns to view analogy as anthropocentric, its dialectic illusory, and its origins as in need of a 'hermeneutics of suspicion'.

27. See Augustine, *De beata vita,* I.4.

28. To take the charge seriously, it suffices to recall that in Roman law a person is a man possessed of civil standing (*Persona est homo statu civili praeditus*). Neither women, nor slaves, nor children were 'persons' in this sense. The connection between role, representation, and person was reestablished in Hobbes's *Leviathan:* "The word Person is latine, instead whereof the Greeks have *prosopon* which signifies the Face, as Persona in latine signifies the *disguise,* or *outward appearance* of a man, counterfeited on the Stage; as a Mask or Visard. And from the Stage, hath been translated to any Representer of Speech and action, as well in Tribunalls, as Theater" (Lev:217). I have discussed this text in more detail in my "The Face of the Hibakusha," in *Writing the Future,* ed. David Wood (London: Routledge, 1990).

29. See the analysis of Siep, "Kampf um Anerkennung." I have further analyzed this issue in *Tradition(s) I.*

30. See G. W. F. Hegel, *Enzyklopädie der philosophischen Wissenschaften im Grundrisse* (1827), vol. 19 of *Gesammelte Werke,* ed. W. Bonsiepen and H. C. Lucas (Hamburg: Felix Meiner, 1989), pp. 13–14.

31. See G. W. F. Hegel, "The Spirit of Christianity," in *Early Theological Writings,* trans. T. M. Knox (Philadelphia: University of Pennsylvania Press, 1981), p. 260.

32. G. W. F. Hegel, *Lectures on the Philosophy of Religion,* 3 vols., trans. R. F. Brown, P. C. Hodgson, and J. M. Stewart (Berkeley: University of California Press, 1984), 1:164.

33. Ibid., 3:192.

34. Ibid., 3:193.

35. See Hegel, PS:808.

36. Jean-Paul Sartre, *Being and Nothingness,* p. 324.

37. Hegel, *Lectures on the Philosophy of Religion,* 1:213 (Hegel's emphasis).

38. As we have seen, in effect, two moves had been made. The generalization of poetics beyond Aquinas's limitations (a move which Eco and others

identified as originally made by Dante) is conjoined with the 'modern' doctrine of personhood developed by Locke, Leibniz, Wolff, and Kant as self-conscious identity through time. Beside Hegel's standard discussion of the latter, see his characterization of Dante in *Lectures on Fine Art*, vol. 2, trans. T. M. Knox (Oxford University Press, 1988), p. 980.

39. See G. W. F. Hegel, *System of Ethical Life*, trans. H. S. Harris and T. M. Knox (Albany: SUNY Press, 1979), p. 146.

40. Ibid., p. 124. Kant's introduction of the question of person in the *Critique of Pure Reason*'s third Paralogism immediately contrasts the identity of person in my own consciousness with that of the standpoint of another person (as object of outer intuition)—a disjunction which contests the link between continuity and substance. See A362.

41. See Kantorowicz, *The King's Two Bodies*. Likewise, see the discussion of this work by Marc Richir, *Du sublime en politique* (Paris: Payot, 1991), ch. 2.

42. J. G. Fichte, "The Vocation of the Scholar," in *The Popular Works of Johann Gottlieb Fichte*, trans. William Smith (London: Trübner, 1889), p. 162.

43. Ibid., p. 163.

44. Compare Heidegger's discussion of Kant, Aquinas, and the issue of *definitio* and *determinare* in BP:86ff. The significance of Hobbes's account of the copula as quantitative equality (and hence the leveling of transcendence by calculation) has also been noted. Finally we should recall the Hobbesian protocols of Hegel's equation of definition and realization: "[W]here the cause [of a subject] are known, there is place for demonstration, but not where the causes are to seek for. Geometry therefore is demonstrable, for the lines and figures from which we reason are drawn, and described by ourselves; and civil philosophy is demonstrable, because we make the commonwealth ourselves." Thomas Hobbes, "Six Lessons to the Professor of the Mathematics," in *English Works of Thomas Hobbes*, p. 7:184.

45. See Levinas, *Ethics and Infinity*, p. 78.

46. Frank, *What Is Neostructuralism?* p. 363. (The cited text is from Schleiermacher.) Likewise, see Frank's *Die Unhintergehbarkeit von Individualität* (Frankfurt am Main: Suhrkamp, 1986).

47. On Heidegger's discussion of this "empty place [*Stelle*] of God," see "The Word of Nietzsche: 'God Is Dead'" in *The Question Concerning Technology*, p. 100.

48. Scheler, *Nature of Sympathy*, p. 121.

49. Jean-Paul Sartre, "The Humanism of Existentialism," *The Philosophy of Existentialism*, ed. Wade Baskin (New York: Philosophical Library, 1965). I literally translate Sartre's original title.

50. See Gadamer's discussion of Aquinas's *De differentia verbi domini et humani*, the doctrine of the Trinity, and his denial that logos and *verbum* coincide, requiring instead a "processal element"—a difference which marks the finitude of discursive rationality (TM:422).

51. See Ludwig Wittgenstein, *Philosophical Investigations*, trans. G. E. M. Anscombe (New York: Macmillan, 1968), §373; *Culture and Value*, p. 23.

52. I have in mind, for example, the failures of such accounts of theoretical primitives as P. E. Strawson's P-predicates, which could account neither for the dignity of such ascriptions nor for the historical mediations and the causal history from which these matters emerge. See P. F. Strawson, *Individuals* (London: Methuen, 1959), pp. 87–105. At most, such predicates are irreducible within the predications in which they are relationally ascribed, like Husserlian perceptual profiles (*Abschattungen*). See ibid., §41.

53. See Hegel, "The Spirit of Christianity," p. 260. In this passage Hegel also acknowledges the Jewish tradition that informs its logic, albeit one that Hegel can only read as "a happy accident." In view of the complicated relations that unite Rosenzweig, Buber, and Levinas in relation (and opposition) to Hegel, it is worth citing the text, its speculation, and doubtless its anti-Semitism in detail: "The most commonly cited and the most striking expression of Jesus' relation to God is his calling himself the 'son of God' and contrasting himself as son of God with himself as the 'son of man.' The designation of this relation is one of the few natural expressions left by accident in the Jewish speech of that time, and therefore it is to be counted among their happy expressions. The relation of a son to his father is not a conceptual unity (as, for instance, unity or harmony of disposition, similarity of principles, etc.) a unity which is only a unity in thought and is abstracted from life. On the contrary, it is a living relation of living beings, or likeness of life" (ibid.).

54. Perhaps the most explicit recognition of the analogical with respect to persons is given in the attempts of Wilfred Sellars in *Science and Metaphysics* (London: Routledge and Kegan Paul, 1968). Having declared analogy to be as essential to the philosophy of science as "it has been to theology and, it would seem, somewhat more fruitful" (p. 18), Sellars devoted a chapter to it in the attempt to find "the way between the Scylla of logical behaviorism and the Charybdis of Cartesianism" by means of "logical reconstruction in accordance with the logic of scientific explanation—which is, of course, just ordinary explanation writ large" (p. 165). Proceeding by phenomenology, conceptual analysis, and transcendental argument (p. 153), Sellars hoped to show how classical non-overt mental 'acts' could then be translated without loss into overt Rylean episodes. Still, as has been seen, the presuppositions of the attempt become portentous. Sellars not only had to presuppose that ordinary explanation and scientific explanation are 'homologously' of a piece, he likewise had to presuppose the phenomenology of prelinguistic acts was reducible (all phenomenology is Cartesian in this respect). Finally, he had to presuppose a logic from which the archive itself had departed after Boethius, namely one in which the logic of relations, predication *per participationem* must be parasitic on the logic of 'substance'.

55. The proximity between Heidegger and Benjamin in this regard was perhaps first seen by Hannah Arendt. See her introduction to Walter Benjamin, *Illuminations*, trans. Harry Zohn (New York: Schocken Books, 1969).

56. Gadamer, TM:424. See Michel Foucault, *The Order of Things* (New York: Random House, 1970), ch. 2. Jean Grondin has recently reemphasized this conceptual inheritance in his reading of Gadamer. See his *Introduction to Hermeneutics*, trans. Joel Weinsheimer (New Haven: Yale University Press, 1995). For further discussion of the relation between Foucault and hermeneutics see my "Kant and Foucault: On the Beginnings and Ends of Anthropology," *Tidschrift voor filosofie*, 47.1 (1985).

57. Ibid., pp. 67f.

58. Johannes Classen, *De grammaticae Graecae primordiis* [1829], p. 99, cited in Adolf Trendelenburg, "A Contribution to the History of the Word Person," *Monist* 20. 3 (July 1910): 350.

59. Heidegger, BP:155.

60. Ibid., p. 157.

61. An insightful analysis of Heidegger's critique of civil society can be found in Peter Slöterdijk, *Critique of Cynical Reason*, trans. Michael Eldred (Minneapolis: University of Minnesota Press, 1987).

62. G. W. F. Hegel, *Philosophy of Mind*, trans. William Wallace (Oxford: Clarendon Press, 1971), pp. 51, 156 (*Encyclopedia of the Philosophical Sciences*, §395, 416).

63. This point is doubtless internal to the logic of the master-slave dialectic, as Hegel himself recognized. It is perhaps even more forcefully made by Lincoln's classic statement on democracy: "As I would not be a *slave*, so I would not be a *master*. This expresses my idea of democracy. Whatever differs from this, to the extent of the difference, is no democracy" (emphasis in original).

64. Aristotle, NE:1156a3.

65. Ibid., 1159b25.

66. Ibid., 1165a29f.

67. Dominique Janicaud, *The Shadow of That Thought: Heidegger and the Question of Politics*, trans. Michael Gendre (Evanston: Northwestern University Press, 1996), p. 123.

68. See Martin Heidegger, "The Anaximander Fragment" in *Early Greek Thinking* (New York: Harper and Row, 1975), p. 18.

69. Emmanuel Levinas, "Revelation in the Jewish Tradition" in *The Levinas Reader*, ed. Seán Hand (Cambridge, Mass.: Basil Blackwell, 1989), p. 199.

70. Ibid., p. 195.

71. Again, on the opposition between person and figure in Levinas's text (and the possibility of its overcoming) see Jill Robbins, "Facing Figures: Levinas and the Claims of Figural Interpretation," in *Transitions in Continental Philosophy*, pp. 283–91.

72. See Emmanuel Levinas, *The Theory of Intuition in Husserl's Phenomenology*, trans. André Orianne (Evanston: Northwestern University Press, 1973), conclusion.

73. Emmanuel Levinas, "Le Dialogue: Conscience de soi et proximité du prochain," p. 354. This text, the most explicit of Levinas's treatment on the topic, origi-

nally appeared in the encyclopedia *Christlicher Glaube in moderner Gesellschaft* (Freiburg im Breisgau: Herder). Here dialogue is distinguished from an act of knowledge or communication and takes on the status of event as transcendence, albeit again beyond "Spinozistic idealism," an event that can miscarry before "the power of domination and the possibility of ruse" (349).

74. Ibid., pp. 356, 354.

75. René Descartes, *Meditations on First Philosophy*, trans. Laurence J. Lafleur (Indianapolis: Bobbs-Merrill, 1960), p. 25.

76. Jean-Paul Sartre, "Faces," in *Writings*, 2:68.

77. Edith Stein, *On the Problem of Empathy*, trans. Waltraut Stein (Washington, D.C.: ICS Publications, 1989), p. 34.

78. Strauss, *Political Philosophy of Hobbes*, p. 56.

79. See Jean-Luc Marion, "Generosity and Phenomenology: Remarks on Michel Henry's Interpretation of the Cartesian Cogito," trans. Stephen Voss, in *Essays on the Philosophy of Science of René Descartes* (New York: Oxford University Press, 1993).

80. See Hans-Georg Gadamer, *The Idea of the Good in Platonic-Aristotelian Philosophy*, trans. Edward A. Bushinski (Pittsburgh: Duquesne University Press, 1953), pp. 150f.

81. Gadamer, *Idea of the Good*, pp. 151–58.

82. See Jacques Lacan, *Le seminaire de Jacques Lacan*, Livre 20, *Encore* (Paris: Editions du Seuil, 1972), p. 103.

83. See Martin Heidegger, *Aristotle's Metaphysics, 1–3: On the Essence and Actuality of Force*, trans. Walter Brogan and Peter Warnock (Bloomington: Indiana University Press, 1998), introduction.

84. Such an account of generosity as a quid pro quo—and despite its theoretical importance for Levinas's work—remains active in Sartre's account. See Aristotle, NE:281ff.

85. See NE:23.

86. Ludwig Wittgenstein, *Tractatus logico-philosophicus* (London: Routledge and Kegan Paul, 1960), 6.42ff.

87. See Ludwig Wittgenstein, "On Heidegger on Being and Dread," in *Heidegger and Modern Philosophy*, ed. Michael Murray (New Haven: Yale University Press, 1978), p. 81.

88. See Hadot, *Philosophy as a Way of Life*, postscript. On Wittgenstein, also see Hadot's "Wittgenstein, philosophie du language," *Critique*, no. 149 (October 1959): 866–81; no. 150 (November 1959): 972–83.

89. See Wittgenstein, *Tractatus logico-philosophicus*, 6.421.

90. See Emmanuel Levinas, "Secrecy and Freedom," in *Ethics and Infinity*, ch. 6.

91. As I have argued elsewhere, this too is part of the Hegelian legacy. See my "Hegel, Hermeneutics, and the Retrieval of the Sacred," *Extensions*, ch. 3.

92. See Adorno, *Aesthetic Theory*, p. 175.

93. Again, the *locus classicus* for this 'reciprocal' relation between summons (*Afforderrung*) and recognition (*Anerkennung*) is Fichte's *Science of Right*, trans. A. E. Kroeger (New York: Harper and Row, 1969), part 1, book 1, para. 3, pp. 5ff. Here it is clear that, contrary to Levinas's gloss, the "Fichtean free ego" does not "undergo the suffering that would come to it from the non-ego" but from another freedom. Fichte's 'voluntarism' always belies itself in an 'unconscious' that escapes it. See my *Tradition(s) I*, ch. 3.

94. Martin Buber, "Afterword: The History of the Dialogical Principle," in *Between Man and Man*, p. 209.

95. J. G. Fichte, "The Way towards the Blessed Life or the Doctrine of Religion," in *The Popular Works of Johann Gottlieb Fichte*, 2 vols., trans. William Smith (London: Trubner, 1889), vol. 2, lecture 3.

96. Ibid., p. 314.

97. See Aristotle's discussion of Heraclitus and Empedocles (NE:1155b) and Heidegger's own varying discourse on Heraclitus. The complexity of Heidegger's texts is reviewed in Derrida, *Politiques de l'amitié*, pp. 367ff.

98. See Derrida, *Politiques de l'amitié*, p. 249.

99. Ibid., p. 63.

100. In invoking an ethics of "good ambiguity" I allude (as has Levinas himself) to the terms of the later Merleau-Ponty in this context and "a rationality that is neither a total nor an immediate guarantee. It is somehow open, which is to say that it is menaced." See Merleau-Ponty, *Primacy of Perception*, pp. 11, 23. It is not accidental that, in Merleau-Ponty's thought, it became increasingly linked to the politics of democracy. See my "Merleau-Ponty, the Ethics of Ambiguity, and the Dialectics of Virtue," in *Merleau-Ponty in Contemporary Perspectives*, ed. Patrick Burke and Jan van der Veken (Dordrecht: Kluwer, 1993).

101. We could question similarly whether when Heidegger transforms the look of the other into our being 'looked at', if he too had not been similarly obsessed with persecution—notwithstanding his own claim that at stake is neither a 'glare' nor an act of a subject. In this regard both Levinas's and Heidegger's accounts remain perhaps uncannily 'stuck' in the problems of the Lacanian-mirror stage.

102. Maurice Blanchot, *Michel Foucault as I Imagine Him*, trans. Jeffrey Mehlman (New York: Zone Books, 1987), pp. 108–109.

103. Hobbes, *English Works*, 4:49.

104. I take this description of Aristotle's account of reciprocity as a '*privilège mutualiste*' from Derrida's *Politiques de l'amitié*, p. 27. While Derrida is right about the problematic character of friendship, both in the fragility of friendship and the venture of friendship, here he views the Aristotelian account too much as a theoretical construction, thereby missing the problem of the Good itself that underlies it.

105. Aristotle, *Eudemian Ethics*, 1239a36. Aristotle's account of the significance of reciprocity is thus less a proof than a semiotics, or better, a symptom-
ology.

106. See Francis Jacques, *Difference and Subjectivity*, p. 162. The affinity with
Habermas is one with which, Jacques claims, "I am happy to concur" (p. xviii).

107. Theodore J. Kisiel has explained the emergence of the term 'equiprimor-
dial' (*gleichursprünglich*) and its proximity to the problem of intersubjectivity
and *Mitsein*, pointing out that the first use of the term occurs in this context in
*Being and Time* (BT:149). Likewise, however, he also (rightly) claims, it is this
very problem of unity and multiplicity that accompanied Heidegger's itinerary
from the 'analogies' of the *Habilitation*. See Kisiel, *The Genesis of Heidegger's* Being and Time (Berkeley: University of California Press, 1993), p. 382. Indeed it
is just this multiplicity that Gadamer has uncovered in the problem of the
Good, the 'dialectic' that emerges between what the medievals would call *analogia attributiva*, directed to a differentiated term, a *pros hen* and the analogy of
proportion, in which no one thing is given priority over another. The dissolution of 'dialectic' makes possible the modern, strictly algorithmic interpretation
of analogy (i.e., as calculation). See Jacob Klein, *Greek Mathematical Thought
and the Origin of Algebra*, trans. Eva Braun (New York: Dover, 1992). The distinction between the analogy of attribution and the analogy of proportionality
is medieval. See the classical study of Cajetan, "The Analogy of Names" in *The
Analogy of Names and the Concept of Being* (Pittsburgh: Duquesne University
Press, 1953). Likewise, see Heidegger's discussion of this treatise (BT:491n).
We will return to Heidegger's refiguration of analogy within modern systematics in ch. 5.

108. For further discussion of the relation between Heidegger and Lacan and
the proximity of Heidegger's appropriation of *aletheia* to Lacan's account see
Jean-Luc Nancy and Philippe Lacoue-Labarthe, *The Title of the Letter: A Reading
of Lacan*, trans. François Raffoul and David Pettigrew (Albany: SUNY Press,
1992), pp. 133ff.

109. Ibid., pp. 136, 142.

110. See my *Tradition(s) I*, pp. 117ff.

111. See Sartre's account of appeal, gift, and generosity and the promise of
reciprocity, N:284ff.

112. See Lacan, Ecrits:29.

113. Merleau-Ponty, *Sense and Non-Sense*, p. 70.

114. Merleau-Ponty, *Signs*, p. 34; translation altered.

## 5. On the Dispensation of the Good

1. Martin Heidegger, *Nietzsche*, vol. 4, *Nihilism*, trans. Frank Capuzzi
(New York: Harper and Row, 1982), p. 191.

2. See Heidegger's analysis of these terms in relation to Suarez. While

Suarez traces this distinction to Augustine, Heidegger claims "basically it is Neoplatonic. Consequently, reference is made to God's asceity" (BP:82). Still, doubtless articulating his own debts to critical modernity (and Kant in particular), he proceeds to call the distinction between *ens increatum* and *creatum* decisive "since the difference between *essentia* and *existentia* must necessarily (and problematically) obtrude itself in reference to the *ens finitum*" (ibid.). In this light too it is worth recalling Wittgenstein's critique of essence, compounded by the 'conventions' of our grammar and the difference or 'heterogeneity' of language games, doubtless still expressing a Kantian inheritance.

3. See Kristeva, *Tales of Love*, pp. 178–81.

4. I have treated this issue more fully in my "The Dispersion of Dasein," *Extensions,* ch. 5.

5. For further discussion of the relation between Heidegger and Wittgenstein, see Michael Murray, "A Note on Wittgenstein and Heidegger," *Philosophical Review* 83 (1974). Murray traces the editing of these materials on Heidegger in Wittgenstein's manuscripts—and in particular the omission of excepts from the manuscripts of Friedrich Waissmann of a section entitled "On Heidegger." The fragment cited in the epigraph to this chapter derives from this. Also see OC §85f; 559.

6. See Jean-Luc Nancy, *The Gravity of Thought*, trans. François Raffoul and Gregory Recco (New Jersey: Humanities Press, 1997), p. 59.

7. See for example, Alain Renault, *System du droit: Philosophie et droit dans le pensée de Fichte* (Paris: Presses Universitaires de France, 1986), p. 171.

8. See Nancy, *Gravity of Thought*, pp. 60f.

9. See Nancy, *Être singulier pluriel*.

10. See Jacques Derrida, *Of Grammatology*, trans. Gayatri Spivak (Baltimore, Johns Hopkins University Press, 1976), p. 51.

11. See Emmanuel Levinas, "Meaning and Sense," in *Collected Papers,* trans. Alphonso Lingis (The Hague: Martinus Nijhoff, 1987), p. 117. This view of the Other as the semantic "*sens de sens,* the Rome to which all roads lead" has been called into question previously. See *Tradition(s) I,* p. 82.

12. See Jacques Derrida, "Form and Meaning," in *Speech and Phenomena.* In this critical 1967 piece Derrida calls into question the link between form and presence and links his discussion explicitly in this regard to the *Enneads,* which, he claims, indicates a certain closure of (by transgressing) metaphysical thought (see p. 127n). Here again the question is linked to the (internal) limitation of construing theoretical predication and formalization simply in terms of such substantial immanence or 'formal' presence.

13. The relation between neo-Platonic thought and Heidegger's criticism of the ontotheological character of metaphysics is treated with respect to Cusanus, in Werner Beierwaltes, *Identität und Differenz: Zum Prinzip Cusanischen Denkens* (Opladen: Deutscher Verlag, 1977). Likewise compare again Gadamer's remarks on Cusanus, TM:434ff. Beyond such premodern accounts,

however—and without contesting their legitimacy—one can further question whether deconstruction's account of the venture (or extension) of modern 'constructivism' was adequate to account for its history. See my "On the Rationality of the Fragment," *Extensions,* ch. 10.

14. See Jean-François Lyotard, *Heidegger and "The Jews,"* trans. Andreas Michel and Mark Roberts (Minneapolis: University of Minnesota Press, 1990), p. 84.

15. See Ernst Tugendhat, "Heidegger's Idea of Truth," trans. Richard Wolin, in *The Heidegger Controversy,* ed. R. Wolin (Cambridge. Mass.: MIT Press, 1993), p. 262. This is a translation of the conclusion of Tugendhat's *Der Wahrheitsbegriff bei Husserl und Heidegger* (Berlin: Walter de Gruyter, 1970).

16. Ludwig Wittgenstein, *The Blue and Brown Books* (New York: Barnes and Noble, 1969), p. 28.

17. See Martin Heidegger, "The Origin of the Work of Art," in *Poetry, Language, Thought,* p. 54.

18. Nancy, *Être singulier pluriel,* p. 57.

19. See *Tradition(s) I,* ch. 2.

20. We have yet to confront the impact of formal notions of theory construction on deconstruction and, in particular, its emergence from the Husserlian version of the Bolzanoan project.

21. Husserl explicitly demarcates the affinity between his account of definite (nomological) multiplicity and Hilbert's complete system of axioms in FTL§31. Without ultimately parsing Heidegger's position on these matters, it suffices to acknowledge that *Being and Time* was surely affected by them, and doubtless in some sense participates in them.

22. Hermann Weyl, *Philosophy of Mathematics and Natural Science,* p. 66.

23. Again, see Jean-Louis Chrétien, "Le langage des anges selon la scolastique," in *La voix nue,* ch. 4.

24. For a similar judgment, see Lacoue-Labarthe, "Transcendence Ends in Politics," pp. 290f.

25. Again, see Tugendhat, *Wahrheitsbegriff bei Husserl und Heidegger.* Likewise, see my "Heidegger, Rationality, and the Critique of Judgment," *Review of Metaphysics* 41.3.

26. See my "On the Rationality of the Fragment," *Extensions,* ch. 10.

27. Levinas is equally clear that the 'economics' of the separation and 'alterity' exemplified in sexuality escapes Freudian reductions to pleasure—an economics still Hobbesian, or reductively egoistic, in any case. See TI:276.

28. MacIntyre, "Contexts of Interpretation," p. 46.

29. For further discussion of the conceptual past of 'phenomenology' see my "On the Right to Interpret: Beyond the Copernican Turn," *Extensions,* ch. 8.

30. See my "On the Agon of the Phenomenological," *Extensions,* ch. 4. The history of Husserl's relation to his 'phenomenological' predecessors is recounted in ch. 7 of *Extensions.*

31. Derrida, *Of Grammatology,* p. 67.

32. See Jean-Luc Nancy, *L'expérience de la liberté* (Paris: Galilée, 1988), p. 205.

33. Scheler, *Nature of Sympathy,* p. 166.

34. Max Scheler, *Ressentiment,* trans. William Holdheim (Glencoe, Ill.: Free Press, 1961) pp. 165–66.

35. In articulating this conflict in these terms, we affirm the lingering effect of post-Kantian debates on aesthetics, and more generally the 'humanistic' in its ethical and political effects. A *locus classicus* for such consideration can be found in Peter Szondi's "Überwindung der Klassizismus," in *Hölderlin-Studien* (Frankfurt am Main: Suhrkamp, 1970).

36. See Scheler, *Formalism in Ethics,* pp. 308, 540.

37. Ibid., p. 476 (Sheler's emphasis).

38. Derrida, *Of Grammatology,* p. 66.

39. See the analysis of this text by Chrétien, *Voix nue,* pp. 259ff.

40. See Pierre Hadot, *Plotinus,* trans. Michael Chase (Chicago: University of Chicago Press, 1993), ch. 6.

41. Edmund Husserl, "The Vienna Lecture," in *Crisis of European Sciences,* p. 291.

42. See Vincent Descombes, *Philosophie par gros temps* (Paris: Minuit, 1989), pp. 170f.

43. Jacques Bouveresse, *La force de règle* (Paris: Minuit, 1987), p. 173.

44. Lyotard, *Différend,* p. 121.

45. J. Alberto Coffa, *The Semantic Tradition from Kant to Carnap: To the Vienna Station* (Cambridge: Cambridge University Press, 1991), pp. 43f.

46. Immanuel Kant, *Metaphysical Foundations of Natural Science,* trans. James Ellington (Indianapolis: Bobbs-Merrill, 1970), p. 6. Kant consistently here restricts the claim to special doctrines of nature.

47. See Immanuel Kant, *Prolegomena to Any Future Metaphysics,* ed. Lewis White Beck (Indianapolis: Bobbs-Merrill, 1950), p. 70.

48. An example of Husserl's reservations about Kant on analyticity can be seen at LI:833: "It is ominous that Kant (to whom we nonetheless feel ourselves quite close) should have thought he had done justice to the domain of pure logic in the narrowest of senses, by saying that it fell under the principle of contradiction. Not only did he never see how little the laws of logic are all analytic propositions in the sense laid down by his own definition, but he failed to see how little his dragging in of an evident principle for analytic propositions really helped to clear up the achievement of analytic thinking."

49. J. N. Findlay, *Axiological Ethics* (London: MacMillan, 1970), p. 17.

50. Coffa, *Semantic Tradition,* p. 18.

51. See Thomas Aquinas, *The Disputed Questions on Truth,* trans. Robert W. Mulligan (Chicago: Henry Regnery, 1952), question 1, article 9.

52. Here I follow—albeit obviously complicating—the analysis of Robert B.

Brandon, *Making It Explicit* (Cambridge, Mass.: Harvard University Press, 1994), ch. 2. For Frege's criticisms of Aristotle and the tradition here see Gottlob Frege, "Boole's Logical Calculus and the Begriffsschrift," in *Frege's Posthumous Writings,* ed. H. Hermes, F. Kambartel, and F. Kaulbach (Chicago: University of Chicago Press, 1987) pp. 16-17: "In Aristotle, as in Boole, the logically primitive activity is the formation of concepts by abstraction, and judgment and inference enter in through an immediate or indirect comparison of concepts via their extension. . . . I start out from judgments and their contents, and not from concepts. . . . I only allow the formation of concepts to proceed from judgments. . . . Instead of putting a judgment together out of an individual as subject and already previously formed concept as predicate, we do the opposite, and arrive at a concept by splitting up the content of a possible judgment."

53. The point can be put another way. Notwithstanding my transcendental origins, both rationally and semantically I depend—factically—on the practices (the meanings or the testimony) of others. To use an example of Putnam's, I may not know the difference between a beech and an elm tree: but knowing that does not imply that there is no difference, nor that we may not refer to these trees (even if only obliquely). *Pace* naive phenomenological accounts couched in the simple descriptions of the *intendit significare,* we must distinguish between the speaker's or thinker's meaning and the semantics of the natural language. This is what Fink's *Sixth Cartesian Meditation* recognized as the problem of natural language (or 'ontic meaning') internal to phenomenological description. Granted the radicality of the transcendental *epochē* "*ontic* meanings just cannot form an analogy to '*non-ontic*' transcendental meanings, for the two cannot be compared with one another" (90). Still, as Fink later admitted, these "ontic-mundane concepts are not dispensible. We must not, of course, *think philosophically* in them, but rather *by means of them predicatively assert* philosophical cognitions" (144) [all emphases are Fink's]. The problem is that the 'natural language' is not uninterpreted: the natural language is not a natural object, nor is it without a history. As I have put it elsewhere, our account of semantically following a rule must include an account of when rationally to give it up, or to change it—and any account of semantics must contain an account of the impact of such changes on meaning. See *Tradition(s) I,* pp. 38f. Also see my "The Philosopher's Text," *Extensions,* ch. 9.

54. For Kant's rendering of phenomenology as "a purely negative science," see Immanuel Kant to J. H. Lambert, September 2, 1770, in *Philosophical Correspondence, 1759-99,* trans. Arnulf Zweig (Chicago: University of Chicago Press, 1967), p. 59.

55. See Paul Engelmann, *Letters from Ludwig Wittgenstein, with a Memoir* (Oxford: Blackwell, 1967), pp. 6-7. Wittgenstein's emphasis.

56. Here is the complete quotation: "Working in philosophy—like work in architecture in many respects—is really a working on oneself. On one's own in-

terpretation. On one's way of seeing things. (And what one expects of them.)" (CV:16).

57. I take these terms from Stuart Hampshire's review of Monk's *Ludwig Wittgenstein: The Duty of Genius.*

58. See, for example, Kristeva, *Tales of Love,* pp. 119f., who sees Plotinus's 'ecstacy' as a loss of the other. Compare, on the other hand, Hadot's defense of Plotinus against R. Harder's charge of autoeroticism in "Le mythe de Narcisse et son interprétation par Plotin," *Nouvelle revue de psychanalyse* 13 (1976): 105f. I have argued that 'friendship' is the broader locus of such questions concerning *eros.*

59. Nicholas Rescher, *Pluralism: Against the Demand for Consensus* (Oxford: Clarendon Press, 1993), p. 2.

60. See Hilary Putnam, "Convention: A Theme In Philosophy," in *Philosophical Papers* (New York: Cambridge University Press, 1971), p. 170.

61. See the above discussion of Hegel and Law (ch. 2), and for further discussion, Hegel's *Science of Logic* vol. I, bk. II, ch. 2A, "Contingency, or Formal Actuality, Possibility and Necessity" (WdL:541ff.).

62. See Ferdinand de Saussure, *Course in General Linguistics,* trans. Wade Baskin (New York: McGraw-Hill, 1966), p. 169.

63. See Derrida, *Speech and Phenomena,* p. 14.

64. See Ludwig Wittgenstein, *Letters to Russell, Keynes, and Moore,* ed. G. H. von Wright (Oxford: Blackwell, 1974), p. 10. See William James, *The Variety of Religious Experience* (New Hyde Park, N.Y.: University Books, 1963), Lectures 6, 7.

65. See the analysis above, ch. 1.

66. See *Tradition(s) I,* pp. 197f.

67. See PH:201. Also see Gadamer's "Reply to P. Christopher Smith," in *The Philosophy of Hans-Georg Gadamer,* p. 526–27.

68. See Scheler, *Formalism in Ethics,* pp. 323–24. Notwithstanding his own traditionalism, as we have seen, here Scheler had also directly related the problem of conscience to the question of tradition, legitimation, and correction: "As the very core of what one's *own individual cognitive activities* and moral experience *contribute to moral insight,* conscience is only *one* form among others of the economization of ultimate moral insight—in contrast to the knowledge of this type accumulated in the past through authority and tradition. Only the *cooperation* of conscience and principles of authority and the contents of tradition with the *mutual correction* of *all* these merely *subjective sources of cognition* guarantees the highest degree of subjective acquisition of this insight (in average cases). But *all* these *sources* of moral insight can be appealed to the insight *itself* and to the evidential *self-givenness* of what is good and not good" (322–23; Scheler's emphasis). Again, while this account is perhaps an improvement on Scheler's earlier traditional communitarianism, the status of its commitments to moral insight and evidential self-givenness doubtless still remain problematical—inter alia in that he forgets the problem of the Good and the ontological

difference at stake within it, a difference that belies simple correlation (and co-alescence) of such cognitive sources. Hence the lingering psychologism in Scheler's appeal to the average case.

69. Levinas's own link to this humanist tradition can be measured by means of his link to Buber. See Martin Buber, "Dialogue," in *Between Man and Man*, pp. 27f.

70. Adorno, *Negative Dialectics*, p. 168.

71. On the question of determinacy and Heidegger's construal of death, see my "The Dispersion of Dasein," *Extensions*, ch. 5. On the lingering stoicism of Heidegger's link between authenticity and the anticipation of death, see Pierre Hadot, *Philosophy as a Way of Life*, p. 96. As in the case of care, here too, I am suggesting, the precedent of Seneca's writing is important (BT:243).

72. See Joyce, *Ulysses*, p. 34. Compare again Derrida's pairing of this text with Husserl's transcendental history in Derrida, *Edmund Husserl's Origin of Geometry*, pp. 102–3.

73. Seneca, *Ad Lucilium: epistulae morales*, ep. LXIII.

74. Arendt, *On Revolution*, p. 222.

75. Seneca, *Ad Lucilium: epistulae morales*, ep. IX. On Kant, see *Tradition(s) I*, pp. 110ff.

76. Ibid.

77. Ibid., ep. IX.

78. Ibid., ep. CII.

79. Boethius, *Consolation of Philosophy*, p. 95.

80. Adorno, *Negative Dialectics*, p. 280.

81. Ibid., p. 362.

82. Ibid., pp. 54–55.

83. Ibid., p. 364.

84. Martin Heidegger, *Schelling's Treatise on the Essence of Human Freedom*, trans. Joan Stambaugh (Athens: Ohio University Press, 1985), p. 158.

85. Heidegger construed the opening of Aristotle's *Metaphysics* (*pantes anthrōpoi tou eidenai oregontai phusei*), standardly construed as "all men desire to know," as "the care for seeing is essential to man's being" (BT:215). See Aristotle, *Metaphysics* 980a21. Compare Adorno's criticisms of this 'translation' in his *Metaphysics: Concepts and Problems,* trans. Edmund Jephcott (Stanford, Stanford University Press, 2000), pp. 20–23.

86. The history of the concept of value, and its origin in von Neumann's positivist invention of the term, is related in Findlay's *Axiological Ethics*, pp. 1ff. The term's etymological diacritics is equally complicated. 'Value' is connected to *valere* (to be worth) and to the medieval English *welden* (to have power over, control—to wield).

# INDEX

STEPHEN H. WATSON is Professor and Chair of the Department of Philosophy at the University of Notre Dame. He is the author of *Extensions: Essays on Interpretation, Rationality, and the Closure of Modernism* and a previous volume to this work, *Tradition(s): Refiguring Community and Virtue in Classical German Thought* (Indiana University Press, 1997). In addition to being the author of many articles, he has co-edited four collections on contemporary Continental thought: *Transitions in Continental Philosophy*; *Phenomenology, Interpretation and Community*; *Reinterpreting the Political: Continental Philosophy and Political Theory*; and *Ipseity and Alterity*.